The Colloquy of Montbéliard

Montbéliard

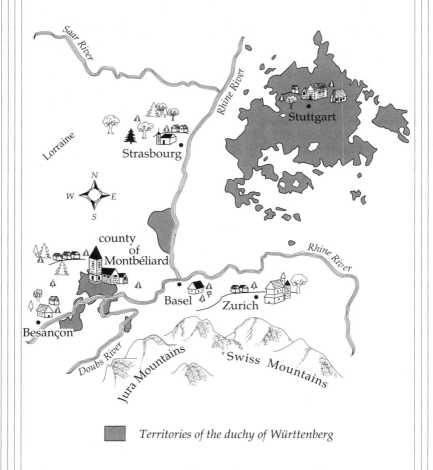

Territories of the duchy of Württenberg

Map by R. D. Kelly-Goss, University of Missouri - Columbia

The Colloquy
of Montbéliard

*Religion and Politics
in the Sixteenth Century*

JILL RAITT

New York   Oxford
OXFORD UNIVERSITY PRESS
1993

Oxford University Press

Oxford   New York   Toronto
Delhi   Bombay   Calcutta   Madras   Karachi
Kuala Lumpur   Singapore   Hong Kong   Tokyo
Nairobi   Dar es Salaam   Cape Town
Melbourne   Auckland   Madrid

and associated companies in
Berlin   Ibadan

Copyright © 1993 by Jill Raitt

Published by Oxford University Press, Inc.
200 Madison Avenue, New York, New York 10016

Oxford is a registered trademark of Oxford University Press, Inc.

Library of Congress Cataloging-in-Publication Data
Raitt, Jill.
The colloquy of Montbéliard : religion and politics
in the sixteenth century / Jill Raitt. p. cm.   Includes bibliographical references and index.
ISBN 0-19-507566-8
1. Religious disputations—France—Montbéliard—History—16th
century.   2. Christianity and politics—History—16th century.
3. Montbéliard (France)—Church history—16th century.   I. Title.
BR848.M7R25   1993
274.4'46—dc20   92-8251

1 3 5 7 9 8 6 4 2

Printed in the United States of America
on acid free paper

ACKNOWLEDGMENTS

Through the years of research that lie behind this volume I have accumulated many debts, all of which I cannot acknowledge here without creating an additional chapter. But I must heartily thank those granting institutions that provided the means for summers of archival research: the National Endowment for the Humanities and the American Council of Learned Societies. The National Endowment for the Humanities also provided the basic grant that allowed me to spend a year as a fellow of the Radcliffe Institute (now the Bunting Institute), which in turn gave me the opportunity to be an associate fellow of Leveret House at Harvard University.

As at the beginning, so at the end of my research and writing, a year's fellowship provided the ideal situation, this time at the National Humanities Center in Research Triangle Park, North Carolina, that humanists' heaven of remarkable collegiality and happy productivity. I owe that year to the National Humanities Center and to a Provost's Research Council Grant from the University of Missouri, Columbia.

The following individuals, libraries, and archives were most generous in helping me to find and copy many of the original manuscripts consulted in the course of my research: Hauptstaatsarchiv Stuttgart; Stefan Strohm, Landesbibliothek, Stuttgart; J. C. Voisin, directeur du service historique, Archives Municipales de Montbéliard, Hôtel de Ville, Montbéliard, France; Micheline Becker, conservateur, Bibliothèque Municipale, Montbéliard; Bibliothèque Publique et Universitaire de Genève and the Institute de l'Histoire de la Reformation and the Musé de la Reformation in the BPU, with special thanks to Peter Fraenkel and Alain Dufour, Directors, and Claire Chimelli and Micheline Tripet, researchers; Archives de Etat de Genève, Hotel de Ville, Geneva; J. Mirroneau, directeur, and Hélène Richard, conservateur des Bibliothèques Municipales de Besançon; Archives Nationales, Paris; Bibliothèque Nationale, Paris; Bibliothek der Universität Tübingen; Stiftsbibliothek, Tübingen; and Herzog-August Bibliothek, Wolfenbüttel.

I am deeply indebted to Ricarda and Karlfried Froehlich, for their hospitality in Tübingen; Ricarda's assistance in finding necessary German manuscripts and her impeccable transcriptions of those manuscripts were absolutely necessary to the progress of this book.

I have also to thank especially Robert M. Kingdon for his unfailing encouragement, advice, and assistance, including the work of his graduate assistant, Glenn Sunshine, who untangled the difficult French hand of the *Instrument* and checked my French spellings and accents throughout this book, bringing them into accord with the standards of the École des Chartes, Paris.

When I had lost references to some of my copies of materials in the Archives Nationales, the directeur général des Archives de France, Jean Favier, very kindly retrieved the correct designation for documents in K 2186 and K 2187.

I am indebted also to Olivier and Nicole Fatio for their friendship, hospitality, and help during my summers in Geneva.

Many colleagues have also assisted me, especially Charles Nauert of the Department of History at the University of Missouri, Columbia; John Headley of the Department of History, the University of North Carolina at Chapel Hill; and Edzard Baumann of the Department of Art History and Archeology at the University of Missouri, Columbia, who kindly obtained for me a copy of a manuscript at the Public Record Office, London.

The efficient assistance of Anne Edwards, research librarian at Ellis Library, University of Missouri, and of my colleagues in the Department of Religious Studies provided the steady support that I needed for research and writing. I must also acknowledge the unique assistance of my secretary at the Duke Divinity School, Sarah Freedman, and of Trish Love, secretary for the Department of Religious Studies at the University of Missouri. To the editors and staff of Oxford University Press, especially Cynthia Read, I wish to express my admiration for their unfailing cordiality and impeccable professionalism.

I am also grateful to the publishers of the following works who graciously allowed me to use portions of my essays that appeared therein:

"The Emperor and the Exiles: the Clash of Religion and Politics in the Sixteenth Century." *Church History* 52 (June 1983).

"The Elector John Casimir, Queen Elizabeth, and the Protestant League." In *Controversy and Conciliation: The Reformation and the Palatinate 1559–1583,* edited by Derk Visser. Allison Park, Pa.: Pickwick Publications, 1986.

"*Probably* They Are God's Children: Theodore Beza's Doctrine of Baptism." In *Humanism and Reform: The Church in Europe, England and Scotland, 1400–1643,* edited by James Kirk. Oxford: Blackwell, 1991.

November 1992   J. R.
Columbia, Missouri

CONTENTS

FOREWORD

The late sixteenth and early seventeenth centuries in Europe may fairly be called an age of confessionalism. It was a period in which the leaders of society spent a great amount of time and energy developing and defending confessions—precise definitions of exactly what they believed to be the essence of the Christian faith. The process began in 1530, with the Augsburg Confession, a carefully crafted summary of Christian belief, drafted for presentation at a meeting of the Reichstag, the legislative branch of the imperial government that then ruled most of Germany. It was presented to that Reichstag by the chancellor of the state of electoral Saxony, Gregory Brück, on behalf of a coalition of "protesting" estates, to demonstrate to that assemblage and to the world that the ideas maintained among those states were true Christian beliefs that did not merit the label "heresy" and thus the persecution proposed by the imperial government. It had been drafted in large part by Philip Melanchthon, Luther's chief assistant in the growing Reformation movement.

This process continued at the ecumenical Council of Trent, in which an assembly of bishops, meeting off and on between 1545 and 1563 under the leadership of papal legates, drafted a series of dogmatic decrees defining with greater precision than ever before the doctrines taught by the Roman Catholic Church. Those decrees, once ratified by popes, were then presented to governments all over the Western world, as a guide to determining which of the competing religious groups were truly Catholic and obedient to the teaching authority of the Roman see.

The process was carried a step further by the "Reformed" churches that looked to Calvin as the most prominent of several leaders. They prepared a series of national confessions of faith, to persuade hostile sovereigns both at home and abroad that they were indeed responsible believers in true Christian doctrine. The best known of these Reformed confessions are the Gallic Confession of 1559, prepared on behalf of a movement led by a group of great French aristocrats of whom the most prominent were members of the Bourbon family; the Scotch Confession of 1560, prepared for the Scottish Lords of the Congregation to help justify their overthrow of the Catholic regency of Mary of Guise; the Belgic Confession of 1561, prepared on behalf of a Dutch movement against Spanish rule that came to be led by William of Orange and the Estates General of the Netherlands; and the Thirty-nine Articles of the Church of England of 1563, adopted by Parliament to justify the religious position advocated by the government of Elizabeth I.

In every case the new confession epitomized the ideas of a religious community. In every case it also supplied a platform for a political entity, whether a political faction, an independent state, or a coalition of states.

Confessions thus became symbols of two types of identity, religious and political. Like many symbols of identity they were devised with care and defended with ferocity. Their constant use is an extremely important indicator of the ways in which public opinion was then manipulated and in which power was legitimated. Their creation and defense required the close collaboration of two types of leaders, lawyers and theologians. Bureaucrats trained in the law actually managed most of these governments but they often found it necessary to draw upon the expert advice of consultants highly trained in theology.

Within the Holy Roman Empire of the German Nation, the rules of this confessional game were defined by the Religious Peace of Augsburg, drafted in 1555. It had ended a period of intensive religious war by allowing each local government within the empire to choose one of two confessions—the Augsburg Confession first drafted by Lutheran leaders back in 1530, or the Catholic confession then in the process of being codified at Trent. A split within the Protestant ranks soon developed, however, with the growth of a Calvinist Reformed movement, building on a base created earlier by Ulrich Zwingli and his followers. Calvin and his associates were quite prepared to accept the Augsburg Confession, but only in a version subject to several interpretations, called the *Variata.* Some German Protestant states lined up behind this version of the Augsburg Confession and the allied confessions presented by Calvinists in other countries. Other states, however, insisted upon a more rigid and restrictive version of the Confession of Augsburg, called the *Invariata,* that was later elaborated in an inter-Lutheran confessional statement called the Formula of Concord, which explicitly excluded Zwinglians and Calvinists.

The tensions between these confessions were particularly acute in the southwestern part of Germany. Three competing governments in that corner of the empire each seized upon a different confession both to assert its own identity and independence and to claim a larger role within the imperial and pan-European political contexts. The duchy of Lorraine became resolutely Roman Catholic and defended its faith in alliance with the papacy and the French Catholic Holy League. The electorate of the Palatine became primarily Calvinist, with some false starts and changes, and defended its faith in alliance with French Protestants, the Swiss cantons, and the Netherlands. The duchy of Württemberg committed itself to conservative Lutheranism and defended its faith in alliance with other Lutheran powers, primarily in eastern and northern Germany.

One particularly acute display of the resulting tensions may be found in the French-speaking county of Montbéliard. It had been converted to a largely Calvinist version of Protestant Christianity. Its immediate neighbors were the Reformed cantons of Switzerland and the duchy of Lorraine ruled by the Guise family, better known as leaders of the fervently Catholic Holy League in France. But Montbéliard itself was ruled by the dukes of Württemberg, and they were determined that it should become an integral part of their Lutheran territories. The confessional debate within the country, therefore, intimately involved the Swiss, the French, and the Germans, as well as attracting attention from other parts of Europe. It reached a climax in 1586, when a public debate was arranged between teams led by the single most prominent spokesmen in Europe for the Calvinist and Lutheran theological points of view. They were Theodore Beza, Calvin's successor as moderator of the church of Geneva and as principal spokesman for Reformed theology, and Jacob Andreae, chief theological adviser to the duke of Württemberg and principal author of the Formula of Concord.

This debate marks an important high point in the entire history of confessionalism, a point at which two of the leading varieties of confessionalism were expressed and defended with unmatched erudition and ferocity. Although the debate was thoroughly documented by participants, it has never been analyzed with the attention it deserves. A full analysis requires unusual skills on the part of the scholar who tackles the assignment. In addition to a full knowledge of the history of the period and mastery of the relevant languages, it requires expert training in the history of dogmatic theology. It requires special skills in interpreting the nuances of eucharistic theology as they had been developed through the Middle Ages and into the Reformation period, since argument over the eucharist was at the center of this particular debate. It requires a mind capable of the analytical "bite," the rigor and clarity that scholars associate with the very best history of theology. It requires detachment and an exquisite sensitivity to various points of view that did not always even try to understand each other. This last quality could be of particular value in our own age of ecumenism. Confessions now rarely serve as political platforms, and they are used less often to define fully religious identity. But they nevertheless remain as barriers that theologians must overcome if we are ever to see reunion of the entire church of Christ.

All of these skills are possessed to an impressive degree by Jill Raitt. She has demonstrated them in earlier publications, most significantly in her book *The Eucharistic Theology of Theodore Beza,* published by the American Academy of Religion. She has developed them in a career of teaching religion at a variety of universities, currently the University of Missouri–Columbia, and in leading positions in several scholarly organizations, most prominently the American Academy of Religion. She has displayed them as a representative of the Roman Catholic community in conversations with theologians of the Lutheran community. These qualities make Raitt the ideal author for this book. They make of the book an important contribution both to historical understanding and to ecumenical dialogue. May it receive the attention it so richly deserves.

ROBERT M. KINGDON

ABBREVIATIONS

AEG   Archives d'État de Genève.

AN-K   Archives Nationales, Paris, Historical Section.

AE   *Luther's Works* (American edition). 55 vols. Edited by Jaroslav Pelikan and Helmut T. Lehman. Philadelphia and St. Louis: Concordia Publishing House and Fortress Press, 1955–.

BN   Bibliothèque Nationale, Paris.

CR   *Corpus Reformatorum.* Edited by C. G. Bretschneider and H. E. Binseil. Halle, 1934–1960.

HAS   Hauptstaatsarchives Stuttgart.

LAS   Landeskirchliches Archiv Stuttgart.

LCC   Library of Christian Classics. 26 vols. Edited by John Baillie, John T. McNeill, and Henry P. Van Dusen. Philadelphia: The Westminster Press,

RCP   *Registres de la Compagnie des pasteurs de Genève.* Vol. 5: 1583–1588. Published under the direction of the Archives d'État de Genève. Edited by Olivier Labarthe and Micheline Tripet. Geneva: Librairie Droz, 1976.

RC   *Registres du Conseil.* References are to original autographs in the Archives d'État de Genève. I owe their transcription to the kindness of Micheline Tripet.

WA   *D. Martin Luthers Werke.* Kritische Gesamtausgabe. Weimar, 1883–.

The Colloquy of Montbéliard

INTRODUCTION

On January 14, 1586, a spy for the English crown sat down to write his report. From Strasbourg Dr. Lobetius wrote to Walsingham, Queen Elizabeth's secretary of state, to let him know how Elizabeth's efforts to form a Protestant League were proceeding.

> You wish to know my opinion concerning what one may expect of the Protestant princes in Germany with regard to the common good and to maintain the common cause against their adversaries. I hope I will have occasion to tell you something more positive than I have been able to tell you heretofore. But to tell you the truth, their reactions are cold and very difficult to warm up, no matter how hard one tries.[1]

Lobetius remarked on the reasons for the resistance of the German princes, namely their laziness and stinginess. He wrote that the prince of Denmark was more cooperative and that some German princes were beginning to open their eyes lest they be surprised with their eyes closed.[2] It is in this context that Lobetius informed Walsingham of the activities of the agents sent by Henry of Navarre for the same purpose, that is, to raise German Protestant support for the Huguenots. One of those agents was the baron de Clervant, who passed through Strasbourg having already visited the prince of Anhalt and the landgrave of Hesse. Hesse was particularly warm and open to the idea of a Protestant League. Clervant was now bound for Württemburg to obtain the support of Duke Ludwig for the same cause. Lobetius extolled the diligence of the agents, who could not be blamed for the lack of response of some of the German princes. After commenting on the need for deep piety and devotion to stir the princes, Lobetius said that without such divinely inspired piety, all their efforts would be in vain. On the other hand, reported the spy, the pope continues his plans boldly to extend his power over all the princes. Among other things that the pope has at heart is the destruction of the city of Geneva, for which he will employ the duke of Savoy. Spanish troops also threaten Geneva, which looks to Bern for protection. Lobetius then turned to the affairs of the Holy Roman Empire and to the next meeting called by the emperor at which both religions of the empire would be represented.[3] The emperor, opposed to all troop levees, was not pleased when he heard about the letter that Queen Elizabeth had written to Duke Casimir of the Palatinate, who was gathering troops in support of Henry of Navarre, leader of the Huguenots. Meanwhile, wrote Lobetius, Gaspar de Schomberg had been in Strasbourg and also Nancy and Metz and other places spying on the followers of Henry of Navarre in order to oppose their plans.

The rest of Lobetius's letter continued to report on the tensions in the empire and in France between Catholics and those "of the religion," that is, the Reformed. He ended the letter with a note saying that Segur[4] had returned from Saxony and brought good news concerning *la cause*. Lobetius hoped for even better news from Heidelberg and from the duke d'Espernon. The *cause* was the same that Lobetius had been addressing throughout, namely, Elizabeth's hope to form a Protestant League, one of whose objects was to aid Henry of Navarre against Henry III of France, still under the influence of the Guise family, architects of the Catholic League.

It is within the perspective of this international setting that the Colloquy of Montbéliard should be understood. It was not simply another theological controversy that failed to reconcile Reformed and Lutheran princes and theologians. Although that is also a conclusion one may draw and the one with which historians have dismissed the Colloquy of Montbéliard, such an assessment fails to consider the complex reasons for the calling of the colloquy.

The religious changes in the first half of the sixteenth century had profound political ramifications in the second half of the century. Goaded by the successes of the Protestant Reformation, the Roman Catholic Church had at last concluded the Council of Trent in 1563. But its decrees were not accepted, promulgated, and implemented at once. In fact, France, torn by the wars of religion and animated by a Gallican spirit, refused to receive the Tridentine decrees. By 1575, German Lutheranism found itself divided among many forms, which the Formula of Concord (1577) attempted to unite. Protestant Christianity was split into factions, each of which drew up confessions to which its constituents had to adhere and which divided the people not only into Catholic and Protestant but into Anglican, Lutheran, Reformed, and Anabaptist as well. All of these divisions were themselves further divided. The notion of tolerance had few advocates, and ruling lords demanded that their own beliefs be taught and practiced by their people on pain of exile, or, in the case of Anabaptists in either Catholic or Protestant territories, death. When one lord succeeded another with a different faith, the people had to follow the faith of the new lord or suffer exile or the ravages of war as in the Palatinate.

In German lands, the political power of the Protestant lords had led to the Peace of Augsburg in 1555, which legitimated Roman Catholics and followers of the Augsburg Confession. "Sacramentarians" were banned from the territories of the Holy Roman Empire. Who were "sacramentarians"? Lutherans labeled as sacramentarians both Zwinglians who did not follow the Augsburg Confession and Calvinists who claimed that they did follow the Augsburg Confession and therefore denied that they were sacramentarians. The legal residence of Calvinists within the Holy Roman Empire persisted as a salient issue.

In 1562, the unsettled state of France erupted into the murderous wars of religion, which ended only in 1593 when the Huguenot leader, Henry of Navarre, succeeded to the French throne as Henry IV, becoming Roman Catholic in order to do so but without losing his Reformed sympathies.

The county of Montbéliard was caught in the net of these bitter disputes and provides a paradigm for many of the religiopolitical problems of Europe. Montbéliard was situated geographically, politically, and religiously in the midst of these controversies and briefly became a focal point for an attempted resolution at least of the Calvinist-Lutheran division with its political ramifications so critical for the conduct of the wars of religion.

The Colloquy of Montbéliard involved a debate between Theodore Beza, called in jest but with some seriousness "the pope of the French Reformed churches," and Jacob Andreae, self-styled "pope of the Lutheran churches." The colloquy took place at Montbéliard, a town within a triangle formed by French Alsace-Lorraine, which remained intensely Roman Catholic, German Württemberg, which became firmly Lutheran and to which Montbéliard belonged as a vassal territory, and German Switzerland, which remained Reformed and from which came its first reformer. Montbéliard was therefore strategically situated geographically and religiously. As we shall see, it was also strategically situated politically.

Religion

Until 1524, Montbéliard was Catholic. In that year, Duke Ulrich of Württemberg, Montbéliard's suzerain, requested that the reformer William Farel, a Frenchman, be sent from Basel to bring Montbéliard to the evangelical religion professed by the Basel reformer, Oecolampadius. The theology of the German Swiss and south German reformers differed from Luther's theology in ways that came to be deeply divisive. While they agreed on the fundamental Protestant doctrines of justification by faith alone and the principle of *sola scriptura,* they disagreed regarding the sacraments of baptism and the Lord's Supper. By 1529, their disagreement had become so profound that a colloquy called by Landgrave Philip of Hesse to heal the breach between the reformers ended in a bitter refusal on the part of the Saxon Luther to shake hands with Zwingli of Zurich and Oecolampadius of Basel.

The primary disagreement concerned what communicants ate when they received the bread consecrated during the Lord's Supper. The question raised by this problem is that of the substantial change of bread into the body of Christ as the Roman Catholic Church taught, or the substantial, real presence of Christ in, with, and under the bread as Luther taught, or the bread as instrument of Christ's offering of himself to the faithful communicant through the Holy Spirit, as the Reformed taught. Luther held that when Christ said, "This is my body," that is precisely what he meant. The verb *is* had to be taken literally and applied to the bread. Ulrich Zwingli, the reformer of Zurich, taught that the Catholic and Lutheran doctrines were unreasonable; bread does not become body, nor does the body of the risen Christ become present on earthly altars. Rather, believers are the objects of divine action and it is they who are changed, not the bread. The church, gathered around the Lord's table, deepens its faith and is itself the body of Christ, the mystical body of Christ. Zwingli therefore taught that the word *is* in the formula "This is my body" means "signifies." Any other interpretation makes a mockery of human intelligence. For Luther, faith accepts the words without trying to understand them: *is* means *is*. As a consequence of these interpretations, Luther taught that regardless of belief or worthiness, whoever receives the consecrated bread receives the body of Christ, substantially present. Zwingli held that only those with faith deepened their union with Christ, already established through faith. As for the substantial body of Christ, said Zwingli, it ascended into heaven and there it remains until the Second Coming. To make the body of Christ present on every altar and in the mouth of every communicant is to deny the truth of Christ's human nature. These differences were further complicated by another form of Reformed theology, articulated by the reformer of Geneva, John Calvin, who did not formulate his doctrine until 1535.

Calvin's doctrine stood between Luther's and Zwingli's. While Calvin agreed with Zwingli that only those with faith received anything more than bread during the Lord's Supper, he agreed with Luther in his use of the word *substantial*. The faithful communicant was united to the substance of Christ, but the union was effected by the power of the Holy Spirit and took place in heaven, where Christ's body was located according to the circumscribed nature of a true human body.

Was the problem of Christ's eucharistic presence limited to the debate of theologians, or did it affect the lives of the laity? What did sixteenth-century lay Protestants know about complicated theological arguments? The Protestant reformers knew that to succeed they must have both the hearts and minds of the people. To well-prepared sermons was added carefully supervised instruction in catechism classes. The people were therefore instructed in these difficult matters and knew very well what they believed and what they did not believe. Not only did the common people understand their confessions of faith, duly drawn up and taught in both school and church, but their lords, those German dukes who are sometimes caricatured as illiterate boors, knew their theology as well and carried on complicated theological debates with their peers. True, theological education for lay people took some decades, but by 1550, it had been effective, and when the Peace of Augsburg was promulgated in 1555, it had profound political and religious repercussions that deeply affected the lives of the laity.

The Peace of Augsburg declared that the followers of two forms of religion would be tolerated in the estates and cities of the Holy Roman Empire: Catholics loyal to the pope in Rome and Protestants who followed the Augsburg Confession. Written by Philip Melanchthon and read before Emperor Charles V in 1530, the Augsburg Confession remains today the primary expression of Lutheran faith.

In 1541, the Holy Roman Emperor Charles V called for a colloquy between Protestants and Catholics at Regensburg. It sought to unite the empire behind Charles as he faced the armies of the Turks advancing on Vienna. But before the Protestants could discuss doctrine with the Catholics, they needed to heal their own differences. To facilitate agreement among Protestants, Melanchthon altered article X of the Augsburg Confession, the article dealing with the Lord's Supper. Instead of saying that the body of Christ is given and eaten as does the 1530 version, the 1541 *Variata* says that the body of Christ is *offered* to communicants. This wording allows for a Lutheran literal eating and for the Reformed interpretation, namely that while Christ is *offered* to all, his body is eaten only by the mouth of faith, not by the physical mouth. The Lutherans therefore opposed the 1541 *Variata* Augsburg Confession.

The political implications proved enormous, since from 1555 through the rest of the century, the Lutherans insisted that only the 1530 unaltered form (the *Invariata*) of the Augsburg Confession served as the basis of the Peace of Augsburg and that the Reformed were therefore illegal in the empire. The Reformed argued that the Peace of Augsburg allowed also those who agreed with the 1541 altered form of the Augsburg Confession.

Politics

The Peace of Augsburg, concluded in 1555, was not only a religious settlement but a political and legal tool that recognized as legal residents within the Holy Roman Empire only Catholics and followers of the Augsburg Confession. Those persons who were neither Catholic nor able to accept any form of the Augsburg Confession (Zwinglians and Anabaptists) were subject to exile or imprisonment or even death. Which form of Christianity, Catholic or "Augsburgian," was enforced in a given area depended on the lord who, under the emperor, governed the territory, or the determination of the magistrates of imperial free cities. This principle was later articulated in the formula *cuius regio, eius religio.*

Meanwhile, a Calvinist form of Protestantism claimed more and more of southern and western France. Alarm seized the Valois kings and the Catholic lords of France, especially the powerful Guise family. They were unwilling to admit the sort of compromise Charles V had drawn up at Augsburg. During the minority of Charles IX, in 1561, the queen regent, Catherine de'Medici, tried to heal France through the Colloquy of Poissy, a theological discussion between Catholics and Reformed. The colloquy failed, and in 1562 the wars of religion began.

At Poissy, the Reformed found their spokesman in Theodore Beza, a Frenchman who became professor of theology in Geneva and Calvin's successor when Calvin died in 1564, just three years after Poissy. At the request of the Catholics at Poissy, Duke Christoph of Württemberg sent Jacob Andreae, bearing the 1530 version of the Augsburg Confession and the Württemberg Confession written by John Brenz. To the Augsburg Confession the Württemberg Confession added the doctrine that the human nature of Christ shared in the divine property of ubiquity, which allowed the body and blood of Christ to be present on every altar and in the mouth of every communicant. Duke Christoph hoped to facilitate a modus vivendi for French Reformed and the Catholics, but also he wanted Antoine of Navarre, then the political leader of the Huguenots or French Reformed, to sign the Lutheran confessions and thereby signal to the German Protestant princes his religious agreement with them. Instead Antoine became Catholic and left leadership of the Huguenots to Louis Condé and Coligny and eventually to his own son, Henry of Navarre, the future Henri le Grand, Henry IV of France.

Henry of Navarre became the effective leader of the Huguenots following the St. Bartholomew's Day massacre of thousands of Protestants in 1572 signaled by the murder of Coligny. Louis Condé had been assassinated three years earlier. Now the two young Henrys, Navarre and Henry Condé, set their faces against Duke Henry of Guise and tried to rescue King Henry III of France from the Guise influence.

Of the three major political forces in France, the Catholic Guise, the Huguenots, and the Politiques, the Huguenots and the Politiques were willing to allow more than one form of Christianity. The Guise, determined to exterminate the Huguenots, formed the Holy League, conspiring with Philip II of Spain and the pope to quash Protestantism in France and, if possible, put a Guise on the French throne. The Huguenots sought allies in England and Germany and favored a Protestant League to oppose the pope and the powerful alliance of Catholic powers.

The struggle in France came to a head in 1585 when the Holy League persuaded Henry III to issue the Treaty of Nemours, which revoked the limited privileges of the Huguenots won during the wars of religion that plagued France after the failed Colloquy of Poissy. The Treaty of Nemours declared that only Catholics would be tolerated in France: *un roi, une foi, une loi.* Huguenots had to convert to Catholicism or leave France within six months. There followed a flood of exiles to England, Germany, and Switzerland. Navarre called upon Duke John Casimir of the Palatinate to raise German troops to invade France. Navarre sent his agent, the baron de Clervant, to Switzerland on the same errand. Elizabeth of England, long in favor of a Protestant League, sent one hundred thousand pounds to Casimir to finance his mercenaries.

Montbéliard

In 1585, the county of Montbéliard filled with French refugees. Count Frederick, whose father, George, had been Reformed but whose uncle and suzerain, Duke Ludwig of Württemberg, was a firm Lutheran, allowed the refugees to remain. Frederick's loyalties were not altogether settled with regard to religion; he was torn between the Reformed theology of his father and his town and the official Lutheran theology he had learned at Tübingen from Jacob Andreae. By the terms of the Peace of Augsburg, neither Count Frederick nor his uncle could tolerate sacramentarians. Were the Reformed sacramentarians? Andreae proclaimed everywhere the identity of Calvinists with Zwinglians so that both would be excluded from the Peace of Augsburg. The Reformed insisted that they followed the altered Augsburg Confession and thus were officially to be tolerated in the empire. Frederick accepted the

French Reformed as fellow Protestants. Should he not help them against the Catholics, especially the hated Guise, whose territory of Lorraine bordered on his own? On the other hand, Frederick had received letters from nearby Catholic towns complaining of the presence of the exiles. These towns also wrote to Archduke Ferdinand and to the Holy Roman Emperor, Rudolf II. Even Henry III, Valois king of France, wrote to Rudolf II complaining of the presence of French exiles in Montbéliard. The French king feared that Montbéliard would be used as a staging ground for sending mercenaries into France. Rudolf wrote imperiously to Frederick that he must send the exiles away. Frederick denied that there were armed Frenchmen in Montbéliard, allowed the refugees to remain, and wrote a long "excuse" to Rudolf.

In December of 1585, the French exiles asked Frederick to be allowed to receive communion under their French Reformed Confession. Frederick refused. They must sign the Augsburg Confession or abstain from communion. The exiles asked for a colloquy to help settle the matter before Easter. In the meantime, the baron de Clervant, sent by Navarre to raise mercenary troops in Germany and Switzerland, stopped by Stuttgart, Ludwig's court, and invited Andreae to participate in a colloquy in Montbéliard. Clervant hoped, and in this reflected the hope of Navarre, that with their theological differences resolved, more German Protestant princes would help the Huguenots with troops and supplies. By 1585, the theological differences between Lutherans and Reformed were so exaggerated that some of the Lutherans felt closer to the Catholics than to the Calvinists. In fact, some of the German Lutheran princes sent troops and supplies to the Catholic Guise, others helped Henry III, and others allowed mercenaries to be recruited for the Huguenot leader, Henry of Navarre.

The Colloquy of Montbéliard was convened to address the problem of a few hundred French exiles who wanted to receive communion under their own confession and from ministers who used a French rather than a German liturgy. The colloquy was also called because the resumption of religious warfare seemed imminent and, for his part, the Huguenot leader, Henry of Navarre, needed German allies. As in 1561, some of the German princes made Navarre's acceptance of the unaltered Augsburg Confession a condition of their cooperation. Navarre hoped that the colloquy would prove to these Lutherans that their theological differences were less important than their common opposition to the pope and the Holy League.

For all these reasons, the colloquy took place. The collocutors discussed the Lord's Supper, which led to a long dispute about the doctrine of the two natures of Christ. They also debated the adornment and music proper in churches, baptism and predestination. Only on music and the adornment of churches could the two collocutors agree to disagree. On the other issues, Andreae accused Beza of holding the doctrines of the "Alcoran" (Koran) and later characterized the Reformed doctrine as devilish and designed to destroy souls. While Beza pointed to agreements on major points and suggested discussing the remaining issues another time, Andreae demanded no less than complete capitulation to his particular theology and then, like Luther at Marburg sixty years earlier, refused the hand of brotherhood to the Swiss Reformed. Won over to Lutheranism, Count Frederick told the exiles that they would have to sign not only the Augsburg Confession but also the Formula of Concord drawn up by Andreae in 1577. The Formula of Concord reaffirmed the 1530 version of the Augsburg Confession and condemned Calvinists by name. There is no indication that the German princes altered their policies in either direction because of the colloquy.

And what of the people of Montbéliard and the French exiles settled there? Did they capitulate and become Lutherans? No. Instead they accepted the French exiles as bourgeois of Montbéliard. Many of them traveled to Basel to receive communion and even to bear their children so that they could be baptized by Reformed rather than Lutheran ministers. Frederick fulminated against their disobedience and against their continual petitions asking him to allow them to have their own confession of faith. The tug-of-war continued into the seventeenth century, when Montbéliard became Lutheran.

This book presents the Colloquy of Montbéliard as a paradigm of the problems that resulted from the political and religious fragmentation that dominated the second half of the sixteenth century. It does so not only in terms of theological differences but also by indicating the influence of those theological differences on political alliances and hence on the development of the nations of Europe.

Notes

1. Original autograph, Public Records Office, London, Reference nos. PFNF 25CL; SP 81/3/PT-1, and summarized in *Calendar of State Papers, Foreign Series of the Reign of Elizabeth,* vol. 20, 297–99. (I owe the following transcription to Glenn Sunshine. The manuscript is extremely difficult to read due to the cramped hand of Lobetius. The translation is my own.) P. 1: "Vous desirez de sçavoir mon opinion touchant ce qu'on / doiz esperer des P[rinces] protestans / en Allemaigne, pour le bien commun et pour maintenir la cause commune, contre / ceulx qui leur sont adverseyres, pour quoy ce prendre je vous diray, que je / souhaiterris avoir occasion de plus esperer que je n'ay faict cy devant. On a à / la verite esté foit froide jusques à present, et tresdifficilz a eschauffer, nonobstant / les diligence dont on a usé."

2. For corroboration of the information in Lobetius's letter and on the effort of Queen Elizabeth to form a Protestant League, see chap. 2, p. 45 (with n. 3) and 54–56.

3. Namely, the Roman Catholics and the followers of the Augsburg Confession. See discussion about the struggle of the Lutherans to exclude the Calvinists from the Peace of Augsburg and of the Calvinists to insist that they too were followers of the Augsburg Confession.

4. Jacques de Ségur-Pardaillan was one of Henry of Navarre's most trusted counselors, his chargé d'affaires and minister of finance. See *Recueil des Lettres Missives de Henri IV,* vol. 2: 1585–1589, ed. M. Berger de Xivrey (Paris: Imprimerie Royale, 1843), esp. 119, 184. See p. xl: "Au mois de juillet [1583] une vaste correspondance en latin commence avec tous les princes protestants de l'Europe. Le roi de Navarre leur envoie comme ambassadeur Jacques de Ségur-Pardaillan, pour solliciter leur appui en faveur des Français de la même communion."

1

Ancient Liberties
and Evangelical Reform

To ordinary folk it might have seemed hardly credible that the baron de Clervant was in Stuttgart, sent by Henry of Navarre expressly to issue an invitation to a theological colloquy to the influential Lutheran rector of the University of Tübingen, Jacob Andreae, one of the two primary authors of the Book of Concord. But to international political insiders, it was not so unusual. Just before his arrival in Stuttgart, Clervant's presence in Strasbourg and his plan to travel to Stuttgart had been duly reported by Lobetius, a spy in the pay of Elizabeth of England, to Francis Walsingham, Elizabeth's secretary of state. At the same time, Henry of Navarre had himself written to Theodore Beza in Geneva, asking him to undertake a task of importance to all of Christendom, a letter confirmed by Count Frederick's invitation to Beza to participate in the colloquy. Why, in short, should a theological debate in the small county of Montbéliard involve the intervention of Henry, future king of France, and the anxious gaze of the virgin queen?

Why was the Colloquy of Montbéliard convoked and by whom? The answer to the second question appears to be quite simple, since a record of the invitation to Theodore Beza can be found in the Registers[1] of the Company of Pastors of Geneva. Another reference occurs in the publication by Jacob Andreae of the *Acta*[2] of the colloquy. Andreae claimed that he was invited by the baron de Clervant, who came to Stuttgart expressly to issue the invitation to the colloquy. At this point, the story becomes more complex than just another colloquy to settle a theological debate. It is even more complex than the need of the people of Montbéliard and their count, Frederick, to end an ecclesiastical struggle between the Lutheran duchy of Württemberg and the Reformed community of Montbéliard. In fact, these seemingly simple invitations conceal a complex political background of international proportions.

The baron de Clervant was a counselor to Henry, king of Navarre, leader of the French Huguenots in the long French wars of religion and the future Henry IV of France.[3] It was as Henry's delegate to the German princes and the Swiss cantons that the baron de Clervant visited Württemberg in January and Montbéliard in February of 1586.[4] Clervant's visit to Andreae was, how-

11

ever, difficult to verify. This elusive bit of information finally came to light in a letter dated January 14, 1586, from Lobetius in Strasbourg to Walsingham in England.[5] No other indication of Clervant's visit to Württemberg exists, to my knowledge, except in the reports of Andreae and Beza.[6] The question then arises, why should Elizabeth of England, through Walsingham, be interested in Clervant's trip to Stuttgart? Equally fascinating is the question of Navarre's interest in the colloquy. Would it not have been enough for Frederick to invite Andreae? Or, more appropriately, why would Frederick not have asked his uncle Ludwig, duke of Württemberg and Andreae's employer, to send Andreae to the colloquy? Why should Henry of Navarre be concerned about the problems of a small county in a Lutheran duchy? The answers to these two questions are interlocked and make the Colloquy of Montbéliard not just an example of the theological problems of the late sixteenth century but also a paradigm for the international intrigue that involved Roman Catholics, Huguenots, and German Lutherans in a complex net that covered not only these major antagonists but included also Philip of Spain, Elizabeth of England, the Holy Roman Emperor Rudolph II, the struggles of the Lowlands, and the papacy.[7]

The history of Montbéliard during the sixteenth century, its reform, and its use as a pawn by its dukes shed light upon the colloquy in 1586 and the years immediately preceding and following it.

Montbéliard: 1524–1573

The year 1524 marks the beginning of the reform of Montbéliard; 1573 is the year of the death of Montbéliard's most important minister during the troubled time following the death of Montbéliard's Reformed Count George and the rule of the county by the Lutheran Duke Christoph. The period 1524–1573 was also chosen by John Viénot for his two-volume history of the reform of Montbéliard from its origins to the death of Pierre Toussain.[8] For the purposes of this study, it will suffice to present a résumé of the Montbéliard story until 1573.

Montbéliard began the sixteenth century as both a fief of Duke Ulrich of Württemberg[9] and an enfranchised town. The town of Montbéliard, with a population of about two thousand in the sixteenth century, was proud of its "ancient franchises and liberties" upon which it often stood against its count or duke. The structure of the magistracy and the rights of the town are important for understanding the relation of the duke of Württemberg and the count of Montbéliard to the town itself. Efforts on the part of Count and then Duke Frederick to abrogate the elective character of the Nine Bourgeois or the rights of citizens to come and go freely were fought by the proud citizens of Montbéliard. Of the Montbéliard government, Louis Renard wrote:

> Before the Revolution of 1789, these were the ancient municipal institutions
> of Montbéliard: Magistracy of the Nine, the Corps of the Eighteen and the

Notables, the Mayor and Procurator—who gave to the old capital its originality, and who made of it for more than five centuries (1283–1793) a kind of little republic and democracy before these were known, of which the Montbéliardais were justly proud.[10]

The "rights and liberties" guaranteed by the charter were indeed extraordinary from the time they were given until their abrogation by the French Revolution, which did little to make the citizens of Montbéliard more free.[11] Those rights that affected the religiopolitical tensions between the citizens and their count in the last quarter of the sixteenth century were the freedom to come and go and even to establish a residence elsewhere without prejudice to their holdings in Montbéliard. The bourgeois had only to return for six weeks out of the year and to maintain his other obligations to the community. Citizens also had the right to buy and sell and to pass on their goods in complete freedom. Should Montbéliard be endangered, the count would have to go to war to defend it. The bourgeoisie had the right to bestow citizenship on whomever they willed except in the case of those enfeoffed elsewhere. Religion and profession were not reasons to exclude someone from citizenship, as Jews and moneylenders were included from the beginning of the bestowal of the charter. More remarkable still, the citizens of Montbéliard were exempt from military service in the army of their count, but they were obliged to defend Montbéliard itself. These franchises and the others in the charter were guaranteed in perpetuity not only by the oath of the count but also through a legal document signed by the count's suzerain.[12] During the sixteenth century, Montbéliard belonged briefly to France, but for most of the early modern period it belonged to the duchy of Württemberg and therefore to the Holy Roman Empire.

The Montbéliard charter, dated May 1283, was granted to the bourgeois of Montbéliard by Count Renaud de Chalon-Bourgogne for the price of one thousand pounds.[13] It remained in effect until 1793.[14] The charter established the Nine Bourgeois, the Eighteen, and the Notables, together with the manner of their election, their duties, and terms of office. The town had nine areas, hence the recurring multiples of nine. The Nine Bourgeois represented their electorate before the count, administered the city, and acted as judges. Their offices were renewable each year when the Nine Bourgeois swore upon the gospel to uphold the rights of the count as well as those of the citizens. On the lighter side, their conviviality was assured since if one of their number was absent, he had to pay a fine of a large bottle of wine to be drunk in a tavern by the other eight. The Eighteen were selected by lot from fifty-four men chosen by the heads of families in each of the nine areas of the town. These Eighteen elected the Nine Bourgeois, seven of whom already served and two of whom were newly elected from the Eighteen. The Eighteen assisted in the government of Montbéliard in such offices as commissioners of fairs and markets, of properties, of security, and so on. The third municipal body was that of the Notables, whose duties were primarily ceremonial. The rights of a bourgeois were either inherited or, in the case of those coming from elsewhere, acquired upon payment of an *entrage,* a sum set by the Nine Bourgeois.[15] The bourgeois paid taxes to the count, who guaranteed them protection. Other categories of Montbéliardais were the *bourgeois-forains,* who were not permanent residents, *habitants-francs,* and *habitants-sujets.*

The count named three categories of municipal officers—the mayor who presided over the tribunal formed by the Nine Bourgeois, the procurator general, and *les chazes.*[16] The mayor had a consultative voice, but the right to determine guilt or innocence and to pronounce sentences belonged to the Nine Bourgeois. In addition, the count appointed three citizens to serve as *les chazes,* who had a voice in sentences that involved the loss of property or imprisonment. Justice was therefore rendered by twelve citizens of Montbéliard. The mayor had other duties, namely to look out for the count's interests, to denounce plots against the count or his council to the procurator general (also appointed by the count), to see to the payment of taxes and debts, to report the presence of foreign soldiers, and so on. The procurator represented the count in legal matters.

Because of its French-speaking citizenry and its unusual privileges, the county was often at odds with its German-speaking duke. These facts alone are not wholly responsible for Montbéliard's problems at the beginning of the sixteenth century. The blundering politics of Duke Ulrich of Württemberg set the scene for many of the difficulties that would emerge in the middle of the century.

After a brilliant beginning as friend and brother-in-law of Emperor Maximilian, who bestowed honors and military eminence upon him, Ulrich allowed his power to go to his head. Heavily in debt for the extravagance of his wedding, attended for several days by sixteen thousand men,[17] Ulrich imposed unpopular taxes on his people. After suppressing a popular revolt, Ulrich enraged the nobility by murdering John von Hutten in 1515.[18] Ulrich responded to the outrage of his people by increasing his tyranny, and he responded to the anger of the emperor by defiance. The result of this high-handed behavior was the loss of his duchy to the Swabian League.[19] Ulrich's daughter Anne, aged six, and her brother Christoph, aged four, were left in Tübingen and became captives of the Habsburgs.[20] To maintain Christoph, who was then removed to Habsburg Innsbruck, the Swabian League took Tübingen, Neuss, and Württemberg. The league then sold the rest of the duchy to Charles V.[21] Ulrich was left only Montbéliard, where he maintained his principle residence from 1520 to 1526.

Intent on regaining his lost territory, Ulrich sought help from some of the Swiss cantons and Philip of Hesse.[22] While in Basel, he came in contact with the native Württemberger and reformer Oecolampadius. In 1524 Ulrich sought Oecolampadius's advice concerning the reform of Montbéliard and in June, Oecolampadius's protégé, William Farel, arrived in Montbéliard.[23] Before the end of July, Farel's success had two results. Oecolampadius sent John Gailing of Ilsfeld to help him, while the archbishop of Besançon sent the father guardian of the Besançon Franciscans to oppose him.[24] Initially, the archbishop seemed to win the day, and first Gailing and then Farel had to leave Montbéliard. Meanwhile, the impoverished Ulrich had managed to raise Swiss troops and at the beginning of 1525 led them toward Württemberg. Fifteen twenty-five was also the year of the Peasants' War. Ulrich tried to make use of the peasants' revolt for his own purposes, but as the Peasants' War failed, so once again did Ulrich.[25] The revolt had another effect, however. It spread beyond Germany and inflamed Montbéliard. The peasants, and even the bourgeois, caught the fever and pillaged convents and monasteries abandoned by their frightened inmates. As elsewhere, the revolt was put down, but at the price of strengthening the already active anticlericalism of many of the people in the countryside and in the towns.

Frustrated in his attempt to regain his duchy and in dire need of funds, Ulrich leased Montbéliard and some nearby territories to his half brother George, who thereby became count of Montbéliard in 1526. The first lesson George learned was that the people of Montbéliard were used to an unusual amount of self-government and that they would deeply resent a heavy hand. George listened to his counselors and governed gently. The evangelical reform was in abeyance since George was still Catholic and Ulrich had not made clear his own position. What Farel had not accomplished and the war could not bring about, the archbishop of Besançon triggered by interdicting Montbéliard because it seemed to him that the town tolerated "Lutheranism." Against the archbishop rallied Count George and the mayor of Montbéliard. Duke Ulrich, at the court of Philip of Hesse, involved Zurich and Bern on the side of Count George. The interdict was lifted in May of 1529. Its effect could not have been other than further to alienate the people of Montbéliard from the Catholic church and to strengthen those who had been converted by Farel and remained true to his reform. In 1528, Count George became a "Lutheran" and employed a German Lutheran preacher at his court.[26]

The year 1529 was important for Montbéliard, although the little county had no knowledge of the crucial debate going on in Hesse despite the presence of Duke Ulrich at the court of Philip of Hesse during the Marburg Colloquy.[27] There Luther and Zwingli could not agree on the doctrine of the Lord's Supper, and thereafter Lutherans derisively referred to Zwinglians as "sacramentarians." The term was later extended to the Genevan reformers and their followers, with what could have been dire results. At the Diet of Augsburg in 1530, the Augsburg Confession was read before Charles V, and in 1531 Melanchthon wrote the less compromising Apology. Luther's followers now had a document against which to measure the orthodoxy of the "Protestants." Among those present at the Diet of Augsburg in 1530 were Count George and Duke Ulrich. Neither could envisage how the document he heard would be used in Montbéliard in the future.

Duke Ulrich seemed no nearer to regaining his duchy in 1534 than he was in 1526. Still in need of cash, Ulrich, with Hesse's help, "sold" Montbéliard to Francis I.[28] The French king knew the value of the little "gateway to the empire" and was willing to help against the Habsburgs. Ulrich retained the right of repurchase, a right he exercised after regaining Württemberg, when Charles V, also aware of the strategic value of the area, insisted that he do so in 1536. But first, Ulrich had to regain his territories. While Charles V was busy in Spain and his brother King Ferdinand was occupied with the Turks, Ulrich and his ally Philip of Hesse successfully invaded Württemberg.[29] The resulting Treaty of Kaadan returned his territories to Ulrich. As head of state, he was now able to "reform" his lands but under the condition that he allow no sacramentarians to remain.[30] For a prince who had learned the Reformation in Basel and Zurich and whose ally was Philip of Hesse, this was not a welcome condition. There is some debate, however, whether the Treaty of Kaadan was lawfully applicable in Montbéliard and its attached areas, namely: the county of Montbéliard itself, the four sovereign principalities of Héricourt, Chastelot, Blamont, and Clémont, the county of Horbourg in Alsace and also in Alsace, Riqueville, and three more principalities in Bourgogne: Granges, Clereval, and Passavant.[31] Since Ulrich's loss of Württemberg in 1519 did not include Montbéliard because Austria had no claim to it or to the Alsatian principalities, the Treaty of Kaadan by which Ulrich regained Württemburg should not have affected Montbéliard and its territories.[32] (But even if this were the case in 1534, Christoph and the emperor took steps to correct the situation. From these documents it would seem that the county and its territories came under imperial law before the Peace of Augsburg, which would involve the county in the same religious difficulties that the Reformed suffered in the empire.)[33]

Ulrich turned to friends in Strasbourg for advice. The reformers Martin Bucer and Wolfgang Capito both recommended two ministers, Jacob Grynaeus and Ambrose Blarer. The optimist Bucer assured Ulrich that the differences between Luther and Zwingli were not so important as the introduction of the Reformation itself. Persuaded by this argument, Ulrich sent Grynaeus to guide the University of Tübingen, while Blarer was to minister to the southern half of the duchy. The Lutheran Erhardt Schnepf, recommended by Philip of Hesse, was engaged to minister to the northern half.[34] Although both pastors accepted the Augsburg Confession, Blarer espoused a Zwinglian interpretation while Schnepf insisted on a Lutheran understanding. The two men worked out a basic formula for the Lord's Supper, the so-called Stuttgart Concord, which freed Blarer from the taint of being a sacramentarian.[35] It also moved Württemberg nearer to the Lutheran camp and loosened the bonds between Ulrich and the German Swiss.

Meanwhile, John Gailing was recalled by Ulrich as his chaplain. There were now four ministers in the duchy of Württemberg, two Swiss whose doctrine was inspired by the reforms in Zurich, Basel, and Strasbourg, and two Germans who sided with Luther. The disagreement at Marburg already divided ministers who considered themselves to be "evangelical," eschewing any other title, for example, "Lutheran." Although theological differences had already appeared, the bitterness of later disputes was not yet evident in Württemberg in early 1535, and the four men agreed not to argue over the problem of what the unworthy received when they communicated.[36]

Problems remained in Montbéliard, however. Count George was responsible for the religion of the area and had therefore to engage a minister capable of stabilizing the Reformation there. Although George preferred the Swiss reform, he had to be careful to ensure that none of the ministers brought to Montbéliard could be expelled as a sacramentarian. To avoid that charge, the church of Montbéliard, its people, and its ministers endorsed the Augsburg Confession. Finally, the clergy had to speak French. When George consulted Ulrich, the duke turned to Grynaeus at Tübingen, who told him about Pierre Toussain, already at Tübingen, who fit every requirement. Recommended also by Blarer and Bucer, Toussain was thirty-six years old, well educated, and a dedicated churchman.[37] He had early made the acquaintance of Oecolampadius and Farel in Basel and then had traveled in Germany, France, and Switzerland, suffering imprisonment for his beliefs in Paris and Metz. When he arrived in Württemberg, Grynaeus and Blarer invited him to assist them. It was thus that Toussain was brought to the attention of Duke Ulrich, who sent him to Count George in Montbéliard.

Toussain's theological convictions were in harmony with Farel and so with those people of Montbéliard who had remained true to Farel's reform from 1524 to 1535 when Toussain arrived. Toussain reaffirmed the Swiss doctrine of the Lord's Supper rather than the doctrine taught by Luther. In doing so, Toussain considered himself to be simply "evangelical," that is, one who is guided by the principle of *sola scriptura*. Like the Swiss, Toussain found no warrant for insisting on the bodily presence of Christ on every altar; indeed, the Gospels affirmed that Christ had ascended bodily to heaven. To deny the circumscription and local nature of the body of the ascended Christ would be tantamount to a denial of the real human nature of Christ; it would be to fall into the heresy of Docetism, which taught that Christ had only the appearance of a body. Toussain, therefore, could not follow Luther in the latter's doctrine of a real bodily presence that required each communicant to eat the body of Christ with the mouth and teeth. The Swiss, following Zwingli and Oecolampadius, believed rather that the communicant received the body of Christ spiritually, that is to say, in faith and through the power of the Holy Spirit. For the Swiss, the bread and wine were symbols of union with Christ but not the bearers of the substance of the body and blood of Christ.[38] They could not affirm that the word *is* was to be taken literally in the formula "This *is* my body; . . . this *is* my blood." Rather, the Swiss reformed believed that *is* meant *signifies*.[39] Toussain preferred not to enter into the kind of debate that these distinctions entailed or to search for formulas like the one devised by Blarer and Schnepf. Until the end of his life, Toussain insisted that he was an Evangelical, a follower of the gospel, first, last, and always. In the Gospels he found the command to do as Christ had done at the Last Supper, and he believed that by so doing he and other communicants were united in a special way to the living, risen Christ. How this was accomplished was not something for Christians to argue over or to use as a basis for excluding one another from the Supper. Rather, Toussain wanted to see all Evangelicals united in a common stand against Roman Catholics.[40]

Toussain may have preferred to stand on common ground and not to dispute the manner in which Christ and communicant were united, but the

Treaty of Kaadan lifted the argument from the area of church discipline and placed it squarely in the realm of politics. No sacramentarian, no one who shared Zwingli's view of the Lord's Supper, could remain in Duke Ulrich's territories. Count George was concerned about this legal requirement, and although he too preferred the Swiss doctrine, he nevertheless asked Ulrich whether or not Toussain was a legal resident in Montbéliard given Toussain's theology. In the spring of 1536, before Toussain had been in Montbéliard a full year, Count George asked him which of the two ministers, Blarer or Schnepf, he favored. Not surprisingly, Toussain said that he stood on the side of Blarer, whose doctrine he knew. Toussain added that he had never heard of Schnepf and so could not say whether he agreed with him or not. In addition, declared Toussain, he was not a Zwinglian either. He simply preached from the gospel.[41] Based on this answer, Count George did not feel that he could give Toussain his wholehearted support although he did not have grounds to dismiss him either. The full reform of Montbéliard did not occur, therefore, until the end of 1538.

During these years, so difficult for Toussain and confusing for his parishioners, neither Ulrich nor George dared anger Charles V by fully supporting the reform in their territories. Toussain preached, brought in schoolmasters, and did all he could, including writing scolding letters to the two rulers, but his own religious zeal was tempered by the political reality understood only too well by George and Ulrich. Count George hoped also that those who had remained Catholic would come to accept the Reformation little by little. To force them to change their religion would have two unfortunate effects: an appeal to imperial authority and the division of the people of the town into factions. George's patience was to prove prudent. In November 1538, Count George suppressed the Mass in Montbéliard and forbade the monks at Belchamp to receive novices or to admit the public to their services. The church of St. Mainboeuf in Montbéliard was closed except for Sunday services and by March 1539 was stripped of relics, statues, and other Catholic accoutrements. On Easter Sunday, April 6, 1539, the Lord's Supper was celebrated according to "evangelical principles."[42]

Politics entered again, however, and in a form that would be repeated until the end of the sixteenth century and into the seventeenth in this tough-minded town. Count George did not like to see those citizens of Montbéliard who remained Catholic traveling to Catholic villages to hear the Mass no longer available in Montbéliard. On August 6, 1539, he published an edict forbidding such travel.[43] The affected citizens appealed to their ancient liberties as bourgeois of a privileged town.[44] Those liberties, it will be remembered, included the right to travel freely to neighboring towns. They accused Count George of trying to gain political power over them under cover of religious zeal. Reformed or Catholic, the people of Montbéliard would not tolerate the loss of privileges, and the argument of the Catholics created a small revolution in the town. Elections were called, and the newly elected governing body favored the Catholics, appealing to Duke Ulrich against the mandates of Count George. Ulrich conceded, and the reforming edicts of Count George were repealed. In this instance, the effort of the ruler of Montbéliard to stop the migration of his people to religious ceremonies outside Montbéliard resulted in the defeat of the ruler.[45] Future battles over the same principle of this same privilege would not be so easily resolved.[46]

The seesaw between Catholics and Reformed could not continue. Count George renewed his efforts to reform Montbéliard. He sent to Geneva to ask for ministers, who began to arrive by the end of 1539. Some of the newly arrived pastors were sent to rural parishes; others remained in Montbéliard. Toussain also wrote to Farel, settled in Neuchâtel, to help choose good pastors for Montbéliard. By 1541, all of Count George's territory was Reformed and supplied with evangelical pastors.

Between 1541 and 1559, Toussain developed schools and the organization of the Montbéliard church, which included the rural parishes. In 1559 Toussain published at Basel *L'Ordre / qu'on tient en l' / Eglise de Mont / béliard, en instrui / sant les enfans, / administrant les saints Sacremens, / avec la forme du / Mariage & des / Prieres.*[47] As Toussain wrote in the preface to the work, the form of the sacraments had been in use, unchanged, for "about twenty years." Viénot comments that Toussain's liturgy was in use in Montbéliard as early as 1535.[48]

Toussain's eucharistic theology can be extracted from his liturgy.

1. To receive communion is to participate in the body and blood of the Savior.
2. One thereby receives grace and the forgiveness of sins as well as the assurance of salvation.
3. Communicants are united in Christ's mystical body, that is, the company of the faithful.
4. Those with true faith who deplore their sins participate worthily and for their salvation.
5. Sinners are not to come to the communion table.

Toussain does not say what happens when a hypocrite, a sinner, an unbeliever receives communion. The thorny issue of the communion of the unworthy or the unbelievers is not addressed here since it would involve Toussain in the sort of scholastic dispute he wished to avoid, namely whether one eats the body of Christ with the physical mouth or the mouth of faith. But the formula pronounced by the minister as he gives communion to each one indicates the role of faith in salvation: "May the faith which you have in the body of Jesus Christ crucified save you. May the faith which you have in the blood of Christ shed for your sins give you eternal life."

No sooner had Count George assured the success of the reform in his territories than he had to leave them. In an argument over Ulrich's debts to him, George was ordered out of Montbéliard by his enraged brother. Duke Ulrich then bestowed Montbéliard on his son, Christoph, soon to be known as "the pious" because of his firm Lutheranism. Christoph had been raised by the Bavarian Habsburgs and accompanied Emperor Charles V from Vienna to Augsburg in 1530. There Christoph saw the duchy of Württemberg bestowed on Charles's brother Ferdinand. To forestall the Bavarian Habsburgs from assisting Ulrich and his heir, Christoph, to regain Württemberg, Charles decided to send Christoph to France. But Christoph escaped during the passage of the court through the Tyrol. Two years later, he joined his triumphant father, who had indeed regained Württemberg with the help of the Bavarian Habsburgs. Ulrich, however, suspected his Bavarian allies of wanting to put Christoph in his place. It was Ulrich himself, therefore, who, in the end, sent Christoph to France.[49] Christoph remained at the court of Francis I for eight years before Ulrich summoned him in the summer of 1542 to become the count of Montbéliard. There seems to have been no need for Christoph to become evangelical when he promised his father to maintain Protestantism in Montbéliard; apparently Christoph had already become a Lutheran.

A well-educated nobleman, Christoph engaged in theological reading and discussion. His reading drew him more to Luther than to the Swiss side of the eucharistic discussions and of the Lutheran theologians, more to Brenz in Württemberg than to Melanchthon in Wittenberg.[50] Christoph preferred the 1530 edition of the Augsburg Confession to the *Variata* edition prepared by Philipp Melanchthon for the collocutors at Hagenau-Regensburg in 1540–1541. The point of dispute between the two versions of the Augsburg Confession was article X, which read in the 1530 *Invariata:* "Concerning the Lord's Supper, they teach that the body and blood of Christ are truly present and distributed to communicants in the Lord's Supper." In the 1540 edition, the *Variata,* this phrase was changed to read: "Concerning the Lord's Supper, they teach that with the bread and wine the body and blood are truly exhibited to the communicants." Although the change seems slight, it had profound and disturbing meaning for the non-Philippist Lutherans since it was done to accommodate the Swiss and Strasbourgians. Bucer and Calvin had come to Regensburg from Strasbourg, and both interpreted the action of the Lord's Supper to be one of offering the body and blood of Christ to the faith of the communicant rather than distributing them as objects to the physical mouths of the communicants whether these latter believed or not.[51] The Lutherans themselves were to split over these differences, and those who followed the *Variata* were condescendingly referred to as Philippists. In 1577, the split thus introduced was resolved in favor of the *Invariata* for those who signed the Formula of Concord.[52]

Christoph had already chosen sides. He turned to Schnepf and in 1543 received from him a translation into Latin of the German Württemberg Church Order prepared by Schnepf in 1536. The Latin version[53] was to serve the needs of the French-speaking clergy of Montbéliard and assure their allegiance to the duke of Württemberg and to the mandate of the Treaty of Kaadan.[54] The moderate *Regula* was not, however, acceptable to the Montbéliard clergy. They had other traditions and were fearful of anything that looked even remotely like a return to the ceremonies of Catholicism such as the celebration of feast days mandated by the *Regula.* Worse still, Christoph had asked Schnepf to send a German minister, presumably to oversee the observance of the *Regula*. John Engelmann, who knew no French, offended the Montbéliard clergy theologically and culturally.

The situation became tense, and Toussain, torn between defending the traditions he had done so much to establish and going elsewhere, wrote to Calvin and Farel for advice on those matters that most disturbed him. Toussain inquired about giving communion to the sick and to those who requested it outside of the celebration of the Lord's Supper. The Lutheran practice of carrying communion to the sick required reservation of the bread and wine, and would that not also imply adoration of the reserved species, a purely Catholic practice? Following the Swiss Reformed, Toussain wanted to have a small congregation gathered around the sick person and the Lord's Supper celebrated in an abbreviated form, which, of course, would include the words of consecration.[55] Another practice allowed by the Lutherans but eschewed by the Reformed was emergency baptism administered by midwives. This practice was, according to Calvin, not only irregular but blasphemous. In fact, wrote Calvin, Toussain must resist this practice even unto death.[56] Bells might be rung, but the observation of feast days was also to be rejected since it so easily led to superstition. Calvin advised the ministers of Montbéliard to stand firm on these matters of principle but to yield wherever else their consciences would allow.

Christoph had also requested that Toussain provide a statement on baptism and the Lord's Supper so that the young count could be sure that his territory was correct with regard to the sacraments. In January 1544, Toussain complied with a confession written in Latin that was brief, simple, and avoided controversial points.[57] Toussain appealed first to scholastic authority with regard to the nature of a sacrament as a visible sign of an invisible grace. Nothing was said about emergency baptism. The paragraph on the eucharist referred to the doctrine of Irenaeus and established the bread and wine as earthly signs of the heavenly reality, namely the body and blood of Christ. These heavenly realities are truly to be given (*dari*) as food for souls. Toussain protected the Reformed eucharistic doctrine without offending Lutheran sensibilities. Indeed, his use of "true" (*vere*) and "given" (*dari*) reassured the Lutherans.

Other points remained a source of contention. Engelmann wanted to impose the feasts of the Virgin Mary and of the apostles, but Toussain refused to allow it and again asked for the advice and help of his Reformed Swiss and German friends. Engelmann carried news of the disobedience of Montbéliard's clergy to Stuttgart and received fresh and harsher orders from Duke Ulrich as well as Count Christoph. Nothing less than complete compliance with the Württemberg Church Order would do. Meanwhile letters from Viret, Farel, and Calvin sustained Toussain and his ministers, advising them to yield where they had to but not on the points of their freedom to assemble and their refusal to allow midwives to baptize. In fact, Calvin urged Toussain to explain everything clearly to Schnepf, relying on his intelligence to understand. Calvin praised Luther's wisdom and did not doubt that the two Germans would support Toussain in the end.[58] In his response regarding baptism, Calvin sketched the lines of the debate as Beza would conduct it in 1586. Midwives should not baptize because they are not ordained to administer the sacraments. No emergency baptism is necessary because salvation does not depend on human activity but on God's election, which establishes a person as part of the covenant with or without the exterior action that is its sign. To make heaven or hell dependent on the administration of baptism is to make the sacrament an object of superstitious magic. Calvin regarded baptism by midwives as "impious and a profanation of legitimate baptism."[59]

Meanwhile, Engelmann was not content to let Toussain's confession regarding the eucharist get by. He asked the test question that would rack Lutheran-Reformed eucharistic debates for the rest of the century: What do the impious receive, the body of Christ or the bread only? The question assumes that the "impious" are those without true faith; otherwise the issue is not as squarely joined as Engelmann intended. Engelmann wanted Toussain to affirm that the *bodily presence* of Christ in the Lord's Supper is independent of the faith of the individual recipient. The Reformed position taught that the *efficacy* of the Lord's Supper depended on the faith of the communicant. Within that general position, the doctrines of Zwingli, Bullinger, and Calvin all differed.[60] In fact, Calvin's doctrine was closer to Luther's than to either of the two Zurichers, and its was Calvin's doctrine that now guided the clergy of Montbéliard. According to this French Reformed teaching, the body and blood of Christ are where Christ has ascended, in heaven. They cannot be physically or corporally present on earthly altars without denying two christological doctrines: the human nature of Christ and his bodily ascension. According to the human nature of Christ, his body, like all human bodies, is locally circumscribed and cannot be in more than one place at a time. According to the doctrine of the corporal ascension of Christ, Christ is in heaven, seated at the right hand of the Father. During communion in the Lord's Supper, Christ offers himself, through the power of the Holy Spirit, to those whose faith prepares their hearts to be united to him. The power of the Holy Spirit is the key to the union of believers in the body of Christ, lifting them to heaven, where they eat the heavenly food and drink the heavenly drink of Christ's ascended body and blood so that the believers become flesh of his flesh and bone of his bone. Unbelievers receive only bread and wine since they have no "mouth of faith" to eat the true body and blood of Christ offered to all. Hence the true body and blood of Christ are *offered* to all regardless of faith or worthiness, but they are *received* only by the faithful. Reception of the true body and blood of Christ, therefore, is dependent on faith.

Toussain knew that Engelmann was trying to draw him out in order to prove to Christoph and Ulrich that Toussain should not be allowed to remain as a minister of the church of Montbéliard. Once again, he appealed to Calvin, who wrote directly to Schnepf, asking him to urge Engelmann to stop his attacks.[61] The result was that both Schnepf and John Brenz[62] wrote to Engelmann counseling a less aggressive attitude, but their appeal was ineffective. As Viénot discovered in letters between Schnepf and Brenz, the two Lutherans were deeply suspicious of the Reformed position and in fact supported Engelmann and other German Lutheran ministers against the French Reformed clergy of Montbéliard.[63]

The struggle between the county of Montbéliard and its rulers continued through the Interim and the Peace of Augsburg. The famous peace of 1555 set the Augsburg Confession as the test of Protestant orthodoxy in the empire. Protestants who affirmed the Augsburg Confession and "Old Believers" or Catholics were the only legitimate residents within the German estates of the empire. As a result, Lutherans were more determined than ever to establish the *Invariata* and thereby to prove that the Reformed were not true followers of the Augsburg Confession and thus were illegitimate within the empire. The Reformed, on the other hand, continually affirmed their orthodoxy on the basis of the *Variata*. The confessional battles waged on a larger scale elsewhere were reflected in Montbéliard.[64]

A five-year hiatus (1553–1558) gave Pierre Toussain some relief when Duke Ulrich died in November of 1550 and his son, Count Christoph, became duke of Württemberg. In 1553, Christoph recalled his uncle George to serve once again as count of Montbéliard. George had persevered in his preference for the Reformed tradition as practiced in Montbéliard, and until his death in 1558 Count George supported Toussain. George's support was not merely verbal. He built a new school, a crucial factor in the development of the reform; he approved Toussain's 1535 liturgy: *L'Ordre qu'on tient en l'Eglise de Montbéliard, en instruisant les enfans et administrant les saints sacremens, avec la forme du mariage et des prieres.*[65] George also provided for scholarships to the University of Tübingen for boys of Montbéliard who wanted to become ministers. Count George's will provided both stipends and money for the building of a college at the university to house Montbéliard students who began to attend there in 1560.[66]

It was during this peaceful time under Count George that a serious theological rupture over predestination distanced Toussain and the Montbéliard clergy from their French Swiss allies, Viret, Farel, and Calvin. In fact, the French Swiss were to stand almost alone with regard to double predestination, an issue raised sharply by Bern, whose council ordered that the argument be relegated to silence in its territories, which included Lausanne. In Lausanne, however, Viret and Beza were supported by Calvin in Geneva and by Farel in Neuchâtel. The controversy resulted in Calvin's treatises and Beza's *Tabula* and the expulsion of Viret and Beza from Lausanne.[67] The Montbéliard ministers, who favored single predestination, were at one with the Lutherans and the Swiss in Bern in opposing Calvin's doctrine of double predestination. They were also opposed to capital punishment for heretics and sided with Castellio against Calvin and Farel over the Servetus affair.[68] Farel broke with Toussain, but Calvin, while disapproving of Toussain's views, would continue to respond to his requests for advice on other issues. When Farel appealed to Count George, George supported Toussain wholeheartedly. As for Toussain, the minister held to his beliefs and grieved for the loss of Farel's friendship and Calvin's esteem. Repercussions of this division would play an important role also in the colloquy of 1586.[69]

The underlying principle of the position taken by Toussain and his clergy, according to Viénot,[70] was that of the integrity of the territorial church. The church of the county of Montbéliard could not be swayed from its faith and liturgy by outsiders. Those who settled in Montbéliard, especially those sent to minister there, would have to conform to the church order approved by Count George. But to assert the integrity of the church of Montbéliard raised another problem: In what way did the county of Montbéliard relate to the duchy of Württemberg? Could a dependent territory assert theological and ecclesiastical independence from its suzerain? This is the issue that would disturb the peace of Montbéliard and infuriate the dukes of Württemberg for the rest of the century. The basis for Montbéliard's claims to a degree of independence lay in the privileges the county and the town had accumulated throughout the Middle Ages. The dukes of Württemberg were not free to command as they willed; they had to respect the treaties and grants obtained in the past by the bourgeois of Montbéliard.

Just how far the duke of Württemberg could push the county of Mont-béliard was tried again and again after the death of Count George in 1558. George's infant son, Frederick, was governed by three Lutheran guardians: the dukes Christoph of Württemberg, Wolfgang of Zweibrucke, and Philip of Hanau-Lichtenberg. Frederick was therefore born of a Reformed father and educated under the direction of ardent Lutherans. During Frederick's minority, the three guardians determined policy for Montbéliard and, in 1559, established a visitation committee consisting of Eberhard Bidembach, Cunmann Flinsback, and Pierre Toussain himself. The committee found that the clergy of Montbéliard conformed to the Augsburg Confession and the Württemberg Church Order except on two points: emergency baptism and the *communicatio indignorum*. The commission also determined that the ministers lacked proper books and therefore provided Bibles, copies of the Augsburg Confession, the Saxon Confession, the Württemberg Church Order, and Melanchthon's *Loci communes*.[71] The perimeters of the battle were now clear. The clergy of Montbéliard would have to yield on two important points that distinguished them from the Lutherans and, at the time, associated them with the Reformed. What is more, they were forbidden to consult the French Swiss theologians or to allow French refugees to become ministers since the Huguenots were Calvinists and would not only reinforce non-Lutheran doctrine but reintroduce dissension with regard to double pre-destination. Christoph decided that the best solution was to impose on Montbéliard the Württemberg Church Order, written by Schnepf and revised by John Brenz.[72] To this end, the church order was translated from German into Latin, and Toussain was then to make a French translation and see to its promulgation.

In February 1560, the Montbéliard ministers were gathered by German Lutheran delegates of the three prince-tutors and told that, *auctoritate magistratus,* they must conform to the Württemberg Church Order or be dismissed. The only concessions were that they need not use Latin chants and that the old people could continue to use Toussain's French catechism. All others must use the Württemberg catechism composed by Brenz. The history of the resistance of the Montbéliard clergy, led by Toussain, is remarkable for their persistence in the face of ducal and theological intransigence. To the petitions of the ministers were added letters from the Montbéliard council, who appealed to the threat to civic order. Disorder would follow if there were a wholesale dismissal of their clergy or even if the people were asked to accept different formulas for the administration of the sacraments. In 1562, Christoph was advised to have the Montbéliard clergy sign the Wittenberg Concord as well as accept the Württemberg Confession with regard to the Lord's Supper.[73] The Wittenberg Concord raised new problems and possibilities since Toussain and his colleagues had no problem with Bucer's understanding of it, which, they thought, gave them some leeway with regard to the Lutheran interpretation. Viénot judged the signing of the Wittenberg Concord to be a Lutheran victory,[74] but if one looks carefully at the interpretation that Bucer appended, it is not so surprising that Toussain agreed to sign it and thereafter always affirmed that he (and the Montbéliard clergy) understood the Wittenberg Concord as did Bucer.[75]

With the signing of the Wittenberg Concord, the ducal guardians and the ministers themselves thought they might enjoy some years of peaceful coexistence. But 1562 marked a far more important event, the massacre at Wassy and the beginning of the wars of religion in France. Montbéliard was a logical place of refuge for French Huguenots, whose presence created problems within and without the county. The kings of France as well as the political and ecclesiastical leaders of nearby Roman Catholic areas suspected that Francophile and Reformed territories within the empire would become staging grounds for Huguenot troops.[76]

Within the county, the presence of French Calvinist refugees raised the same problems that had caused the painful arguments with Farel and Calvin. In addition to the difference about double or single predestination, the Calvinists were much less flexible concerning the Lord's Supper than Toussain and the other clergy in Montbéliard were willing to be.[77] Since this sort of division was just what had created the situation the guardian-tutors had tried to avoid, the presence of professing Calvinists in Montbéliard caused Duke Christoph to intervene again. All refugees were to be examined with regard to their beliefs and their intentions concerning residency in Montbéliard. Toussain himself testified to his belief in single predestination and God's universal salvific will. Toussain then assured Christoph that the ministers and council of Montbéliard had dismissed four of the clergy who held Calvin's teaching of double predestination. Viénot summed up the theological parties in Montbéliard in the 1560s: "There were the intransigent Calvinists, the strict Lutherans and, equally distant from both, the 'Evangelicals' represented by Toussain and his friends."[78] The evangelicals wanted to teach the simple gospel; they accepted the Augsburg Confession as conformed to God's Word and they accepted also the Wittenberg Concord of 1536 and most but not all of the Württemberg Church Order of 1559. Toussain's French confession of faith and his liturgy continued to be favored and to be used by the evangelicals.

In 1568, Duke Christoph died and was succeeded by his son, Ludwig. Ludwig had been raised at Tübingen in a time and under the rectorship of a man given to confessional disputation. Jacob Andreae was rector at Tübingen and was not one to tolerate deviance among Lutherans, much less allow Calvinists any quarter. Ludwig would do all he could to unite his duchy not only as Lutheran but indeed as the peculiar type of Lutheranism taught by John Brenz and Jacob Andreae. Württemberg Lutheranism supported the eucharistic doctrine taught in the 1530 Augsburg Confession by a doctrine of their own, ubiquitarianism.[79] The consequences for Montbéliard were grave. Since Frederick was still underage, Montbéliard continued to be governed by the three ducal guardians, principally Duke Ludwig.

In the meantime, Toussain's son, Daniel, was driven from his ministry in Orléans by the wars of religion. Daniel was a Huguenot, a minister of the French church, and therefore a Calvinist. But this fact was not a problem to the people and clergy of Montbéliard, among whom Daniel found not only welcome but popularity, to the degree that all agreed he should succeed his aged father as superintendent at Montbéliard.

The unanimity in Montbéliard was not reflected in Stuttgart, however, and in 1571 Duke Ludwig asked his theologians to investigate Daniel Toussain.[80] The theological delegation to Montbéliard was led by none other than Jacob Andreae.[81] The state of confessional theology, of disputes among Lutherans and between Lutherans and Calvinists, meant that alert clergy were now more highly trained in theological fine points and in the polemics engendered by the increasingly frequent disputes. Andreae and Daniel Toussain were of a different breed than Pierre Toussain and Brenz, just as Ludwig was a more intransigent (but not a more pious) Lutheran than his father, Christoph. Since the agreement of 1562, the demands on the Montbéliard clergy had become more precise. Not only were they to adopt the Württemberg Church Order, they were also to adopt Württemberg theology in its entirety, including the doctrine of ubiquity. The result was to unite the ministers of Montbéliard against Andreae. Differences between Montbéliard evangelicals and French Calvinists ceased to matter so much as the theological focus became eucharistic and christological. Only two ministers in the county supported ubiquity, L'Archer at Héricourt and Leger Grimault at Montecheroux.

Andreae's first act was to examine the recent arrival from France, the man who had become the most prominent of the ministers, Daniel Toussain. Wasting no time, Andreae asked D. Toussain about his eucharistic doctrine, because, said Andreae, there can be peace only where there is truth.[82] Toussain saw through this ploy and immediately turned to the real issue. He accused Andreae of imposing new conditions on Montbéliard, in fact of asking the clergy and people to give up their own traditions and adopt those of Württemberg, which now included condemning the French Calvinists and the Reformed of the Palatinate. The debate then turned to the nature of Christ's presence in the Lord s Supper, with the predictable outcome that Toussain was discovered to be a Calvinist or, as Andreae would have it, a Zwinglian, that is, a sacramentarian. He could not, therefore, be allowed to remain in Montbéliard.

Andreae had to decide how to bring the rest of the clergy into line, and to that end, he prepared a confession that would be imposed upon the council and clergy of Montbéliard. All but two of the council signed the statement drawn up by Andreae and his theological assistants. Many of the ministers, fearing their dismissal, also signed. Others refused, and still others asked for time to consider what they should do. Two signed and then withdrew their signatures. Pierre and Daniel Toussain spoke for all. Daniel affirmed the adherence of the Montbéliardais to the terms of the 1562 agreement, including the Augsburg Confession and the Wittenberg Concord. He eloquently pointed out that neither the Augsburg Confession nor the Wittenberg Concord contained condemnations of other Protestant groups such as the Swiss or French Reformed churches. The confession that Andreae wanted them to sign did condemn these churches.[83] Andreae had claimed that he wished to bring peace to Montbéliard; the result of his first visit was to bring confusion and distress.

The answer to Andreae's appeal was a firm refusal. A new minister was therefore sent to Montbéliard, a German Lutheran from Stuttgart, Henry Efferhen. Pierre Toussain was "retired," and Daniel sent back to France.[84] As they realized what had transpired, the citizens reacted. The Nine Bourgeois, in the name of the people, asked the prince-guardians to allow them to retain their ministers and to practice their religion as they had done for nearly fifty years, thirty-seven of them under the ecclesiastical leadership of Pierre Toussain. The next day the Württemberg commissioners answered by accusing the citizens of Montbéliard of sedition. The commissioners did not transmit the citizens' request to the princes; instead, they threatened that had they done so, the princes would have been very angry.[85]

Daniel Toussain returned the attack. He had no objection to the teaching of the Augsburg Confession, but he could not accept Andreae's doctrine of the ubiquity of the body of Christ. Nor had he any problem with the Wittenberg Concord as long as Bucer's explanations were included. Finally, he could not condemn Zwinglians and Calvinists. The eucharistic issue turned also on the *manducatio indignorum.* Bucer had maintained that the faithless, as a category distinct from the unworthy, did not receive the body of Christ, while Andreae, declared Toussain, taught that everyone, even those without faith, received the true body of Christ.

Since the issue of the Wittenberg Concord became central to the eucharistic argument between the Württemberg theologians and the ministers and people of Montbéliard, it is appropriate to understand why Daniel Toussain insisted that the 1571 agreement (like that of 1562) include Bucer's commentary and not just the text of the Concord itself.

The explanation of Martin Bucer is found in a book published in 1561 containing eucharistic essays by Farel, Bucer, Melanchthon, Brenz, and Peter Bocquin. The selection from Bucer consists of his explanation of each of the chapters included in the Wittenberg Concord.[86] With regard to paragraph III, Bucer speaks of three kinds of persons who may present themselves for communion:

> Above all, there are three sorts of persons who may take the Sacrament. The first are all those who condemn and ridicule it, who are not only impious, but who do not believe the Lord. These know and feel that they receive nothing but bread and wine and in fact, that is all that they do receive because they pervert the words and institution of the Lord. The second group believe that by these words the Lord offers them his body and they accept the same sacramentally, so that at the same time they receive the reality of the sacrament [*rem sacramenti*] but not, nevertheless, that gift of God which depends upon a worthy reception. These make themselves guilty of the body and blood of the Lord who nevertheless want to receive it and do receive it because they embrace the words and institution of the Lord. They do not eat truly, as Augustine said, that is they do not fully enjoy this vivifiying food for which they are not sufficiently prepared mentally. The third are those who not only believe the institution of the Lord and prepare themselves to receive this sacrament, but at the same time, with a lively faith, prepare for it, think about it and embrace it. These last thereby receive the virtue and joy of this food.[87]

The distinctions made here are interesting indeed and allow Pierre Toussain to maintain a *manducatio indignorum* while denying a *manducatio infidelium*. It is a position between Calvin's and Luther's and merits study in itself.[88] It also makes clear why the ministers of Montbéliard insisted that their acceptance of the Wittenberg Concord was according to Bucer's understanding of it.[89]

Bucer's explanation of baptism also supported the two Toussains and the Montbéliard clergy. Bucer affirmed that baptism is necessary because God commands it and because no one is saved without the action of God. But "we do not know what that action of God is in infants" any more than we know what was the nature of the movement of John in his mother's womb.[90] We do know that infants do not have the use of intelligence and yet whatever God does in them must be similar to faith and love. But the point is, said Bucer, that infants are not made holy and saved except by divine action in them.[91] Finally, he wrote, while baptism should be administered publicly on certain days, when someone is in danger of death, the ministers should see to it that he or she is baptized. Bucer did not specifically exclude midwives or laymen from administering emergency baptism, but he implied the Reformed doctrine by saying that "the ministers should see to it."[92]

Only two years remained to Pierre Toussain. They were years spent trying to maintain the church of Montbéliard in the same belief and liturgy that he had fostered during the thirty-seven years he had served as its principal minister. Since the Montbéliardais could find no relief within the duchy of Württemberg, they looked elsewhere. In December 1571, they wrote to Theodore Beza in Geneva and the church at Neuchâtel for advice. Beza advised them to remain as peaceful as possible and to utilize the services of the pastors assigned them when they could do so in good conscience.[93] The ministers of Neuchâtel were more aggressive and advised the Montbéliardais to boycott the services of the Lutheran ministers. If they did not wish to delay baptisms, pregnant women should go to Reformed towns to have their babies, which, in fact, some of the women of Montbéliard did.[94] Advice from both correspondents counseled the Montbéliardais to make use of their ancient treaties with Bern to exert pressure on the duke of Württemberg. Beza also advised that in their acceptance of the Augsburg Confession they stipulate "as Melanchthon explained it," which meant, of curse, the *Variata* and the Apology and excluded the interpretation of Andreae with its condemnation of Zwinglians as well as Anabaptists. The battle had now passed beyond Montbéliard, and the two major combatants were engaged—Jacob Andreae from Württemberg/ Tübingen and Theodore Beza from Geneva.

Less than two years later, in January 1573, Andreae and three associates (Hans Conrad von Ulm, Heinrich Hans von Mundolsheim, and Balthasar Bidembach) were in Montbéliard, commissioned to examine the ministers and schoolmasters and to dismiss any whom they found to be "Calvinist" in their eucharistic doctrine. As Viénot recalls, the commissioning of Andreae and his colleagues came within months of the St. Bartholomew's Day massacre. Refugees from France flowed into Reformed areas in the empire, including Montbéliard. These refugees were Huguenots, Calvinists. But Duke Ludwig was not listening to appeals from Reformed[95] leaders to unite the Protestant powers against the Catholic powers. In fact, as we shall see,[96] Lutheran princes tended to listen as closely to the French crown as they did to the appeals of the Huguenots. Meanwhile, Charles IX of France wrote to Ludwig asking him not to allow the refugees to remain in his territories. Ludwig communicated this request to the council of Montbéliard. The Montbéliardais responded by making the French refugees bourgeois and therefore legitimate citizens. Ludwig then countered that the French could stay only if they accepted the Augsburg Confession and the Württemberg Church Order.[97]

Returning among the refugees was Daniel Toussain, escaped from the devastation at Orléans. But he could not remain and a few days later left for Basel. Before the end of 1573, Pierre Toussain, aged seventy-five, had been dismissed and died within months.

Andreae and the other commissioners had demanded that the council, the clergy, and the schoolmasters sign a formula that included the *manducatio indignorum*. They condemned the minister Floret's explanation of the formula of 1571. On January 12, 1573, an act of concord was signed.[98] The act began by acknowledging the commissioners sent by George Frederick, marquis of Brandenburg, and Charles, marquis of Baden, the guardians of Count Frederick. Called before the commissioners were the Nine Bourgeois, the Eighteen, and the Notables, as well as other officers of Montbéliard. Before the signing, Andreae, speaking in German, reprimanded the gathered citizens and ministers. His harangue was then translated into French. Andreae rehearsed the events of 1571 and 1572. He reproached the Montbéliardais for not accepting his efforts to bring "peace and union." Now, the guardian princes had again sent Andreae and Bidembach to smooth out the difficulties besetting the Montbéliard church. Their mission had no other end, said Andreae, than to bring "peace and to introduce the Confessions of Augsburg and Württemberg with the latter's Ecclesiastical Ordinances plus the Concordat of 1536 between Luther and Bucer."[99] In addition, due to Pierre Toussaint's great age, they were to install Henry Efferhen as superintendent of the Montbéliard churches. The articles themselves included subscription to the Lutheran canon: Scripture plus the three creeds (Apostles', Nicene, Athanasian), the Augsburg and Württemberg Confession (the two are given in the singular) with the Apology of the Augsburg Confession. This body of confessional material was called by Andreae "the creed of our time by which the churches of this county and the adjoining lands are distinguished from the papists and other sects."[100]

The Montbéliardais must also accept the Wittenberg Concord, especially with regard to the Lord's Supper.[101] Specifically, they must accept that the body and blood of Christ are truly and substantially exhibited and received with the bread and wine, not by a natural or local or inclusive union but in a heavenly and mysterious sacramental union.[102] Second, while there is no "enduring conjunction" of the bread and wine with the body and blood of Christ beyond the celebration and communion of the Lord's Supper, the sacramental union does guarantee oral manducation by the unworthy as well as the faithful.[103] As pointed out above, however, Andreae's insistence on the use of the Wittenberg Concord, while intended to neutralize the appeal of the Montbéliardais to the document, in effect left open the door to the use of Bucer's explanation of it and thereby to a Reformed interpretation, with its distinction between the impious and the infidel.[104] That this explanation was included means a degree of capitulation on the part of the commissioners since it both allowed for and denied oral manducation.

The article on baptism and Bucer's explanation from the Wittenberg Concord leave this issue also open to the Reformed interpretation. While the explanation urges that infants in danger of death be baptized, it reserves the office of baptism to ministers. No mention is made of midwives. In fact, the opening sentence safeguards a Reformed interpretation: "One must understand here a necessity stemming from the ministry and command of God, and not the necessity of salvation, for doctor Luther and his followers themselves believe that the power of Christ can save even those who are not baptized."[105]

As we shall see, Bucer's explanation of baptism accorded in this instance with Calvin's and Beza's, but in the next few lines, Bucer allowed for not only the remission of original sin but the gift of the Holy Spirit at the time of baptism. The Genevans could not allow that the Holy Spirit was bestowed on every child that received baptism. To do so would be to tie the gift of the Spirit to the sacrament regardless of the ability of the baptized to respond to the word in faith.[106]

A final paragraph was added to the act signed in Montbéliard in 1573. Ordination was proscribed for any who refused to accept this act plus the Württemberg Church Order. Signatures followed and included not only the

German commissioners but the pastors and ministers of the county and districts belonging to Montbéliard. Among these were Pierre Toussaint, Henry Efferhen (now listed as superintendent of Montbéliard), and André Floret.[107] The Nine Bourgeois signed, as did the Eighteen and six of the Notables.[108] The next morning, however, through their spokesman, Pierre Paget, the Montbéliardais appealed. They protested that the articles on the Lord's Supper and baptism would scandalize the weak and asked that those articles be "softened." They requested that a document be drawn up affirming the confession sent by Duke Christopher to the Council of Trent and assuring that nothing in the act implied the condemnation of any other churches. Finally, they requested that their "ancient liberties, franchises, and good, praiseworthy and ancient customs" be respected.[109] With these requests duly recorded, the act of concord was received at Montbéliard.

It seemed that the Lutherans had won, and, indeed, it is on that note that Viénot ends his volume. But the faith of the Montbéliardais was not so easily changed nor their ceremonies replaced by the Württemberg liturgies. The struggle would continue, in fact, into the seventeenth century.

Between 1573 and the colloquy in 1586, the most significant year to illustrate this struggle is 1577. In 1577, Count Frederick took over the government of Montbéliard. In 1577, Jacob Andreae, backed by Duke Ludwig, tried to persuade other German Protestant princes to sign, and to have their clergy sign, the Formula of Concord.[110] Frederick had been educated at the University of Tübingen, whose rector was none other than Andreae, who with Martin Chemnitz was one of the chief "formulators." Frederick was nonetheless the son of Count George, who, until his death, was a firm adherent of the Montbéliard tradition.[111] Frederick found his position difficult also because he knew the mind of the Montbéliard clergy and people.[112] Moreover, he was disposed to help the French Reformed refugees. Duke Ludwig's insistence that the Formula of Concord (*Corpus doctrinae*) be signed by the Montbéliard clergy and magistrates made Frederick's position more painful, but in the end he obeyed Ludwig and supported the Württemberg agents who presented the formula for signature on October 9, 1577.[113] Although twenty-two of the clergy signed, five refused. The bourgeoisie of Montbéliard were sufficiently upset with the consenting clergy and the imposition of the formula to write to Swiss Protestant cities to ask advice. The Company of Pastors of Geneva received such a letter in which they were asked to evaluate the Epitome of the Formula, which had been translated into French. The company was also asked to intercede with their prince.[114]

On March 21, 1578, Frederick received a long petition with at least thirty-five signatures.[115] The petitioners reminded Frederick of his father, Count George, who was so respectful of the privileges and of the bourgeois and of the Reformed religion of Montbéliard. They appealed to the accord of January 1573, which they all had signed and which contained an article on the Lord's Supper conformed to the Augsburg Confession as interpreted in the Wittenberg Concord. They begged Frederick not to force them to act contrary to their consciences by condemning other Reformed churches or to give their neighbors, especially their Roman Catholic neighbors, occasion to accuse them of inconstancy with regard to religion. The problems of the bourgeoisie of Montbéliard with their count continued into the next century. Specific instances occurred in 1586, 1587, 1588, 1589,[116] 1594,[117] and 1613.[118] The battle between the bourgeoisie and Frederick came to a head in 1586–1587 but apparently did not settle the issue of a confession of faith for the French church in Montbéliard, but that is part of the story that follows the colloquy.

Notes

1. *Registres de la Compagnie des Pasteurs de Genève*, vol. 5: 1583–1588, ed. Olivier Labarthe and Micheline Tripet (Geneva: Librairie Droz, 1976), 110–11: "Le jeudi suivant, après le Consistoire, la Compaignie fut assemblee en la maison de M. Chauve au College, où il fut advisé que M. de Beze accompaigné de M. de la Faye se representeroit au plus tost à Montbelial [sic] pour conferer avec Jacobus Andreae de Tubingue qui s'y debvoit aussi trouver, suivant le desir que Monseigneur le comte dudict Montbelial en avoit, qui le pourchassoit à toute instance." For the invitation itself, see *Registres* 5, 111, n. 67.

2. Jacob Andreae, Acta Colloquij Mont / tis Belligartensis: / Quod habitum est, Anno Christi 1586. / Favente Deo Opt. Max. / Praeside, / Illustrissimo / Principe ac Domino, Domi- / no Friderico, comite Wirtember- / gico et Mompelgar- / tensi, &c. / inter clarissimos viros, D. Ia- / cobum Andreae, Praepositum & Cancellarium Aca- / demiae Tübingensis: & D. Theodorum Bezam, Pro- / fessorem & Pastorem Geneven- sem, / Authoritate praedicti Prinici- / pis Friderici, &c. nunc Anno Chri- / sti 1587. publicata. / Haec acta candide et bona fide consi- / gnata, vanissimos de hoc Colloquio sparsos rumores, inprimis vero / Epistolam quandam, vanitatibus et calumnijs re- fertam, & typis ex- / cusam, abundè refutabunt. / Cum privilegio. / Tubingae, / Per Georgium Gruppenbachium, / Anno M.D. LXXXVII [hereafter Acta]. P. A2(v) of the preface attributed to Count Frederick says that Frederick invited the two theologians to engage in a colloquy in his castle. P. A1(r) of Andreae's account of the colloquy itself informs us: "Anno Domini 1586. die 13. Ianuarii, cum serenissimi Domini, D. Henrici Regis Navarreni Legatus, N. Baro de Cleroan Stutgardiam venisset, & D. Iacobum Andreae quoque adesse cognovisset: misso ad ipsum nuncio viro Nobili, eum ad Colloquium familiare vocavit." (See ch. 2, pp. 49ff. for a discussion of the meaning of this invitation through Navarre's agent, the baron de Clervant.) For a discussion of the letter mentioned in the title see Chap. 6, pp. 160–64.

3. C. Mazauric, "Claude-Antoine de Vienne, Sieur de Clervant (1534–1588)," *Annuaire de la Société d'histoire de la Lorraine*. 67–68 (1967–1968): 83–152. This is the best account of Clervant's life available. I owe the reference to Alain Dufour, publisher, Librairie Droz S.A., Geneva.

4. Edouard Rott, *Histoire de la représentation diplomatique de la France auprès des cantons Suisses, de leurs alliés et de leurs confédérés*, vol. 2: 1559–1610 (Bern: A. Benteli, 1902), 368. This entry reads: "Claude Antoine de Vienne, Sr de Clervans. Mission extraordinaire du roi de Navarre auprès des cantons évangéliques et de la république de Genève. Février-Avril 1586. A peine eut-il traversé le Rhin, en octobre 1585, que le Sr de Clervans s'affrançit de la réserve dont il n'avait cru devoir se départir pendant son sejour en Suisse. Projets de contre-ligue et de levées de reitres furent exposés par lui avec succès, tant à Heidelberg et autres cours voisines, qu'à

Francfort, à Strasbourg et enfin à Montbéliard, où il se rendit au commencement de février 1586 en vue de stimuler le zèle des huguenots qui s'y étaient réfugiés." Clervant's course then took him to Basel, Geneva (end of February), Bern, and finally to Henry III's agent Fleury in Soleure, whom he tried to convince that his mission was peaceful, although he had been sent to raise troops. He told Navarre not to expect much from the tight-fisted Swiss, and in April went on to Germany. Cf. Eugène Haag and Émile Haag, *La France Protestante* IX, (Paris, 486), which says that Clervant was at a baptism on February 8, 1586, according to the register of the Montbéliard church, and adds: "C'est à son instigation que le comte tent le colloque auquel assista Beze, dans le vain espoir d'opérer la fusion des deux Églises réformées."

5. Original autograph, Public Records Office, London, Reference nos. PFNF 25CL; SP 81/3/PT-1, and summarized in *Calendar of State Papers, Foreign Series, of the Reign of Elizabeth,* vol. 20, 297–99. Lobetius was one of Walsingham's many agents who were located throughout Europe and paid a small stipend to provide the English government with information.

6. To confirm Clervant's visit to Andreae, I checked archives in Paris, Montbéliard, Besançon, Stuttgard, Tübingen, Basel, and Geneva. Political historians may find interesting this lack of direct reference in the correspondence of the principals involved.

7. For a fuller treatment of Elizabeth of England's involvement in these issues see my "The Elector John Casimir, Queen Elizabeth, and the Protestant League," in *Controversy and Conciliation: The Reformation and the Palatinate 1559–1583,* ed. Derk Visser (Allison Park, Pa.: Pickwick Publications, 1986), 117–45. See also W. Brown Patterson, "The Anglican Reaction," in *Discord, Dialogue, and Concord: Studies in the Lutheran Reformation's Formula of Concord,* ed. Lewis W. Spitz and Wenzel Lohff (Philadephia: Fortress Press, 1977), 150–65. See also chap. 2, nn. 37, 38.

8. John Viénot, *Histoire de la Réforme dans le pays de Montbéliard depuis les origines jusqu'à la mort de P. Toussain,* 1524–1573, 2 vols. (Paris: Librairie Fischbacher, 1900).

9. For source material on Württemberg, see Christian Friderich Sattler, *Geschichte des Herzogtums Wurtenberg unter der Regierung der Graven,* III–V (Tübingen: Georg Heinrich Reiss, 1771–1772). For studies on aspects of Württemberg under Ulrich, see Werner-Ulrich Deetjen, *Studien zur Württembergischen Kirchenordnung Herzog Ulrichs 1534–1550: Das Herzogtum Württemberg im Zeitalter Herzog Ulrichs (1498–1550), die Neuordnung des Kirchengutes und der Kloster (1534–1547)* (Stuttgart: Calwer Verlag, 1981).

10. Louis Renard, "L'Ancien 'Magistrat' de Montbéliard," in *Mémoires de la Société pour l'histoire du droit et des institutions des anciens pays bourguignons, comtois et romands, (travaux) 1958–1959,* fasc. 20, special number: *Le pays de Montbéliard et les régions voisines dans l'histoire et dans l'économie* (Dijon: Société pour l'histoire du droit et des institutions des anciens pays bourguignons, comtois et romands), 117: "Telles ont été, avant la Révolution de 1789, les anciennes institutions municipales de Montbéliard: Magistrat des Neuf, Corps des Dix-Huit et des Notables, Mairie de justice—qui ont donné à la vieille capitale du Pays son originalité, et qui en ont fait pendant un peu plus de cinq siècles (de 1283 à 1793) une sorte de petite république et de démocratie avant la lettre, dont étaient fiers les Montbéliardais d'autan. Et ils en avaient le droit."

11. Alexandre Tuetey, *Étude sur le droit municipal au XIII et au XIV siècle en Franche-Comté et en particulier à Montbéliard,* Extrait des mémoires de la Société d'Émulation de Montbéliard (Montbéliard: Henri Barbier, 1865), 110: "Il résulte

d'un examen général de la charte de 1283, que les privilèges accordés par le comte de Montbéliard, étaient extrêmement étendus; les franchises conçues dans le sens le plus large et le plus libéral, constituaient pour ces bourgeois une liberté civile des plus complètes, au point que la Révolution française qui a introduit partout une transformation si radicale dans les institutions, n'a opéré peu de changements à Montbéliard. Elle fut même accueillie par les habitants avec froideur; ce fait n'a rien d'anormal, car le gouvernement qu'ils avaient eu jusqu'alors devait faire naître en eux plutôt des regrets que le désir d'un nouveau régime, sont ils n'éprouvaient pas le besoin."

12. Ibid., 118–23.

13. Renard, "L'Ancien 'Magistrat' de Montbéliard," 109.

14. Through the kindness of the director of historical services, J. C. Voisin, archivist of the Archives Municipales de Montbéliard, I have been able to examine originals of the confirmation of Montbéliard's franchises by Count George in 1554, another confirmation by Duke Christoph in 1558 and again in 1570 by the tutors of Frederick, and also the physically impressive document of the oath of fidelity sworm before Count Frederick on May 9, 1587.

15. When French refugees fleeing the persecution begun by the St. Bartholomew's Day massacre arrived in Montbéliard, they were given citizenship to protect them from extradition by Count Frederick's Lutheran guardians. The cost of citizenship in 1570 was ten Basel pounds (Tuetey, *Droit municipale*, 151), although this sum changed continually, as one can see from the *Départemente du Doubs, Ville de Montbéliard, Inventaire sommaire des Archives communales Antérieures à 1793, Series AA: Actes constitutifs et politiques de la commune*. The original documents are preserved in the Hôtel de Ville of Montbéliard.

16. Renard, "L'Ancien 'Magistrat' de Montbéliard," 115–16: *"les Chazés, habitants de l'endroit ou du voisinage, sans doute possesseurs d'un morçeau de terrain, chęzal, d'ou peut-être ce terme de chazés; ce pouvait être aussi des gens casés, placés là, à coté du "Magistrat", pour modérer, tempérer ses pouvoirs."*

17. Viénot, Histoire de la Réforme 1: 3. Cf. Martin Brecht and Hermann Ehmer, *Sudwestdeutsche Reformationsgeschichte: Zur Einfuhrung der Reformation im Herzogtum Württemberg 1534* [hereafter *SR*] (Stuttgart: Calwer Verlag, 1984), 195–96.

18. Brecht and Ehmer, *SR*, 196.

19. For a brief and lively account of Ulrich's relations with the Swabian League and the Hapsburgs, see Thomas A. Brady, Jr., *Turning Swiss: Cities and Empire 1450–1550* (Cambridge: Cambridge University Press, 1985), 92–115.

20. Brecht and Ehmer, *SR*, 196.

21. Brady, *Turning Swiss*, 112; see also 189–91; Viénot, *Histoire de la Réforme* 1:4–5.

22. Viénot, *Histoire de la Réforme* 1:5. See Brady, *Turning Swiss*, 104, who credits Charles V's agent, Maximilian von Bergen, for Ulrich's failure to persuade the Swiss to provide him with troops. (See 103, n. 9, for the various names given Bergen.)

23. Brecht and Ehmer, *SR*, 197. Cf. Karl Bauer, "Die Stellung Württembergs in der Geschichte der Reformation," *Blätter für Württembergische Kirchengeschichte* 38 (1934): 3–51, and "Die Bedeutung der Württembergischen Reformation für den Gang der deutschen Reformationsgeschichte," *Blätter für Württembergische Kirchengeschichte* 38 (1934): 267–80.

24. Viénot, *Histoire de la Réforme* 1:17.

25. Brecht and Ehmer, *SR*, 197. See also Heiko A. Oberman, *Masters of the Reformation: The Emergence of a New Intellectual Climate in Europe*, trans. Dennis

Martin. (Cambridge: Cambridge University Press, 1981) (Original German: *Werden und Wertung der Reformation* [Tübingen: Mohr, 1977]), 252–53.

26. Viénot, *Histoire de la Réforme,* 1:33.

27. Ibid. But see Oberman, *Masters of the Reformation,* 269ff., esp. 270, where Oberman, following Köhler, affirms that Ulrich's Swiss–South German alliances were at the bottom of Philip of Hesse's encouragement of a colloquy between Zwingli and Luther.

28. Brecht and Ehmer, *SR,* 199.

29. Ibid., 192, 199–202.

30. Ibid., 147–48; 200–206; 236–37; 270–71; 281. But see Oberman, *Masters of the Reformation,* 253, n. 43, with regard to the Treaty of Kaadan and its effect on religion in Ulrich's territories. Oberman and Brecht and Ehmer both cite Wilhelm Bofinger's "Kirche und werdender Territorialstaat: Eine Untersuchung zur Kirchenreform Herzog Ulrichs von Württemberg." I am inclined to think that the Kaadan treaty of 1534 was influential. It may also be taken as an indication of the terms of the Peace of Augsburg of 1555 and the continuing ambiguity regarding the "Calvinists." For the political background on the year 1534 in Württemberg, see Volker Press, "Die württembergische Restitution von 1534—reichspolitische Voraussetzungen und Konsequenzen," *Blätter für württembergische Kirchengeschichte* 87 (1987): 44–71, esp. 62.

31. *Johann Jakob Mosers Mompelgardisches Staatsrecht,* ed. Wolfgang Hans Stein, trans. George Anders (Stuttgart: W. Kohlhammer Verlag, 1983) (this is a 1720 unpublished disputation, *De Comitatu Principali Montepeligardo,* plus a longer 1772 manuscript: *Einleitung in das Furstlich Mompelgardische Staatsrecht,* p. 1: "Johann Jakob Moser ist als der Vater der deutschen Staatsrects in die Geschichte eingegangen"; p. 32 (quotation from Duke Leopold Eberhard, 1714): "La Principauté de Montbéliard est un composé des Comtez et Seigneuries suivantes, sçavoir 1. de la Terre qu'on appelle Comté de Montbéliard in specie, 2. des quatre Seigneuries Souveraines, sçavoir Héricourt, 3. Chastelot, 4. Blanmont, 5. Clémont, 6. Du Comté de Horbourg, situé en Alsace, 7. de la Seigneurie de Riqueville située aussi en Alsace, 8. des trois Seigneuries situées en Bourgogne, sçavoir Granges, 9. Clereval, 10. Passavant."

32. Ibid, 120: "Als dieser Herzog [Ulrich] hernach anno 1519 unglucklich wurde und alle seine Wurttembergische Lande verlohre, ja diese gar anno 1520 an Oesterreich verkaufft wurden, verblieben ihm doch die Mompelgartische und Elsassische Lande, an welche auch Oesterreich nie keine Praetension machte, noch machen konnte. Dahero auch der zwischen Oesterreich und Wurttemberg anno 1534 geschlo ene Cadanische Vertrag und de en Folgen das Mompelgartische gar nichts angiengen."

33. Ibid. 174: "Erstgemeldter Herr Geheimer Archivar Sattler berichtet ferner, dass, als Herzog Christoph Mompelgart an seinen Oncle, Graf Georgen, uberlassen, hatten die Interessenten den Kayser ersucht, es zu genehmigen, Herzog Christoph seiner Lehenspflicht zu erlassen und Graf Georgen zu belehnen, welches der Kayser auch bewilliget habe."

34. On Blarer and Schnepf, see Martin Brecht, "Herkunft und Ausbildung der protestantischen Geistlichen des Herzogtums Württemberg im 16. Jahrhundert," *Zeitschrift fur Kirchengeschichte* 80, Band 1969, vierte folge XVIII, heft 1, pp. 164–65. For the complicated background to this necessarily simplified account, see Brecht and Ehmer, *SR,* 203–6. For Ulrich's influence on the University of Tübingen, see Oberman, *Masters of the Reformation,* 253–59. See also Hermann Ehmer, "Erhard Schnepf: Ein Lebensbild," *Blätter für württembergische Kirchengeschichte* 87 (1987): 72–125, esp. 81–86.

35. Brecht and Ehmer, *SR*, 206–9, lays out the background and the issues. Viénot, *Histoire de la Réforme* 1: 37, n. 1, gives the formula: "Wir bekennen, dass der Leib und das Blut des Herren in Abentmal warhaftig, das ist, substantive und essentialiter, nit aber quantitative, qualitative und localiter gegenwertig seie und dargereichet werde." Viénot notes also how quickly evangelical theology fell back into scholasticism. Nor was this formula original; it was, in fact, the same formula rejected by Zwingli and accepted by Luther at Marburg. (See Brecht and Ehmer, *SR*, 207, for the Marburg formula.) The difficulty was that while God, considered a pure spirit, was believed to be present substantially and essentially only, a body is experienced to have also quantity and qualities and must be located. The eucharist presented peculiar problems since medieval Christian belief was that the body of Christ, through the Incarnation, is also God's body and that the whole Christ is present sacramentally in the eucharist. Even the word *warhaftig* is important in this brief formula since Calvin would later make a crucial distinction between *en vérité* and *en réalité*. (See p. 79 and the article by Joseph Tylenda, "Calvin and Christ's Presence in the Supper—True or Real," *Scottish Journal of Theology* 27 (February 1974): 65–75.

36. See pp. 27–28.

37. For extended information about Pierre Toussain and his career in Montbéliard, see Viénot, whose two-volume work on Montbéliard concludes with the year of Toussain's death, 1573. Cf. Brecht and Ehmer, *SR*, 267–69, esp. 268: "Die weitere Geschichte der Mompelgarder Kirche ist eng mit der Person Toussains verbunden."

38. The manner of the effectiveness of these symbols varies among the Swiss reformed. See B. A. Gerrish, "The Lord's Supper in the Reformed Confessions," *Theology Today* 23, no. 2 (July 1966): 224–29.

39. The dispute over the Lord's Supper will be analyzed in detail in chap. 3. See also Walther Köhler, *Zwingli und Luther: Ihr Streit uber das Abendmahl* (Leipzig: Verein für Reformationsgeschichte, 1953).

40. Viénot, *Histoire de la Réforme* 1:52–53.

41. Ibid., 54.

42. Ibid., 64.

43. Ibid., 67.

44. See n. 14.

45. Viénot, *Histoire de la Réforme* 1:67–68.

46. See pp. 173, 187.

47. Viénot, *Histoire de la Reforme* 1:74. See the following pages in Viénot for part of the text. On pp. 77–78, Viénot sets Farel's and Toussain's baptismal liturgies in parallel columns and notes that Toussain leaves out Farel's reference to predestination. On pp. 78–81, Viénot gives the liturgy of the Lord's Supper. In Viénot, *Histoire de la Réforme,* vol. 2, illustrations facing pp. 174 and 176 reproduce the original title pages. The publisher was Jaques Estauge.

48. Ibid., 75, n. 3.

49. Ibid., 87–89.

50. Friedrich Hertel, ed., *In Wahrheit und Freiheit: 450 Jahre Evangelisches Stift in Tübingen* (Stuttgart: Calwer Verlag, 1986), 53, with n. 24 and esp. n. 37 from Balthasar Bidembach's funeral oration for Christopher: "Er hat in Mompelgard alle opera Lutheri, des mannes Gottes, teutsch und Lateinisch, sovil damals im truck gewesen, dessgleichen alle bucher des ehrwurdigen herrn Brentii und andere mehr, mit sonderm fleiss und iudicio aussgelesen . . . auch der papisten und zwinglischen bucher vil gelesen, und eins gegen dem andern, alles aber gegen dem wort Gottes gehalten, gewegen [=abgewogen] und probiert."

51. The *Invariata* reads: "De Coena Domini docent, quod corpus et sanguis Christi vere adsint, et distribuantur vescentibus in coena Domini, et improbant secus docentes" (CR XXVI, 278). The *Variata* reads: "De Coena Domini docent quod cum pane et vino vere exhibeantur corpus et sanguis Christi vescentibus in Coena Domini" (CR XXVI, 357).

52. For further discussion of the Formula of Concord, see ch. 6.

53. Ecclesiasticorum rituum et caeremoniarum ducatus wirtenbergensis Regula, in usum quorundam parachorum, germanice nescientum, e germanico in latinum versa (hereafter *Regula*) (Tübingen: Ulrich Morhardt, 1543).

54. Viénot, *Histoire de la Réforme* 1:93–100, for a summary of the Württemberg Church Order.

55. On the controversy regarding communion for the sick and especially the controversy between Toussain and Engelmann and the role of Schnepf and Brentz, see Hermann Ehmer, *Valentin Vannius und die Reformation in Württemberg* (Stuttgart: W. Kohlhammer Verlag, 1976), 57–70. Ehmer takes exception to Viénot's assertion that it was Christoph who imposed the Württemberg Church Order on Montbéliard. Rather, argues Ehmer, Christoph appealed to Ulrich as well; see 63, n. 17.

56. Viénot, *Histoire de la Réforme* 1:103, n. 3.

57. Viénot, *Histoire de la Réforme* 2:19. Because of the interesting features of this confession, as well as its brevity, it is worth reproducing: "Divus Augustinus libro X de Civitate Dei, item Pontificii in jure canonico de consecratione dist. II; et doctores scolastici libro IV Sententiarum sic definiunt sacramentum et omnium consensu dicunt esse sacrae rei signum et invisibilis gratiae visibilem formam. Baptismus igitur est sacramentum, hoc est, ut illi definiunt, sacrae rei signum et invisibilis gratiae visibilis forma. Signum et forma visibilis est aqua materialis et actus baptismi exterioris. Res autem sacra et invisibilis gratis quae cum signo datur, est remissio peccatorum et communicatio spiritus sancti per Christum Jesum. Sic coena Domini est sacramentum, hoc est, ut illi testantur, sacrae rei signum et invisibilis gratiae visibilis forma. Signum et forma visibilis est panis et vinum, coena, res autem sacra et invisibilis gratia quae cum signo datur est corpus Christi pro nobis traditum et sanguis ejus pro nobis fusus. Quemadmodum etiam Irenaeus scribit Eucharistiam duabus rebus constare, altera terrena, altera coelesti, terrenam vocat elementa et res visibilis in coena, hoc est panem et vinum, coelestem autem rem vocat, quod alii rem sacram et invisibilem dicunt, hoc est panem et vinum offerri, sed una cum elementis et signis id est cum pane et vino, veritatem ipsam et res ipsas sacras et coelestes hoc est verum corpus et verum sanguinem Domini in cibum animarum nostrarum vere dari et exhiberi, nos illis in Coena vere pasci et refici credimus et profitemur."

58. The year was 1544. Luther was still two years from his death, and the split among the Protestants was evidently not considered irreparable, at least by Calvin. See F. Ehmer, *Valentin Vannius,* 64–70. See also B. A. Gerrish, "John Calvin on Luther," in *Interpreters of Luther: Essays in Honor of Wilhelm Pauck,* ed. Jaroslav Pelikan (Philadelphia: Fortress Press, 1968), 67–96. See esp. 73–74, in which Gerrish establishes that Luther's most vicious anti-Swiss invective appeared only in 1544, when he published his *Short Confession on the Holy Sacrament.*

59. CR XXXIX, 705–6. *Pace* Jane Dempsey Douglass in her fine book *Calvin, Women and Freedom* (Philadelphia: Westminster Press, 1985), and the thesis she maintains there. Calvin might have contemplated a day when women had the same freedom as in Eden, but he wanted women in his churches to be passive.

60. Gerrish, "The Lord's Supper," 224–43, for a sensitive handling of the differences among the three theologians.

61. Viénot, *Histoire de la Réforme* 1:112. See F. Ehmer, *Valentin Vannius,* 68.

62. John Brenz, one of the most important of the second-generation Lutheran reformers and the most influential of the Württemberg churchmen between 1550–1570. See Gerhard Schafer and Martin Brecht, "Joannes Brenz 1499–1570: Beitrage zu seinem Leben und Wirken," *Blätter für Württembergische Kirchengeschicte* 70 (1970): (The entire volume is dedicated to Brenz on the four hundredth anniversary of his death.)

63. Viénot, *Histoire de la Réforme* 1:112–13. The perimeters are now set. The arguments and efforts of the two sides continued until the colloquy itself. I shall refer only briefly to material available in Viénot and pick up the story again in detail only in 1573, the year of Toussain's death, which marked the end of Viénot's study of Montbéliard.

64. See F. Ehmer, *Valentin Vannius,* in which Ehmer mentions several times that future Lutheran-Calvinist disputes and efforts to come to a common doctrine were foreshadowed in Montbéliard in 1543–1544. For an in-depth study of the later and more bitter struggle in the Palatinate, see Walter Hollweg, *Der Augsburger Reichstag von 1566 und seine Bedeutung für die Entstehung der Reformierten Kirche und ihres Bekenntnisses (Beiträge zur Reformationsgeschichte Bd. 8)* (Neukirchen-Vluyn: Neukirchener Verlag, 1964).

65. Viénot, *Histoire de la Réforme* 1:194.

66. Ibid., 250–52; and Moser, *Mosers Mompelgardisches Staatsrecht,* 138: "Graf Georg machte anno 1555 8.Martii eine Stifftung mit einem Capital von 10,000f. davon in dem Herzoglich-Wurtembergischen Theologischen Stipendio zu Tubingen 10 arme Knaben aus den Graf- und Herrschafften Mompelgart, Reichenweyher und Horburg in der Theologie auferzogen und, wann sie zu Kirchen oder Schulen Tuchtig waren, dieselbe vor andern in solchen Landen befordert werden sollten." Cf. Hertel, *In Wahrheit und Freiheit,* 53–54, with n. 111. See also John Viénot, *Le Livre d'immatriculation au collège des Montbéliards a Tubingue* [n.p.]: Imprimerie "JE SERS," (1931), which lists the students of the college from 1560 to 1775. For the studies of the seminarians at Tübingen as well as an astonishing note on their doctrinal variety and the foundation of the Montbéliard college, see Brecht, "Herkunft und Ausbildung der protestantischen Geistlichen," 163–75, esp. 168–70. Cf. Martin Leube, "Die Mompelgarder Stipendiaten im Tübinger Stift," *Blätter für Württembergische Kirchengeschichte* 20 (1916): pp. 54–73, for the sixteenth century.

67. Paul-F. Geisendorf, *Théodore de Bèze* (Geneva: Alexandre Jullien, 1967), 74–75, 99–103.

68. On the trial of Servetus, see T. H. L. Parker, *John Calvin, a Biography* (Philadelphia: Westminster Press, 1975), 117–23. For the polemical battle between the Genevans and Castellio, who fled to Basel, see Sébastien Castellion, *De haereticis an sint persequendi et omnino quomodeo sit cum eis agendum,* LUTERI & BRENTII, *aliorumque multorum tum veterum tum recentiorum sententiae,* facsimile reproduction of the 1554 edition with an introduction by Sape van der Woude (Geneva: Librairie E. Droz, 1954), introduction.

69. See ch. 5, p. 135.

70. Viénot, *Histoire de la Réforme* 1:206.

71. Ibid., 213.

72. For a history of the Württemberg Church Order, see Martin Brecht, *Kirchenordnung und Kirchenzucht in Württemberg vom 16. bis zum 18. Jahrhundert* (Stuttgart: Calwer Verlag, 1967), esp. 9–52.

73. Viénot, *Histoire de la Réforme* 1:226–28.

74. Ibid.

75. For a discussion of the role of Bucer, his lost "confession" sent to Montbéliard, and the role of the Wittenberg Concord see F. Ehmer, *Valentin Vannius*, 65–67. See also H. G. Haile, *Luther, an Experiment in Biography* (Garden City, N.Y.: Doubleday, 1980), 130–47.

76. See ch. 2, pp. 46–47.

77. Viénot, *Histoire de la Réforme* 1:281ff.

78. Ibid., 287: "Il y avait les calvinistes intransigeants, les luthériens stricts et, à égale distance des uns et des autres, les "évangeliques" représentés par Toussain et ses amis."

79. See chap. 4 for the christological consequences of this doctrine.

80. Viénot's first volume presents these events, together with excellent archival documentation in vol. 2 (nos. 139–60, pp. 231–316), which carries the dispute through 1573 and includes the Wittenberg Concord with Bucer's Explanations.

81. Rosemarie Müller-Streisand, "Theologie und Kirchenpolitik bei Jakob Andrea bis zum Jahr 1568," *Blätter für Württembergische Kirchengeschichte* 60–61 (1960–61): 224–395. See also Robert Kolb, "Jacob Andreae," in *Shapers of Religious Traditions in Germany, Switzerland, and Poland, 1560–1600*, ed. Jill Raitt (New Haven: Yale University Press, 1981), 53–68, and Robert Kolb, *Andreae and the Formula of Concord: Six Sermons on the Way to Lutheran Unity* (St. Louis: Concordia, 1977).

82. Viénot, *Histoire de la Réforme* 1:304. Cf. ibid., vol. 2, no. 140 bis: Colloquium cum Magistro Daniele Tossano Montbelgardi institutum, p. 240: D. Jacobus: Verum concordia non est perpetua nisi cum veritate.

83. Viénot, *Histoire de la Réforme* 1:309–11. The condemnation of the Reformed churches was included in the formula of Concord of 1577, largely composed by Andreae. See *Concordia Triglotta: The Symbolical Books of the Ev. Lutheran Church, German-Latin-English* (St. Louis: Concordia, 1921) [hereafter *Triglot Concordia*], *Epitome*, 806–9 (Zwinglians named); 816–17 (Calvinists named); 838–43 (lists errors of Anabaptists, Schwenkfeldians, New Arians, Anti-Trinitarians); *Thorough Declaration*, pp. 970–75, in which the words of Beza at Poissy are cited as one of the errors of the sacramentarians. The argument then condemns the *Variata* edition of the Augsburg Confession and proceeds to name Martin Bucer and to condemn Bucer's explanation of the Wittenberg Concord (pp. 976–77). The following pages continue the Reformed-Lutheran arguments, drawing upon Luther's works to substantiate the position taken in the *Declaration* to p. 1015. The article on the person of Christ follows the same pattern to p. 1049. With sacramentarians are named Zwinglians (1014–15). Finally, *The Visitation Articles of 1592* also names Calvinists specifically along with other "erroneous doctrines" concerning the Lord's Supper, baptism (1154–55), and predestination (1156–57).

84. Daniel Toussain was first recalled to Orléans. He went from there to Neuchâtel and then was called by the Elector John Casimir to Heidelberg, where he continued to serve the Reformed church with distinction.

85. Viénot, *Histoire de la Réforme* 1:312–13. Cf. ibid., vol. 2, no. 142, pp. 248ff., especially pp. 249–50 (speaking of the Augsburg Confession and the Peace of Augsburg): "et pour ce ont les electeurs, princes et etats du St-Empire dressé et constitué une paix publique au faict de religion, soubs laquelle seulement les deux religions cognues à ung chascung sont comprinses; dont si entre lesdicts ministres ung ou plusieurs enseignans ou dogmatisans signament en l'article concernant la Ste-Cène de N.S. aultrement qu'il est porté et declaré par ladite confession d'Augsbourg et concordat susdit, estoyent soufferts et parmis, il conviendroyt au prince et seigneur du pays et non à ses sujets en donner déculpe et rendre raison où il affiert; quoy con-

sidéré, lesdicts bourgeois doibvent facilement comprendre qu'à eulx n'appartient en ce prescrire ordonnance à leur magistrat et supérieur qui ne leur veut commander chose contre Dieu, ains est enclin les faire avoir la vraye posture de la pure et sincère doctrine de son saint Evangile." On this basis, the commissioners judged that Daniel Toussain could not remain in Montbéliard (p. 251): "lesdits seigneurs princes curateurs ne peuvent iceluy Tossaint ny ses semblables souffrir ès églises contre la paix publique pour le faict de la religion constituée."

86. *Scripta / Eruditorum / Aliquot virorum de / Controversia Coenae / Domini. / Anno M.D. LXI.* (No editor, no place and no publisher given.) The introduction to Bucer's explanations of the Wittenberg Concord is by Conrad Hubert and declares that he has in hand an autograph emended many times by Bucer himself. Hubert claimed that he was moved to publish this edition in order to correct others that have appeared and are very corrupt. In the others, negatives are given as affirmatives and a mutilated text for a complete text. ("Praesertim cum aliquot illius libri corruptissime in lucem editi sunt, in quibus negantia pro affirmantibus posita sunt, et mutilata pro integres: idque multis in locis.") Hubert's explanatory page is printed between a preface by Jean Sturm and the text of Bucer. [It is my guess that the book was printed in Strasbourg or Heidelberg. I would also suppose that it was available to Daniel Toussain in 1562.) Included in the book are a 1544 confession written by Bucer in Strasbourg and another written in England in 1550. Both affirm the role of faith that receives what Christ offers (the word Bucer prefers is *exhibere*), namely, his real and present self. Melanchthon is represented in the book by his 1559 *Judicium de controversia Coenae Domini,* a letter to Crato, and a portion of his 1556 commentary on Colossians 3. A telling treatise in this collection is *Sententia Ioan. Brentii desumpta ex ipsius exegesi in Ioannis Evangelium.* In this work, Brenz ascribes efficacy with regard to the sacrament to faith: "Aliud est donare, aliud distribuere, aliud accipere. Deus donat per Sacramenta donum distribuitur: homo fide accipit" (p. 68). The last part of the book contains the theses presented at Heidelberg by Peter Bocquin. The whole collection seems to be against Heshuss and Westphal.

87. Ibid., pp. 5–6, B iiii and verso: "Omnino enim tria genera hominum Sacramenta sumere possunt. Quidam, qui omnia hic contemnunt et rident, qui prorsus impii sunt, nec quicquam Domino credunt: hi nihil quam panem et vinum agnoscunt et sentiunt, eoque nec amplius percipiunt: quia pervertunt verba et institutionem Domini. Alii, verbis hic Domini porrigentis corpus suum credunt, eaque idem Sacramentum accipiunt, ut simul rem sacrmenti percipiant, nec tamen donum hoc Dei digni perpendunt: hi ea indignitate reos se faciunt corporis et sanguinis Domini, que tamen sumere volunt, et sumunt: quia verba et institutionem Domini amplectuntur: non manducant autem revera, ut Augustinus dicit, hoc est, non fruuntur plene hoc cibo vivifico, quem in mentem non satis demittunt. Tertii sunt, qui non credunt tantum institutioni Domini, et accommodant se illi sacramento sumendo, sed simul viva fide omnia expendunt, considerant, et amplectuntur: indemque virtutem et iucunditatem huius cibi solide percipiunt. Sic se habet etiam verbum Evangelii, id ex se et institutione Domini, est verbum salutis, quibuscunque annuncietur vel credatur. Hoc audiunt quidam sine omni fide: hi, cum illud non intelligunt, quantum ad ipsos attinet, nihil percipiunt, quam inanem strepitum verborum. Alii credunt et intelligunt, nec tamen rite in animo illud recondunt: isti Evangelium, etiam ut verbum salutis est, audiunt, ac ita in eo salutem audiunt et assumunt, et in eo meditantur, atque elabi illud animo sinunt [*sic*], fructum vero verbi seipsos destituunt, quo feliciter perfruuntur, qui illud audiunt corde perfecto, et perpendunt digne: qui sunt tertii et optimi generis auditores." Cf. the French version used at Montbéliard and

reproduced in Viénot, *Histoire de la Réforme* 2:296–303. Bucer likens the reception of the Lord's Supper to hearing the Word and draws complete parallels so that his meaning cannot be misunderstood.

88. Haile, *Luther*, 143–44. Although Luther had planned to ask Bucer and the south German delegates to Wittenberg to affirm that the body of Christ was not only offered to unbelievers but received by them, he did not do so but rather accepted the statement of Bucer and Capito. This is remarkable since to admit that anyone does not receive the body and blood with the bread and wine is to deny oral manducation and the *communicatio indignorum*. Was Luther aware of this? If so, what made him willing to accept Bucer's position? Had his sleepless night convinced him that concord was more valuable than insisting on complete agreement? See Haile's explanation of Luther's change of mood, pp. 145–47. See also the texts gathered by Ernst Bizer in "Martin Butzer und der Abendmahlsstreit: Unbekannte und unveroffentlichte Aktenstucke zur Entstehungsgeschichte der Wittenberger Konkordie vom 29. Mai 1536," *Archiv für Reformationsgeschichte* (1938): 203–37; and (1939): 68–87. Haile has no reference to Bizer's material.

89. Bizer's two articles (see n. 84, *Scripta Erud.*) make still more understandable the Montbéliard ministers' insistence on Bucer's interpretation of the Wittenberg Concord. According to Bizer's text, Luther tacitly allowed a lengthy defense of Oecolampadius's doctrine and in the process distinguished not just "offering" and "receiving" but, still more subtly, "receiving" from "eating." By this means, the unworthy could "receive" the body and blood of Christ with the bread and wine, but they did not "eat" it since their faith was either absent or so defective that they were incapable of receiving the benefits of Christ, which (as Calvin and Beza consistently taught) could not be separated from Christ himself: To "eat" Christ is to "eat" the benefits of Christ, namely, life everlasting. But Christ and his benefits can be given only by the Holy Spirit working through faith.

90. Ibid., 8.

91. Ibid., 9.

92. Ibid.

93. Viénot, *Histoire de la Réforme,* vol. 2, no. 150 for complete text.

94. Ibid., no. 151, esp. p. 279: "il vaut mieux s'absenter et délayer le saint batême, ou bien donner ordre de bonne heure que les femmes aillent faire leurs couches en lieu ou purement l'Evangile est préché."

95. I justify my use of "Reformed" by Andreae's use of the term in his Preface to the *Acta,* e.g., p. 2: "Gallicas Ecclesias, quas ipse reformatas appellabat."

96. See chap. 2.

97. Viénot, *Histoire de la Réforme* 1: 340–41.

98. Ibid., vol. 2, no. 158, pp. 292–308. This piece contains Bucer's explanations in French. Viénot does not indicate the source of the translation, but it is faithful to the 1561 Latin text given on p. 28 n. 87. The following is from vol. 2, p. 299: "Car il y a en tout trois sortes de gens que peuvent reçepvoir les sacrements: Les ungs qui contempnent et mesprisent icy et se mocquent de toutes choses, lesquelx sont du tout meschans, et ne croyent aulcunement au Seigneur. Ceulx-là ne recognoissent et ne perçoivent rien aultre chose que du pain et du vin' tant seulement; pourtant qu'ilz pervertissent les paroles et l'institution du Seigneur. Les aultres croyent aulx paroles du Seigneur ouffrant icy son corps, et prennent les signes par telle foy qu'ils percoipvent aussy les choses signifiéez. Et touteffois ne considerent point ce don là du Seigneur comm'il affiert, ceux'cy par telle indignité se font culpables du corps et du sang du Seigneur, lesquelx toutesffois [*sic*] ilz veuillent reçepvoir et les reçoipvent pour

ce qu'ilz embrassent les paroles et l'institution du Seigneur, mais ilz ne mangent point vrayement, comme dict St- Augustin, c'est-à-dire, ilz ne jouissent point plainement de ceste viande vivifiante, laquelle ilz ne reçoipvent point assez en leurs espritz. La troisième sorte est de ceulx qui ne croyent pas seulement à l'institution du Seigneur, s'accommodans à reçepvoir ce sacrement, mais lesquelx pésent, considèrent et embrassent quand et quand toutes choses par une vive foy et, de là, reçoipvent vrayement la vertu et doulceur de ceste viande. Ainsy est-il de la parole de l'Evangile lequel de soy mesmes et par l'institution du Seigneur, est la parole de salut à quelconques gens qui soit annoncé, ou lesquelx y croient, aulcuns l'oyent sans aulcune foy, lesquelx ne l'entendans, tant qu'à eulx touche, ilz ne reçoipvent rien, fors un vain bruict de paroles; les aultres croyent et entendent et touteffois ne le serrent point comm'il appartient en leurs coeurs. Ceulx icy oyent aussy l'Evangile, comme estant la parole de salut, et ainsy ilz oyent et y reçoipvent leur salut, mais d'aultant qu'ilz ne le pésent et ne le méditent pas comm'il appartient, ains le laissent escouler de leur coeur, ilz se privent eulx mesmes du vray fruict de la parole, duquel ceulx-la sont heureusement jouyssans qui l'oyent d'ung coeur parfait et le contemplent comm'il affiert, et ceulx-cy sont de la troisième et meilleure espèce d'auditeurs."

99. Ibid., 293.

100. Ibid., 295: "comme le symbole de notre temps par lequel les églises de ce comtey [*sic*] et seigneuries adjoinctes soient discernéz d'avec les papistes et aultres sectes." Andreae spoke no French, and Viénot tells us (2:293, n. 1), "Le peuple de l'ancient pays de Montbéliard n'a jamais parlé allemand." The text here was translated for the people by the chancellor of Montbéliard.

101. Ibid.

102. Ibid., 296.

103. Ibid., 297–98.

104. Ibid., 299. The version used at Montbéliard is the following: "Ainsy est-il de la parole de l'Évangile lequel de soy mesmes et par l'institution du Seigneur, est la parole de salut a quelconques gens qui soit annonce, ou lesquelx y croient, aulcuns l'oyent sans aulcune foy, lesquelx ne l'entendans, tant qu'a eulx touche, ilz ne recoipvent rien, fors un vain bruict de paroles." From a letter written by Pierre Toussain to the pastors of Geneva, Lausanne, and Neuchâtel on January 22, 1573, it is clear that Toussain felt they had not agreed to the *manducatio impiorum:* "Et quod doctrinam attinet, mallemus (laus sit Domino Deo) quidvis perpeti, quam vel ubiquitatem, vel impiorum manducationem approbare, aut eas ecclesias, quae non sunt confessionis Augustanae, improbare, etc."

105. Viénot, *Histoire de la Réforme* 2:301: "Il faut icy entendre de la necessité du ministère et du commandement de Dieu, et non pas de la necessité du salut, car le docteur Luther et les siens croyent que ceux mêmes qui ne seroient pas baptisez peuvent estre sauvez par la vertu de Christ. Mais il fault que ceux-cy ne contempnent pas le baptesme et de là ilz veuillent que les enffans [*sic*] soient baptisez, et veu qu'il est dict de telz enffans qui sont en l'église, ce n'est pas la volonté du Père qu'il en périsse l'ung d'iceulx, il appart que, par le baptesme, les enffans ont la rémission du péché originel et la donation du Saint Esprit, qui est avec efficace en eulx selon leur mesure."

106. See ch. 5, pp. 145–46.

107. See Beza, *Correspondance* 14 (1573), no. 1028, pp. 233–34). This is a letter from Beza to Nicolas Pithou, who took refuge in Montbéliard after the St. Bartholomew's Day massacre. Beza says that he is sending a letter to Floret encouraging him and advising prudence and moderation. Beza also mentions a letter to the "*maistres bourgeois.*" Both letters are lost. See also nos. 996, 1002, 1003.

108. Ibid., no. 1002. Beza commented on the unusual proceeding in Montbéliard, namely, that they were required to sign the articles one by one: "c'est chose nouvelle et inusitée en tous lieux, tant en Allemagne qu'ailleurs, de faire soubsigner les particuliers un par un à quelque confession." The editors (n. 3) comment on the fact that it seems that even lay persons were required to sign.

109. Viénot, *Histoire de la Réforme* 2:303–8. (Viénot found the whole of this long document in the archives of the mayor of Montbéliard.)

110. For more on the Formula of Concord, see pp. 58 and 167.

111. Letter of Frederick, count of Montbéliard, to Beutterich, resident of Montbéliard and agent of Duke John Casimir, October 8, 1577 (Hauptstaatsarchiv Stuttgart, Bestand A 63, Bü. 54). Beutterich had advised Frederick not to sign the Formula of Concord, at least not before conferring with him orally or by writing, letter of Beutterich to Count Frederick, October 7, 1577 (Hauptstaatsarchiv Stuttgart, Bestand A 63, Bü. 54). Frederick answered that he had in mind the electors who had signed the Formula of Concord and urged him to do so, among them his uncle and suzerain, Duke Ludwig. He had also in memory his very dear Lord and father "et de plus d'anstant que de fut treslouable memoire l'illustre Prince mon trescher seigneur et pere tenoit a son vivant le mesme party." Frederick assured Beutterich that he had also in mind his "cousin," Duke Casimir. Frederick's memory of the former and his respect for the latter urged him not to sign.

112. See the letter to Ludwig from the schoolteacher Claude du Mourier, Montbéliard, October 10, 1577: "Tresillustre prince, et excellent Seigneur Claude de Morier [*sic*] Maistre d'escole en ce lieu de Montbéliard treshumble et obeissant serviteur de vostre excellence satisfaisant à l'ordonnance qui luy fut hier faicte au soir par Monsieur le chancellier de donner par escript les causes et raisons pour lesquelles il ne peut hier signer ce qu'il ouit lire, dict et remonstre en toute humilité et reverence qu'à cause de l'imbecillité de son esprit et memoire il n'a peu tellement comprendre tout les poincts de doctrine contenus au livre duquel il ouit hier la lecture qu'il en puisse rendre presentement raison n'ayant differé signer pour aultre chose que pour le scrupule de certaines façons et manieres de parler par luy cy devant non entendues qu'il ont engendre en sa conscience." Mounier continues to explain that he is over sixty years old, has never aspired to the ministry and is content to teach the "petits Abécédaires." Mounier pleads that he not be discharged because he refused to sign the formula. Mounier's letter was copied in German for Ludwig (Hauptstaatsarchiv Stuttgart, Bestand A 63, Bü. 54).

113. Although Frederick had promised Beutterich that he would listen to his advice, there is no evidence as to whether or not he did.

114. *Registres de la Compagnie des Pasteurs de Genève au temps de Calvin*, vol. 4: 1575–1582, ed. Olivier Labarthe and Bernard Lescaze (Geneva; Librairie Droz, 1974), 99–102, dated November, 1577. Note 94 says that Duke Christoph of Württemberg sent Lucas Osiander to ask the magistrates and pastors of Montbéliard to sign the Formula of Concord. See also the long note on p. 106, which speaks of the many towns of Germany that had written to Geneva about the condemnation of the Calvinists in the Formula. There it is claimed that "many lords, princes and republics have refused to sign it," among them Montbéliard. Beza and Salvart decided that something must be done, and several publications appeared by March 1578.

115. Archives Nationales, Paris, Historical Section [hereafter AN-K], K 2186. Some of the signatures are written over others; some appear to be initials but may belong to a name already entered. I have registered the most conservative count.

116. See chap. 6 for the years 1586–1589.

117. Charles Duvernoy, *Éphémérides du comté de Montbéliard.* . . . (Besançon: Imprimerie de Charles Deis, 1832), 21, 485, 48, 53, 164, 167, 168, 171, 173, 184, 188, 435, 316, 157. This book is arranged according to months rather than years, so that, for example, the events of April are gathered regardless of the year, hence the seemingly erratic pagination above.

118. D. v. Kolb, "Luthertum und Calvinismus in Württemberg," *Blätter für württembergische Kirchengeschichte* 32 (1928): 151–52. Kolb reports that people from Montbéliard are still going to Basel and other towns to take communion in the French church.

2

The Political Background

The story of Montbéliard is not only part of the complex history of France and the empire; it is involved in the history of all of Europe. Its problems are a microcosm of the problems of people affected by religious quarrels in the last quarter of the sixteenth century. At least three forms of Protestantism were represented in Montbéliard during the fifty years previous to the colloquy of 1586: the evangelicals faithful to Pierre Toussain and his simple confession of faith, the French refugees who followed the Gallican Confession, and the Lutheranism of the town's suzerains. Montbéliard was often, therefore, a focal point for heated exchanges between its count, Frederick, and the Holy Roman Emperor, Rudolph II.[1] Montbéliard featured in correspondence between the king of Navarre and the Palatinate elector, John Casimir.[2] Meanwhile, Duke Ludwig of Württemberg, William, Landgrave of Hesse, other Lutheran princes, and the king of Denmark were contacted by Queen Elizabeth with regard to a Protestant League.[3] The architects of the Catholic League, the powerful Guises, were concerned about Montbéliard as a staging ground for attacks against Henry III of France, while Montbéliard's Catholic neighbors, especially those in the Guise's Lorraine, complained to Rudolph and to Henry III about the Huguenot refugees sheltering there.[4]

The political history of Europe in the last quarter of the sixteenth century is a complex weave out of which it is not easy to pluck the pertinent threads. The relations between Henry III and Navarre are complicated enough, but they are interwoven with the development of the Catholic League[5] and the alliances to counter it. Strengthened by Phillip II of Spain's identification of his own cause with that of the league, it concluded on January 2, 1585, the Treaty of Joinville. By reserving succession to the French crown to Cardinal Charles de Bourbon and guaranteeing Henry of Guise a yearly subsidy of fifty thousand écus, the stage was set for the capitulation of Henry III to the Guise and the signing of the Treaty of Nemours concluded July 7, 1585. Nemours provides a moment at which the pattern was particularly clear.[6] The treaty was the cause of Navarre's more intense pursuit of the French wars of religion and of tangled diplomatic relations with the areas on France's eastern border, including Savoy, Lorraine, the Swiss cantons, and the German western duchies. The treaty itself represented the capitulation of Henry III to the Catholic League, a capitulation brought about by Catherine de' Medici.[7] The terms of the Treaty of Nemours were the culmination of Guisard policy: Henry of Navarre, secretly excommunicated by Sixtus V on June 27, 1585,[8] was excluded from succession to the French throne in favor of Cardinal Charles de Bourbon. France was to have one religion, Catholicism.[9] Reformed pastors had to leave France within a month; Reformed laity were to abjure their faith or leave France within six months. They might sell their property within that time or receive its income. The conditions of Nemours were reinforced on September 9, 1585, when the newly elected Sixtus V publicly excommunicated Henry of Navarre and thereby excluded him, in the eyes of the Catholic church, from the rights to all his territories as well as succession to the French throne.[10] On October 7, 1585, Henry III made the conditions of the treaty more harsh, cutting to two weeks the time the refugees had to leave France.[11]

The results of these actions on the part of the French crown were to increase the flood of refugees across France's borders into Protestant territories, one of which was the county of Montbéliard. Count Frederick of Montbéliard allowed passage to those who wished to move farther from France and residence to those who wished to remain in Montbéliard. The magistrates of neighboring Catholic areas were disturbed and wrote to Archduke Ferdinand. He wrote in turn to Frederick telling him not to give refuge to such dangerous people, who, he said, intended to scheme against the French Catholics.[12] On December 7, 1585, Duke Ludwig wrote to Frederick in the same vein, warning him that if he did not send the French exiles on their way, the duke of Guise, in league with the king of Spain, might take the presence of the French exiles as an excuse to invade the area of Alsace, including Montbéliard. Within three years, Ludwig's political knowledge proved accurate. Ludwig also told Frederick that he would incur imperial wrath if he continued to harbor the exiles. And indeed, on December 16, 1585, Emperor Rudolph II also warned Frederick "in a friendly way" to obey at once and to send away the French refugees. If Frederick did not obey, he would fall under Rudolph's displeasure and incur punishment (*Kaiserlichen ungnad und straff*).[13]

Frederick immediately turned to Elector Palatine John Casimir for counsel.[14] He complained that the reports from neighboring Catholic cities to Ludwig, Ferdinand, and Rudolph II were groundless. Frederick then composed a long apology to the emperor, which he sent to Casimir, asking Casimir to correct it and to advise him before he sent it to Rudolph. In his apology, dated January 20, 1586, Frederick argued that he had not allowed the refugees to settle in his lands. Bad neighbors had sent in false reports. Frederick then said that those temporarily in his lands were well-known honest people from Burgundy. Others were learned gentlemen and craftsmen, not soldiers. In short, they were "poor miserable exiles who, like me, pray God that Montbéliard were far enough away [from France] that they could be at home, at peace and safe."[15] Frederick argued that he was only doing his Christian duty, that his compassion accorded with God's command to love and to treat others as we should wish to be treated if we were afflicted for our sins with exile.[16] After further arguments, Frederick suggested that if the emperor continued to listen only to Frederick's enemies and to threaten him, "I would have to take my case to my relatives and take steps to protect myself against these unfounded charges."[17]

Letters continued to fly back and forth among Frederick, John Casimir, and Ludwig. John Casimir wrote to Rudolph II, and Ludwig wrote to Archduke Ferdinand. Casimir also instructed his ambassador to the Deputationstag meeting in Worms to inform the representatives of the estates of the empire concerning Rudolph's pressure on Frederick. Ludwig agreed with Frederick that the Protestant princes should ally with Frederick if Rudolph II refused to relent. Casimir wrote to Frederick on April 18, 1586, suggesting that he write to Saxony, Brandenburg, Hesse, Württemberg, and other allies. This matter, wrote Casimir, involves all the Protestant estates. Frederick should also write to Basel, Hanau, and other neighboring cities to find out who was responsible for the bad reports. When these cities denied that the French refugees were troublesome (as they in fact did write by May 15, 1586), Frederick should send copies to Rudolph II.[18] Meanwhile, Duke Ludwig had written to Frederick on April 21, reminding him that even he had "not always been trustworthy, especially *regarding religion* and even more in other matters, he had been slippery and undependable."[19] Ludwig was referring to Frederick's tolerance, if it may be so called, of Montbéliard's resistance to the Württemberg theology and also, perhaps, to Frederick's support, in money and arms, of the Calvinist Henry of Navarre.

The influx of refugees increased the pressure on the ministers of Montbéliard to conduct services according to the liturgy of either Toussain or the French Reformed church. In either case, they would be subject to discipline for departing from the Württemberg ecclesiastical ordinances and the letter of the unaltered Augsburg Confession. The French refugees were therefore barred from communion in the Lord's Supper unless they conformed to Lutheran theology and practice, something they would not do after leaving France for their Reformed faith. They petitioned Count Frederick to be allowed to take communion according to their own liturgy on Christmas Day 1585. Frederick denied their petition, but he was open to the suggestion of a colloquy to explore the possibility of agreement between the French Reformed and the Lutherans on the difficult subject of the Lord's Supper.

Although Count Frederick himself invited Beza to participate in the colloquy to be held at Montbéliard in late March 1586,[20] behind Frederick was Henry of Navarre. The colloquy could serve a larger purpose than the comfort of local refugees; with Beza and Andreae as the collocutors, it might answer the theological objections of the Lutheran dukes to a Protestant league.[21] It was Navarre's agent, the baron de Clervant, who invited Jacob Andreae to the colloquy.[22] It was also Clervant who, during a visit to Montbéliard in early February, urged Frederick to call the colloquy.[23] According to a letter from Henry of Navarre himself to Beza, Clervant and du Fresne[24] were to inform Beza of a mission of great importance to all of Christendom. On February 25, 1586, Henry wrote:

Msr. de Besze, Because the bearer of the preceding had an accident on the way and was wounded, I have been advised to send you this word through Beringen,[25] my valet de chambre and to ask you to take the greatest care and diligence in that which I have recommended by Sr. de fresne [sic] and particularly in that which Mr. de Clervant will give you to understand on my part and concerning which we are asking something necessary and important to us and in which all Christianity has an interest.

Henry added several lines in his own hand telling Beza that in this instance, he had to overcome himself. Henry asked God to bless Beza and signed the letter with his own hand at Nerac.[26]

Several letters from Henry of Navarre to Beza from this period are preserved in the Archives Tronchin. The first (AT 2, no. 3) of interest here is dated November 27, 1585. In it Henry speaks of something that will be good for his house, the crown of France, and Henry himself. Henry does not say what it is but asks for Beza's advice. Presumably the bearer of the letter will explain what it is. I would like to think, of course, that it is the colloquy. Letter no. 4 is cited above. The next letter (no. 6) is undated but tells Beza to believe its bearer, "*sr du fresne conseyler au grand conseyl,*" as he would believe Henry himself. The matter in hand was secret, which may account for the lack of reference in official correspondence.[27] It is likely, however, that du Fresne also urged Beza to accept Frederick's invitation to participate in the colloquy in spite of Beza's ill health. Efforts on the part of the Geneva Council to have Frederick delay the colloquy until April 10 met with no success even though the council argued that Beza had just arisen from his sickbed.[28]

Published accounts of the calling of the colloquy are found in Andreae's *Acta*[29] and in Beza's *Responsio.*[30] According to Andreae, the legate of Henry of Navarre, the "baron de Cleroan [sic]," visited Andreae in Tübingen on January 13, 1586. With Clervant was an interpreter, the Baron Malroy, since Andreae did not speak French nor could Clervant understand Latin.[31] Clervant's mission was to persuade Andreae to participate in a colloquy. Andreae at first demurred, saying that he had no business mixing in French politics. Clervant countered with an illustration drawn from the Old Testament in which priests were consulted by the king. The two joked that then Andreae should wear a pectoral cross with twelve stones for the twelve tribes of Israel. The conversation grew serious, however, when Clervant spoke of the Augsburg Confession and the points of conflict between the Lutheran and the French churches. Surely, argued Clervant, both had not thrown off Rome's tyranny only to give scandal by their lack of agreement.

Clervant's next remarks show signs of either Andreae's editing or Clervant's diplomacy. The disagreement, said Clervant, centered on the Lord's Supper, while on the other matters there seemed to be accord. Clervant then proposed that they agree that the words of institution mean that Christ does what he says, leaving the mode of presence to divine omnipotence and wisdom. God can do what he says, what he promises, and in ways that exceed human understanding, argued Clervant. Andreae answered that that was exactly what the Lutherans had been saying from the beginning of the unhappy controversy. Andreae blamed their differences on intractable Zwinglians and launched into a theological argument that would be repeated during the colloquy.[32] Besides, said Andreae, the Lord's Supper was not the only article that divided the Lutherans and the French. Others were the person of Christ, baptism, and predestination. Clervant declared that the French churches did not know that these other points were problems.

To keep their meeting brief, Clervant asked whether or not Andreae would be willing to meet with Beza for an informal colloquy, at either Strasbourg or Montbéliard, so they could dicuss these matters peacefully. Andreae readily complied, hoping that if they could not agree, at least they could understand one another and stop hurling false accusations back and forth.

Andreae's account further explained that Clervant met Lucas Osiander and asked him to encourage Andreae to attend the colloquy and approved of Osiander's attendence as well. Then Clervant went on to Montbéliard, where, Andreae claimed, unknown to himself, Clervant stirred up the French exiles to ask Frederick for a colloquy between Andreae and Beza. But Frederick would not call a colloquy, claimed Andreae, unless Beza wrote to request it. When Beza had done so, said Andreae, Frederick wrote to Ludwig, duke of Württemberg, making the request formally. Thus it was that on March 13, 1586, Andreae received a formal invitation to the colloquy "so earnestly sought by the French refugees."[33]

In his *Responsio,* Beza gave a different account and furthermore asserted that Clervant himself denied Andreae's version. Beza was constrained, however, not to offend Count Frederick, who had approved Andreae's *Acta,* indeed had encouraged its publication and provided a preface for it. In Beza's *Responsio,* the baron de Clervant said that the *Acta* were inaccurate. In the first place, he (Clervant) had no commission from Navarre about Montbéliard, nor had he any knowledge of the colloquy prior to his visit to Württemberg. Rather, he had come to Tübingen on the general business of peace between the Lutheran and Reformed churches.[34] It was Andreae who mentioned the possibility of a colloquy at Montbéliard. Clervant had objected that it would be better to have a synod called by princes and attended by a number of learned men since a discussion between two private persons would not bear much weight. Andreae responded that since he (Andreae) was called the "pope of Germany" and Beza was called the "pope of France," an agreement between the two of them would indeed be weighty and others would then also be able to agree.[35]

Beza then claimed that Andreae had been urging just such a conference for four years even though Beza himself had not much confidence that the results would be worth the trouble. The French exiles in Montbéliard insisted, however, and Count Frederick made it clear that he wanted it and would be gratified to have Beza come. Beza then conferred with the churches of Bern and Zurich as well as his colleagues in Geneva. The Swiss agreed that although they could not expect much from Andreae, Frederick wanted it badly and it would be best to obey him. The magistrates of Bern and Geneva, who had received letters from Frederick, also favored Beza's participation.[36] Beza referred to Andreae's motive for the colloquy as yet another occasion to stir up the Lutheran princes against the Reformed and to persuade the former not to send help to the French Huguenots. In fact, Andreae had added fuel to the anti-Reformed polemic of some Lutheran preachers through a recently published book.[37] How much could the Reformed expect from such a man, especially when Andreae had already declared that he could not be persuaded that anything he had taught was wrong or open to discussion?[38]

The calling of the colloquy is therefore a problem in itself. Whose account is true, and why do the accounts differ on points that could be verified by the audience? At once it must be said that in such a highly charged polemical and political situation, not only will versions differ in order to give their writers some advantage, but sorting out truth from embroidery and downright falsehood is simply not possible. The best one can do is to find what corroborating material may support one side or the other. That Clervant was in Tübingen is true. What he and Andreae said to one another is a matter of adjudication between the two accounts. First, it would seem that Clervant was in Württemberg for two reasons, the first and most important being to persuade Ludwig to help Navarre through a Protestant league or at least to get Ludwig to persuade the duke of Brandenberg and other Lutheran princes not to help the Guise and their Catholic League. The second reason was related to the first and may have been either to explore ways of resolving the problems between the Lutheran and the Reformed (Beza's version) or to persuade Andreae to participate in a colloquy (Andreae's version). Why? Because if the theological differences between the Huguenots and the Lutherans could be resolved, the German princes might come to the aid of the French.

On the Swiss side, there was no doubt about the primary reason for accepting the invitation to travel to Montbéliard. Responding to a letter from Beza that he had received on February 5, Abraham Musculus wrote from Bern on March 9–10, 1586:

> As to the colloquy with Jacob Andreae, we are also of the opinion that we should in no way refuse it. Nor that we hope such a heavily controverted matter can be defined in this way, but we suspect that our adversaries know as well as we that danger from the Antichrist [the Pope] and his followers menaces everywhere on account of which they themselves recognize that a firmer union with us is necessary.[39]

Musculus added that he would be glad to go as a hearer and witness but doubted how much theological help he would be. There is no mention in Andreae's *Acta* or Beza's *Responsio* of anyone speaking other than the two principles, with the exception of Faius's whispered intervention.[40]

Musculus had good reason to doubt that the eucharistic controversy could be resolved through a colloquy of a few days. The history of such efforts was already long. The Marburg Colloquy of 1529 marked the most obvious beginning of tension between Lutheran and Swiss Reformed Protestants and made the Lord's Supper the focal point of their controversy.[41] From that point on, the theological tension not only increased but developed into a political distinction that was exercised when Duke Ulrich regained Württemberg. The Treaty of Kaadan specifically outlawed sacramentarians, that is, Zwinglians. Between the 1530s and the Peace of Augsburg in 1555, German Lutheran princes tried to enforce the outlawing of sacramentarians. The Peace of Augsburg declared that only followers of the Augsburg Confession and Catholics could legally reside in the empire. Which of the two was to be allowed within a particular area was up to the ruler, hence the development of the principle *cuius regio, eius religio.*

In 1557, the two future Montbéliard collocutors met under more friendly and hopeful circumstances. While in Germany trying to raise support among the German Protestant princes for the French Reformed imprisoned in France, Beza attempted to formulate a confession of faith on the Lord's Supper that might serve to unite the Lutherans and the Reformed. Beza and Farel met with Andreae and Diller in Frankfurt and Göppingen in May of 1557.[42] There they agreed on a formula that was later bitterly rejected by Bullinger and Peter Martyr in Zurich because it referred to the presence of the *substance* of Christ in the Supper: "We confess, therefore . . . in the Supper of the Lord not only the benefits of Christ, but also the very substance of the Son of man, by which I mean the true flesh (which the eternal Word assumed in the perpetual unity of his person, in which he was born and suffered and rose for us and ascended into heaven) and that true blood which he poured out for us."[43] The confession presented to Andreae in Göppingen affirmed that the flesh and blood of Christ are not merely presented symbolically or proposed to the memory but are truly and certainly represented and offered. The symbols are not therefore bare but are conjoined to that thing (*res*) that attains to God promising and offering, whether to the faithful or to the infidel.[44] The Swiss side is then presented through an explanation of the symbolic or sacramental nature of the union of the signs with the signified. The mode of the conjunction of the faithful with the signified is not physical or local or through the diffusion of the human nature of Christ but is spiritual, that is, effected through the power of the Holy Spirit.[45] It should also be noted that the *substance* of Christ is *offered* to both faithful and infidel. Nothing is said about who *receives* it.

This peaceful agreement was shattered on both sides. The Zurich theologians were incensed by the use of the word *substance,* while only a few months later, at Worms, the Catholics declared that they could not conduct a colloquy with representatives of such widely different eucharistic theologies, especially if the Lutherans accommodated Swiss eucharistic theology. This latter move seemed to have been made when a delegation representing the French Protestant church arrived at Worms to seek the intercession of the Protestant German princes with Henry II on behalf of imprisoned Huguenots. For both of these occurrences, it is worthwhile understanding events at Worms in the fall of 1557.

There the divisions among the Lutherans became painfully evident.

Worms was a last effort on the part of King Ferdinand to heal the religious breach in the empire, at least sufficiently to gain strength in his continuing war with the Turks. To that end, he invited Roman Catholics and followers of the Augsburg Confession to meet in theological debate.[46] The colloquy failed principally because of Lutheran disunity, especially between the followers of Flacius Illyricus at Jena (represented at Worms by Erhardt Schnepf) and the followers of Philip Melanchthon. While they disagreed over a number of points, the chief dispute was over article X of the Augsburg Confession. The president of the colloquy, Julius Pflug, asked the Lutherans to try to resolve their difficulties prior to the conference.[47] The Flacians and Philippists therefore met on September 5, and Schnepf began his campaign to have specific groups condemned.[48] He was successfully opposed by both Brenz and Melanchthon. The colloquy opened on September 11 amid considerable pomp. Melanchthon responded to the opening address of Bishop Helding and claimed that all present stood by the 1530 Augsburg Confession.[49] But the problem of the two versions of the Augsburg Confession was exploited by the leading Roman Catholic theologian, Peter Canisius. Canisius asked not only for an explanation of the two versions but also that the Lutherans condemn such eucharistic doctrine as Roman Catholics and followers of the Augsburg Confession found unacceptable.[50] Canisius and Bishop Helding played the game of the Jena theologians, backed by Elector John Frederick of Lower Saxony, who were determined to anathematize all who did not agree with their interpretation of the *Invariata* Augsburg Confession.[51] Arguing against specific condemnations were John Brenz of Württemberg and Melanchthon.[52] When Melanchthon's party continued to prevail and no specific condemnations were forthcoming, the Jena theologians submitted formal protests.[53] The division was past healing at this point, and president Pflug was asked to exclude the Lower Saxon theologians for their intransigence regarding anathemas.[54] But to do so would be to destroy the colloquy, which was meant to be between the Catholics and the followers of the Augsburg Confession. The Jena theologians could not be faulted on the score of holding to the Augsburg Confession. Their refusal to participate or their exclusion meant the failure of the colloquy.

It was after the departure of the Jena delegation that the four Reformed representatives—William Farel, John Budé, Gaspard Carmel, and Theodore Beza—arrived.[55] Their mission was to gain the intercession of the German princes with Henry II of France on behalf of 135 imprisoned Huguenots.[56] Since no support would be forthcoming without a confession of faith, a brief statement was drawn up and signed on October 8 by the four Reformed delegates and by Melanchthon, Brenz, Pistorius, Diller, Marbach, Karg, and Andreae. The document contains specific condemnations of those following Servetus, the Anabaptists, who include the "Stenckfeldians [*sic*]," the Libertines, the Epicureans, and the "papist idols."[57] It affirms the adherence of the French Protestant church to the 1530 Augsburg Confession with the exception of article X. It then lays out the following particulars: They (the French Protestants) condemn the papist doctrines and affirm that they follow the words of Paul: *Panis est koinonia corporis* (the bread is communion with the body). The Son of God is truly present and makes those who eat in faith his members.[58] The Lutherans, including Brenz and Andreae, signed this statement and expressed the hope that the Lord's Supper might be the subject of a future colloquy. The Reformed and Lutheran delegates then addressed a letter on behalf of the French to Palatine Elector Otto Henry and Count Palatine Wolfgang, to Christoph, duke of Württemberg, and to Philip, landgrave of Hesse.[59] Although the princes did not respond favorably to the request due to the intervention of emissaries from the cardinal of Lorraine,[60] they did so the following spring.[61]

The German Protestant princes, especially Christoph of Württemberg and excepting Elector John Frederick, were not willing to concede the failure of the Worms colloquy.[62] They hoped that without the contentious theologians, they might themselves work out a means of Protestant unification. The Frankfurt Recess of 1558 might have succeeded were it not for the advice of those same contentious theologians to their princes. Before the end of 1558, through the Book of Refutation, Duke John Frederick of Lower Saxony and his Jena theologians had succeeded in naming themselves as the sole conservors of Christian orthodoxy and anathematizing, by name, those they considered heretics.[63] Under the label of "adiaphorists," the Philippists, or followers of Melanchthon, were included among the heretics. Supporting their doctrine of the Lord's Supper, the Jena theologians included the ubiquity of Christ's body, a doctrine that was flatly unacceptable to many Lutherans as well as to the Reformed. August of Saxony, Melanchthon's duke, rightly felt attacked and asked the faculty of Wittenberg to respond.[64] It is not necessary to follow further the arguments in this inter-Lutheran war; it is sufficient to note that the condemnations were effected with the predictable result of promoting further divisions among Lutherans.

Failure though Worms may have been for Ferdinand and for the disunited Lutherans, it was in some sense a success from the point of view of the Reformed. Since no decision resutled that was binding in imperial law concerning which version of the Augsburg Confession had to be endorsed and since many Lutherans rejected the Jena anathemas, there remained the possibility for the Reformed within the empire to claim the German Protestant princes as allies and themselves as adherents of the Augsburg Confession. And in fact, three and a half years later at Naumburg (January 1561), the German Protestant princes declared that the 1530 Augsburg Confession could be understood according to the *Variata* version of article X. In addition, in response to the appeal of Elizabeth of England through her envoy, Christopher Mundt, the princes declared themselves to be of the same faith as the church of England. They sent an appeal on behalf of the French Protestants to Charles IX of France, and they invited the churches of Denmark, Scotland, and Sweden to join them in their declaration of belief.[65] The unanimity of the German Protestant princes disturbed two factions, the Catholics and the ultra-Lutherans of Jena, who thus continued to play into the hands of the Catholics. The Catholics sought, successfully, to break this unity later that same year at Poissy.

In France, Catholics faced Reformed directly. Although French Protestants had been called "Lutherans" in the early decades of the Reformation, by the 1550s they were recognized as belonging to *"la religion prétendue reformée."* The problems the Reformed of France faced were different from, although not unrelated to, those faced by the Reformed in the empire. The Peace of Augsburg had no counterpart in France. Nevertheless, the position of Reformed groups within the empire, vis-à-vis the "Religionsfriede" of 1555, had some influence on the French situation and vice versa. If the Reformed were formally accepted in the empire (Naumburg pointed in that direction), an argument could be made for their acceptance in France. On the other hand, to exclude the Reformed from among those who followed the Augsburg Confession was part of the Catholic strategy of divide and conquer. The strategy was used effectively at Worms; it was used effectively four years later at Poissy through the introduction of Lutheran theologians into what was billed as a colloquy between the French Catholic and the French Reformed churches.[66]

After the death of Henry II in 1559, Catherine de' Medici, his widow and regent for the eleven-year-old Charles IX, attempted to bring the Reformed and the Catholics together at Poissy in 1561. Less than one year later, France was torn apart by the wars of religion. At Poissy, Theodore Beza and Jacob Andreae, who had met amicably at Göppingen and at Worms in 1557, were again participants. This time, however, both had weightier responsibilities. Beza was the primary spokesman for the Reformed; Andreae was sent there by his duke at the invitation of Antoine, king of Navarre, once recognized as the leader of the Huguenots but by 1561 a declared Catholic. Once again, the primary issue was the Lord's Supper. Once again, the Augsburg Confession, this time in its *Invariata* form, was offered as a means of conciliation between the Reformed and the Catholics.[67] The agent who offered it was Andreae, sent specifically to perform this function by Duke Christoph of Württemberg, who also provided the Württemberg Confession. At Poissy, Beza's theology was less open to Andreae's favorable interpretation than the Göppingen formula had been.[68] Indeed, the Lutheran got on better with the Catholics at Poissy than with his fellow Protestant from Göppingen days. But the possibility of a theological liaison between the Catholics and the Lutherans over the real presence in the eucharist was not a serious threat given other theological and political differences.[69] From this point on, Andreae and Beza became more and more inimical, especially through the battle for the Palatinate in which Brenz and Andreae made clear their double doctrine of ubiquity and the "majesty" of Christ's human nature, two doctrines the Swiss found contradictory to the reality of Christ's humanity.

Before turning to the meeting between Andreae and Beza at Montbéliard, the examination of two events will serve especially well as examples of the increasingly bitter polemical and political battles between the Lutherans and the Reformed: the Augsburg Diet of 1566[70] and the publication of the Formula of Concord in 1577.[71] Both also provide an opportunity to relate the Lutheran-Reformed and intra-Lutheran disagreements with the efforts of the

Reformed to engage all the Lutherans in an anti-Catholic, pro-Protestant league.[72] It is not surprising that the roots of this movement are both manifold and difficult to find. It is not surprising because the Protestants were scattered through Europe and felt vulnerable in the face of the combined power of Rome and the Habsburg empire. The Council of Trent appeared to most Protestants to be a potentially powerful instrument since its enforcement would mean the triumph of the Catholic church. What could be more reasonable than for the Protestants to form a solid front against the Catholics? At the same time, political realities and loyalties prevented such a league. The Peace of Augsburg as well as their feudal obligations to the emperor bound the German Protestant princes. They could not form a political alliance without breaking their oaths to the emperor. Their one attempt to do so, the Schmalkald League, had ended in disaster in 1546 with the victory of Charles V at Mühlberg and the imposition of the hated Interim. The situation was further complicated by the 1555 Peace of Augsburg, which bound territories within the empire to either follow Catholicism or adhere to the Augsburg Confession.

But the Protestants outside the empire were under no such constraints, and it was the Swiss Protestant cantons, together with France, England, and Denmark, that moved to encourage the German Protestant princes to join them against the Catholic powers. While there is evidence that Elizabeth of England was interested in such an alliance from the time of her accession,[73] and again in 1561, it was in 1577 that she began an urgent campaign and to this end sent envoys to the courts of Denmark and of the German Protestant princes.[74] Although Elizabeth declared that her intention was to stop the Catholics from overcoming Protestants and enforcing the decrees of the Council of Trent, her policy was determined more by politics than by religion. Especially after the St. Bartholomew's Day massacre and the "house arrest" of Henry of Navarre and the duke of Alençon, Elizabeth feared a Catholic alliance that would attempt the rescue of Mary Stuart at the cost of Elizabeth's throne and English civil war. Elizabeth was more concerned to keep France and Spain off balance and the Lowlands from the French than she was to be the protectress of Protestants. On the other hand, Walsingham, her ambassador to France and then her secretary of state, seems to have been much more genuinely concerned about the protection of the Huguenots, whose religion he fervently shared.[75]

When, in January of 1561, Elizabeth heard of a gathering of German Protestant princes at Naumburg,[76] she sent Christopher Mundt to ask them to consider a Protestant "Confederation" to withstand the pope's efforts to break Protestantism through the Council of Trent.[77] The queen's envoy received a courteous hearing, especially since Christoph of Württemberg had already widened the idea of a Protestant League beyond the empire and thought of including Denmark (whose king had been invited to Naumburg), Sweden, England, and Scotland. He too wanted to mount firm resistance to the actions of the Council of Trent.[78] It was clear, however, that before the German princes could form any sort of alliance, they must overcome the serious disagreements that had driven them apart at Worms. The Naumburg meeting was another effort on the part of the German Protestant princes to resolve their differences concerning article X of the Augsburg Confession. Philip of Hesse nearly succeeded in having the *Variata* edition accepted on the grounds that the *Invariata,* especially in some of its recensions, would allow for transubstantiation.[79] The union of the princes, their willingness to sign a formula based on the 1530 Augsburg Confession but acceptant also of the editions published since then, was countered once again by the duke of Weimar Saxony. John Frederick protested that the princes' statement must include condemnations of those who did not adhere to the *Invariata* and that the *Variata* must be disavowed. As had his theologians at Worms, John Frederick walked out of the assembly.[80] The rest of the princes signed the Naumburg articles on February 8. On the previous day, they had addressed a letter on behalf of the Huguenots to Charles IX in which they included a copy of the Augsburg Confession.[81] The outcome of Naumburg looked propitious, but theological disputes, this time in the Palatinate, renewed the divisions among the Lutheran princes, prodded by their theologians.

Although Lutheranism had been introduced into the Palatinate in 1545 by Frederick II, it was not until 1556 that Frederick's son, Otto Henry, declared Lutheranism to be the official religion of the Palatinate. In 1559, Frederick III became elector and, through the appointment of theologians and advisers, allowed the Reformed element to dominate. According to his letters, Frederick was convinced that Luther had not moved far enough from the Catholic doctrine of the Lord's Supper, nor was he convinced that Lutherans had done enough to reform moral behavior.[82] Frederick also hoped to reconcile Protestants in the empire, but the internal result of his policy was to set Reformed against Lutheran in the Palatinate itself. Tilemann Hesshus, on Melanchthon's recommendation, had been given positions of extraordinary influence at Heidelberg,[83] where he tried to pit his strict Lutheranism against the Reformed strengthened by Frederick III. When, in 1559, Frederick III stripped Hesshus of his offices, including that of pastor, Hesshus became one of the Reformed Palatinate's most bitter and constant foes. Nevertheless, the fall of Hesshus signaled the triumph of the Reformed in Heidelberg, and by 1563 Zacharias Ursinus and Caspar Olevian had produced the Heidelberg Catechism, a major Reformed document.[84]

Developments of this kind could not but worry Frederick's neighbor, Christoph of Württemberg, and in 1564 the Maulbronn Colloquy engaged Jacob Andreae against Ursinus as principal collocutors. The colloquy, like those before it and those to follow, did nothing to heal the theological divisions, especially regarding the Lord's Supper.[85] Maulbronn did, however, draw more attention to the Reformed doctrine of the Palatinate and to the question of the legality of the situation. Once again the problem became politically urgent: Could the *Variata* version of the Augsburg Confession be allowed as a legal base within the empire?[86] The matter was taken before the Augsburg Diet of 1566,[87] where Frederick III defended his position successfully largely because Duke Christoph of Württemberg and the duke of Brandenburg hoped not to alienate Frederick further.[88]

Frederick's victory in the Palatinate was to undergo a severe test when he died in 1576 and was succeeded by his son, Ludwig VI, a Lutheran who followed the *Invariata* Augsburg Confession. Reformed theologians were driven out of the Palatinate except in that part of it ruled by John Casimir, the second son of Frederick III. In their places came Lutheran theologians, including Balthasar Bidembach from Württemberg. It would take more than a few years to change the Palatinate, however, and when Ludwig VI died in 1583, his brother John Casimir became regent elector and returned the territory to the Reformed tradition. It was now the turn of the Lutheran theologians to be dismissed. Among the theologians replacing the Lutherans in Heidelberg was Pierre Toussain's son, Daniel Toussain.

Within this history, what is the significance of the Reichstag of 1566? Frederick III hoped it might provide an opportunity for a middle ground for the reunion of the fractured Lutherans and even of the Lutherans with the Reformed. The basis of Protestant belief was, after all, the sufficiency of Christ as God's promise grasped by faith. Other doctrines may be disputed, but Frederick wanted to call them *"Nebendisputationen."*[89] These doctrines ought not be a basis for Protestant disunion, he said. Further, argued Frederick, disputes over such matters had been tolerated in the early church as Peter and Paul agreed to disagree and as Jerome and Augustine disagreed without dividing Christendom.[90] However reasonable such a position seems to be, it was not so taken by Frederick's peers, especially Wolfgang of Zweibrücken, who, like the Weimar faction, desired doctrinal conformity on all points, especially those most hotly disputed, namely the Lord's Supper and Christology.[91] Other electors were less intransigent and, in the hope of winning Frederick back to "orthodox" Lutheranism, namely an endorsement of the *Invariata* version of the Augsburg Confession, refused to press him so hard. These two influential electors were Christoph of Württemberg and Joachim of Brandenburg. The result was a de facto interpretation of the Peace of Augsburg as allowing the *Variata* form of the Augsburg Confession. The increasingly Reformed Palatinate was now safely included in the empire.[92] This interpretation was not noted by the Lutherans as a Reformed success, however, and the theologians of Württemberg continued to call for conformity to the unaltered form of the Augsburg Confession and condemnation of those who refused so to conform.[93] In other words, Württemberg in the 1560s had joined those who sought conformity through condemnation. Brenz and Andreae no longer supported the Wittenberg Lutherans who opposed specific condemnations; they had moved to the side of those hard-line Lutherans who wished to name names.[94]

Serious differences among Lutherans and continuing bitterness between Lutherans and Reformed moved the German Protestant princes to declare a truce in 1568 and to forbid their theologians to engage in controversy. One might as well ask a waterfall to flow upward. Controversies not only continued but became more bitter. At the same time, Andreae continued his efforts, begun at Maulbronn, to label all Reformed as "Zwinglian" and to persuade princes sympathetic to the Reformed to adhere exclusively to the *Invariata* Augsburg Confession and even to the Württemberg ubiquitarian theology. Andreae proposed to William of Hesse a colloquy between Lutherans and Zwinglians. The Lutherans were to be Andreae, Nicholas Selnecker, and Chemnitz. The Zwinglians were to be Beza, Rudolf Gwalther, and Ursinus. The principal text of the debate was to be the Wittenberg Concord with Bucer's declaration. The collocutors were to determine how much of Bucer's declaration was approved and what errors it contained.[95] Beza declined to participate, citing his distrust of such colloquies, the failure of the Maulbronn debate serving as an example.[96]

Although Andreae failed to persuade William of Hesse to convene a colloquy, he did not fail to publish ever-more condemnatory books. In fact, Andreae was determined, it seemed, to gain those parts of Germany to ubiquitarian Lutheranism that were either Reformed, like the Palatinate, or Philippist, like Wittenberg. It was in the context of this second goal that Andreae and Beza engaged in a polemical exchange that foreshadowed the issues, arguments, and appeals to John Damascene and other authorities that would be used at Montbéliard fifteen years later.[97] In March 1571, Beza wrote a long letter to William of Hesse that later became two prefaces, one against Andreae, which appeared as the preface to a book by Christoph Hardesheim published in Geneva, and the other as the preface to Lambert Daneau's 1581 refutation of Martin Chemnitz's *Examen libri de duabus in Christo naturis.* . . .[98]

In spite of the divisions among the German Lutherans, Andreae and Chemnitz, through the Formula of Concord (1577) and the Book of Concord (1580), succeeded in drawing together many of the Lutheran factions and even in condemning by name those deemed guilty of doctrinal errors.[99] The formula affirmed the *Invariata* and condemned, among others, the Reformed.[100] The Formula and the Book of Concord were intended primarily to unite Lutherans, and this was indeed the result in many, but not all, of the German estates.[101] One-third of the Lutheran territories in Germany did not adopt the Formula of Concord in spite of Andreae's devoted efforts. When the king of Denmark received beautifully bound copies of the Book of Concord from his sister, he carried them to the fire and burned them. He then made it a capital offense to import, sell, or even own the Book of Concord.[102] Henry of Navarre appealed to the king of Denmark's rejection of the Book of Concord against the request of some German Protestant princes to make Navarre's acceptance of it a condition of their help in the critical year, 1585.[103] The bourgeoisie of Montbéliard also appealed to the lack of unanimity among Lutherans to plead their case against signing the Formula.

Before turning to the Colloquy of Montbéliard itself, the polemical language and intolerance of the period require comment. Tolerance is so little a mark of the sixteenth century that any expression of it is remarkable.[104] As theologians engaged in controversy, they anathematized one another in the harshest terms they could employ. The attitude of many controversialists was often based on the conviction that they alone possessed the truth and all others were deluded—"dreamers" at best and "devils" or "Turks" or "Mohammedans" at worst. Their opponents were not only wrong, they deceived others and were dupes or even conscious agents of the devil. Thus the Jena theologians and their duke claimed that they alone guarded the truth and that all others, including Lutherans who disagreed with them, were worthy of damnation. During the interchange of postcolloquy publications, Andreae's language worsened while Beza's language and arguments became less polemical.[105]

The reasons for this difference between Lutheran and Reformed are worth exploring and lie as much in the realm of politics as in religion. Where a religion is supported by the state, it can afford to be triumphalist and harsh toward all the contenders whose place in the state is less secure or even, as with the Anabaptists, illegal. Only in Scotland did the Reformed have a secure base in a state large enough to give them the sense of invulnerability enjoyed by Lutherans and Catholics in the empire. Elsewhere, the Reformed fought for every toehold they could find: the Lowlands, England, France, Poland. Even in the Protestant cantons of Switzerland, doctrines differed depending on the origin of the Reformation in each city-state. The need to support one another politically was more important than doctrinal differences, as the relation of Bern to Geneva demonstrates. The two cities differed on the doctrine of predestination, and Bern was not always a stable partner even politically, but in the long run the Swiss cities supported one another, especially against the Roman Catholics. In the Reformed tradition, the strongest sign of tolerance of some theological differences is the Harmony of Confessions, which was the 1581 response of the Reformed churches across Europe to the Formula of Concord.[106] This work contained the confessions of Reformed groups from Poland to England, from France to the Lowlands. The doctrines these confessions contained were similar but not identical. The need to stand together against the Lutheran concord outweighed the need to find one confessional expression that could be signed by all.[107]

Other sufferings were visited upon those who did not conform to the territorially supported religion. These ranged from the extreme of having to move one's household to an area where one's religion was either dominant or tolerated to traveling elsewhere to receive communion or even to give birth in order to assure that the baby would be baptized by a minister of one's own faith.[108] The hatred that religious zeal can enkindle made soldiers and even crowds of nonmilitary people more rapacious when their rulers fought over territories as occurred in the Palatinate, in France, and in the Lowlands. In the Lowlands, Catholic soldiers terrorized Protestants. In France, Protestant troops vandalized and terrorized Catholics and vice versa,[109] while in the Palatinate Lutherans and then Calvinists burned and pillaged the same unfortunate Protestant villages depending on which form of Protestantism was favored by the reigning duke. If it can be argued that soldiers in the sixteenth century behaved as have soldiers in all times and places, it can also be argued that religion did nothing to soften their behavior.

Notes

1. Jill Raitt, "The Emperor and the Exiles: The Clash of Religion and Politics in the Sixteenth Century," *Church History* 52 (June 1983): 145–56.

2. Ibid.

3. Raitt, "The Elector John Casimir," 117–45.

4. For an idea of the rumors in Paris on this point, see René de Lucinge, *Lettres sur les debuts de la Ligue* (1585), ed. Alain Dufour (Geneva: Librairie Droz, 1964) [Lucinge was Charles Emmanuel's ambassador to the court of France], 269: "Ilz tiennent qu'il vient aux huguenotz douze mille reistres et six cents harquebusiers françoys qui les attendent à Mombelliard pour leur fayre escorte en France." But see the letters to Henry III (January 4, 1586) and to Villeroy, Henry's secretary of state (January 6, 1586), from Fleury, Henry's ambassador to Savoy. Fleury assured Villeroy that while there were indeed troops in Montbéliard, they were no more than 100 or 120. Fleury also calmed fears about the immediate arrival of the "*reistres,*" or cavalry, from Germany (BN 500 Colb.' 427, fas. 399–401).

5. Girolamo Ragazzoni, Eveque de Bergame, *Nonce en France: Correspondance de sa Nonciature 1583–1586* [hereafter Ragazzoni], ed. Pierre Blet, S.J. (Rome: Gregorian University Press, 1962) 137. The instructions given by the cardinal of Como, secretary to Gregory XIII, include a section on the pope's preference for war over peace in France: "In evento che V.S. habbi mai a venir a termini di persuadere il Re a pace o a guerra con li suoi ribelli, come facilmente potrà occorrere più d'una volta, per l'inconstantia et volubilità de le cose di la, avvertirà d'inclinar sempre più a la guerra chè a la pace, perchè con li nimici di Dio non si doverebbe mai tener pace, et maggiormente poiche si è veduto con la esperienza di tanti anni, et massime ultimamente, che il Re ha sempre più guadagnato con la guerra che con la pace." See also the introductory section: "Le Nonce Entre le Roi et la Ligue," 52–64. Unfortunately for this study, Blet frequently saw fit to omit parts of Ragazzoni's letters that refer to the Huguenots and to replace the text with brief and unsatisfying summaries. See p. xi, where Blet says that he has reproduced only "important" texts. See also the fine book by De Lamar Jensen, *Diplomacy and Dogmatism: Bernardo de Mendoza and the French Catholic League* (Cambridge: Harvard University Press, 1964), esp. 29–72.

6. Jensen, *Diplomacy and Dogmatism,* 70: "The principal terms of the treaty were the following:

"(1) All previous edicts of pacification were superceded.

"(2) The practice of any other religion than the Roman Catholic was forbidden in France.

"(3) All ministers of any other religion should leave the kingdom within one month.

"(4) Heretics were not allowed to hold any public office.

"(5) Within six months all subjects of the king must make profession of the Catholic religion or leave the realm.

"(6) The chambres mi-parties were to be abolished.

"(7) Surrender of the fortified places conceded to the Huguenots in the Peace of Monsieur was demanded."

7. Ragazzoni, no 163, p. 403: Ragazzoni to the cardinal of Como (secretary of Gregory XIII), [Paris, April 18, 1585]: "trovandosi il Re Chr.mo . . . abbandonata da

la Nobiltà principale et da buoni soggetti di guerra, et non trovando anco copia di soldati privati, crescie tuttavia la opinione quasi commune, che il Re debba accordarsi con questi signori sollevati al meglio che potrà, il che pare che la Regina madre senti, che si debba fare in ogni modo, et così Mons. di Lione, che è stimato horamai più de la parte di Guisa, che di quella del Re." See also p. 137, *Instruction of the Cardinal of Como,* in which Ragazzoni is advised never to deal with the king alone but always to include Catherine: "Et a questo fine avvertira V.S. di far l'istesso capitale de la Regina madre che del Re, non trattando mai con l'uno, che non tratti ancor con l'altra, se non ci sarà impedimento. Et potrà mostrare a lei di conoscer et creder che ogni cosa dipendi da consiglio, valore et autorità sua."

8. Ragazzoni, 91–93. The decision taken by the Inquisition was not promulgated by a papal bull until September 9, printed on September 23, 1585. The prince of Condé was included in the condemnation.

9. See Ragazzoni, 62–63, for the extent to which the league represented an action against Henry III as much as against Navarre and Henry III's dislike and distrust of the Guise and their ambitions, a distrust and dislike shared by the queen mother.

10. Henri IV, *Recueil des lettres missives, de Henri IV.* 2:87ff. for Henry of Navarre's letters to Henry III, Catherine de' Medici, the Swiss cantons, and German dukes, among others. Cf. Jean-Pierre Babelon, *Henri IV* (Paris: Fayard, 1982), 345–47. Ragazzoni, 62–64, describes the league as a threat to Henry III, a threat about which the latter complained in a letter to the cardinal d'Este on April 2, 1585. Neither Gregory XIII nor Sixtus V would give full approbation to the Catholic League, but Sixtus V's excommunication of Navarre signaled approval of Charles of Bourbon's claim to be heir to the French throne. See n. 7 above. Cf. Jensen, *Diplomacy and Dogmatism,* 72–73.

11. N. M. Sutherland, *The Huguenot Struggle for Recognition* (New Haven: Yale University Press, 1980), 364–65, summarizes the terms of the July 7 treaty and the October 7 declaration.

12. AN-K 2186, dr. 1. I gratefully acknowledge here the paleographic assistance of Ricarda Froehlich, who transcribed most of the German letters and helped with the translations. I also thank the editors of *Church History* for permission to quote from "The Emperor and the Exiles," *Church History* 52 (June 1983): 152–53.

13. AN-K 2186, dr. 1, fonds Montbéliard. Archduke Ferdinand to Count Frederick, December 5, 1585; Duke Ludwig to Count Frederick, December 7, 1585; Emperor Rudolph II to Count Frederick, December 16, 1585.

14. AN-K 2186, dr. 1. Count Frederick to Elector Palatine John Casimir, January 6, 1596.

15. "vnnd inn summa arme Elende vertribene leutt, die (wie Ich selbsten) von Gott wunschten, dass Mompelgart inn seiner gelegenheit annderst beschaffen, vnnd also entlegen, dass sie nicht alhie, sonnder daheimbden beij dem Irigen ruig vnnd sicher sein mochten" (Frederick to Rudolph II, January 20, 1586, AN-K 2186).

16. *Ibid.:* "Dass Ich aber mitt Ihnen ein christliches mittleiden hat, beschicht aus der von Gott selbs anbevolhener liebe, auch behertzigung, dass (da Gott vor seie) sein Allmacht vnns vnnserer vilfeltigen sunden wegen mitt der gleichen ruthen vnnd Exilien heimsuchte, wir ebenmessige christliche Bruderlich Hospitalitet gern suchen."

17. Ibid.: "Dann Ich sonnsten solches an meine nechstuerwannte clags weis gelangen zu lassen vnnd vff mittel, wie Ich dergleichen vngegrunten antragens verhaben sein mochte, zutrachten notturffsignlich getrungen wurde."

18. Casimir to Frederick, January 23 and April 18, 1586. On April 10, 1586, Frederick wrote to Basel, Strasbourg, Murbach, Calmar, Schlettstatt, Besançon,

Entsisheim, and the governor of Burgundy. On May 5, 1586, Schlettstatt responded, followed by Strasbourg on May 10 and Reychenweyh on May 11 (AN-K 2186).

19. "Dann solte gleich E.L. selbsten, auch annderer zuuersicht entgegen, ain mahl vonn Inen, (welche nitt allezeitt so offennbar, sonnder wie *in religione,* allso vill mehr auch in annderen hanndlungen schlupferig vnnd ongewis)" (Duke Ludwig to Count Frederick, April 21, 1586, AN-K 2186, dr. 1; the emphasis is Ludwig's).

20. AEG, *Registres du Conseil* (hereafter RC), Vol. 81, f. 47r: "Au reste à aporté à m. de Beze des lettres de m.le conte de Montbéliard par lesquelles il l'invite à la conference avec Jacob Andreae luy assignant jour au 23ieme du prochain." See chap. 1, no. 1. See also Jacques Auguste de Thou, *Histoire universelle . . . depuis 1543, jusqu'en 1607,* vol. 9, bk. 85 (Paris: n.p., 1734), 597–98. It is disappointing that de Thou reported the colloquy only by rumor. His inaccuracy is evident from his saying that Beza published his response four years after the colloquy. Of more interest is de Thou's understanding of the reason for the colloquy (p. 598): "Avant le depart de ces Ambassadeurs, la guerre étant déjà allumée parmi nous, les Protestans regardoient les secours d'Allemagne presque comme leur unique ressource. Cependant comme les Églises de la Confession Helvetique & de Genève, suivie par les Protestans de France, étoient fort animées alors contre celles de la Confession d'Augsbourg, les princes d'Allemagne qui la suivoient, s'étoient extremement refroidis. Pour les concilier, Frideric de Wirtemberg comte de Montbéliard, fort zelé pour les Protestans de France, & assez favorable à leur doctrine, à ce que bien des gens croyoient; excité d'ailleurs par Claude Antoine de Vienne sieur de Clairvant, menagea une conférence à Monbéliard entre les deux églises Protestantes."

21. The Huguenots' chief ally in Germany was John Casimir, regent elector of the Palatine. Casimir was to lead German cavalry into France. That he had problems arising from Lutheran-Reformed theology is attested to by Lucinge, *Lettres . . . Ligue,* 155: "Le duc de Cazimir, qui venoyt pour le Roy de Navarre, est empeché a desmesler le different pour la religion contre le duc de Virtemberg et quelques autres de ses voysins, comme je croy V.A. aura sceu, mais le Roy en a eu lettres asseurées." (Casimir is wrongly identified as the "Duc de Deux-Ponts" in n. 4.)

22. Original autograph, Public Records Office, London, Reference nos. PFNF 25CL; SP 81/3/PT-1, p. 1, and translated in *Calendar of State Papers, Foreign Series, of the Reign of Elizabeth,* vol. 20, 297. On January 14, 1586, Lobetius (an agent in Strasbourg working for the English government) wrote to Walsinham: "Le Sr. de Clervant a esté vers le prince d'Anhalt et vers les landsgraves / qu'il a trouvez fort gratieux et de bonne volunte. Il va a present trou- / ver le duc de Virtemberg. Et ainsy vous entendes qu'il ne tiendra a admonition / diligence et sollicitation que les choses n'aillent bien." (M. de Clervant has been to the prince of Anhalt and the landgrave, whom he has found most gracious and well inclined. He is now going to the duke of Württemberg. Thus you will see that it is not for lack of diligence and solicitation that things do not go well.) This letter verifies Clervant's presence in Stuttgart in the second week of January and thereby substantiates Andreae's claim in the preface to his 1586 *Acta* that it was indeed Clervant who invited him to the colloquy. Cf. Rott, *Histoire,* 368, which affirms that although Clervant did not remain in Montbéliard for the colloquy, nevertheless, it met "at his instigation, in the hope that it might help along the union of the two reformed churches" (Calvinist and Lutheran). See also chap. 1, nn. 3, 4.

23. Mazauric, "Claude-Antoine de Vienne," 126: "Nous trouvons ce dernier [Clervant], en février 1586, à Montbéliard, ou, le 8, il presente au baptême Zacharie de Jaucourt avec Nicole de Vienne comme marraine. C'est à son instigation que le

comte de Montbéliard convoque le colloque, auquel assiste Théodore de Bèze, dans le vain espoir d'opérer la fusion des deux églises protestantes."

24. Henry IV, *Recueil des lettres missives* 2:183 in a letter from Henry of Navarre to De Fleury, "Conseiller du Roy, Mon Seigneur, et son Ambassadeur en Suisse." Henry wrote on January 20, 1586: "Mais se presentant la commodité du sr de Fresne, present porteur, conseiller au grand conseil de sa dicte Majesté"; since de Fresne was sent to Fleury on January 20, he was therefore in Switzerland in January 1586. See also p. 423 for the date January 1, 1589; and the note with its citation from Amyrault, *Vie de Francois, seigneur de la Noue,* 309): "De Fresne, que les édits de la Ligue avoient contraint de sortir hors du Royaume, et qui s'estoit retiré à Lausanne, sçachant que la Noue estoit à Geneve, s'y alla habituer pour avoir l'avantage de communiquer souvent avec luy.' Il est probable que ce fut la Noue qui donna alors M. de Fresne au roi de Navarre." Cf. David Buisseret, *Henri IV* (London: Allen and Unwin, 1984), 97: "Pierre Forget, sieur de Fresnes is identified as a member of Henry's "conseil des affaires." On the other hand, see Yves Cazaux, *Henri IV,* vol. 1, *Ou la grande victoire* (Mayenne: Albin Michel, 1977), 272, where Philippe de Fresne-Canaye is called the "conseiller au grand conseil," an appointment delayed because de Fresne was "de la religion" [Reformed]. Both de Fresnes, Canaye and Forget, served Henry of Navarre before and after his accession to the throne of France. See Michel de la Huguerye, *Mémoires inédits de Michel de la Huguerye,* vol. 3, 1587–1602 (Paris: Librairie Renouard, 1880), 290. De la Huguerye reports that he was in Geneva with La Noue (who lived there) and Du Fresne-Canaye, identified in a note as Philippe Canaye. Philippe Canaye de Fresne was in Geneva with de La Noue at the beginning of 1586, according to F. E. Sutcliffe in his introduction to *François de La Noue, discours politiques et militaires* (Geneva: Librairie Droz, 1967), xvi. It was Canaye de Fresne who oversaw the publication of La Noue's discourses, providing them with a dedicatory letter to the king of Navarre written on April 1, 1587, from Lausanne.

25. Pierre de Beringhen. See *Dictionnaire de biographie française,* vol. 6, col. 20.

26. Archives Tronchin (in the Bibliothèque Publique et Universitaire de Genève), vol. 2, Lettres Autographes de 1500 a 1600, no. 4: "Monsr. de Besze. Parce que le porteur de la precedente a faict maulvaize rencontre par le chemin et a este blesse j'ai advise de vous faire ce mot seullement par Berenges mon varlet de chambre et vous prier de vous employer le plus soigneusement et diligemment que vous pourrez en ce que je vous ay recommande par le Sr. du Fresne et particullierement en ce que Mr. de Clervant vous en fera entendre de ma part, et dont nous avons besoing comme de chose qui nous est necessaire et importante, et en quoi toute la chrestiente a interest en quoi me promettant de votre bon zele et fidelite, que vous n'obmettrez rien de ce qui sera en votre pouvoir que je ne vous en diray davantage, si ce n'est pour me recommander a vos bonnes prieres et vous assurer de mon amitye. Comme aussy je prie le Createur vous tenir Monsr. de Besze en sa saincte et digne garde. De Nerac ce 25ieme fevrier 1586. *Monsr. de besze il faut en cest oeuvre sy necessayre vous vayncre vous mesmes. Je suys votre mylleur et plus afectione amy Henry*" (emphasis mine to indicate that these words were written in Henry's own hand).

27. I can find no official commission for either du Fresne or Clervant in this regard. Indeed, it has been a long search to find anything to corroborate Clervant's presence in Stuttgart; see chap. 1, nn. 5, 6. The lack of commission and the secrecy regarding Navarre's part in the colloquy also corroborate Beza's report of Clervant's account of his visit to Andreae.

28. AEG, RC, vol. 81, f. 47r (original autograph of secretary Gallatin, February 28, 1586): "Au reste a aporte à m. de Bèze des lettres de m. le conte de Montbéliard par

lesquelles il l'invite a la conference avec Jacob Andreae luy assignant jour au 23ieme du prochain. Sur quoy ont esté adresser lettres de la pars de messieurs audit Sire conte pour le prier de differer jusque au 10 de apvril prochain à cause de asperté du temps, et de ce que ledit Sr de Bèze est relevé fraichment du maladie. Et [il?] respondat est pria requerir messieurs de Bern d'[octroyer] oultrouir Mr. Musculus pour aller avec ledit Sire de Bèze ce que esté approuvé." See also RC, p. 5, pp. 110–12, esp. n. 67: "Frédéric de Wurtemberg, comte de Montbéliard après sa lettre personnelle à Bèze . . . avait encore écrit au Conseil lui demandant de laisser partir le réformateur et de faire en sorte qu'il soit à Montbéliard le 23 mars. Le Conseil répondit au comte de différer la conférence jusqu'au 10 avril les intempéries rendant le voyage difficile et Bèze n'étant pas rétabli d'une récente maladie. La Seigneurie demandait en outre qu'Abraham Musculus de Berne accompagnât Bèze au Colloque. . . . La demande du Conseil de surseoir la conférence au 10 avril ne fut pas acceptée par le comte qui devait se rendre le 20 avril en France à la tête de la délégation des princes allemands et qui attendait Jacob Andreae le 13 mars à Montbéliard."

29. *Acta, Praefatio,* pp. a2v–a3r, and 1–9: *De occasione colloquii Mompelgartensis.*

30. AD ACTA / COLLOQUII / MONTISBELGARDENSIS / TUBINGAE EDITA, / Theodori Bezae / Responsionis, pars / prior. / Edito Secunda [hereafter *Responsio*]. Genevae, / *Excudebat Joannes le Preux.* / *M.D. LXXXVIII.* I also have the first edition, 1587, but crucial pages are missing in my copy. I have therefore used the 1588 edition. The two editions have identical texts but vary in page numbers because of the difference in the format. The French translation will be referred to as *Response*, while Beza's responses recorded in Andreae's *Acta* will be referred to as Resp.A., *Praefatio*, 3–6.

31. At least Andreae claimed that Clervant could not understand Latin. I assume he meant *spoken* Latin since Clervant's diplomatic missions, especially in Germany, would presuppose his ability to read and perhaps to write Latin.

32. See chap. 4.

33. *Acta,* 7: "tanto studio a Gallis expetatur."

34. Although Clervant may have come with the general idea of discussing peace between the churches, it is possible that Andreae made that general idea specific by suggesting the colloquy.

35. Beza, *Responsio,* 4.

36. Ibid.

37. Beza may have been referring to *Solida Refutatio com-* / *pilationis Cinglianae,* / *Quam Illi Con-* / *sensum Orthodoxum* / *Sacrae Scripturae et Veteris Eccle-* / *siae, de controversia sacramentaria, ap-* / *pellarunt, in lucem ediderunt, & aliquo-* / *ties recoxerunt. Conscripta per Theologos Wirtembergi-* / *cos: in gratiam eorum, quibus gloria Christi Servato-* / *ris, & sua aeterna salus cor* / *di est* (Tübingen: Georg Gruppenbach, 1584). In this work, Calvin is directly attacked and the Calvinists likened to Turks and followers of the "Alcoran" (p. 45).

38. *Responsio,* 5–6.

39. Archives Tronchin, vol. 5, fol. 204–5 [autograph]: "Quod collocutionem cum Iacobo Andreae concernit, nos quoque in ea sententia sumus, ut illam nullo modo recusandam esse censeamus. Non quod speremus hanc tantam controversiam hac ratione definiri posse, sed quod suspicamur nostros illos adversarios intelligere quanta non tantum nobis, sed et ipsis ab Antichristo eiusque affectis pericula undiquaque immineant, propter quae aliqua ipsis firmiore nobiscum coniunctione quam maximé sit opus: eamque ob causam illos in hoc esse ut licet tota illa controversia penitus tolli nequeat, ratio tamen ineatur, qua pax aliqua tollerabilis inter nos coëat, ut coniunctis viribus communem hostem fortis et foelicius oppugnemus."

40. See chap. 3, p.

41. For an account of the Marburg Colloquy, see Köhler, *Zwingli und Luther.*

42. For the text and informative notes on this effort and its repercussions in Zurich, see *Correspondance de Théodore de Bèze,* vol. 2, 1556–1558, ed. F. Aubert, H. Meylan, and A. Dufour (Geneva: Librairie E. Droz, 1962), 66–71, 75–103, 243–53. Another interesting letter occurs on pp. 110–12. It is dated September 24, 1557, and is from Andreae, then at the Colloquy at Worms, to Beza. The two theologians were still friends. Beza himself attended Worms and in early October joined William Farel, John Budé, and Caspar Carmel in a letter to German princes, including the duke of Württemberg, concerning the legation on behalf of the French Reformed to the French court.

43. Ibid., 243–48 for the entire confession. The quotation given above is on p. 244: "2. Credimus ac profitemur in Coena Domini non omnia modo Christi beneficia, sed etiam ipsam Christi substantiam, ipsam, inquam, veram carnem Filii hominis, quam Verbum aeternum in unitatem personae assumpsit, in qua natus et passus pro nobis resurrexit et ascendit in coelos, et verum illum sanguinem quem fudit pro nobis, non significari tantum aut symbolice, typice vel figurate duntaxat tanquam absentis memoriam proponi, sed vere et certo exhiberi et applicanda offerri, adjunctis ipsi rei symbolis minime nudis, sed quae quod ad Deum ipsum promittentem et offerentem attinet, rem ipsam semper vere ac certo conjunctam habeant, sive fidelibus, sive infidelibus proponantur." In spite of the use of *substance,* this paragraph carefully adheres to the *Variata* principle that Christ is offered to all. The word *dare* does not appear.

44. Beza, *Correspondance,* 2:244: "Fatemur ergo in Coena Domini non omnia modo Christi beneficia, sed etiam ipsam Filii hominis substantiam, ipsam, inquam, veram carnem (quam Verbum aeternum in perpetuam unitatem personae assumpsit, in qua natus et passus pro nobis resurrexit et ascendit in coelos) et verum illum sanguinem quem fudit pro nobis, non significari duntaxat aut symbolice, typice vel figurate, tanquam absentis memoriam proponi, sed vere ac certo repraesentari, exhiberi et applicanda offerri, adjunctis symbolis minime nudis, sed quae quod ad Deum ipsum attinet promittentem et offerentem, semper rem ipsam vere ac certo conjunctam habeant, sive fidelibus sive infidelibus proponantur."

45. Ibid., 245.

46. Julius Pflug, *Correspondance,* vol. 4, L'Épiscopat (II) Julliet 1553–Septembre 1564, ed. J. V. Pollet (Leiden: Brill), 1979, no. 719, for a letter of invitation to Pflug from the Catholic estates. See nos. 722 and 723 for Ferdinand's invitation to Pflug to moderate at the colloquy and Pflug's refusal for reasons of health. Ferdinand reiterated his invitation (nos. 728, 737). In a letter (to John Gropper?) dated July 2, 1557, Pflug wrote that he would have to go to Worms and that he would take Michael Helding with him (no. 739). See nos. 749 and 750 for Ferdinand's intructions to Pflug.

Cf. J. Broderick, S.J., *Saint Peter Canisius, S.J.: 1521–1597* (Baltimore: Carroll Press, 1950), 389, which gives the names of the official collocutors: Catholic: Michael Helding, John Delphius, Jodocus Ravesteyn, Martin Rithovius, Peter Canisius, and Frederick Staphylus; Protestant: Philip Melanchthon, John Brenz, John Pistorius, George Karg, James Runge, and Erhardt Schnepf. Broderick's chapter on "The Conference at Worms" purports to be the first treatment of this colloquy in English and also to be scholarly and ecumenical and does not appeal to older Catholic accounts "in which Protestants are too often furnished with hoofs and a tail" (385). Broderick does not quite succeed, but minus his evaluations, the account is reliable. To the official list of participants should be added those who seconded them and indeed added their signatures to official documents. Among these is Jacob Andreae: *CR* IX, 278.

47. Pflug, *Correspondance*. For an introduction to the Diet of Ratisbon (1556) and the Worms Colloquy (1557), see pp. 205–23. For Pflug's invitation to the Protestants to arrive early in order to discuss their differences, see Ferdinand's letter to Pflug (no. 751). That the Catholics were not of one mind was revealed by Pflug in a letter to George Gienger (no. 746). In the same letter, Pflug spoke of his reluctance to participate in the colloquy.

48. Broderick, *Saint Peter Canisius*, 397. Cf. Pflug, *Correspondance* 4:217–18.

49. *CR* IX, 266. After affirming the creeds of the early church, Melanchthon said: "Eamque doctrinam affirmamus comprehensam esse in confessione Ecclesiarum nostrarum, quae exhibita est imperatori Carolo V. in conventu Augustano anno 1530. Hanc confessionem fatemur omnes pio consensu amplecti. Et ab eo non discessimus nec discessuri sumus." See also *CR* IX, 276–277, for a statement signed by Brenz and Melanchthon concerning the question whether the body of Christ taken in the Holy Supper descends into the belly (an corpus Christi in coena sacra sumptum in ventrem descendat?). The answer is that the body of Christ neither descends to the belly nor is torn by the teeth. In the second statement (277–78) and signed by Melanchthon, Brenz, Andreae, Marbach, Pistorius, Diller, Eber, and Runge: "Nec fit conversio substantiae panis. Cum autem facta sumptione panis descendit in ventrem, et alteratur, estque iam cibus corporalis, desiit ratio sacramenti. . . . Nec Lutherus ponit conversionem substantiae panis, sed ponit synecdochen, videlicet, sumpto pane et vino vere sumi corpus et sanguinem Christi. Ad hanc synecdochen congruunt et Pauli verba, quae tantum de usu instituto loquuntur, panis est koinonia corporis, id est, quo nobis communicatur corpus Christi." It should be noted that nothing in this statement would bother Calvin or Beza.

50. Broderick, *Saint Peter Canisius*, 403 for a version of Canisius's address. Cf. Pflug, *Correspondance* 4:219–20.

51. *CR* IX, 213–15, which is an excerpt from the instructions given his theologians by the Duke of Saxony. In it, he specifically commands them to see that certain "heretics" are condemned by name: "so dem Colloquio verwandt, sich offentlich und einhelliglich zu der Ausgb. Confess., Apologia und schmalk. Artikeln bekennen und obligiren, daneben aber auch ausdrucklich und nahmhaftig verdammen alle Irrthume, neue und alte, so mit solchen oftgedachten Confession und Artikeln sich nicht mehr vergleichen, namlich," and there follows a specific list of those to be condemned. Cf. Broderick, *Saint Peter Canisius*, 408–9. Bishop Helding then repeated the question regarding specific groups (Zwinglians, Calvinists) and individuals (Flacius Illyricus, Osiander). Did the Lutherans consider these to be followers of the Augsburg Confession? (Broderick, *Saint Peter Cannisius*, 408, and Pflug, *Correspondance* 4:220–21.)

52. *CR* IX, 319–21. To the elector August, Melanchthon wrote an account of his and Brenz's defense against the condemnations and of the actions of the Jena delegation.

53. *CR* IX, 284–95. This long protest in German contains the specific condemnations and was signed by Schnepf, Morlin, Sarcer, Strigel, and Stossel on September 20, 1557. The formal declaration of their inability to participate further—directed to the president of the colloquy, Julius Pflug, in Latin—is dated October 1, 1557 and signed by Schnepf, Morlin, Strigel, and Stossel (314–17). See esp. 315: "Etsi igitur non solum mandata Illustrissimi Principis nostri, Ducis Saxoniae in promptu habebamus, quae diserte et severe praecipiebant, ne ad colloquii societatem nos adiungeremus, nisi omnibus sectis et corruptelis communi consensu damnatis, sed etiam aliis non levibus neque infirmis causis in eandem sententiam ducebamur."

54. Broderick, *Saint Peter Canisius*, 409–10.

55. Beza, *Correspondence,* vol. 2, nos. 112, 114, 115. Number 114 responds to the German theologians' request for a statement of their faith; no. 115 is a copy of their letter to the German princes named above and is the same as that in CR IX, 332–34. For Calvin's wish that the Swiss might have attended from the beginning and his unhappiness that Bullinger's intransigence prevented a Swiss presence at Worms, see Heinrich Heppe *Geschichte des deutschen Protestantismus in den Jahren 1555–1581,* vol. 1, *Die Geschichte des deutschen Protestantismus von 1551–1561 entstehend* (Warburg: R. G. Elwertscher Druck und Verlag, 1852), 157. Heppe gives Carmel's name as Johannes (247), while in Beza's letters Carmel signs himself Caspar, given as Gaspard by the editors of the *Correspondance* (p. 113, n. 8).

56. See Heppe, 1:246ff., for an account of the arrest of the French Protestants in Paris and the protest of the Swiss cities sent to Henry II and with the envoys to Worms as well.

57. Beza, *Correspondance* 2:116–17, contains notes that explain each of these categories. Number 120 (pp. 131–38) contains Beza's account to the Zurich pastors of the writing of this confession (Bullinger had forbidden Beza to sign any more confessions with Lutherans after the Göppingen affair of May 1557). Beza tells the Zurichers that Melanchthon required a brief statement since everyone knew that article X was a matter of dispute. Melanchthon's strategy, according to the editors of the *Correspondance* (n. 11), was to distance the Reformed delegates from the clearly heretical sects and to affirm that the Reformed and Lutherans were essentially of one mind.

58. CR IX, 332–34 (cf. Beza, *Correspondance,* vol. 2, no. 114): "nihil habere rationem sacramenti nisi in usu instituto. Et constantissime affirmamus, filium Dei missum esse, ut per eum colligatur Ecclesia, et adesse eum suo ministerio, et in Coena testificari, quod faciat nos sibi membra. Et verba Pauli sequimur, qui ait, *panis est koinonia corporis,* id est, est illa res, quam cum sumimus, filius Dei vere adest, et facit nos per fidem sibi membra." Cf. Beza, *Correspondance,* vol. 2, no. 120, for Beza's long letter to the Zurich pastors explaining this confession. Beza was still smarting from the rebukes of Bullinger and Martyr over the Göppingen confession of May 1557. The long, disapproving answer of the Zurich pastors is dated December 15, 1557 (no. 124, pp. 145–53).

59. CR IX, 335–36, Cf. n. 27.

60. Beza, *Correspondance,* vol. 2, no. 129, n. 6 (p. 164); no. 135 (pp. 179–82). Cf. Heppe, *Geschichte des deutschen Protestantismus* 1:245–65.

61. See Hans Petri, "Herzog Christoph von Württemberg und die Reformation in Frankreich," *Blätter für Württembergische Kirchengeschichte* 55 (1955): 5–64. For Henry II's acerbic response to the letter on behalf of the imprisoned French Protestants, drafted by Melanchthon and sent by Christoph, see p. 32.

62. Pflug, *Correspondance* 4:345–48, for Pollet's introduction concerning the Frankfurt Recess. Cf. Heppe, *Geschichte des deutschen Protestantismus,* 1:266–97, for a full account of the Frankfurt Recess. (Pagination in Heppe's second edition [1865] is the same.)

63. Hans-Werner Gensichen, *We Condemn: How Luther and 16th-Century Lutheranism Condemned False Doctrine,* trans. Herbert J. A. Bouman (St. Louis: Concordia, 1967), chap. 10: "Condemnation as Practiced by the Gnesio-Lutherans." This chapter gives a good history of the Philippist-Flacian dispute from 1556 to 1561. The full title of the Book of Refutation is given by Jean Janssen in *L'Allemagne et la Réforme,* vol. 4: *L'Allemagne depuis le Traité de Paix d'Augsbourg en 1555 jusqu' à la Proclamation du Formulaire de Concorde en 1580,* trans. E. Paris (Pans: Librairie Plon, 1895), 36: *Johann Friedrichs V, des Mittlern, Herzogen zu Sachsen, in Gottes Wort, prophetischer*

und apostolisher Schriftgegrundente Confutationes, Widerlegungen und Verdammgung etlicher ein Zeit her zuvider demselzen Gotteswort und heiliger Schrift, auch der Augsburgischen Confession, Apologien und der schmalkalkdischen Artikeln, aber zu Furderung und Wideranrichtung des Antichristlichen Papstthums eingeschlichenen und eingerissenen Coruptelen, Secten und Irrthumen. Jena, 1559.

64. See CR IX, 731 and 738 for Melanchthon's reactions.

65. Heppe, *Geschichte des deutschen Protestantismus,* 1:404ff.

66. But see the discussion of this very point by Donald Nugent in *Ecumenism in the Age of the Reformation: The Colloquy of Poissy* (Cambridge: Harvard University Press, 1974), 204ff. Frederick III of the Palatinate was convinced, however, that the cardinal of Lorraine had declared Calvinists as well as Zwinglians outside the Peace of Augsburg (*Briefe Friedrich des Frommen Kurfursten von der Pfalz* vol. 1, ed. August Kluckhohn (Braunschweig: C. A. Schwetschke and Son, 1886), no. 150, pp. 251–52. See also Felicitas Rottstock, *Studien zu den Nuntiaturberichten aus dem Reich in der Zweiten Halfte des sechzehnten Jahrhunderts: Nuntien und Legaten in ihrem Verhaltnis zu Kurie, Kaiser und Reichsfursten* (Munich: Minerva Publikation, 1980), 293 [this section deals with the 1566 Augsburg Reichstag and is cited here to indicate the continuation of the policy of maintaining Protestant divisions: "aber mit dem Ausscheren des Kurfursten von Sachsen in dieser Frage war bereits ein Weg beschritten, der die Gefahr von Religionsgesprachen wie auch den Zusammenhalt der Protestanten verminderte. Soweit konnten die papstlichen Gesandten mit August von Sachsen zufrieden sein." See also Hollweg, *Der Augsburger Reichstag von 1566,* 164–65.

67. For texts of letters and documents sent from Duke Christoph to Antoine, king of Navarre, as well as summaries and other texts relating to Poissy, see Sattler, *Geschichte des Herzogtums Wurtenberg,* pt. 4, pp. 172–203, esp. nos. 63, 64. See also Petri, "Herzog Christoph von Württemberg," 40–52. See Nugent, *Ecumenism in the Age of the Reformation,* 208–19 for a detailed discussion of the many confessions present at Poissy and which one the delegates were asked to sign. Nugent includes references to Beza's *Correspondance,* vol. 3.

68. Nugent, *Ecumenism in the Age of the Reformation,* The most famous incident at Poissy was Beza's declaration that the body of Christ is in heaven and as far from earth as is heaven. This speech alienated Catherine and the Catholics with whom Beza had seemed almost reconciled in meetings before the general gathering. Beza's speech shocked the Lutherans to whom it was reported, some of whom used it to convince others that the Reformed were "Zwinglians."

69. Janssen, *L'Allemagne et la Réforme,* 4: 225–26. Although I cannot endorse Janssen's theses, I found the primary material he cites abundant and deserving of consideration. The possibility of a theological liaison can be found in the cardinal of Lorraine's interest in the Augsburg Confession; see H. Outram Evennett, *The Cardinal of Lorraine and the Council of Trent: A Study in the Counter-Reformation* (Cambridge: Cambridge University Press, 1930), 276ff. See also Beza, *Correspondance,* vol. 3, for Beza's reports on Poissy; p. 168, n. 18, discusses which confession, Augsburg or Württemberg, Beza was asked to sign.

70. The best study of this diet is Hollweg, *Der Augsburger Reichstag von 1566.* See also Volker Press, *Calvinismus und Territorialstaat: Regierung und Zentralbehorden der Kurpfalz 1559–1619* (Stuttgart: Ernst Klett Verlag, 1970), esp. 237–38.

71. On the Formula of Concord , see n. 100.

72. Janssen, 4:90. Complicating this picture were the wars of religion in France and the fate of the Lowlands, a part of the Holy Roman Empire. Were the Reformed areas of the Lowlands included in the Peace of Augsburg? Such questions were on the

mind of the Reformed German elector, Frederick III of the Palatinate. See *Briefe Friedrich des Frommen,* esp. vol. 2.2., e.g. Frederick's concern over the St. Bartholomew's Day massacre (670–81), and his concern for the Lowlands (vol. 2.1, nos. 664, 665; vol. 2.2, no. 765).

73. Conyers Read, *Mr. Secretary Walsingham and the Policy of Queen Elizabeth,* 3 vols. (Oxford: Oxford University Press, 1925) vol. 1, p. 298. See also *Briefe Friedrich des Frommen,* vol. 1, p. 43, no. 19 (March 28, 1559) and 47, #22 (April 3, 1559). Both letters record the arrival in Heidelberg of Christopher Mundt, sent from Elizabeth of England to Germany to discuss a union of Protestant princes. The Kluckhohn collection of Frederick III's letters is remarkably rich in doctrinal matters.

74. For Elizabeth's efforts to form a Protestant League, see Patterson, "The Anglican Reaction," 150–65; Raitt, "Elector John Casimir," 117–45; and Gensichen, *We Condemn,* 163–67. See also Read, *Mr. Secretary Walsingham* 1:298–305. That Elizabeth earlier (1569–1570) contemplated such a league with some seriousness is documented by ibid., 82–83.

75. Ibid., 197.

76. Kluckhohn, *Briefe Friedrich des Frommen,* vol. 1, pp. 155–66, no. 113, is an account of the gathering of German princes at Naumburg. Kluckhohn adds, in the lengthy n. 3 (pp. 155–58), a discussion of article X of the Augsburg Confession, the changes it underwent, and a report of Frederick III that many of the German princes signed various versions of the Augsburg Confession. Cf. Heppe *Geschichte des deutschen Protestantismus* 1:364–439.

77. The text Mundt brought to Naumburg (Feburary 7, 1561) and the reply given him by the princes assembled there (February 8, 1561) are reproduced in Heppe, *Geschichte des deutschen Protestantismus* 2, *Beilage,* 132–37.

78. In fact, it was to Naumburg that papal nuncios came to invite the Protestant princes to send delegates to the last session of Trent. The princes rejected the invitation, partly because the pope had called them "well-beloved sons," a characterization they found inappropriate, and also because they considered that the emperor, not the pope, had the right to call the kind of council they had been asking for, one that was free and not controlled by the pope. Janssen, *L'Allemagne et la Réforme,* 4:146–150. Cf. Heppe, *Geschichte des deutschen Protestantismus* 1:395–99.

79. Evennett, *The Cardinal of Lorraine,* 353–54, esp. n. 5, and pp. 208, 217. See also the account in Heppe, *Geschichte des deutschen Protestantismus* 1:365–439. For a view of Naumburg through the eyes of Philip of Hesse and Henry Bullinger, see Beza, *Correspondance,* vol. 3, no. 173 (pp. 105, with n. 7).

80. Heppe, *Geschichte des deutschen Protestantismus* 1:390–91.

81. Heppe, *Geschichte des deutschen Protestantismus* 1:403. A copy of the *Augustana* was also sent to Antoine, king of Navarre and still a Protestant, in response to his appeal for help for the Huguenots.

82. Janssen, *L'Allemagne et la Réforme,* 4:203–4, citing A. Kluckhohn, *Briefe Friedrich des Frommen.*

83. Janssen, *L'Allemagne et la Réforme,* 4:45–46: These positions were first professor of theology, pastor of the church of the Holy Spirit, superintendent general and president of the ecclesiastical council.

84. For a discussion fo the nature of the Heidelberg Catechism and the major influences on it, see Derk Visser, "Zacharinus Ursinus and the Palatinate Reformation," in *Controversy and Conciliation: The Reformation and the Palatinate 1559–1583,* ed. Derk Visser (Allison Park, Pa.: Pickwick Publications, 1986), 1–20. Visser is well informed on Ursinus and the Palatinate reformation.

85. Kluckhohn, *Briefe Friedrich des Frommen,* vol. 1, pp. 504–5, no. 275, gives other bibliographical references to Maulbronn. See also Heppe, *Geschichte des deutschen Protestantismus* 2:71–96. Heppe gives a session-by-session account and concludes with the bitter publication of each side's version of the colloquy even though a complete protocol had been kept that should have obviated disagreement at least about what was actually said. See also the 145 pages of letters and documents that follow Heppe's text, including a letter from Beza to William of Hesse in which Beza complains of the protocol from Maulbronn: "Et quod ille de notarijs dicit, non potest non esse mihi vehementer suspectum, quum illus constet in Mulbrunensi collatione nihil veritum ipsius quoque prothocolli acta corrumpere" (Beilagen no. 24, p. 120).

86. Hollweg, *Der Augsburg Reichstag von 1566,* 144. Hollweg cites Christoph, who wrote to Frederick III: "ob sie den churfursten pfalzgraven expresse der Augspurgishen Confession anhengig hielter oder nit." "Item ob er des religionefridens vehig." Cf. Janssen, *L'Allemagne et la Réforme,* 4:222–23), who cites letters among the Lutheran princes and Frederick's responses with regard to Frederick's "Calvinism." The Lutheran princes would have liked to outlaw Frederick as a follower of a "sect" and therefore as outside the terms of the Peace of Augsburg. Frederick countered by insisting that the Protestants needed to unite against the Catholics.

87. The Swiss Protestant states were worried about this diet, and to counter its possible religious repercussions, Bullinger's confession was circulated and sent to Heidelberg. It was accepted and became known as the Second Helvetic Confession, one of the foundational documents in the Reformed tradition. See *Registres de la Compagnie des Pasteurs de Geneve,* vol. 3, 1565–1574, Annex 23–27, pp. 194–205. Cf. *Correspondance de Théodore de Bèze,* vol. 7 (1566), ed. H. Meylan et al. (Geneva: Librairie Droz, 1973). Many of the letters are appropriate, but see esp. no. 508, pp. 253–55, with notes. See also no. 520, in which Beza sends Bullinger a letter from John Knox approving the Second Helvetic Confession. For Frederick III's viewpoint, see Kluckhohn, *Briefe Friedrich des Frommen,* vol. 1, entries for 1566.

88. Hollweg, *Der Augsburger Reichstag von 1566,* 145. For a shorter account of the history of the 1566 Reichstag, see Brecht and Ehmer, *SR,* 372–78.

89. Hollweg, *Der Augsburger Reichstag von 1566,* 139.

90. Ibid.

91. Ibid., 141–44.

92. For the Catholic interpretation of the 1566 Augsburg Reichstag and its relation, on one hand, to the *Religionsfriede* and the Council of Trent and, on the other, to the emperor's concern to keep the German princes united so that he could face the Turks, see Rottstock, *Studien zu den Nuntiaturberichten,* 94–171, esp. 109ff., 141ff. See also ibid., 295, and the attitude of August of Saxony, who "erkannte die Gefahr, die einer Verurteilung des Calvinismus für die Augsburger Konfession heraufbeschworen wurde."

93. As late as December 6, 1591, voices were still raised against the Calvinists as excluded from the Peace of Augsburg: "Die Calvinisten werden nicht im Religionsfriden begriffen, gebürt ihnen frembde Arrianishe Phrases in ihren *Thesibus* zu gebrauchen." Hauptstaatsarchiv Stuttgart, A 63, Bü. 67: "Die Ritterschaft dieses Chur-Craiss Abschid zu Württemberg [*sic*] den 6. December anno 1591."

94. Ibid. This manuscript is dated December 6, 1591, and indicates that the campaign to exclude Calvinists from the Peace of Augsburg continued to the end of the sixteenth century. "Die Calvinisten werden nicht im Religionsfriden begriffen, gebürt ihnen frembde Arrianische Phrases in Ihren Thesibus zu gebrauchen: Christus est Creatura item Baptismus non salvos facit melius est mori sine Baptismo quam docere Baptismum salvos facere."

95. Heppe, *Geschichte des deutschen Protestantismus,* vol. 2, 23, pp. 118–19: "1) Es solte den Theologis Concordia Buceri mit dem Luthero und den Wirtenbergern getrossen sambt denen darbei hehorigen *Declarationibus* eiusdem Buceri vorgehalten und von ihnen vernommen werden, wass ein oder das ander Theill darin approbirt, und was dsie improbirten, und aus wass ursachen, 2) Wass ferner eyn Theill dem andern vor Errorum quantum ad illam materiam bezichtige."

96. Beza's letter is cited in n. 87.

97. Beza, *Correspondance,* Vol. 7, no. 282.

98. Ibid. The entire text is reproduced (pp. 60–92) with the excellent notes characteristic of the volumes of Beza's *Correspondance* published by Librairie Droz.

99. For studies of the Book of Concord, see *Bekenntnis und Einheit der Kirche: Studien zum Konkordienbuch,* ed. Martin Brecht and Reinhard Schwartz (Stuttgart: Calwer Verlag, 1980). See also Jobst Ebel, "Jacob Andreae (1528–1590) als Verfasser der Konkordienformel," *Zeitschrift fur Kirchengeschichte* 89 (1978): 78–119, and Lewis W. Spitz, "The Formula of Concord Then and Now," in *Discord, Dialogue, and Concord,* for background and bibliographical notes. For a taste of a polemical "history" of the Book of Concord, see *Concordia Concors. / De / Origine et Progressu For- / mulae Concordiae Ecclesiarum / Confessionis Augustane, / Liber Unus: / In Quo Eius or- / thodoxia, Scripturae Sacrae, Oecumenicis Symbolis, Toti Antiquitati / Puriori, et primae illi, minimeque variatae confes- / ioni Augustanae, ex asse consona: Modus item agendi, in eo conscribendo, sufragiis mu- / niendo, & tandem promulgando ovservatus, legitimus, & in Ecclesia Christi hactenus / usitatus fuisse, Christiano lectori evidenter & perspicue demonstratur: & Rodolphi Hospiniani Tigurini Helvetii convitia, mendacia, & ma- / nifesta crimina falsi deteguntur ac solide / refutantur.* The work was issued with the authority of the Saxon elector and the approval of the theologians of Leipzig, Wittenberg, and Württemberg. It was edited by Leonhard Hutter (Wittenberg: Clement Berger, 1614).

100. *Triglot Concordia.* For the rejection of the Variata, see p. 777, no. 3; p. 847, no. 5; p. 851, no. 3. For condemnations of Calvinists as well as Zwinglians, see p. 817. On p. 973 (Sol. Decl. VII, 2–3), Beza's words at Poissy are quoted as an example of erroneous doctrine. Zwinglians, sacramentarians, anabaptists, and others are named throughout the formula, and Calvinists are clearly included under the first two categories in such sections as the *Sol. Decl.* VII as noted earlier. The Visitation Articles of 1592 are included in *Triglot Concordia* (pp. 1154–57); they list the "false and Erroneous Doctrine of the Calvinists" and include a number of points under each of the following headings: the Holy Supper, the Person of Christ, Holy Baptism, Predestination, and the Providence of God. The Visitation Articles are not included in *The Book of Concord: The Confessions of the Evangelical Lutheran Church,* ed. and trans. Theodore G. Tappert (Philadelphia: Muhlenberg Press, 1959).

101. For a list of the princes and city councils who signed the preface of the Book of Concord in 1580, see Tappert, *The Book of Concord,* 14–16. Among them are Duke Ludwig and Count Frederick of Württemberg-Montbéliard.

102. Trygyve R. Skarsten, "The Reaction in Scandinavia," in *Discord, Dialogue, and Concord,* ed. Lewis W. Spitz and Wenzel Lohff (Philadelphia: Fortress Press, 1977), 140–41. These laws of Frederick II of Denmark may be the harshest reaction of any Lutheran ruler.

103. Henri IV, *Recueil des lettres missives* 2:437–43. On February 15, 1589, Henry finally gave an answer to the German Protestant princes who had sent him the Book of Concord in March 1585. The princes were the duke of Saxony, the marquis of Brandenburg, the duke of Bavaria, the duke of Brunswick, the duke of Mecklenburg,

and the duke of Württemberg. Henry said that the wars had kept him too busy to give the Book of Concord the attention it deserved. In his response in 1591, Henry affirmed his approval of the Augsburg Confession (p. 440), but he found the arguments in the Book of Concord too subtle and too acerbic to accord with charity and the ways of the ancient church (p. 441). Henry also objected to certain theologians in Germany who, in a manner hardly Christian, attacked the afflicted Reformed churches (p. 442). Henry repeated his appeal to a Christian council, free from the bitte4r of such ambitious theologians and under the authority of Christian princes (p. 442).

104. See Heinrich Bornkamm, "Das Problem der Toleranz im 16. Jahrhundert," in *Das Jahrhundert der Reformation: Gestalten und Krafte* (Göttingen: Vandenhoeck and Ruprecht, 1966), 262–91.

105. See pp. 00–00.

106. Jean-François Salvard (with the help of others, including Beza), Harmonia confessionum fidei . . . (Geneva: Petrus Santandreas, 1581). See Frédéric Gardy, *Bibliographie des oevres théologiques, littéraires, historiques et juridiques de Théodore de Bèze* (Geneva: Librairie Droz, 1960), 184–85. The claim that Calvinists are the least tolerant of the Protestants is largely based on the case of Servetus in Geneva. The circumstances are sometimes misrepresented. Rarely is it pointed out that Geneva put fewer "heretics" to death than many other Protestant territories.

107. On the other hand, the Augsburg Confession continued to be used ambiguously. The German Protestants who sent troops with Casimir into France justified their actions religiously by appealing to the Augsburg Confession. The German Protestants who sent troops into France to fight with the armies of the Guise and ostensibly on the side of Henry III claimed their loyalty to the Augsburg Confession and denied that the "*abominable secte de Calvin*" followed the Augsburg Confession. This group also claimed that they wished to protect God's chosen king (Henry III) against the lawlessness of those who wished to overthrow him; M. L. Cimber and F. Danjou, eds., *Archieves curieuses de l'histoire de France depuis Louis XI jusqu'à Louis XVIII*, series 1, vol. 2 (Paris: Imprimerie de Bourgogne et Martinet, 1836), 108. This is part of a 1586 "Responce faicte par les Seigneurs Allemans estans au service du Roy" (pp. 106–10). Those who *manu proprio*, signed the *Responce* are Philibert, marquis de Bade; Jean Philippes Reingraff, Friderich Reingraff; Georges, compte de Leiningen, seigneur de Wluesterbourg et Chambourg, tousjours franc; Christofle, baron de Bassompierre; seigneur de Harroue; Albert , comte de Dietz.

108. Duvernoy, *Éphémerides*, 468–69.

109. See Natalie Zemon Davis, "The Rites of Violence," in *Society and Culture in Early Modern France* (Stanford: Stanford University Press, 1975), 152–87.

3

The Lord's Supper

The controversy over the Lord's Supper was central to the Colloquy of Montbéliard; in fact, it was the only topic that the Swiss delegation had expected to discuss, according to Beza's report. This position is borne out by Clervant's remarks to Andreae that the French church thought that the Lord's Supper was the only problem between Lutherans and Reformed.[1]

The setting of the colloquy is described by Andreae in his *Acta*. The hall was filled with "a great number of French exiles" and was presided over by Count Frederick. Two tables had been set a little apart from each other. At the first table sat Frederick and Hector Vogelmann, the ecclesiastical superintendent of Montbéliard, with the Württemberg team: theologians Jacob Andreae and Lucas Osiander and the political representatives Johann Wolfgang von Anweil and Frederick Schütz. The Swiss collocutors sat at the second table: theologians Theodore Beza and Anthony de La Faye from Geneva, Abraham Musculus and Pierre Hubner from Bern, and Claude Albery from Lausanne, and political representatives Antoine Maris from Geneva and Samuel Mayer from Bern. No remark was made by either party about the place of Count Frederick among the German theologians. Admitted as hearers were the Montbéliard ministers of the French church, Richard Dinot and Samuel Cucuel, along with those French refugees who could follow the Latin discourses.[2]

In his welcoming address, the ecclesiastical superintendent of Montbéliard, Hector Vogelmann, set the tone of the colloquy. He explained that the French nobles, refugees from the French wars of religion, had often asked for such a meeting concerning some articles of religion and the use of the French language in the liturgy. Out of compassion, Prince Frederick had forwarded their petition to Duke Ludwig of Württemberg, who responded by sending his theologians and several politicians to participate in the colloquy.[3] As he closed his address, Vogelmann invited Beza to say whatever he had most on his mind.

As Andreae reported it, Beza admitted that the colloquy had been called for the sake of the French exiles living in Montbéliard. Beza then requested that everything be taken down in writing to assure careful speech and fair play. He agreed to the format suggested by Andreae, that is, that written theses should serve as the basis of discussion. Beza also agreed that the theses should be confirmed only from the Word of God, after which the dogma under dispute would be set forth.[4] Finally, Beza asked that the debate remain on one point until they agreed or it became clear that they could not agree.

After thanking God and the prince profusely, Andreae responded. He reiterated that the sole norm was to be the Word of God. He objected to Beza's request that everything be written down. Andreae argued that doing so would delay proceedings and inhibit free discussion. He assured Beza that he need not fear foul play since each side was committed to seeking only the truth. Andreae than moved to the presentation of the Württemberg theses. The Swiss would be given time to respond in writing and then to draw up their own theses. When that had been done, the conversation concerning the theses could begin.[5]

The opening remarks require comment. Particularly important to this study, and indeed a problem of this period from the point of view of the history of theology, is the declared principle of *sola scriptura*. Both collocutors claimed that the Word of God was to be the sole norm. Throughout this colloquy, the interpretation of that norm must be kept in mind. By 1586, the major confessions had been ratified. In 1566, the Second Helvetic Confession had been adopted by the Swiss and also by the French at La Rochelle in 1571 as in harmony with their own French Confession of 1559. In 1580, the Lutheran Book of Concord was published. Each church considered its confessions to be drawn from Scripture and the correct interpretation of the Word of God. Both groups of theologians accepted the first five ecumenical councils as true to God's Word and appealed to these councils and to the church fathers in confirmation of an increasingly important claim: confessional orthodoxy. Although no Protestant would admit that any of these secondary "norms" had the unique authority of Scripture itself, in fact, the confessional positions of the churches were firmly entrenched.

The argument concerning a record of the colloquy also proved central in the polemic that followed the colloquy and ended only with Andreae's death in 1592. Beza lost the argument and never ceased to call foul thereafter since there was no notarized protocol. Andreae countered that even a signed protocol could not prevent calling the report in question, as the aftermath of the Colloquy of Maulbronn proved.[6] Another area of dispute was the introduction of points other than those appropriate to the discussion. Both Andreae and Beza protested, from time to time, that the other did not remain on the topic, confusing the issue before either agreement or the impossibility of agreement had been reached. The only materials presented in the *Acta* as they were at the colloquy are the theses that were written out and preserved independently as well as being incorporated into the *Acta*.

The Württemberg Theses

The pattern established in the first set of theses were followed throughout. The first group of Württemberg theses presented points on which the Lutherans judged there was no controversy. The second set were considered controversial theses. In the third set, the Lutherans gave their summary of Reformed points that they deemed contrary to Scripture.

The "noncontroversial theses" began with the declaration that all the faithful, even outside the liturgy, eat the flesh of the Son of Man spiritually, by faith, for salvation, as John 6 makes clear. But the eating of the sacrament of the Lord's Supper is another kind of eating and is not always salutary since when it is taken perniciously it is judgment. Andreae concluded that although the two eatings are not the same, spiritual eating is necessary if sacramental eating is to be salutary. Both sides agree, stated thesis II, that Capernaitic[7] eating of the flesh of Christ is a damnable doctrine. In thesis III, both likewise condemn the Roman Catholic doctrine of transubstantiation. Thesis IV declared that the Lutherans, as well as the Reformed, deny that the presence of the body and blood of Christ is physical or local or inclusive. The six Lutheran theses unacceptable to the Reformed may be summarized as follows:[8]

V. The true body and blood of Jesus Christ are truly and substantially present and distributed with the bread and wine and taken orally by all who use the Sacrament, whether worthy or unworthy, good or bad, faithful or infidel, the former to life and the latter to judgment.

VI. The words *in, with,* and *under the bread* indicate the presence of the true body. The same thing is indicated by the terms *substantially, corporally, really, essentially,* and *orally.*

VII. The words of institution declare the presence of Christ's real[9] body and blood.

VIII. Christ is no liar.[10]

IX. Christ is God-man in one inseparable person to whom nothing is impossible. All power in heaven and earth is given him. What he wished to do, he could do: *Quod vellit, possit, ergo fecit.*[11] He wished to give himself to be eaten; therefore he did so.

X. The mode of Christ's presence is not expressed in Scripture. But this much can be said: It is supernatural and incomprehensible to human reason and therefore it is not to be disputed. God can find many ways to make the body and blood of Christ everywhere available other than the natural and physical mode, which is the only mode understood by human reason. Christ's words are simply to be believed.

The Württemberg theologians judged the following propositions to be contrary to Scripture:

1. That the words of Christ are not to be taken simply (*òti to reto*) as they sound but must be interpreted in the light of other passages.

2. That the mouth receives only bread and wine, while Christ is eaten by faith. That by faith believers ascend to heaven and there are made partakers of his body and blood since Christ's body is in heaven and will remain there until the last day.

3. That God is not able, by his omnipotence, to make the body of Christ present in more than one place at one time.

4. That Christ is not more present to participants in the eucharist than he was to Abraham of old.
5. That in the Supper the virtue, operation, and merit of the absent body and blood of Christ are dispensed.
6. That among those eating unworthily (and therefore taking judgment to themselves) are numbered those also who are weak or stupid in faith or suffer other weaknesses but who nevertheless have true faith.
7. That oral manducation leads to stercoranism.[12]

When the Swiss received these written points, they went off to draw up their own theses and to draft replies to the Lutherans. The next morning was therefore given up to study, and the meeting began again after the midday meal.

When the colloquy resumed, Beza stressed that those participating were not doing so as official representatives of their churches but as private persons. He then submitted the Reformed theses and replies. Beza's theses do not follow the pattern of Andreae's theses but rather the pattern established in Beza's *Confessio fidei* and at Poissy, and that he would repeat in his 1593 *De controversiis:*[13] (1) the signs, (2) the signified, (3) the conjunction of the signs and the signified, (4) the reception of the signified, (5) the effects of communion, and (6) the causes of the salutary effects. In Andreae's *Acta,* Beza's theses and responses are not simply presented but are accompanied by refutations in the form of marginal notes. For the sake of clarity, however, I shall first present Beza's written theses, antitheses, and responses to the statements considered contrary to Scripture by his opponents. I shall then summarize Andreae's part of the discussion, which followed the presentation of the written material. Beza's *Responsio* provides the source for his side of the argument as he answered Andreae's marginalia. Finally, I shall briefly describe Andreae's *Epitome* (1588) and Beza's reaction to it.

The Swiss Theses

The Signs

Beza began by distinguishing two uses of the word *sacrament.* The narrower meaning refers to those things that the senses perceive, that is, that bread and that wine. By the Lord's institution and commandment, they are removed from their common and natural use and given a spiritual and sacred signification. This signification is not bare and empty, nor is it a mere remembering, but it really attains to God; what is signified, namely Christ's body and blood, is offered to souls. Beza then asserted that he and Andreae agree on the foundation of this thesis, the words of institution, with one exception. For the Reformed, what is offered is received by faith, not by the mouth. Oral manducation had been the major point of contention from the beginning of the Protestant disagreements about the Lord's Supper.

The Signified

Thesis II says only a little more than the first, listing those things signified. Besides the signification of the body and blood by the bread and wine, the Passion of Christ is signified by the breaking of the bread and the pouring out of the wine. Through Christ's institution of the sacrament the significations have the power of presenting the signified realities to the mind. The foundation of thesis II is Christ's command to do what he did, so that the rites as well as the elements are part of the institution of the Lord's Supper and must be observed lest the signification be vain and empty.

The Conjunction of the Signs and the Signified

With regard to this point, Beza repeated his application of the narrower meaning of the word *sacrament* and introduced the Aristotelian category of "relation," or *habit:* "Since sacraments by their narrower signification (as it is said) are signs, we put the sacramental conjunction in the mutual relation and habit of the signs and the things signified by which, as these things impinge upon the senses, from Christ's ordination, they are taken from their common and natural use and applied to signifying and offering to us sacred and divine realities."[14] This is the heart of Beza's doctrine as he developed it out of Calvin's theology of the Lord's Supper and answered the difficult question of how Christ is present sacramentally.[15] The foundation of this thesis, Beza argued, is the truth of Christ's body. Since that body is a human body and is therefore circumscribed and localized, it requires a sacramental presence by relation or habit rather than by substance. Beza employed the Aristotelian *predicamenta,* or "categories," to explain his sacramental theology but not to provide its foundation, which remained the witness concerning Christ's human nature given in Scripture and expressed in the creeds of the apostolic church.

Beza held that the more one insists on the truth of the body of Christ, the more one must give up the notion of consubstantiation. The rest of Beza's argument on this point dealt with the localization of Christ's body in heaven according to the account of the Ascension and the promised return of Christ on the last day.

The Reception of the Signified

Beza explained the reception of the signs and the signified through the analogy of eating ordinary food. The purpose of ordinary eating is to nourish the body; the purpose of sacramental eating is to nourish the soul. Therefore just as the mouth of the body eats physical food, so the mouth of the soul eats spiritual food. The mode of receiving the body of Christ is therefore spiritual. This is the basis of what Beza called sacramental metonymy, whereby earthly elements signify heavenly realities that are offered to the soul and are truly received through the instrument of faith by the power of the Holy Spirit. The arguments Beza adduced to substantiate this position will be discussed in the context of his responses to Andreae's marginalia.

The Effects of Communion

Beza said that the Lord's Supper was not instituted for the sake of the bread and wine but for the salvation of human beings. The mystery therefore lies in the union of Christ and the faithful, not in the supposed union of the body of Christ with the bread. Through the sacrament, which requires and confirms penitence and faith, a spiritual conjunction with Christ is deepened and strengthened through which Christ gives all his gifts and benefits to the faithful. The Holy Spirit, the bond of charity, effects this mystical union so that Christ is head of the members of this body united to him and is the source of their increasing unity and spiritual growth into eternal life.

The second effect is the condemnation of the unworthy, that is, those who through ignorance of this mystery or through incredulity and impenitence, eat condemnation, not from the Supper itself but from its unworthy use. It is at this point that the consistency of the Reformed doctrine results in a disturbing corollary. Since faith comes by hearing God's word and the action of the Holy Spirit on the mind, a degree of mental development seems to be necessary. Those, therefore, who have not reached the age of reason or who are deprived of the use of reason are not qualified to use the sacrament of the Lord's Supper.[16] The Lutherans objected to this corollary in the sixth of the propositions given above as "contrary to Scripture." The Lutherans had grasped only one part of the Reformed doctrine, which is offset by the Reformed principle that God's action is not dependent on human activity, including preaching and the sacraments, or the lack thereof.[17] These activities are done because Christ commanded that they be done and so to despise them is to despise Christ. Nevertheless, God's grace is not dependent on these actions.

The Causes of the Salutary Effects

The causes of the salutary effects are, first, the Holy Spirit, who with ineffable power effects the union of the faithful with Christ, a union called by St. Paul "a great mystery." The Holy Spirit, who is the Spirit of Christ, does this through the life, suffering, death, resurrection, and ascension of Christ in whom the faithful believe. The instrumental causes are the minister doing as Christ commanded, the words of institution, the signs themselves, and the sacramental rites. Faith, given by God, is the principal instrumental cause. None of these instruments, however, has any intrinsic efficient power apart from the working of the Holy Spirit and the command of Christ. Beza said that these last two theses concerning the effects of the Lord's Supper do not require proof. The theses were signed by Theodore Beza, Abraham Musculus, Anthony Faius, Peter Hubner, and Claude Albery on March 22, 1586.[18]

On the same day, Beza presented his antitheses and responses to the propositions labeled "contrary to Scripture." The first antithesis made clear that the fundamental difference between the Lutherans and the Reformed remained the same as it had been at Marburg in 1529, namely the interpretation of the words of institution. The Lutherans insisted that the words were to be taken literally (*kata to reto*), while the Reformed taught that they involve a trope, or figure of speech, which requires clarification from other scriptural passages, notably John 6. The final arbiter in the interpretation of all Scripture, as Beza frequently reiterated, is the analogy ("afterword" to the word of God) of faith contained in the Apostles' Creed.

But to admit a privileged instrument of interpretation is to allow for gradations of valid instruments and disagreement about the authority of various of the church fathers such as Augustine, Tertullian, Cyril, and John Damascene. Andreae and Beza exemplified this problem as they discussed the early church fathers' use of the terms *substantially, corporally, essentially,* and *in, with, and under* the bread and wine. Both agreed that the fathers used them, but they disagreed as to what the terms meant. Andreae took the fathers to affirm the Lutheran interpretation of the words of institution, while Beza argued that the fathers meant that Christ is truly offered to the faith of the communicants, not to their mouths. The terms *orally* and *sensually* are not patristic, and Beza simply rejected them. *Sensually* was denied also by Andreae, but Beza pointed out to him Luther's endorsement of the *Ego Berengarius* formula, which includes this term as descriptive of the way the priest handles and eats the true body of Christ.[19]

A principle on which the Reformed stood firm against the Lutherans was that Christ offers himself through hearing the Word and receiving the sacraments. In both, the effective agency is the Holy Spirit working through faith to unite the believer to the full reality of Christ. This is the union, said Beza, to which Paul referred in Ephesians 5, and it is indeed a great mystery. Since the salutary communication of both word and sacrament depends on the Holy Spirit and faith, there is likewise no essential difference in the content of the sacraments of the Old and New Testaments although the external signs differ. The New Testament offers "greater" sacraments only in that they are more specific and their substance, Christ, has appeared. The main difference between word and sacrament in both dispensations lies in the impact of the sacraments on all five senses rather than on hearing alone as when one listens to preaching. Whether one speaks of word and sacrament or of the Old and New Testaments, the difference is a matter of clarity and strength of appeal, not of the substance of what the faithful receive, namely the whole Christ who is inseparable from all his benefits. In all cases, the result for those without faith and for the impious is the same, condemnation, not because they have orally eaten the body of Christ but because they have misused both word and sacrament.

Beza then drew out the analogy of the Lord's Supper to an ordinary meal. Just as one physically eats and drinks to sustain physical life, so one spiritually eats and drinks spiritual food to sustain spiritual life. The error of the Lutherans, argued Beza, is that they confuse these two kinds of eating and demand reception of the essential body of Christ in the mouth with the substance of the bread.

In order to sustain this position, Beza continued, the Württemberg theologians also maintained that the body of Christ is ubiquitous, which involves them in christological heresies. Beza charged that the Württembergers destroyed the humanity of Christ by insisting on the communication of properties between the natures of Christ so that his humanity is endowed with the properties of his divinity. Contrary to true humanity, the human nature of Christ then becomes omnipotent and omnipresent. On the contrary, argued Beza, according to the doctrine of the Ascension, Christ is now in heaven and there his body remains circumscribed and limited to one place as are all true bodies. From thence he will return on the last day. Beza insisted that this doctrine does not deny that Christ, as Logos, enjoys all the divine properties or that this man who is God may not also be said to be omnipresent and ubiquitous. But it is to assert that the human nature of Christ is bound by the limitations common to all bodily creatures. To say otherwise, said Beza, is to teach that God can share divine properties with creatures. But omnipotence is proper to God alone and cannot be given wholly or partially to a creature, even to the created humanity of Christ. The argument given here in brief form was elaborated in Beza's *Responsio,* in which he answered Andreae's charge that the Reformed blasphemously deny God's omnipotence.

In Beza's answer to Andreae's tenth point, he mentioned the covenant: "The mode by which the signified thing [*res*] is joined to the signs by divine ordination explains the naming of the signs, and shows it to be relative depending on God's pact. Such a relation has a place even in human and ordinary contracts. But the mode of reception of the signified thing . . . is truly, as we confess with the Apostle, a great mystery, and therefore to be believed and adored, not minutely examined."[20] Beza then argued that if Christ's body and blood are essentially present with the bread and wine but differ from the latter merely by being invisible, then there is no longer a presence in mystery but a purely natural presence. Behind these arguments lay an understanding of essence as another term for nature. Beza therefore introduced the category of relation, which allows for things essentially unlike (bread/body) to be brought together in a relationship that may be either natural, as the relation of Peter to the rock on which he sits, or supernatural, as the relation of Peter to Christ to whom he is united through faith. Through the category of relation the nature of a sign and the nature of that which is signified are maintained.

In his fourth response to the statements considered by the Württembergers to be contrary to Scripture, Beza wrote: "We confess that Christ, God and man, who could not otherwise be a Mediator, was not man in act before the real incarnation. Nevertheless we teach that he was present to the faith of Abraham, (which is called the substance of things which are not) not by an illusory opinion, but truly and efficaciously, just as he was present to the other holy patriarchs."[21] Beza concluded this argument by a reference to Augustine: "The sacraments of the old times were equal to ours *in re,* but different in their signs."[22]

The next response was trenchant and typical of the Reformed doctrine. Beza claimed that Christ and his benefits are so inseparable that through faith, the mind receives both not only in the Lord's Supper but in the word and in baptism as well.

Beza simply denied the charge that he rejected or considered unworthy those of imperfect faith. Perfect faith is not possible as long as one is in this fleshly life. In fact, the Lord's Supper strengthens faith. But this response did not adequately answer the charge Andreae had made. "Imperfect faith" may be variously interpreted. Andreae had asked not about the perfection of faith but about the mental ability of communicants. The problem was both theological and pastoral. Was communion to be given to a person lacking sufficient intelligence to understand what is offered in the Lord's Supper? One of the functions of the minister's examination of communicants on the eve of the celebration of the Lord's Supper was to determine whether or not the individual was in an appropriate state of mind and conscience to come to the Lord's table.

Finally, to Andreae's indignant denial that oral manducation involves stercoranism, Beza responded that while the defenders of transubstantiation and consubstantiation do not intend anything so blasphemous, it is difficult to see how they can avoid it if they insist on oral manducation. If Christ is literally eaten by the mouth and crushed by the teeth, does he then just melt away?

These responses are signed by the five Swiss delegates.[23]

Andreae's Eucharistic Theology

In this section, I shall summarize Andreae's eucharistic theology as it appears in the discussion following the presentation of written theses by both sides. Because the discussion moves erratically from point to point and would be tedious to follow in the order in which it actually took place, I have gathered Andreae's principal arguments under five headings: (1) the words of institution, (2) Christ in the Old and New Testaments, (3) Christology as it appears in this section, (4) sacramental principles, and (5) use of philosophical terms. An alternate organization might have been according to the theses, as in Beza's case, but since Andreae's theses overlap, this does not seem useful. Beza's five points, on the other hand, imply the theology they explicate.

At the beginning of the discussion, Andreae summed up the controversy under two principal points: the true and real presence of the body and blood of Jesus Christ in the Holy Supper of the Lord, and the true and sacramental reception of that body and blood by eating and drinking the sacrament. In Andreae's *Acta,* the 137 pages that report the discussion between Andreae and Beza are devoted to proving Andreae's position. Of those 137 pages, Beza was given only a quarter of the space, and often his remarks were reduced to one or two lines.

The Words of Institution

The starting point was simple: the literal acceptance of the words of institution, "This is my body, take and eat." Andreae argued that the Lutherans were following the apostles, who, when Christ was forsaken by those who could not accept what he said, turned to him asking, "To whom shall we go? You have the words of life." Andreae quoted Calvin, who also affirmed that the Lord's Supper is a mystery to be experienced rather than understood. Further, Andreae asserted, since the words are to be taken literally, John 6 may not be used to support a symbolic interpretation. Although in John 6, *eat* (*manducate*) does mean *believe* (*credete*), it refers to spiritual manducation by faith, not sacramental eating. Spiritual eating occurs whenever one believes that Christ's body was given up for us and his blood poured out for our sins. It is always salutary and must, of course, accompany sacramental manducation lest one eat condemnation. But the two modes of eating are different and must not be confused. In fact, Andreae claimed that Calvin, in his commentary on John 6, says that the eating of the Lord's Supper and the eating in John 6 are not the same. Andreae was referring to Calvin's comment on John 6:53: "This sermon does not refer to the Lord's Supper, but to the continual communication which we have apart from the reception of the Lord's Supper." Andreae did not extend his use of Calvin to include Calvin's comment on John 6:54: "So it is certain that He is now treating of the perpetual eating of faith. At the same time, I confess that there is nothing said here that is not figured and actually presented to believers in the Lord's Supper. Indeed we might say that Christ intended the holy Supper to be a seal of this discourse. This is also the reason why John makes no mention of the Lord's Supper."[24]

Christ in the Old and New Testaments

The Lutherans reacted sharply to the Reformed contention that the patriarchs of the Old Testament also ate Christ, who was as present to them in their sacraments as to Christians in theirs. Andreae argued that there is no sacramental manducation of the body and blood of Christ in the Old Testament because it contains only figures of realities to come. Indeed, the blood of calves is a figure of the true blood of Christ but its reality is simply calves' blood. Nevertheless, because of their faith, the patriarchs enjoyed the benefits of Christ: grace, forgiveness of sins on account of Christ who will be immolated, and the hope of eternal life. Andreae explained that the Old Testament and New Testament sacraments are the same in their principal efficient cause and their final cause, but they differ in matter and form.[25] That is, Andreae allowed that both gain their effectiveness from the primary agent, God, and both are means of grace, but their content and the manner in which their effects are realized differ. There is, therefore, as great a difference, argued Andreae, between the Old and New Testaments as there is between the figure and the reality which the figure signifies. Finally, what could be more absurd than to say that the patriarchs had the reality of Christ when Christ had not yet been born?[26]

To Beza's challenge that the patriarchs could as easily possess Christ who had not yet been born as the benefits of the actions of that same unborn Christ, Andreae responded that with regard to his benefits, Christ is "the same yesterday, today and forever," and "the lamb that is slain from the beginning of the world." Andreae explained that the benefits of Christ have, as their foundation, the Christ who is to come. Since Christ is foreshadowed in the Old Testament, the Logos conferred benefits on the patriarchs not on account of the shadow (the sacraments of the Old Testament) but on account of him who was represented by the shadow. Forgiving sins, after all, is the work of God, not a human being. So just as a Christian can participate in Christ's merits by faith without Christ being present, so could the patriarchs.

Christological Arguments

The problem of the Lord's Supper cannot be separated from the fundamental theological doctrine of the person of Christ and so, although the portion of the *Acta* dealing with the latter question is longer than the section on the Lord's Supper, it is instructive to see what aspects of Christology were so intrinsic to the eucharistic debate that they could not be postponed but were included in this section. These questions may be taken under two closely related headings—the two-natures, or *communicatio idiomatum,* debate, and the Resurrection/Ascension.

With regard to Christ's bodily nature, Andreae said that Christ's body is like other human bodies except that, according to Scripture, it has properties and prerogatives by which it is superior to all creatures, even angelic creatures. Just as there is an analogy and proportion between inanimate and animate bodies, in the same way there is an analogy and proportion between animate bodies and a deified body, as the fathers have said. As an example, Andreae said that a table is to the eye as the eye is to a glorified body. Just as the eye does not cease to share bodiliness and dimensions with the table just because the eye sees by virtue of the soul and the table does not, so the body of Christ, united personally to the Son of God, has properties that other animated bodies do not. It does not, however, cease to be a body and to share in the properties of animated bodies.[27]

While there is one Christ, not two, one on earth and the other in heaven, nevertheless, the consideration of his body or his humanity is double. Considered simply as body, the true and essential body, like our bodies except for sin, retains the essential properties of a true body and never relinquishes them. Thus considered, the body of Christ is now in heaven, that is, in the state of another age, with God the Father and not on earth.[28]

But, Andreae argued, in another way, as the divinized body of the God-man, Christ's body is able to be on earth. Scripture, when it speaks of Christ's absence (as with all that is said of Christ), must be understood not *simpliciter,* as if he were in no wise present, but *secundum quid,* that is, by the mode of the true body or property of a body without respect to anything else.

Andreae's complex use of scholastic terms requires comment. Andreae was arguing that Scripture must be understood to be speaking of Christ's body not simply but in a certain way (*secundum quid*), that is, as a body only. When Scripture refers to Christ's body simply, and not "in a certain way," said Andreae, it does so as the body of the God-Man, or the deified body. So when Scripture speaks of Christ's absence, it means the absence of the body of Christ purely as corporeal. Otherwise the body of Christ as divinized is able to be present everywhere; it is ubiquitous.[29]

Confusion arises because, according to scholastic tradition, to speak of anything purely is to speak of it *simpliciter.* To speak of it in relation to something else is to speak *secundum quid.* Andreae's explanation was clumsy, and he promised to speak of it further in the discussion of the person of Christ.

Another explanation for Christ's ubiquity is found in the Lutheran interpretation of what the fathers called the *communicatio idiomatum.* Andreae cited John Damascene, who attributed divinization to the body of Christ in such a way that he excels the angels even bodily. Cyril supported the same doctrine, according to Andreae, when he wrote that Christ vivified others by using his body, touching people and speaking to them. That means, affirmed Andreae, that Christ acted with divine power through his body since to vivify is a divine property.

In his understanding of Philippians 2, Andreae carried on the same argument. When he explained the term "in the form of God" (*in forma Dei*), he said that the words clearly teach that Paul is here speaking of Christ according to his humanity.[30] It is one thing to be *the* form of God; another to be *in the form* of God. Christ is the form of God as God; he is in the form of God as man. *In forma Dei* then signifies the communication of the form of God to human nature through the personal union. Nevertheless, the form of God was put off so that Christ could cover himself with the habit and condition of a servant. This does not subtract from the truth and circumscription of his body, and yet the man Christ rules all things spiritually and is present to them, governing them, in a heavenly manner beyond human comprehension.[31]

Taking the same doctrine from another point of view, Andreae said that from the Incarnation Christ was both in the womb and at the right hand of God since God's right hand is God and Christ is God. God is most high in majesty, not in place or location. Even as man, Christ's majesty remains, although hidden under human form. There is not, therefore, such a great difference in Christ before and after the Resurrection. The Creed places the exaltation after the Resurrection because the exaltation refers to the putting off, through his death, of the form of a servant and allows Christ's majesty to appear.[32] Andreae summed up his argument by affirming three states of Christ: humility, glory, and dispensation, or *oeconomias.* The third category covers the forty days when Christ confirmed his apostles' faith by appearing among them.[33] But, said Andreae, more of this in its proper place, namely in the discussion of the person of Christ.

Sacramental Principles

Andreae's fundamental sacramental principle is the common and undisputed one: The Supper has to be for both soul and body since the mind is in the body. The whole person, body and soul, is refreshed spiritually by this food and drink. But what the sacramental mode unites and where, therefore, the mystery lies, is a point of continual disagreement between Andreae and Beza. For Andreae, the bread and the body of Christ are united. For Beza, the faithful communicant and Christ are united. In the first case, there is a mystical presence of Christ's body; in the second, there is a mystical union or marriage of the faithful and Christ.

Andreae, however, denied that the Württembergers taught consubstantiation of the body with the bread, but rather a sacramental conjunction of the body and the bread. He would not allow that such a conjunction constituted a relation between the two substances (bread and body), and he was loath to speak of sign and signified; rather, he called this union of bread and body a miracle: "this is a truly miraculous mode of presence, that the body of Christ, existing and remaining in heaven according to the mode of a true body (*secundum quid*), without any local motion, by another mode is present (*simpliciter*) in all places, is distributed and received wherever the Lord's Supper is celebrated.[34] Andreae denied that such a presence is physical, local, or relative, but rather said that it is mystical and, as such, to be believed rather than understood.[35]

Andreae discussed the causes and effects of the Lord's Supper in an extended debate with Beza concerning the testament and the seals of the testament. Andreae declared that the words of institution are the testament, and since this is so, Christ spoke clearly and without figures. To Beza's denial that the Supper is the testament, but rather its seal, Andreae quoted Luke and then rehearsed the aspects of a testament that Luther had taught fifty years earlier.[36] The testator is Jesus Christ. The words of institution are the formula by which the will of the testator is made known. The heirs are the believers, and their legacy is the remission of sins and life eternal. The apostles are the witnesses, and the seal is the bread and wine and body and blood of Christ by which the promise is guaranteed. While Andreae knew that figures are used to illustrate and to explain, Christ needed no figurative language in such a solemn declaration.[37]

Unfortunately, Beza did not pick up Andreae's division of the testament into parts that so nearly correspond to the way Beza organized his own interpretation; rather, Beza pressed Andreae on his first declaration, that the Lord's Supper is the whole testament. Beza asked whether or not baptism is a testament. Andreae answered that baptism is not called a testament primarily because Scripture does not so call it. Christ is one in all the sacraments but not according to the same *ratio*. So in God's word, baptism is not a testament but the laver of regeneration and renovation in the Holy Spirit.

Andreae next insisted that a sacramental sign is such only when it is joined with what it signifies as the seal is affixed to the parchment of the testament. Neither is worth anything by itself; each is effective only as a part of the whole, which together they make up. Beza then cited Bernard of Clairvaux's analogy of the ring to illustrate the use of a trope with regard to Christ and the eucharist in the church.[38] Andreae insisted that in the analogy of the ring, Bernard demonstrated the end and use of the sacraments, not the way in which Christ is present in the Lord's Supper. To prove this, Andreae quoted Bernard: "In the sacrament of the altar, you ought to attend to three things, the species of bread, the truth of the flesh, and the virtue of spiritual grace." You can never use Bernard, Andreae admonished Beza, to support your argument that there is a trope in the words of the testament of Christ.[39]

Arguing for the *manducatio indignorum,* Andreae said that the presence of Christ and the effects of that presence must be distinguished. The effects are determined by faith or incredulity; the presence itself is not so determined. Further, that Christ is the judge is not the result of incredulity but is an office given Christ by the Father.[40] So Christ is the judge and incredulity is the cause of judgment, which proceeds from the body of Christ who judges the sin of incredulity. This, affirmed Andreae, is parallel to mercy, which is the cause of conferring life on the faithful. Christ is therefore the source of life as savior and of death as judge.

At this point, according to Andreae's *Acta,* Beza demanded that he pose his argument in a syllogism. Andreae conceded: Whoever eats the bread of the Lord's Supper, eats the body of Christ. The impious eat the bread of the Lord's Supper. Therefore the impious eat the body of Christ.[41] Beza immediately objected that the first premise is exactly what was being debated and so cannot be used as the principle upon which the rest of the argument is built. Andreae countered by quoting 1 Corinthians 10: "The bread which we break is the communication [*koinonia*] of the body of Christ." But this will not do as a proof of the primary premise, insisted Beza, because the word *communication* is pivotal to the debate itself. The effort to conduct the debate according to basic logic and the use of syllogisms proved fruitless.

Andreae continued his argument for the *manducatio indignorum.* As the word enters the ear when the gospel is read, so the Sacrament enters the mouth. Both have diverse effects for which the sun provides a simile. One cause can have diverse effects as when the heat of the sun hardens mud and softens wax. So Christ both judges and vivifies. The cause of damnation is in the recipient, not in or from God. Damnation cannot be defined; it falls between two causes, the person in whom is its cause and God who damns. Christ is not the source of damnation in the same way that he is the source of life. Incredulity proceeds from the devil and a perverse will. But faith is the instrumental cause of salvation and God's gift through the Holy Spirit.

To these arguments, Beza responded that incredulity is the efficient cause of damnation and that Christ is the cause of life and salvation only.[42]

The argument that ensued involved the use of philosophical terms and, in the *Acta* at least, Andreae demonstrated a surer knowledge of Aristotle's efficient causality. In fact, Faius had to lean over the table to correct a hasty

denial of the nature of an instrumental cause into which Beza had blundered.
Beza objected that since faith is not a cause that works through its own power,
it is not an efficient cause. Faius whispered that an instrumental cause belongs
in the category of efficient causes. Andreae then gave a classic example of
primary and instrumental efficient causes:

> The *ratio* of efficient causes is not the same. For some are principal causes,
> having their efficiency in themselves; others are instrumental. Thus God is
> according to himself and absolutely the efficient cause of all creatures for
> which he required no instrument. Now in the creation of human beings,
> instruments are used, husband and wife. But faith is not among the efficient
> causes that work by themselves, but rather, as we have said, it is an instru-
> mental cause which, without Christ as the efficient cause, is unable to offer
> salvation.[43]

Andreae argued that the power of God must not be separated from the
word of God. Who hears the word receives both the word and the power of
God for life or death. Actually, both Andreae and Beza were close on this
argument. They agreed that incredulity damns and that Christ exercises the
office of judge and pronounces sentence. But they disagreed on how Christ is
received in the Lord's Supper. For Beza the important union is that of Christ
with the believer. To be united with Christ in faith is to be united to the very
source of life. For Andreae the sacramental union of the bread and the body
of Christ is determinative so that whoever takes the sacrament into his or her
mouth takes the body of Christ, who is then either life or judgment according
to the faith or lack of it with which Christ is received.

Andreae summed up: Faith plus Christ equals salvation. Incredulity plus
Christ equals damnation. Andreae then requested that they cease using philosophical terms that were not understood by the audience. He was the first to
break this rule, however, as he proceeded to discuss the double power of
Christ's body to be in heaven *secundum quid* and everywhere *simpliciter*.

Andreae had raised the likeness of the sacrament to the preached word in
their union of word and power. Beza had insisted that the word and sacrament
are also alike in what they offer, namely the whole Christ to be spiritually
eaten by faith. Both word and sacrament depend on the Holy Spirit and faith
to prepare the mind to grasp the word and to eat the body. Andreae objected
to this degree of likeness between word and sacrament because it is a denial of
the *manducatio oralis,* that is, of the Lutheran and Roman Catholic doctrine
that whoever receives the sacrament of the Lord's Supper eats the real, substantial body of Christ. Andreae argued that faith does not effect Christ's
presence or absence, but it does determine whether or not it is salutary for a
given individual. Andreae insisted that even those without faith receive
Christ, but to their condemnation.

Against this position, Beza argued that just as one can hear a foreign
language without understanding it, that is, the sound can penetrate the ear but
its significance is lost upon the mind, so the word of God and the Lord's
Supper can be presented to the ear and the mouth, but neither is received into

the soul without faith through which the word and sacrament are grasped for salvation. Andreae countered that Paul said that faith comes by hearing, not hearing by faith. Paul proceeded from the effect to the cause, so preaching precedes faith, not vice versa. Paul was speaking of exterior rather than interior hearing, as may be seen by the context, for preaching and hearing are correlates. So those who hear the preaching and do not believe are damned. Those who hear and believe receive salvation. The difficulties inherent in this argument are not further discussed in this context, but it is clear that the nub of the problem is why, of those who hear the preacher, to some faith is given and to others it is not. The problem is one of the free grace of God and of election.

At the end of the discussion of the Lord's Supper, Andreae demanded that Beza consent to the Lutheran doctrine in toto. In fact, he asked Beza to consent to the Württemberg Lutheran doctrine, which included the teaching on the ubiquity of Christ's body, a doctrine not even accepted by all Lutherans. Andreae would yield on no point nor would he allow that some of the points in dispute might be left open and the major points agreed on for the sake of peace, as Beza often suggested. To Andreae, all points were major points.

Philosophical Language

As the *Acta* report the proceedings of the colloquy, Andreae used more technically philosophical language and used it with more assurance than did Beza.[44] On the other hand, Andreae was scornful of Beza's demand that the debate proceed by way of syllogisms, and the few that Andreae used are, to say the least, simplistic. In each case, his first premise was the heart of the debate and so could not be used as a first premise, which must be above debate. Beza recognized this problem in his *Responsio*.[45] It is difficult to know whether Andreae was simply unskilled in logic or despaired of its application.

Beza's *Responsio*

In the *Responsio,* which consists primarily of Beza's answers to Andreae's marginal comments printed in the *Acta,* the two theologians are not seen to be any closer, but aspects of their theologies are brought out that are not found in either the theses or the discussion as reported in the *Acta*. In this section, then, I shall go through Beza's text, in which he gives the theses, antitheses, and statements judged by the Lutherans to be contrary to Scripture as they appear in the *Acta* followed by the marginalia and Beza's answers to those marginal comments that he felt to be more damaging than the report of the discussion itself. I shall not dwell on points sufficiently covered elsewhere, although some repetition may be unavoidable.

To Beza's first thesis, Andreae's marginalia made three objections in order to establish a real difference between spiritual and sacramental manducation:

(1) Christ said, "Take and eat," which rules out an interpretation in the light of John 6; (2) the sacrament can be taken unworthily by those without faith, while spiritual manducation is the exercise of faith; and (3) the two are not different soley because of their exterior forms but also with regard to what is offered through the forms. To the first point, Beza answered that if one does not interpret the words of institution according to John 6, there is no way to avoid a Cyclopian eating. If there is no figurative understanding, then, as Augustine says, Jesus would be commanding a horrendous crime. And how, argued Beza, does Andreae interpret John 6 itself, which also contains the words *flesh* and *blood?* How is it that Andreae interprets one passage literally and allows the other a figurative interpretation? Beza followed this argument at some length, developing it from his reading of Augustine, Cyril, and Chrysostom. Beza and Andreae used the same authorities, and it is clear that as the Scriptures are variously interpreted, so are the major fathers of the church. Both sides used the same authorities to uphold opposing positions.

Beza also accused Andreae of a sophistry that is called in the schools *petitio principii,* or presupposition of the principle. Andreae presupposed as true and proven the very things called in question, namely oral manducation. He then argued that oral manducation differs from spiritual manducation, which is itself, for Andreae, established through oral manducation.[46] Beza concluded his argument by referring to a passage in Irenaeus: The body and blood of Jesus Christ are heavenly things not with regard to their substance, but with regard to their sacramental use. Irenaeus calls the bread and wine "earthly" even though with regard to their use they are separated from common things. Beza was here protecting the human nature of Christ from the kind of divinization that would destroy its human reality, and at the same time Beza considered it to be "uncommon," just as the bread and wine were put to "uncommon" use.[47]

In his response to the second marginalis, Beza distinguished *spiritually* from *naturally, corporally,* and *orally.* What is given into the mouth or hand is corporal and received corporally and naturally, while what is offered by the Holy Spirit is received by a mind endowed with faith and is truly spiritual. Therefore only by the faithful is Christ truly received, while the unworthy receive only bread and wine, not discerning the body and blood offered with the bread and wine. To Andreae's third argument, that not only the signs differ but also what is offered and received, Beza countered that the flesh and blood of Christ are offered and received in sacramental and spiritual "eating" even though the manner of offering differs.

The second thesis was Andreae's denial that Lutherans could be accused of Capernaitic[48] eating. On this point, the Lutherans agreed with the Reformed. In the margin Andreae asserted that Beza was setting up a straw man by constantly accusing the Lutherans of teaching Capernaitic eating. "For in this mystery the *ratio*[49] of the body of the Lord is wholly spiritual . . . which clearly denies the crass thoughts of Capernaitic types."[50]

Beza wrote that the denial of the Lutherans is useless since it is not possible, in effect, to have an oral manducation of the essence of Christ's body and blood that is not Capernaitic. Andreae's insistence on oral manducation is flatly opposed, in Beza's mind, to a sacramental and therefore spiritual manducation. For Andreae, the word *sacramental* demands oral manducation, and once again the difference lies in the notion of each regarding the locus of the sacramental union. In his refutation, Beza continued to oppose corporal and tangible to spiritual. If, as Andreae argued, Lutherans consider the body of Christ in a spiritual manner, then it cannot be touched because it is in being tangible that a body differs from an intangible spirit. Andreae cannot claim that Christ's body is essentially present, for it is of the essence of a body to be tangible and quantified. What Andreae is trying to say, wrote Beza, is that Christ is present. But what kind of presence does he mean? Beza then defined kinds of presence: (1) definitive: without circumscription, proper to spirits; (2) repletive: without definition, proper to divinity and therefore nontransferrable; and (3) local: circumscibed, proper to bodies. Beza contended that Luther tried to transfer repletive presence to the human nature of Christ in his doctrine of ubiquity.[51] But this cannot be done because

> if the humanity itself of Our Lord Jesus Christ, because of the hypostatic union, is everywhere repletively, that is, filling all things without being comprehended by any, it follows that neither will the body of Christ be In, Under, or With the holy bread, because of the institution which the Lord began when he instituted the Holy Supper, since he would have been there just as much from the very moment of the hypostatic union, present not only with this bread and wine, but also with all things as long as they endure.[52]

This argument will play a much larger role in the discussion of the person of Christ, but it has its place here and underlines the inseparability of the two doctrines.

Thesis III is the mutual denial of transubstantiation. Although there were no marginalia, Beza added a paragraph likening consubstantiation and transubstantiation and charging both with being Capernaitic. Beza contended that consubstantiation differs only in being more absurd.

Thesis IV turns on the Lutheran denial that the presence of the body of Christ is natural, physical, or local or that it involves inclusion in the bread. Beza admitted that he did not see how the *substance* of the body and blood could be *really* present with the bread and wine except in a natural and local manner. Even the glorification, while it made Christ immortal, did not remove his human nature. Beza refused to apply a third mode, a sacramental mode, that could mediate between a natural and corporal presence and a purely mental presence. In fact, a third mode was available to Beza in his own doctrine of the relational presence of Christ to the believer.[53] If both sides could have admitted that a sacramental presence escapes natural categories of body and mind just as it transcends space and time, there might have been concord. But neither was willing to make such a concession nor investigate the possibilities inherent in the partial doctrines of each. It is a poignant "if only." The marginalia of thesis IV are brusque—for example, "It is not a question of what you see or do not see, but of what Christ commanded, take and eat, this is my body." Beza is still more brusque: "Dr. Andreae says nothing here worthy of response."[54]

With thesis V, the opposition becomes total. This thesis presents the Lutheran doctrine concerning the real, substantial presence and oral manducation with its concomitant doctrine of the *manducatio indignorum*. Beside Beza's denial of all three, Andreae filled the margin with comments. He first accused Beza of ambiguity and trickery in his use of the word *present,* by which Christ is really offered to all but really received only by those with faith. Beza's contention that it is the soul and not the mouth that receives Christ was opposed by Andreae with the words of institution. His third remark was that for those without faith, the sacrament is not complete since, as Beza taught, they receive only bread and wine or the signs alone. Finally, where Beza asserted that the unworthy are culpable of the body and blood of the Lord not because they have taken it but for having held it in contempt, Andreae moved the negative so that the last phrase read: "because they have taken it, not for having held it in contempt."[55] Beza defended the Reformed concept of "present" as unambiguous since what is offered is offered to the soul, not the mouth: "We call it sacramental presentation or "praebition" when what is presented to our eyes (sign) signifies another to our mind, so that what is signified is presented to the understanding and therefore also received by the understanding. . . . But whatever is presented to the understanding need not first be presented to the body."[56] Against the second argument, Beza ran through the Old Testament and the Gospel account of John the Baptist to show that faith is necessary for ceremonies to be efficacious. He ended with Augustine: "Believe and you have eaten." His principle was that the gospel is the same gospel whether it is preached or offered with signs and ceremonies. Christian faith can have no other object whether or not the word *faith* is expressed. It was not necessary at the institution of the Lord's Supper for Christ to explain all of this. Beza said that nothing is more ridiculous than to measure the integrity of the word or sacraments by what is received rather than by what is offered. Finally, Beza affirmed that incredulity prevents complete reception.

Thesis VI dealt with the words used by the Lutherans in their formula: *in, with, under: substantially, corporally, really, essentially, orally.* Beza agreed that the terms were used by the Fathers, but since they have been abused by the Lutherans to support consubstantiation, the Reformed prefer not to use them. *Really* taken for *truly* is admissible, but *orally* is to be entirely rejected since it is like the *sensually* of the "papists." Andreae found nine separate points requiring comment:

1. The words are ancient.
2. Lutherans are against a local understanding of Christ's presence.
3. They also eschew a false use of the old terms.
4. Lutherans do not teach consubstantiation but rather a sacramental and supernatural presence.
5. Both Reformed and Lutherans apply the words *substantial, corporal,*

and *essential* to what is given in the Sacrament, not to the mode of conjunction of the signs and signified, or the manner of the presence. In other words, they are properly used when applied to the body of Christ, not to the manner of its presence or of the sacramental conjunction. There is also agreement on the careful use of *really* and *truly*.
[7 and 8 repeat old arguments.]

9. Andreae denied that the Catholics use the term *sensually* with regard to the Lord's Supper, even though Andreae agreed that "the papists" doctrine was gross.[57]

I shall not give all nine of Beza's responses, for much of the material is repetitive. To Andreae's second point, Beza answered that the question is not whether two things can be united in the same place; they can. But the question is whether or not a true body, composed of its members, can be present in a given place according to its essence (or as the schools say, by its first act) without being there according to what it is.[58] As often as Andreae denied that to be in a place and to be there locally are the same for the body of Christ, Beza maintained that Andreae's denial falsifies the body of Christ. "When Andreae says that the saints and God are both in the same place, he proves that he reduces the humanity of Christ to his divinity."[59] However much Andreae denied that he taught consubstantiation, that is in fact what he teaches, charged Beza. Beza then recalled Luther's approval of the Ego Berengarius formula, which uses the word *sensually* of the manner in which the priest handles the body of Christ.[60]

Thesis VII deals with the interpretation of the words of institution. Beza affirms that all passages of Scripture must be related to the analogy and rule of Christian faith comprised in the Apostles' Creed. The argument here does not differ from its presentation in the theses and antitheses of the *Acta,* except that Beza gives his definition of consubstantiation: "How else can one define consubstantiation except by the real conjunction of two substances [essences] on earth, that is of the body, In, Under, or With the bread and of the blood In, With or Under the wine, even when one denies that the presence is natural or local?"[61]

Thesis VII affirmed that Christ does not lie. Right, said Beza, but you apply the argument incorrectly. The marginalia here infer that the Swiss deny Christ's omnipotence, and Beza accused Andreae of calumny. Insofar as Christ is God, he is omnipotent, stated Beza. It is, on the contrary, Andreae who has written that the divinity of the man Christ is not the eternal essence common to the Father and the Holy Spirit, but that it (divinity) is communicated to him by the Second Person. Further, Beza said that Andreae wrote that "this communicated divinity, which is the gifts distributed by the Holy Spirit to the saints in measure, is given to Christ without measure."[62] Beza promised to discuss this further in the section on the person of Christ.[63]

Thesis IX dealt with the omnipotence of Christ:[64]

> We believe also and we teach that nothing is impossible to Christ, God and Man, but in such a way that the exposition of these words and what one

draws from them must be examined by the rule of faith. We say then, in the first place, that this omnipotence is one, and that there are not two, one uncreated, proper to the Deity and which cannot be transferred to any creature and the other created which would be a quality infused into the humanity of Christ.[65]

Andreae objected that the Lutherans do not teach a created omnipotence. There is only one, eternal, infinite omnipotence, but it has a double aspect in Christ who, according to his humanity, is not omnipotent but through personal participation in the divine nature is omnipotent. Beza countered that the humanity of Christ is not omnipotent, but that Christ the man is omnipotent in the word just as the humanity is not the deity, but this man Jesus is God.

Andreae objected that Beza's statement was ambiguous. Beza explained:

God is omnipotent, but nevertheless, his power cannot make effectively things that he has not determined to make or that are contrary to those he has decided to make. The reason is not that he lacks omnipotence, but that he is not a liar. For to be changeable, to change one's will, proceeds from weakness and not power, and is appropriate to one able to lie. We put in this rank the unchangeable circumscription and locality of the body of Christ, that is, the body of Christ with its limits and contained in a certain place, insofar as God has established that what Christ has at one time taken to himself shall never be abolished. And this would obtain if the substance of the body of Christ could be, either before or after the glorification, in many places all at once.[66]

Andreae reduced this entire argument to a denial by Beza of Christ's omnipotence. Actually, Beza is in line with the classic argument of the *via antiqua* that God's omnipotence does not include the creation of contradictions.[67]

To hold Andreae to the affirmation of a created omnipotence given to the man Christ, which Andreae had denied teaching, Beza quoted from Brenz's *Recognitio:*

A difference between Christ and Peter cannot be established from the fact that we say that Christ the man is God since we say that Peter is God. . . . From this saying of the Gospel, the word is made flesh, which is said of Christ and not of Peter, a difference between them is established, because the Son of God fills the man Peter with his essence as he does the man Christ, but nevertheless he does not communicate to Peter all his properties, but only some of them.[68]

Beza then quoted from Andreae's *In Apol. adversus Ingolstadianas:* "Between the indwelling of God in the saints and in Christ there is one difference: to the saints God distributes his gifts *dimensa,* but to Christ *immensa.*"[69]

Beza misquoted Brenz although he did not distort the meaning, for Brenz did not posit the difference in Christ and Peter in the indwelling of the Son of God who by essence or divinity fills all things. The difference lies rather in the lifting up of the Son of man into the fullness of God's power and majesty. But Beza did distort the doctrine of Brenz and Andreae by insisting that the omnipotence given Christ is created. What the Lutherans of Württemberg taught is that although Christ as man is finite, he whose humanity is assumed by the Word is made capable of infinite gifts, which include the omnipotence and omnipresence of the divinity: *finitum capax est infinitum.*[70]

But Beza would not grant this and held that a finite being is capable only of receiving finite gifts. He argued that the properties that Christ and Peter share are either created or uncreated. The second possibility is blasphemous. Beza said that the scholastics correctly observed that the divine omnipotence cannot be communicated to any creature. Nor is the soul of Christ omnipotent except insofar as it is the instrument of the omnipotent word in unity of person. The humanity of Christ is not omnipotent, but the man Christ is so in the word. It must be remembered, insisted Beza, that the strength of the instrument and of the one who uses the instrument are two strengths in number, not one only communicated to the instrument.[71]

Andreae charged, still in the marginalia of thesis IX, that Beza attributed to the Holy Spirit what Christ had attributed to his own flesh. Beza answered that the Holy Spirit is the essential power of the Father and the Son. What is attributed to the Holy Spirit is not taken from Christ. Christ's humanity was sanctified by the Holy Spirit at baptism and anointed by the Father, affirmed Beza. The preservation of a distinct and active role of the Holy Spirit throughout their theology was one of the distinctive strengths of the doctrine of Calvin and Beza.

Thesis X declared that Scripture does reveal in what manner the worthy and unworthy communicate. One can say only that it is supernatural and incomprehensible to human reason and ought not to be disputed. Beza had opposed this in his antithesis by speaking of the sign joined with (related to) the signified by a divine command. Therefore the manner of communication is relational and has its likeness in human contracts. Andreae objected in the margin that relation is a human fantasy and that there is no likeness between human contracts and the sacraments.

To these objections, Beza answered that relation cannot be denied since a sign has to be related to that which it signifies, and he quoted both Andreae himself and Augustine's letter 23 to support his argument. Andreae, in the *Acta,* had agreed that there is a sign and a signified, but he vehemently denied a conjunction by relation. Beza retorted that only a sorcerer could deny that the two are related. As for civil contracts, they differ from sacraments in their signs and in what they signify, but they are alike in the way that they relate the sign and signified. To support this thesis, Beza turned to Bernard and a passage that Beza found "golden":

> One can give a ring just for the sake of the ring, which then has no significa-
> tion. Or one can give a ring in order to invest someone with an inheritance.
> The ring is then a sign of such a kind that the one who received it can say that
> the ring is worth nothing in itself; it is the inheritance that I am looking for. It is
> in this way that the Lord, as he drew near his passion, wished to invest his
> disciples with his grace, giving them an exterior sign of his invisible grace.[72]

This passage does indeed make clear the relation of the sign to the signified, but Andreae could cite Bernard for his purposes as well.[73] Andreae continued to deny that any relation existed between the sign and the signified, preferring to assert their identity, a doctrine that put him in the Catholic camp. His rejection of the word *sign,* and his insistence that one must speak of the whole sacrament and not of the elements by themselves, lent itself to the Catholic doctrine of transubstantiation.[74]

Andreae had accused Beza of attributing Christ's eucharistic presence to the faith of the believer rather than to the power of God. Such a charge, responded Beza, is a calumny since both sign and signified are truly present and offered. Faith does not cause the sacramental conjunction, Beza argued. Indeed, Christ offers himself to all who approach with or without faith. But faith does enable reception. Such faith is not from the human spirit; rather, it is itself the gift of the Holy Spirit and of Jesus so that all glory and praise belong to God: Father, Son, and Spirit.[75]

"Contrary to Scripture"

The same method was followed with regard to the articles considered by the Lutherans to be contrary to Scripture and which Beza defended. The first article concerned the interpretation of the words of institution. Andreae agreed that obscure passages require clarification in the light of less obscure passages, but he denied that the words of institution are obscure. Beza wrote that the words of institution are certainly clear when they are understood to involve sign and signified and thus the relation of sacraments. He cited examples of heretics who claimed that certain passages should be taken literally: So the Arians took literally Christ's assertion that "the Father is greater than I" and the Anthropomorphites took literally "your hands fashioned me." No, said Beza, Scripture has to be understood in the light of the rule of faith, which protects the faithful from the errors of heretics.

The second article involved Christology only, and the points made there will be better handled in the section on the person of Christ. Article III was discussed in the responses to thesis IX and to these, Beza referred Andreae.

The problem of Abraham is renewed in article IV, where, among other arguments, Beza quoted Brenz's *Suevicus syntagmatus* (*sic*) which was written, said Beza, before Brenz had become a ubiquitarian. The passage is very much the same as the argument given by Beza:

> While Christ was indeed remote from carnal eyes and ears in the time of the paschal lamb, he was nevertheless most present to faith by whose wings he flew from this world into a spiritual [world], and according to the nature of the vision of God, saw those things that are Christ's. For as God sees all future things as present to himself, thus faith makes most present to itself and sees something far beyond the grasp of this world.[76]

But the context of this passage denies the similarity of Old and New Testament realities. The patriarchs, wrote Brenz, saw Christ in faith; they did not grasp him in reality as communicants do now in the Lord's Supper.[77]

Beza's Confession on the Lord's Supper

Although it preceded his responses to the theses and articles in the *Acta,* Beza placed the confession on the Lord's Supper at the end of his responses on this topic. This confession, written by Beza and signed by his colleagues, received its share of marginalia in the *Acta.* In the first response to Andreae's marginalia, Beza defended himself by asserting that he and his companions are speaking as private persons because they do not feel they can speak for all Christians. Beza asked Andreae why he considered himself authorized to impose the Formula of Concord on churches that had nothing to do with his appointment as a minister. Beza accused Andreae of persuading the princes to give him that authority in spite of the churches. Beza was sent with the approval of Geneva and Bern, but he was not delegated to speak for them in a formal way, hence he spoke for himself only. In this brief exchange, the pride and independence of the Swiss cities and of their churches are set against the sometimes unwilling subservience of those regions bound to observe the religion of their princes and to obey the ministers appointed by their princes.

An interesting liturgical note occurs in another of Beza's responses, in which he charged that Andreae did not follow Christ's commands, for Andreae still used little round hosts, which he placed in the mouths of communicants rather than in their hands; nor did Andreae break the bread properly.[78]

Another point deserves comment. Beza wrote that Andreae restricted the name of Christ to his humanity. "But we all know," said Beza, "that Christ, by his divinity dwells in us by a special virtue and grace of which the Lord's Supper is the pledge and witness. At the same time, according to his humanity, in power and authority, Christ governs the church from heaven through the Holy Spirit.[79] Here Beza used the doctrine of the mystical union of the faithful with Christ to prove that the name "Christ" should not be restricted to the humanity.

Andreae compared the sacrament with the birth of Jesus from Mary by which she bore the man in one way and God in another. To this Beza responded that the hypostatic union is entirely different from the sacramental conjunction. The deity and humanity are two totally diverse natures. But the body and blood of Christ are limited corporal entities, as are bread and wine. So if the body and blood and bread and wine are substantially joined, they must be present in the same way, essentially and actually. Their reception therefore must also be the same, that is, natural, visible, sensible. This is the conclusion one must come to if one accepts consubstantiation. Beza protested that during the Last Supper, Christ was not yet glorified, so that only a spiritual reception was possible. As was that one, so must ours be.

Andreae accused Beza of making the reception of the body of Christ relative, which is simply wrong. (Andreae transposed what Beza said of the conjunction of the signs and signified to the manner of reception, which was Andreae's error, not Beza's.) Andreae also protested that the members of Christ are joined to him really, not relatively, so the conjunction must be real and not relative. This argument was weak also since it assumed that *real* excludes *relative* and that Christ must be joined with the bread in the same way as with the faithful.

Returning to his defense of the contract as the type of relation that also obtains in the sacrament and of the sign of the contract that offers what it signifies, Beza used the example of a house key. While the house key is not the house, yet in a sense it is since it is the sign of ownership and handing it over is equivalent to handing over the house. In no way, however, are the key and the house substantially united. In the same way, a husband offers himself with the wedding ring and Christ offers himself in the gospel. In all of these, there is no substantial union but rather a relation.

Beza at last dealt with the sacrament in regard to both time and space, neither of which, he said, prevents the spiritual reception of Christ. The Holy Spirit unites the faithful with Christ who is in heaven and also effects the union of Christ with the patriarchs of the Old Testament. The ability to overcome both time and space is a spiritual one, impossible if the limitations of corporality are maintained. Here also occurred one of the rare mentions of sacrifice in relation to the Lord's Supper. Just as the patriarchs enjoyed Christ in their sacraments through faith and hope, so Christians now, with the eyes of faith, see the sacrifice of Christ as though it were taking place now, and they take his body and blood as truly by faith as though they grasped it with their hands.

To thesis VI, Andreae again objected that Beza was substituting the Holy Spirit for the body and blood of Christ and their efficacy. Beza answered with an exposition of trinitarian theology. The Holy Spirit is the essential and immanent power of the Father and the Son, proceeding from both without separation from either but distinguished from both. His office is to regenerate Christians, to illumine and guide them to the truth, to move and to console them, and in short to be the author of all the good movements of the saints and to distribute to them diverse gifts. All of this is done in the name of the whole Trinity. Furthermore, Jesus taught that the Holy Spirit "will take what is mine and teach you." But the point here is that one must be careful to attribute divine activities to divine persons and not to attribute to flesh and blood what is proper to God alone. With regard to Christ, one must neither divide the person nor confuse the natures.[80]

The last argument is also important. Andreae wanted the sacraments to possess an intrinsic power. He objected that "the substance of the sacrament is dissolved if this intrinsic sacramental power is removed."[81] Beza built his rebuttal around God's use of instrumental causes: the pastor, the words, the bread and wine, the actions. The most important of instrumental causes is, of course, faith. If the sacraments are assumed powerful in their own right, or intrinsically, then Andreae was forging idols. Only God himself can work the effects attributed to the sacraments; such power may not be given even to angels.

Finally, Beza responded to the preface that Andreae inserted into the *Acta* between the sections on the Lord's Supper and the person of Christ. Beza said that he wanted each side to draw up points of agreement and disagreement after each section was debated. Beza pleaded for the best means to achieve a peaceful agreement. He then presented his own list of agreements and disagreements.

Agreements and Disagreements

With regard to the sacramental presence, we agree on the following:

1. The Lord's Supper is composed of two things, the signs and the signified.

2. By the Lord's command, the signs are bread and wine and the signified are his body and blood.

3. Jesus Christ and his benefits are inseparable.

4. The signs and the signified are joined by a sacramental conjunction.

5. The signs are not bare and empty but present to both worthy and unworthy what they signify.

6. The fathers have said that the body of the Lord is In, Under, and With the bread.

There is disagreement on the following:

The mode of conjunction of the signs and the signified.

1. The Württembergers teach that there is a real and substantial conjunction of the bread and the body so that with the bread, the body is received into the mouth by both the worthy and the unworthy. The Swiss affirm a sacramental conjunction, which they teach is relative so that the body remains in heaven and the bread on earth. The body therefore is not presented in its corporal essence to the mouth of the worthy and the unworthy.

2. The Württembergers understand by the words In, With, or Under the bread and wine, the real and sacramental conjunction of substances here on earth. The bread is taken in a natural way by the mouth, while the body is also taken orally, but in an incomprehensible manner that is neither natural nor local. The Swiss teach that these words indicate a relative conjunction or a correspondence between the bread and the body by which the signs are offered to the mouth and the body and blood of the Lord to the soul.

There is agreement on the reception of the sacrament.

1. All who approach receive the signs orally, but the worthy unto life and the unworthy unto condemnation.

2. The spiritual reception by faith, proper to those who approach worthily and who alone receive the signified thing (*res*), is salutary.

3. The manner of receiving the signified things is incomprehensible and a mystery better adored than too much investigated.

There is disagreement on the mode of manducation.

The Württembergers teach oral manducation of the body of Christ by both the worthy and the unworthy, the former to life and the latter to condemnation. The Swiss teach that the signified things are presented to the soul and so are received spiritually only by the faithful, since only they possess the instrument by which Christ and his benefits may be received. Consequently, the unworthy are culpable of the body and blood of the Lord not because they have taken them unworthily but because they have rejected them by their incredulity and impenitence.[82]

This summary, which is not given in Andreae's *Acta,* is remarkable for its fair treatment of the points of the opposition, arranging them according to the two points that Andreae insisted were primary in the dispute. In the introduction to these lists, Beza said again that since they agreed on so many major points, some degree of concord could be achieved. The disputed points, while their importance was recognized, ought not to be allowed to overshadow the basic agreement or to cause such serious and bitter dissension. It was in the hope that a modus vivendi could be achieved that Beza and his companions had come to Montbéliard.

It is clear, however, from the demands made by Andreae as reported by himself in the *Acta* and still more by his remarks in the *Epitome,* that Andreae had expected nothing less than complete capitulation to the Lutheran doctrine on all points. If Beza could not be converted, the Montbéliardais could be, either by argument or by the imposition of a common confession and church order by the Württembergers with the approval of the ruling count and duke, Frederick and Ludwig.

Andreae's *Epitome*[83]

The last word in this exchange is taken by Andreae, who in 1588 published his *Epitome*[84] in Latin and also a vernacular and far less gentlemanly version, *Kurzer Begriffe.*[85] In this summary, which is indeed brief, Andreae reduced the discussion to two major points, the interpretation of the words of institution and the third mode of Christ's real presence and oral manducation, which, argued Andreae, is between a purely spiritual and a crassly physical and local presence and eating. These were not new arguments, but several points are worth noting. The first is that the whole of Beza's theology of sacramental signs is completely ignored. Second, the "third mode" is presented with excellent arguments. This is the "sacramental mode" that might have provided ground for real agreement.

Andreae's arguments are clear, and he gave a fair summary of Beza's principal objections to the Lutheran doctrine of ubiquity. These four objections were based on (1) the true localized body of Christ, which is in heaven and allows for only a relation with the bread, (2) the scriptural passages that assert Christ has left the world and will return, (3) St. Paul's written statement that he wished to leave this world, to be freed so that he could be with Christ, and (4) the fathers' discussion of Christ's absence from earth. These points are taken by Beza to be in flat contradiction with a real conjunction of the flesh of Christ with the bread.

Andreae wrote that Beza's problem was that he refused to admit that the flesh of Christ could be present in any way other than locally and circum-scriptively. This is due to Beza's inability to rise above purely human sense perception and reason. This is also the basis for his assertion that God cannot effect another kind of real presence that is heavenly, sacramental, and to be believed rather than understood. Andreae then met Beza on his own ground and accused him of falsely applying the *analogia fidei*. The Creed does not present the birth, passion, death, resurrection, and ascension of a mere man, but of the Logos incarnate so that the body of Christ is a deified body. Such a body, argued Andreae, differs from an animate body as much as an animate body differs from an inanimate body.

There are two problems here. Andreae would not clarify what he meant by a sacramental presence beyond asserting that God can give spiritual gifts through physical means. Andreae would not investigate the relation of sign and signified, apparently because that would seem to yield something to Beza. But he did concede that the body and blood presented with the bread and wine are spiritual gifts. Second, Andreae did not answer the charge that if Christ's body is deified, it ceases to be a human body.

Andreae's discussion of the "deified body" led to consideration of God's omnipotence and what Andreae considered to be Beza's "blasphemous" de-nial of it. In this context, however, Andreae insisted that what God's omnipo-tence makes present is not the human body of Christ as it is localized and absent but that body of Christ made present mystically in a mode beyond human comprehension.

Here, once again, Andreae and Beza might have worked toward agree-ment if their opposition had not been so bitter. For the mode of presence is sacramental, and therefore both mystical and relational. The difference be-tween them is that while the Lutherans said that Christ is mystically present to the congregation on earth, Beza said that the congregation of the faithful is lifted to heaven to be mystically united with Christ.

In the last two pages of this section of the *Epitome,* Andreae summoned Beza before Christ's tribunal on the last day to answer for his blasphemies. Andreae also insisted that there can be no peace and no agreement, not even a truce, between them since Beza corrupted true doctrine and led souls astray. Beza must not be believed when he wrote that the Lutherans and Calvinists agree on more points than those on which they disagree. There is no agree-ment at all on any point with regard to the Lord's Supper, insisted Andreae, who turned to the next section of the colloquy, the person of Christ.

Notes

1. See ch. 2, p. 49.
2. Armand Lods, "Les Actes du Colloque de Montbéliard (1586): Une polé-mique entre Théodore de Bèze et Jacque Andreae," Mélanges de la Société de l'histoire du Protestantisme Français, *Bulletin Historique et Littéraire,* 46 (1897): 197. There is no further information about those who or how many attended the colloquy

other than the participants. Whether they persevered throughout the debates, how they reacted, other than in a few instances, is not recorded.

3. This is still another quite simple version of the calling of the colloquy that bypasses the role of Clervant, but, since it is part of Andreae's narrative, it cannot be seen as anything other than a simplification.

4. That this condition was met by neither party is a matter of discussion. See pp. 160–61.

5. It should be noted that Andreae kept at his table not only Count Frederick but also control over the proceedings and the formulation of the theses.

6. The Colloquy of Maulbronn took place in 1564 between Brenz (with Andreae) and Zacharius Ursinus with other theologians of the Palatinate. See above, p. 56. See also Beza, *Correspondance* 5:50–52, with bibliographical information in n. 8.

7. *Capernaitic* refers to John 6:22–71, esp. 6:52, in which the Capernaites ask, "How can this man give us his flesh to eat?" *Cyclopian,* a reference to the monster Cyclops, who devoured Odysseus's sailors in Homer's *Odyssey,* has the same meaning. These derogatory terms infer that communicants eat, cannabalistically, the natural body of Christ. See p. 82 for Calvin's interpretation of John 6:54.

8. When I follow the numbering of the document, I use, as does the document, roman numerals. When I summarize, collapsing several theses into one, I use arabic numerals.

9. Throughout I have been careful to translate *vere* as "true" and *realiter* as "real" since these are technical terms for each side.

10. See below, p. 92.

11. This scholastic argument was used in the Middle Ages on behalf of the Assumption of the Virgin Mary: Christ wanted to have his mother with him as a complete person, that is, body and soul; what he wanted to do, he could do and, the argument goes, he therefore did do.

12. Stercoranism means that what passes into the mouth proceeds through the belly and out onto the dungheap. *Stercora* is Latin for dung.

13. See Theodore Beza, *De controversiis in Coena Domini.* See p. 133 n. 82.

14. *Acta,* 20–21: "Signa, sive symbola, sive sacramenta, cum angustiore significatione haec vox accipitur, appellamus in hoc argumento res in sensus externos incurrentes; ex Domini institutione & mandato à communi & naturali usu rebus spiritualibus & sacris nobis significandis, destinatas."

15. See my *Eucharistic Theology of Theodore Beza: Development of the Reformed Tradition,* AAR Studies in Religion no. 4 (Chambersburg, Pa.: American Academy of Religion, 1972, 1987).

16. Western tradition condones this position with regard to the eucharist; no condemnation attaches to ignorant use, however, only to malicious use.

17. Jill Raitt, "Three Inter-related Principles in Calvin's Unique Doctrine of Infant Baptism," *The Sixteenth Century Journal* 11, no. 1 (Spring 1980): 51–61, esp. 59.

18. *Acta,* 27. Beza and Faius were ministers from Geneva; Bern sent Musculus, a minister, and Hubner, a professor; Albery was a professor from Lausanne.

19. *Luther's Works* (American Edition), vol. 36, Robert H. Fischer, ed. (Philadelphia: Muhlenberg Press, 1961), 301–301. In his "Confession Concerning Christ's Supper" (1528) (*AE* 36, 151–372; *WA* 26, 261–509), Luther wrote: "Therefore, the fanatics are wrong, as well as the gloss in Canon Law, if they criticize Pope Nicholas for having forced Berengar to confess that the true body of Christ is [']crushed and ground with the teeth.' Would to God that all popes had acted in so Christian a fashion in all other matters as this pope did with Berengar in forcing this confession." See below, n. 57.

20. *Acta,* 32: "Modum, quo res significata ex divina ordinatione cum signis coniungitur, ipsa signorum appellatio explicat, et ostendit esse Relativum ex Dei pacto; quod et in ipsis contractibus humanis et ordinariis locum habet. Modum autem perceptionis rei significatae . . . vere mysterium magnum esse, cum Apostolo profitemur, ac proinde credendum, et adorandum, non perscrutandum."

21. Ibid., 33–34: "Ad IV: Christum Deum et Hominem, ut qui Mediator alioqui esse non potuerit, fatemur quidem actu non fuisse hominem ante realem incarnationem: sed tamen fidei Abrahami, (quae dicitur hupostasis rerum quae non sunt) non illusoria opinione, sed vere et efficaciter, ut et caeteris sanctis patribus, praesentem fuisse docemus."

22. "Unde merito Augustinus asseruit; veterum Sacramenta, re paria fuisse nostris, signis autem diversa."

23. Ibid., 35.

24. John Calvin, *Calvin's New Testament Commentaries,* vol. 4, *The Gospel according to St. John,* ed. and trans. T. H. L. Parker (Grand Rapids, Mich.: Eerdmans, 1961), pt. 1:1–10, p. 170.

25. It is clear that Aristotelian metaphysics was the common mode of analysis in the universities, including Tübingen, where Andreae was rector.

26. It is interesting to note that while Andreae argued for the omnipresence of Christ's human nature, he would not allow that it is also omnitemporal. On the other hand, Beza argued for the omnitemporality of Christ but denied the omnipresence of his human nature.

27. *Acta,* 69–70.

28. Ibid., 136: "Quapropter etsi unus est Christus, et non duo, alter in coelis, alter in terris: duplex tamen corporis, seu humanitatis eius consideratio est. Altera, quatenus verum, et essentiale corpus, nostris corporibus, excepto peccato, simile est; quod essentiales proprietates veri corporis retinet, et nunquam deponit. Et hac ratione consideratum corpus Christi, duntaxat nunc in coelis, hoc est, in statu alterius seculi est, cum Deo patre, et non in terris."

29. Ibid., 138. An opportunity was missed here. Had Andreae spoken of a *sacramental* body, he and Beza might have come to some agreement.

30. This is precisely the question. Beza would say that it refers to Christ the *man,* not to Christ's humanity. This is another instance of the concrete-abstract problem.

31. *Acta,* 94–96.

32. Ibid., 84–85.

33. Ibid., 149–50.

34. Ibid., 180: "Et hic vere miraculosus modus praesentiae est, quod corpus Christi propter veri corporis modum in coelis existens et permanens, absque omni locali motu alio modo in omnibus locis adsit, distribuatur, et percipiatur, ubi Coena Domini celebratur. Qui modus praesentiae neque physicus aut localis, neque sketikos, est et relativus, sed mysticus, sicut antiquitas locuta est: Mysterium quod creditur, non autem intelligitur."

35. Ibid.

36. Martin Luther, *Treatise on the New Testament* in AE 35, pp. 84–85; WA VI, 356–57.

37. *Acta,* 47–48.

38. Ibid., 59. See below, p. 94, nn. 72–73, in which these arguments are repeated.

39. Ibid., 63: "Tria quippe in Sacramento altaris attendere debes, speciem panis, veritatem carnis, et virtutem gratiae spiritualis. Hactenus Bernhardi verba. Nihil igitur

similitudo annuli facit ad confirmandum tropum in verbis Testamenti Christi; quem neque Bernhardi, neque Christi verba admittunt." See p. 95, n. 74.

40. Ibid., 109: "Quod vero ad effectum huius sacramentalis praesentiae attinet, aliud est praesentia, aliud effectus praesentiae. . . . Incredulitas autem non facit Christum iudicem et condemnatorem: sed pater constituit eum iudicem."

41. Ibid.: "Quisquis manducat panem Coenae Dominicae, is manducat corpus Christi. Impii manducant panem Coenae Dominicae. Ergo impii quoque manducant corpus Christi. Et sic non respuendo, sed recipiendo Christi corpus, iudicium manducant."

42. Ibid., 126. This affirmation is consistent in Reformed theology. For the Reformed, Christ can be *only* life-giving since Christ and his benefits, while distinct, are inseparable.

43. Ibid., 128: "Causarum efficientium non est eadem ratio. Aliter enim se habent principales, et καθ'άυτσ efficientes: aliter instrumentales. Sic Deus est καθ'άυτσ et absolute causa efficiens, omnium creaturarum, ad quas creandas nullo instrumento indiguit. Nunc in creatione hominis utitur instrumentis, Mare, et Foemina. Non autem est fides ex causis καθ'άυτσ efficientibus salutem; sed duntaxat, sicut diximus, instrumentalis, quae sine Christo efficiente causa, salutem praestare non potest."

44. How much of this accuracy and assurance may be due to editing his remarks for publication there is no way of knowing. According to Andreae's biographers, he was actually not very skilled in philosophy, while Beza had the opposite reputation. See Kolb, *Andreae and the Formula of Concord,* 10: "His [Andreae's] antagonists later called him a theological lightweight because he had had so little formal theological training." See also Walter Kickel, *Vernunft und Offenbarung bei Theodor Beza: Zum Problem des Verhaltnisses von Theologie, Philosophie und Staat* (Neukirchen: Neukirchener Verlag des Erziehungsvereins, 1967). The main point of this volume is that Beza was a skilled Aristotelian and as such at the origin of Reformed scholasticism.

45. See p. 89.

46. *Responsio [Response].* The Latin edition of 1588, p. 34 (French, p. 46) has a clearer technical vocabulary, e.g., *verrissime* for *realement.* In this passage, *real* is used twice in the French where it describes the reality of a denied physical contact and then the reality of the spiritual union. Therefore *real* is not opposed to *spiritual,* but rather *physical* is opposed to *spiritual,* which is itself qualified to mean "by the power of the Holy Spirit" rather than mental, as indeed Calvin used the word *spiritual.* In the Latin edition of 1588, *verissime* rather than *reelement* modifies the spiritual conjunction.

47. The generic term "uncommon quality" applied to the bread, wine, body, and blood could be specified as a "sacramental quality."

48. See n. 7.

49. I have chosen not to translate the difficult term *ratio.* Here it means more than "understanding" or "plan" or "rationale," although "rationale" perhaps comes closest.

50. *Responsio,* 33, marginalis 2: "sed quod per omnia spiritualis sit ratio corporis Domini:[sic] in hoc mysterio: quae cum Capernaitarum crassis cogitationibus aperte pugnat." (*Response,* 48: "La difference n'est pas en ceci seulement: mais en ce, qu'en ce mystere nous considerons le corps de Christ d'une Façon du tout Spirituelle, laquelle repugne entierement à erreur grossier des Capernaïtes.") For Luther's understanding of John 6, see Ian D. Siggins, *Martin Luther's Doctrine of Christ* (New Haven: Yale University Press, 1970), 214–21.

51. Ibid., 236–37. Siggins describes Luther's use of these terms and Zwingli's arguments against Luther's doctrine of ubiquity. Siggins also gives a fine explanation of Luther's ambiguous use of *communicatio idiomata* (pp. 230–43).

52. *Responsio,* 35: "Etenim si ratione hypostaticae unionis humanitas quoque Christi ubique est repletive, non idcirco fuerit corpus Christi In, Sub, vel Cum illo sacro pane, neque sanguis, In, Sub, vel Cum illo sacro vino, quia sacram suam Coenam sic instituerit Dominus: sed quoniam non modo cum illo pane & vino, sed etiam cum omnibus rebus ab ipso unionis hypostaticae momento adfuerit & adest, & aderit quandiu res illae stabunt." (*Response,* 50–51: "Car si l'humanité mesmes de nostre Seigneur Iesus Christ à cause de l'union hypostatique, est partout repletivement, c'est à dire, remplissant toutes choses sans estre nulle part compris, il s'ensuiura que, ni le corps de Christ ne sera point Dedans, Soubs ou Avec ce pain Sacré, ni le sang Dedans, Soubs ou Avec ce vin sacré, à cause de l'institution qu'en a faict le Seigneur en instituant sa Saincte Cene, mais d'autant qu'il aura esté, que dés le moment de son union hypostatique, il est et sera present, non seulement avec ce pain et ce vin, mais aussi avec toutes choses tant qu'elles dureront.")

53. See my *Eucharistic Theology of Theodore Beza* for an analysis of Beza's relational doctrine of the presence of Christ in the Lord's Supper.

54. *Responsio,* 36, marginalis 1: "Non quaeritur, quid vos videre, aut non videre positis: sed quid Christus dicat, & iubeat: Accipite, Manducate: Hoc est corpus meum"; p. 37: Nihil his adfert D. Andreas, quod refutationem mereatur." (*Response,* 52: "Il n'est pas question de ce que vous voyez, ou ne voyez pas, mais de ce que Christ a dit et commandé, PRENNEZ, MANGEZ, ceci est mon corps"; p. 53: "Le D. André ne dit ici rien digne de responce.")

55. Ibid., 37: "ut rei fiant corporis et sanguinis Domini: non quae sumpserint, sed quae contempserint. Manducando, non negligendo, aut contemnendo accipiunt iudicium." (*Response,* 54, marginalis 4: "qu'ils sont faicts coulpables du corps et du sang du Seigneur, non pour l'avoir pris, mais pour l'avoir mesprise. Ils prenent leur condamnation, non pas en le mesprisant, mais en le mangeant. 1 Cor. 11.)

56. Ibid., 38: "Nulla est aequivocatio in Praebendi verbo, quum exprimamus non ori sed menti hanc praebitionem fieri. Sacramentalis enim praebitio dicitur in qua aliud videtur, (nempe signum) aliud intelligitur, ac proindi menti praebetur & mente percipitur, nempe res significata. Quod autem menti praebetur ab ea apprehendendum, minime semper necesse est praesens ibi adesse, ubi situm est eius corpus, cuius menti praebetur. Immo interdum ne in rerum quidem natura existere illud oportet ad perceptionis veritatem & efficaciam. Nec enim phantasticum & imaginarium fuit quod de Abrahamo dicitur, illum videlicet, non corporis certe, sed mentis & fidei oculis, diem Domini vidisse, & propterea gavisum. Et patres testatur diserte Paulus eandem atque nos escam edisse, & eundem potum bibisse, nempe Christum: quod oculis fidei subsistant, ea etiam quae sperantur, ex Dei verbo, ac proindi quae reipsa nondum videntur, Heb. 11.1. (*Response,* 54: "Il n'y a aucune ambiguité en ce mot *Presenter,* puis que nous adioustons que ceste presentation se fait, non pas à nostre bouche, mais à nostre ame. Car nous appellons Presentation ou Prebition Sacramentelle, celle en laquelle une chose se presente à nos yeux (a savoir le signe) pour nous en signifier une autre en nostre esprit, laquelle par consequent estant presentee à l'entendement, se reçoit aussi de l'entendement, à savoir la chose signifiee. Or n'est-il pas tousiours necessaire que ce qui est presenté à l'entendement pour estre receu par lui, soit present là où est le corps, à l'entendement duquel il est presenté. . . . Car ce qui est dit d'Abraham n'est point phantastique ni imaginaire, à savoir qu'il a veu le iour du Seigneur non des yeux du corps, mais des yeux de l'esprit et de la foy: et s'en est resioui.")

57. Jean de Montclos, *Lanfranc et Berenger: La controverse eucharistique du XIe siècle* (Louvain: Spicilegium Sacrum Lovaniense, 1971), 171–72. Berengarius was

brought to Rome in 1059 and made to pronounce what is called the "Berengarian Profession of Faith," which contains the following: "Ego Berengarius . . . Consentio autem sanctae Romanae et apostolicae Sedi, et ore et corde profiteor . . . verum corpus et sanguinem Domini nostri Jesu Christi esse, et sensualiter non solum sacramento, sed in veritate manibus sacerdotum tractari, frangi et fidelium dentibus atteri, jurans per sanctam et homousion [*sic*] Trinitatem, et per haec sacrosancta Evangelia."

58. "Essence" and "what it is" are the same.

59. *Responsio,* 40: "Deinde quosum istud sanctorum & Dei coëxistentium exemplum, nisi ut manifestissime appareat, Humanitatem Christi ex hoc ipsius dogmate, in Deitatem manifeste transformari?" (*Response,* 58: "En apres que veut dire autre chose cest exemple de la coëxistence des saincts et de Dieu, sinon pour faire voir tout ouvertement, qu'il transforme par son opinion, l'Humanité de Iesus Christ en la Divinité, sans qu'il s'en puisse excuser?")

60. On the *Ego Berengarius,* see n. 57.

61. *Responsio,* 42: "Immo consubstantiatio, quinam aliter definiri potest in hoc argumento quam Realis duarum essentiarum in terris, id est corporis In, Sub, vel Cum pane, & sanguinis In, Cum, vel Sub vino coniunctio, quantumvis alterius praesentia, nec Physica, nec Localis statuatur? Deinde ut etiam Realem illam praesentiam D. Andreae largiar, annon tamen aderunt panis & vinum ut praesentis corporis & sanguinis, rerum videlicet signatum analogia nisi *sketikè* & relative?" (*Response,* 61: "comment se pourroit autrement definir en cest argument la Consubstantiation, que par la conionction reelle de deux substances en terre, à savoir du corps, Dedans, Dessoubs ou Avec le pain, et du sang Dedans, Avec ou Soubs le vin, encores qu'on ne die que la presence de l'un soit naturelle, ou Locale?") Note that in Latin *essentiarum* is translated by *substances* in the French edition.

62. Ibid., 43: "*effusa dona, in sanctis quidem dimensa, in Christo vero immensa.*" (*Response,* 62: "*ceste Divinité communiquee, sont les dons distribués, aux Saincts par mesure, mais à Christ sans aucune mesure.*"

63. Beza has Andreae on this one, since what is communicated is not proper to the giver, that is, is not a distinguishing mark of the entity involved. Thus what is divine is "proper" to the divinity and cannot be communicated to creatures. This is most evident in the case of limited creatures like saints; the main tradition in Christology also argues that it is the case with the created human nature of Christ. While the human nature can belong to a divine person, it cannot acquire infinite divine properties since it is a finite, created nature.

64. I shall present this section as a dialogue in which Beza first gives his antithesis as Andreae presented it in the *Acta,* followed by Andreae's marginal comment correctly cited by Beza and then answered in his *Responsio.*

65. *Responsio,* 43: "Christo Deo & Homini, nihil esse impossibile, & ipsi profitemur: sed ita, ut huius dicti interpretatio, & quod inde colligitur, ad fidei normam examinetur. Affirmamus ergo primum, istam Omnipotentiam unicam esse, non autem duplicem, quarum una sit increata, Deitati propria, & in nullam rem creatam transferenda: altera creata, quae sit qualitas in Christi humanitatem infusa." (*Response,* 62–63: "Nous croyons aussi et enseignons, que rien n'est impossible à Christ Dieu et Homme: mais en telle sorte qu'il faut que l'exposition de ces mots et ce qu'on en tire par consequence, soit examiné à la regle de la foy. Nous dison donc en premier lieu que ceste Toutepuissance est une, et non pas qu'il y en ait deux, l'une desquelles soit non creée, [*sic*] propre à la Deité, et qui ne se puisse transferer à aucune creature: et l'autre creée qui soit une qualite infuse en l'Humanité de Christ.")

66. Ibid., 44: "Deinde Deum ipsum ita dicimus esse Omnipotentem, quod ad

potestatem per se consideratam attinet, ut tamen ea non possit *Actu,* quae non facere decrevit: aut iis, quae decrevit, contraria sunt. Ratio eius rei est, non quod non sit Omnipotens: sed quia posse mutare voluntatem, ac proinde mutari, non esset potentiae, sed infirmitatis, & eius, qui mentiri posset. In his autem numeramus, corporis Christi immutabilem circunscriptionem [*sic*] & localitatem: quia Deus constituit, ut quod semel assumpsit, nunquam aboleat: quod fieret, si vel ante, vel post glorificationem, simul pluribus, nedum omnibus locis, corporis Christi substantia esse posset."
(*Response,* 63–64: "Dieu est tellement Toutpuissant, eu esgard à la Puissance considerée en soy, que toutesfois elle ne peut faire en EFFECT, [*sic*] les choses qu'elle n'a point deliberé de faire: ou qui sont contraires à ce qu'elle a deliberé. La raison de cela est, non pas qu'il ne soit Toutpuissant mais d'autant que pouvoir changer de volonté, et par consequent estre muable, procede d'infirmité et non pas d'aucune Puissance, et convient à celui qui peut mentir. Nous mettons en ce rang l'immuable circonscription et localité du corps de Christ immuablement borné en ses limites, et contenant un certain lieu, d'autant que Dieu a establi que ce que Christ a une fois pris à soy il ne abolisse iamais: ce qui adviendroit si la substance du corps de Christ pouvoit estre, soit devant, soit apres la glorification, en plusieurs lieux tout ensemble, tant s'en faut qu'elle puisse estre par tout.")
67. See chap. 4, pp. 119–20 for further discussion of this point.
68. *Responsio,* 45–46: "Ecce enim totidem haec D. Brentii verba pag. recognit 46.*Non potest hac ratione inter Christum et Petrum discrimen constitui, ut dicamus Christum Hominem esse Deum quin dicamus Petrum esse Deum. . . .* Et mox. *Ex isto Evangelii dicto, Verbum caro factum est, quod de Christo dici ur* [*sic*] *non de Petro, discrimen Christi et Petri eo statuendum est, quod Filius Dei sua essentia implet hominem Petrum, ut et hominem Christum, non tamen communicat Petro omnes suas proprietates, sed tantum nonullas. Item, Ut in Christo Divi- / nitas tota inhabitat secundum Essentiam, Potentiam et Praesentiam, sic tota inhabitat in Petro.*" (*Response,* 66: "Car à fin qu'on n'en doubte, voici les propres mots du D. Brence. *On ne peut pas mettre difference entre Christ et Pierre en ce regard, que nous disions que Christ Homme, est Dieu, et que nous ne disions pas que Pierre soit Dieu. . . . Et peu apres. De ces mots de l'Evangile, la Parole a esté faicte chair, qui s'entendent de Christ et non pas de Pierre, il faut recueillir la diference qui est entre Christ et Pierre, en ce que le Fils de Dieu remplit de son essence, est homme Pierre, comme il fait Christ Homme, et toutesfois ne communique pas à Pierre toutes ses proprietés, mais seulement quelques unes.*") In his French edition, Beza gave p. 40 as a reference to the *Recognitio;* in the Latin, he gave p. 46. In the copy I have, *Recognitio/ Propheticae & Aposto-/licae Doctrinae, de Vera/ Maiestate Domini Nostri Ie-/su Christi, ad dexteram Dei/ Patris sui omnipo- /tentis. / In hoc Scripto refutatur liber Henrici Bullingeri,/ cui author rirulum fecit: Fundamentum fir-/mum, cui tuto fidelis quivis inniti/ potest, &c.* / Authore Ioanne Brentio. (Tübingen: Ulrich Morhard, 1564), the quotation is from pp. 41–42: "Quod ergo est inter Christum et Petrum discrimen. Uterque enim est homo, et in utroque est Deus. Dicis, illud est discrimen, quod Christus non tantum sit homo, verumetiam Deus: Petrus autem tantum sit homo, et non Deus. Recte. Sed ut melius, quae dicis, intelligam, age recenseamus, quae habent inter se communia, et quae peculiaria: ut cognoscamus, qua in re consistat discrimen. In Christo inhabitat divinitas, eacque tota secundum essentiam, potentiam et praesentiam. Sed et sic tota inhabitat in Petro. Ubicuncque enim est Deus, ibi totus est, quippe qui sit simplicissimus, nec dividatur in partes, ut pars Dei sit in Petro, pars in Philippo, pars in Bartholomaeo. Non potest igitur hac ratione inter Christum et Petrum discrimen esse, ut dicamus, Christum hominem esse Deum. Petrum au- / tem non esse Deum."

69. *Responsio,* 46: "Sed & ipse D. Andreas, In Apol. adversus theses Ingolstadianas, *inter inhabitationem dei in sanctis et in Christo,* (inquit) UNUM *est discrimen, quod Sanctis distribuat sua dona dimensa, Christo vero immensa."*

70. Brenz, *Recognitio,* 38–40: "Nam si filius Dei habet suam omnipotentiam communem cum filio hominis, quae in unam personam assumpsit, nihil amplius aut vetat aut impedit, quo minus habeat etiam cum ipso communem omnipresentiam suam. . . . Quare cum filius Dei in incarnatione contulerit in filium hominis omnipotentiam suam, negari non potest, quin etiam contulerit in eum omnipraesentiam suam, et evexerit ipsum in eam maiestatem, qua omnia coram praesens intuetur et gubernat. . . . Nam si non piget Cinglianos, Philosophica sua somnia de finito et infinito, et de mensura capacitatis identidem inculcare, cur nos pigeret coelestia spiritus sancti oracula, semper nobis ob oculos ponere, ne quis nos per Philosophiam et inanem deceptionem depraedetur? . . . Maxime ergo omnium docet, quod humanitas Christi non solum ea sit capacitate, ut facta sit omnipotens, verumetiam, ut facta sit omnipraesens. Si enim caro Christi facta est capax verbi, . . . quod non etiam facta esset capax omnipotentiae et omnipraesentiae?"

71. This is a more important point, and more debatable, than either Beza or Andreae realized or, as may have been the case, cared to discuss. While an instrument has its own strength, as the tensile strength of a saw, it works because of the communicated strength of the primary cause. Thus a saw cuts only because it is applied to the wood by the carpenter. The effective agent is the carpenter, and in a sense it is the strength and intelligence of the carpenter, who uses an appropriate instrument, that is communicated to that instrument so that it can do the work intended by the primary agent. The same is true of the divine and human natures in Christ. The human nature is an *instrumentum coniunctum* and thus works divinely. Sacraments are also instruments, but not conjoined. The eucharist presents a peculiar kind of sacrament since the bread and wine are separate instruments through which the conjoined instrument of Christ's body is made present. It is indeed curious to see which of the medieval doctrines and traditions Beza and Andreae choose to use and which they prefer to ignore.

72. *Responsio,* 49: "*datur annulus absolute propter annulum & nulla est significatio: datur ad investiendum de haereditate aliqua & signum est, ita ut iam dicere possit qui accipit, annulus non valet quidquam, sed haereditas est, quam quaerebam. In hunc itaque modum passioni appropians Dominus, de gratia sua investire curavit suos, ut invisibilis gratia, signo aliquo praestaretur."* (*Response,* 71–72.)

73. *Acta,* 63. Andreae continued the Bernard quotation to show that it referred to the ordination of priests and the consecration of bishops. Andreae then argued that Bernard taught the same real presence of Christ in the eucharist as did Andreae: "Tria quippe in Sacramento altaris attendere debes, speciem panis, veritatem carnis, et virtutem gratiae spiritualis. Hactenus Bernhardi verba."

74. *Acta,* 145. Andreae quoted the Corpus Christi hymn: "Sic in Coena Domini sumit unus, sumunt mille, tantum iste quantum ille; sumunt boni, sumunt mali; sorte tamen INAEQUALE; et sumptus non consumitur: sicut dictum pium et vetus sonat."

75. In the Latin edition (p. 50), at the end of his response to the marginalia on thesis X, Beza added a brief refutation of Andreae's fourth point. This is one of the few instances in which the Latin edition of 1588 adds material to the French edition of 1587.

76. *Responsio,* 54: "Quod amplius? Si nobis non credit D. Andreas, credat Suevico Syntagmati, id est ipsi D. Brentio nondum Ubiquitario, cuius verba sunt. *Remotus quidem erat agni paschalis tempore Christus ab auribus et ab oculis carnalibus,*

praesentissimus tamen erat fidei, quae motis alis suis ex hoc mundo in Spiritualem transvolat, ac pro natura visus Dei, quae Christi sunt videbat. Sicut enim Deus omnia etiam futura sibi praesentia videt: ita fides rem longissime pro mundi captu positam sibi praesentissimam facit & videt."

77. Brenz 3:41–56.

78. *Responsio*, pp. 59–60.

79. *Responsio*, 62–63: "Ludit Sophistice D. Andreas in Christi appellatione pro Christi Humanitate. Christum enim alioqui, licet verum Deum & Hominem, neque ab humanitate sua unquam separatum, tamen non secundum carnis essentiam, sed sua divinitate, non tantum Essentialiter, sed etiam peculiari energia & gratia in sanctis suis habitare (cuius gratiae tessera & pignus est Coena Domini) quis Christianus negarit? Sed & caelitus Christum humanitatis illius suae imperio & potestate Ecclesiam regere, & membra sua adhuc in terris posita sui Spiritus virtute fovere & mirabiliter conservare, quisnam Christianus inficiatur?" (*Response*, 93: "Le D. André se ioue du mot de Christ, en le prenant pour l'Humanité de Christ. Car qui est le Chrestien, qui ait iamais nié que Iesus Christ, quoy qu'il soit vray Dieu et vray Homme, et non iamais separé de son Humanité, habite en ses saincts? non pas selon l'Essence de sa chair, mais par sa divinité: et ce non par s'unir en Essence, mais par une vertu et grace particuliere, de laquelle la Saincte Cene nous est un certain gage et tesmoignage: et qui est d'avantage le vray Chrestien, qui ait iamais nié, que Iesus Christ selon l'auctorité et puissance de son Humanité, ne gouverne du ciel son Eglise, et entretienne et conserve miraculeusement ses membres qui sont encores ici en la terre, en les conservant par la vertu de son S. Esprit?")

80. Further discussion of these points is better left to chap. 4.

81. *Responsio*, 71, marginalis 3: "Sublata hac intrinseca vi sacramentali: substantia sacramenti dissolvitur." (*Response*, 107: "Cest vertu Sacramentele interieure estant ostée, la substance du Sacrement est renversée.")

82. *Responsio*, 75–77: "*1) Sacramentum Coenae Domini constare duabus rebus, nempe Signis et Rebus significatis. 2) Signa esse, ex Domini institutione, panem et vinum: Res autem significatas, illud ipsum corpus traditum pro nobis, et illum ipsum sanguinem pro nobis effusum. 3) Beneficia Christi in legitimo sacrae huius actionis usu non esse separata ab ipso Christo, a quo proficiscuntur. 4) Haec signa et res significatas non alia ratione quam coniunctione Sacramentali copulari. 5) Quod ad Deum nobiscum paciscentem attinet, et semper veracem, nunquam nuda esse signa, sed utraque haec Sacramentaliter six coniuncta, vere semper quibusvis accedentibus, sive dignis sive indignis praeberi. 6) Hoc sensu, id est huius Sacramentalis coniunctionis respectu veteres patres dixisse, corpus Domini esse In, Sub et Cum pane. In his autem non consensum est. 1) Quod Reverendi Domini collocutores Wirtembergenses censent in Sacramentali coniunctione tam signa, quam res significatas suis substantiis et re ipsa in terris, quamvis non physice nec localiter, tamen vere simul et inseparabiliter copulari: ac proinde ori quorumvis, sive dignorum, sive indignorum accedentium exhiberi. Collocutores autem alterius partis in coniunctione Sacramentali, quam duntaxat relativam faciunt, docent res significatas, id est corpus et sanguinem Domini, non alibi nunc quam in coelis esse et permanere, quorum signa sunt in terris, ac proinde illas quidem menti, ista vero ori quorumvis accedentium praeberi. 2) Istis phrasibus, In, Cum, et Sub pane et vino R.D. collocutores Wirtembergenses intelligi censent illam suam Sacramentalem coniunctionem realem Substantiarum in terris, qua fiat, ut utraque illa, nempe Signa quidem Physice et localiter: corpus autem et sanguis Domini, nec Physice nec localiter, sed imperscrutabili quodam modo vere et simul in terris adsint, et ori quorumvis accedentium praebeantur. Alterius autem partis Collocutores docent, illis phrasibus*

nullam aliam coniunctionem, quam illam relativam exprimi. In altero autem capite de perceptione Sacramentali Signorum et rerum significatarum consensus est. *1) Signa, sicut quibusvis, sive dignis sive indignis accedentibus praebentur, ita a quibusvis sumentibus ore recipi, a dignis quidem ad vitam, ab indignis vero ad condemnationem. 2) Solam Spiritualem perceptionem per fidem, et digne accedentium propriam, quae res significatas accipiant, esse salvificam. 3) Perceptionis illius rerum significatarum modum esse imperscrutabilem, et, ut loquitur Paulus, vere mysterium magnum et adorandum non perscrutandum,* In hoc autem non est consensus. *Quod R.D. Collocutores Wirtembergenses, sicut utraque simul et inseparabiliter, ut dictum est ori quorumvis accedentium praeberi censent: sic etiam credunt a quibusvis eodem oris instrumento, nec tamen (quod ad res significatas attinet) physico et locali, sed imperscrutabili modo percipi, a dignis quidem ad vitam, ab indignis ad condemnationem. Alterius autem partis Collocutores docent, sicut soli menti res signatae praebentur: ita a solis fidelibus, (ut qui soli unicum illud mentis instrumentum afferant, quo Christus cum suis beneficiis apprehenditur) spiritualiter percipi: ac proinde indignos fieri reos corporis et sanguinis Domini, non quod illa indigne sumpserint, sed quod ea per suam incredulitatem et impoenitentiam repudiarint."*

83. *Epitome / Colloquii / montisbelgartensis / inter D. Iacobum Andreae et D. / Theodorum Bezam, Anno Domini 1586. / Mense Martio celebrati. / In qua Ecclesia Christi fide- / liter monetur, ut ab horribilibus erroribus Calvinistarum / sibi caveat: quos illi de infrà scriptis articulis / fovent, atq. summo studiio propa- / gare conantur.* (Tübingen: George Gruppenbach, 1586). [Note the addition of two categories that were not debated at Montbéliard nor addressed by Beza in any of his works on the colloquy.

84. See chap. 4, n. 60, for the French title.

85. *Kurzer Begriff / des Mümpelgarti- / schen colloquii oder Gesprächs welches / zwischen* D. Iacobo Andreae, *unnd* D, Theodoro / Beza, um Martio des 1586 Jars ist gehalten / worden. / *Darinnen die Kirch Christi trewlich ver- / warnet würdt sich zuhüten vor den grewlichenn / irtthumen der Calvinisten welche sie von den nach= / volgenden Articeln haben.* . . . Gestellt / Durch Iacobum Andreae D. Probst / unnd Canzlern zu Tübingen. Tubingen bey Georg Gruppenbach. 1588. [This edition contains the same two additional categories as the Latin above.]

4

The Person of Christ

The doctrine of the person of Christ became the major theological sticking point between Reformed and Lutheran theologians in the second half of the sixteenth century. From the Maulbronn Colloquy of 1564 through the bitter battles about the meaning of *kenosis* in the first quarter of the seventeenth century, discussions of the Lord's Supper, which meant discussions of the manner of Christ's presence, became christological arguments. Reformed and Lutheran theologians affirmed the presence of the person of Christ and agreed that Christ offered himself to communicants who received the bread and wine. The arguments began when one asked in what way communicants were thereby related to the human and divine natures of Christ, which quickly became the question of the relation of the natures of Christ to each other and to Christ's person.

The arguments did not end there, however. Although both Lutherans and Reformed agreed that faithful communicants received the body and blood of Christ,[1] they fought over where and how this occurred and over the language used to express their beliefs. During the course of the long polemical wars, both sides accused one another of ancient heresies and cited patristic and scholastic sources to bolster their arguments. Neither side succeeded in persuading the other (or, it seems, many of their audiences or readers) to change a theological position previously held. The people of Montbéliard remained true to the doctrine that had first converted them.

The Colloquy of Montbéliard provides an example not only of the relation of politics to religion in this troubled time but also of the polemical debate that went on in the period among Protestants and also between each of the major Protestant churches and the Catholics, especially in the empire. The Counter-Reformation gained momentum after the last session of the Council of Trent (1562–1563), and its advocates took a leaf from the Reformers' book and staged debates as a means of trying to persuade princes and the councils of free imperial cities to remain steadfast Catholics or return to the Catholic fold. Of course the Protestants worked just as hard to maintain and even to increase the areas they had already gained, often by the means of public debates so effective in the past. Nor could the Protestants' common need to unite against the Catholics, strengthened by the doctrinal and reform decrees of Trent, provide sufficient motivation to overcome theological differences.

110

On the contrary, the polemics between Protestant groups were often more acrimonious than those between Protestants and Catholics. Certainly the polemical exchanges during the Colloquy of Montbéliard were bitter; those carried on through the resulting publications were still more condemnatory and unyielding.

Because of the length of the debate over the person of Christ and because the pattern of the colloquy has already been laid out in chapter 3, I shall provide here a summary and analysis of each side rather than give a blow-by-blow description. According to Andreae's *Acta,* The Württemberg team presented twenty-one theses. These were followed by eight propositions ascribed to the Reformed and considered by Andreae to be "contrary to Scripture." Beza presented no theses on the person of Christ but only responses to the Lutheran theses and propositions. His responses were printed in the *Acta,* accompanied by Andreae's marginal comments. Beza's answers to Andreae's marginalia formed his 1587 *Responsio,*[2] to which Andreae replied in his 1588 *Epitome.*[3] The *Epitome* rarely advanced a new argument; its burden was polemical to a degree worthy of comment in its proper place.[4]

The Württemberg Christology

The differences among Lutherans regarding the person of Christ were acknowledged in the Formula of Concord, and the blame for those differences was placed on the sacramentarians, beginning with Zwingli at the Marburg Colloquy of 1529.[5] The "majesty" of Christ was also discussed in the Formula of Concord,[6] as one would expect when its two principal authors were Jacob Andreae and Martin Chemnitz. Indeed, the majesty of Christ provided the concept within which the *communicatio idiomatum* could be explained, and although it does not go as far as Andreae went in his *Acta,* the formula claimed that properties are shared between the natures of Christ.[7] It quoted lengthy passages from Luther, who, although he asserted a communication of properties between the natures, did not make that communication direct but only through the person of Christ.[8] To this principle the *Formula* remained true.[9] Thus far, Lutherans and Reformed could agree on the communication of properties in the person of Christ, but they were driven to disagree regarding the application of that doctrine to the Lord's Supper.

The twenty-one Württemberg theses (A) may be summarized under eight points:

1. The Son of God, the Word, assumed a human nature consisting of a soul and body so that the one person of Christ possesses two natures, a divine nature to which is attributed infinite properties and a human nature with finite properties.
2. The two natures retain their proper essences and are not mixed or confused, nor do they form a third entity as, for example when sugar and water are mixed into hydromel or sugar water.

3. In addition to the human nature Christ received from Mary, he also received gifts proper to his office as mediator and through which even his human nature is endowed above the angels and all other human beings.
4. While the divine and human natures are not mixed but remain distinct, they belong to the person of Christ to whom their properties[10] are communicated and of whom the properties of both natures may be predicated. The fathers of the church called this communication of properties a *communicatio idiomatum.*
5. This true and real (that is, not merely verbal) communication of properties does not allow the human nature of Christ to stand by itself apart from the person of Christ nor to alter its essence so that it is equal to the divine nature. Nevertheless, the personal union of the natures allows for divine properties, such as omnipotence, omniscience, omnipresence, and vivifying power not only to be predicated of but to be communicated really to Christ's human nature, which therefore participates in these divine properties without losing its distinctive humanity.
6. During his life on earth, Christ exercised the properties of one nature and of the other according to his will. Thus the *majesty of Christ* (which includes his omnipotence, and so on, revealed at his resurrection and ascension and expressed in the term "seated at the right hand of the Father") was veiled during the time of his servanthood on earth but was not lost at any time. In his miracles, flashes of Christ's majesty were revealed even during his life on earth.
7. Thus it is truly said that the Word was made flesh, that God suffered on the cross, and that Jesus raised the dead and redeemed humankind. For the one person of the Son of God made flesh did these things and is to be adored even in his humanity.
8. It is also the Son of God made flesh who is everywhere present in the church and especially in the Holy Supper, in which his body and blood are given to be eaten by all who take the bread and wine.

Following the twenty-one theses (reduced to the eight given above) were the doctrines which the Württemberg theologians believed were taught by the Calvinists and which the Lutherans condemned (B). These were eight in number but may be summed up in the following five points:

1. The *communicatio idiomatum* is merely verbal, not real, so that the humanity of Christ does not share in the omnipresence of the divinity.
2. It follows from (1) that "God suffers" means only that the humanity of Christ suffered.
3. The logical result of this teaching is the heresy of Nestorius: There are two Christs. Beza therefore implies a human Christ who suffers and a divine Christ who does not suffer.
4. The Calvinists are also guilty of Arianism because the divinity in Christ is subject to growth and decline and made less than the divinity of the Father, while the person of Christ is made a median (*medius*) between the divinity and human beings.

5. The humanity of Christ does not share divine attributes and therefore his flesh is not to be adored.

The theses and the statements were written out and signed by Jacob Andreae and Lucas Osiander.

The Reformed Response[11]

Beza, in the name of his companions, agreed to the first two theses. He chose to read into the third (contained in A2) a formula that Andreae disapproved in a marginal remark, namely that "the properties never depart from their subjects." To agree to this reading of thesis III would be to accept the Reformed position that the divine and human properties are not shared between the natures of Christ but only through the person of Christ. Beza attempted the same tactic in response to thesis IV (A3). Beza interpreted it to mean that the Lutherans distinguished between the "grace of union," by which "that man is God," and "habitual grace," which is the seat of those gifts with which Christ is endowed above all other creatures. Andreae's *marginalis* protests that the nature of the grace of union is exactly what is in dispute.

Andreae's thesis V allowed for a communication of properties by which is attributed to the whole person what is proper to either nature. The thesis went on to declare that what is proper to one nature can be said of the other. If no more than the first part were claimed, the Reformed and the Lutherans would have had nothing to dispute. But Beza interpreted even this part of the thesis in his own terms. He took the person of Christ to be the same as the person of the mediator, of whom divine and human attributes indeed may be predicated. As to the second part, Beza continued to deny that what is proper to one nature may be attributed to the other nature. All attribution must be in the concrete, he argued; it must be to the person, Christ. It may not be predicated in the abstract, that is, from the humanity to the divinity or vice versa. To this assertion, Andreae reacted by filling the margin with objections and arguments. All of the marginalia may be reduced to an insistence on a real communication of attributes from the divine nature to the human nature and a rejection of Beza's insistence that attribution be to a concrete subject only. Beza claimed that Andreae's incomprehension of correct Christology stemmed from his incomprehension of the difference between concrete and abstract terms.[12] In his *Responsio,* Beza expanded on this difference using Thomistic arguments and even citing Thomas Aquinas.[13] Beza wrote that the word *humanity,* which is abstract, represents human nature as it is in itself, distinct by its essential properties from all other natures. Furthermore, these properties are inherent in human nature as in a subject from which they may not depart. The concept *humanity* is forged by the understanding that abstracts it from individuals or even from one individual by setting aside individuation or subsistence. The individual or individuals are then said to belong to the species "human being."[14]

The argument, as presented in the *Acta,* did not advance until Beza responded to theses VIII and IX taken together. There Beza argued that Andreae confused the hypostatic union with its effects. Within the union, that is to say, in the person of Christ, there is a real communication of properties since both divine and human natures, with their properties, belong to the person of Christ the mediator. But the effects of the union do not include a communication between the natures so that the humanity can be ubiquitous, omnipotent, and so on. That is why the Reformed say that the communication of properties is verbal, that is, a matter of predication. The Reformed taught that it is correct, therefore, to say that in Christ God suffered and that Christ the man redeemed sinners, raised the dead, and so on. Andreae objected to this argument and this time accused Beza of the Samosatian heresy, labeling both Paul of Samosata and Beza as those who deny the communication of properties.[15]

Andreae's thesis X used the similes of incandescent iron[16] and the union of soul and body to exemplify the exchange of properties in the hypostatic union. Beza said that Andreae employed these similes inappropriately and not as the fathers had used them, namely to indicate likenesses, not to provide exact equivalents. The communication of properties in burning iron and even in the soul's animation of the body cannot be taken as duplicates of the hypostatic union. In the similes, Beza explained, both elements are created; in the hypostatic union, a finite reality is united to an infinite being. Beza concluded that the two natures (*ousiae*) must be kept distinct but not separate in the person of Christ. There is one Christ, Beza argued, who possesses two wills and actualities (*energiae*), two realizations (*energemata*), but only one result (*apotelesma*) since the person is unique. This is the way, said Beza, to understand Athanasius and therefore to remain orthodox.

Andreae responded by saying that the two natures in Christ perform actions that are not divided but rather are directed to one end. Although the point was debated later in the colloquy, the issue here is that the functions of the natures are united, therefore the natures themselves must share properties. Because Beza insisted that the two natures and their actions must be kept distinct but not separated, Andreae accused Beza of Nestorianism and said that Athanasius never taught that the two natures of Christ produce two actions. The refusal of either collocutor to hear the nuances of the other's argument is painfully clear.

In response to thesis XI,[17] Beza discussed habitual grace, which, he said, sums up the gifts given to Christ's created nature. Among the gifts are Christ's power, which in the divinity is absolute and infinite but in the humanity is a created gift. In the marginal note, Andreae denied that Christ's power should be enumerated among his created gifts. Beza cited Cyril, Gregory of Nyssa, and Damascene[18] in support of his view; Andreae denied that the Orthodox Fathers said any such thing and added Tertullian to the list. Andreae accused Beza of taking whatever suited his argument from the Fathers instead of reading them honestly. The example used by Damascene was the raising of Lazarus. Beza understood Damascene to say that the divinity in Christ raised Lazarus while the humanity wept. But because the divinity and the humanity belong to the one person Christ, one can say that God wept and Jesus the man raised Lazarus from the dead. Andreae argued rather that the power of the divinity would not have raised Lazarus without the human nature and that when the man cried, God also wept even though it is not proper to God to cry.[19]

The same basic arguments are then given with regard to the other properties disputed during the colloquy: Christ's knowledge, presence, ability to vivify, and, as a corollary, the appropriateness of the adoration of Christ's humanity. In the course of the dialogue, however, some points require comment. Among these is the dispute over Phillippians 2:5–11 and the interpretation of the term "form of a servant." The Württembergers taught that the term meant the hiding or "exinanition" of the divine majesty communicated to Christ's humanity from the moment of his incarnation. As Andreae put it, "The form of a servant is not the humanity, but the servile condition of the man Christ."[20] Andreae and Chemnitz taught that during Christ's life on earth, he hid his divine properties, summed upon under the term *majesty,* except for such moments as the Transfiguration and the working of miracles. This voluntary suppression of manifestations of his divinity amounted to Christ's putting on the "form of a servant." When he ascended into heaven to sit at the right hand of the Father, he put off the form of a servant and began the period of his manifest majesty or glory. Christ in glory manifests his majesty by exercising the fullness of his powers, which include omnipotence, omniscience, and omnipresence.

Against this doctrine, Beza affirmed that "the form of a servant" refers to Christ's humanity just as "the form of God" refers to the divinity. Beza interpreted "form" as "essence" or "nature," not as "appearance" or "likeness." As a man on earth and even now in his glory, said Beza, Christ's humanity remains finite, however gifted with knowledge and power. Christ never put off, indeed cannot be divorced from, the form of a servant, namely his humanity, which is forever in the created, finite form of a servant, that is, a human being. Christ's humility in his incarnation was indeed rewarded by resurrection and glory, but in his manhood, that is to say, in his human nature and therefore as God's creature. His divinity, hidden from his incarnation until his resurrection, could be manifested but not augmented, humbled, or glorified. The divine form or nature remains eternally infinite in all its properties.

Related to the interpretation of the "form of the servant" is the question of the gifts given the man Jesus Christ. Andreae distinguished an absolute ubiquity proper to the infinite essence and a participated ubiquity that the infinite essence may share with a finite nature united to it. Understood in this way, such divine properties are not against but above the nature privileged to share in them.

This teaching could also be interpreted by Beza to mean that while the Holy Spirit does indeed indwell the faithful, the finite capacity of each determines the finite dimensions of the accompanying gifts; what is given from uncreated largesse is received as created gift. Beza's interpretation, in fact, has much in common with that of Peter Lombard.[21] The vocabulary of the scholastics and of Beza speaks of Christ's grace of union, which is unique to the God-Man and of further created gifts proper to Christ's human nature.

Andreae, on the other hand, taught explicitly that the same Holy Spirit dwells in the man Christ and in holy persons who are Christ's members, "but not by one and the same participation or communication. For in the man Christ, all are without measure, that is, uncreated, immense, and infinite. In all other holy men, Christ's members, all are created, measured, finite, communicated gifts."[22] The man Christ therefore is able, like the Holy Spirit, to be ubiquitous. Andreae attempted to prove his argument by an interesting syllogism:

> Whoever fills all, is everywhere present.
> The man assumed by the Son of God in the unity of person fills all.
> Therefore that assumed man is present everywhere.[23]

The syllogism is interesting on two counts. Its second premise assumes that its terms are given or at least accepted, while it is precisely the nub of the argument between Andreae and Beza. Secondly, the use of the term *assumptus homo* sounds an alarm. The usual term, after the acceptance of Damascene's enhypostatic position, is *assumed humanity* because *man* points to a complete individual, which includes a human person. It is not *a* man, therefore, but rather the *humanity* of Christ that was assumed by the person of the Word as Beza often repeated. The danger of Nestorianism, as understood by both Andreae and Beza, lurks in the term *assumed man* more clearly than in Beza's insistence that the natures of Christ be kept distinct but not separate.[24]

With regard to the presence of Christ, Beza said that all the gifts given Christ were above nature, or "hyperphysical," and not contrary to nature, or "antiphysical." But to possess any infinite attribute is to demolish the nature of the creature, absorbing it in the nature of the creator who alone is infinite. In other words, said Beza, an infinite attribute cannot be shared except in a finite form, which is a contradiction, a lie, and therefore an impossibility since God is Truth. Beza said that to be a true man, Christ must have had on earth and continue to have in heaven a circumscribed local presence. The human nature of Christ cannot share in the ubiquity of the divine nature. Beza insisted further that those created gifts given Christ such as his knowledge and grace were subject to growth as Matthew 24 says: "He grew in wisdom and grace." These gifts reached their fullest when Christ entered into glory, but even then they did not become infinite since Christ retained his finite human nature.

On the contrary, Andreae argued in the margin, the communication of the divine majesty has nothing to do with circumscription, nor does it abolish the human nature but rather exalts it into the highest grade of glory at the right hand of God.[25]

Along the same line, Andreae and Beza agreed that Christ is adorable.[26] But Beza denied that the human nature, as distinct from the person of Christ, is to be adored. Andreae insisted that the humanity of Christ is adorable because it is united to the divinity in the person of Christ. In this instance, Beza accused Andreae of Nestorianism because he seemed to make a separate entity of Christ's humanity.

In close connection with these arguments is one that occurred further on in the colloquy but has its logical place here, namely, whether the humanity of Christ is capable of infinite gifts: *finitum capax infiniti aut non?* The discussion occurred within the context of the hypostatic union and its identity with (Beza) or distinction from (Andreae) the communication of properties. By claiming that the union and the communication are the same, Beza sought to preserve the integrity of the natures as natures and the communication of properties only to the person of Christ. The distinction on which Andreae insisted was one that posed the hypostatic union as first in the order of causes even though it was simultaneous with the communication of properties, which, in terms of causality, followed the union and was therefore distinct from it. In this context, Andreae insisted also that the human nature was able to receive divine properties.[27] Since this is a complicated argument and is also exemplary of controversial theology at the end of the sixteenth century, I shall reproduce it here.

BEZA: If by communication you mean the union, I concede that not only omnipotence, but also the rest of the attributes are communicated to the human nature. Therefore since the human nature is united with the divine, and God and man are one person, therefore it [humanity] is also united with omnipotence, since it cannot be separated from the Deity.

ANDREAE: As I declared and demonstrated above, the union of the natures and the communication of properties differ in many ways. For the communication of properties is like the effect and consequence [of the union]. Even though they are simultaneous in time, in the order of nature they are related as prior and subsequent.

On the other hand, since the union of natures is not a bare and simple union, but a true and real communication, by which the divine gives, and the human receives, thus the communication of properties is not such a union, by which nothing proper to the natures may be communicated to the other, but rather a true and real communication, by which the word has communicated himself and all that is his to his assumed nature.

BEZA: Union and communication are one;[28] and as suffering is not communicated to the divine nature so that it has it IN ITSELF, thus also omnipotence is not communicated to the humanity in Christ so that it [the humanity] has it IN ITSELF. Otherwise the Deity is crucified; thus the humanity is made omnipotent. But since the former is not the case, neither is it the case that the humanity is made omnipotent as you claim.

ANDREAE: I have sufficiently demonstrated that the union of the natures and the communication of idioms or properties are not one and the same. As I said above, because of the diversity of the natures, there is no common basis for these propositions that the divinity is crucified and the humanity is made omnipotent. And what is more, I have shown that it is not the same thing to say that the human nature is made omnipotent and that the divinity is made passible or was crucified.

For because of the immutability of the divine nature, it receives IN ITSELF neither perfection nor imperfection. But human nature IN ITSELF is able to receive, and in the person of the Son of God, it truly receives the highest majesty which is proper to the deity: as I have declared in the words of the Holy Fathers.[29]

In other words, Andreae posited different modes of the *communicatio idiomatum* for the humanity and for the divinity so that the union of the natures and the communication of properties could not be identical. Beza countered with the doctrine that the hypostatic union is the same for both natures since each belongs equally to the person of Christ. This is true, said Beza, even though the assuming nature excels infinitely the assumed nature and even though the self-subsisting Word provides subsistence for the humanity. Andreae denied that the basis of the communication is the same because the divinity is unchangeable and therefore can receive nothing whether perfect or imperfect, while the humanity is changeable and so may receive whatever the divinity communicates to it.[30]

In answer to one of the dogmatic statements attributed by Andreae to the Reformed and declared contrary to Scripture, Beza condemned and rejected a merely verbal communication of properties because it would imply that the hypostatic union was not real. On the other hand, he also condemned the idea that the two natures shared properties. Beza affirmed that while the basis of the hypostatic union and of the communication of properties is the same because both pertain to the unity of the person, nevertheless what that means for each nature, even in the union itself, is very different. The assumed human nature receives its very subsistence from the Word, the Logos.[31]

The Logos, as Second Person of the Trinity, is not subject to change and therefore the humanity can add nothing to it, continued Beza. The appropriate way to understand the words *God suffered* is to say that God, that is, the flesh united to the deity, suffered. Or again, one may affirm that Christ is all-powerful, that is to say, that the deity united to the humanity is all-powerful. This is not to divide the persons as did Nestorius but to divide and hold distinct the natures that are inseparably united in the person of Christ. By this last statement, Beza claimed he avoided the heresy of Eutyches, who failed to distinguish the natures in Christ but rather reduced the humanity to the divinity. Beza then quoted Luther's sermon for Christmas Day based on the first chapter of the Epistle to the Hebrews: "The humanity of Christ is like that of another holy and natural man, for he did not always think, say, will and argue as though he were some omnipotent man. Those who make him thus imprudently confound the two natures and their operations."[32]

To this Andreae claimed that Beza was damned out of his own mouth because he did not merely distinguish but separated the two natures of Christ. With regard to the text from Luther, Andreae said that that quotation referred only to Christ in the state of exinanition, that is to say, when his majesty was hidden under the "form of a servant."

In relation to the Lord's Supper, an important distinction is made by the two collocutors. Andreae claimed that Christ's presence in the Lord's Supper is due to the hypostatic union because through it his humanity participates in the divine omnipotence and omnipresence. Beza countered that he did not attribute the sacramental presence of Christ to the hypostatic union but rather to the words of institution by which Christ established the sacrament.

The Continuing Discussion on the Person of Christ

It is interesting to note that throughout the *Acta,* the length of Andreae's speeches compared with Beza's is at least four lines to one and often it is an even greater proportion—as much as four pages to a few lines. Beza, in the preface to his published *Responsio,*[33] complained that Andreae had enriched his own remarks while changing Beza's for the worse. If, however, the *Acta* provide even a partially accurate picture of what actually took place, Andreae held the floor at length while Beza sometimes responded in a dozen words or less.[34] As Andreae opened the discussion on the person of Christ, he tried to fix blame for the christological controversy on the Reformed. Andreae said that it all began when the Reformed denied that Christ can will to be bodily where he wishes. Andreae claimed that the Reformed denied not only the power of Christ the man but also the absolute power of God. Andreae cited Peter Martyr and Lambert Danaeus[35] as well as Beza,[36] each of whom said that God could not will Christ's body to be in many places at the same time. And indeed the Reformed did argue that God cannot will a contradiction since that would be against God's truth. A body, they argued, because of its corporal nature, must be located in one place at one time.

From the Middle Ages through the sixteenth century, the principle of contradiction held whether it was interpreted through the *via antiqua* or the *via moderna.* In the first interpretation, the principle of noncontradiction was based on the nature of the Creator; in the second interpretation, it was based upon the created order that God chose to establish. Both traditions, however, allowed for the miraculous contravention of the natural order as in the Roman Catholic doctrine of transubstantiation, which posited a miraculous existence of the accidents of bread and wine after the substance in which they inhered was changed into the substance of the body and blood of Christ. Neither Andreae nor Beza entered into the philosophical basis of his own argument, nor does either speak of the "miraculous" so much as of the "supernatural" or "hyperphysical." Andreae, however, indicated that he favored the *via moderna* when he used the phrase common to that tradition, *potentia absoluta.*[37] But even in the "modernist" tradition, the absolute power of God to do other than he has done was discussed to establish the contingency of creation, not to posit two powers in God or the existence of some order other than the created order.[38] Andreae was probably not referring to the medieval doctrine but rather to an idea of God's power that derived from it, namely, that God could countermand the created order and even support what, to the human reason, is a contradiction, namely, that something finite can receive something infinite.[39]

The problem was not new in the late sixteenth century; it had long roots stemming from the first christological controversies regarding the union of the divine and human natures in Christ. *Finitum infiniti capax* (*aut non capax*) was also discussed with regard to infused charity: Was it created (grace) or uncreated (the Holy Spirit)? Behind such questions was the problem of the necessity or flexibility of created natures, hence the problem of God and contradictions. Can God make a contradiction? Can God make a stone without gravity, a fire that does not burn, water that runs up? The *via antiqua* said that God must be true to the divine nature; because creation reflects the Creator, action follows nature. To allow a creature to act contrary to its nature would be to lie, that is, to declare something to be other than it is. Something that rises rather than falls is possible, but it is not possible to call it a stone. Something that gives light but does not burn is possible, but it is not fire. The *via moderna,* on the contrary, taught that the stability of creation is due to God's will, not to God's own nature. God, *potentia ordinata,* will not make fire that does not burn, but that is not because it is impossible to God, who could choose (*potentia absoluta*) to make stones without weight, water that runs up, and fire that does not burn. Beza's Christology followed the *via antiqua:* A finite nature cannot share infinite properties, nor can properties of one nature be shared with another without destroying both natures. Andreae's doctrine of ubiquity relied on the purely speculative side of the *via moderna:* The finite can participate in infinite properties, nor would such a sharing alter the specificity of either nature. I say "speculative" because, in practice, the modernists based their theology on the *potentia ordinata* and the *pactum,* or covenant, God made with the church that the sacraments would be effective, that is, that God's promise to the church and the sacramental sine qua non *causality* would not be arbitrarily or capriciously curtailed or altered.[40]

Beza's Christology followed the *via antiqua* in other ways as well. He insisted on an enhypostatic Christology[41] in which the person of the Word assumed an apersonal human nature for which the person of the Word provided a subsistence that supported the integrity of the human nature. The person of the Word was therefore the person of Christ, who possessed two integral natures. Communication of the powers of those natures was directly only to the person; the natures could not share with each other. The integrity of each nature would be destroyed by this mixing of the infinite and the finite. On this point, Beza praised the scholastics and linked the integrity of Christ's two natures to the truthfulness of God.[42]

Andreae declared that the omnipresence of the humanity of Christ posits contraries rather than contradictories and hence is not against the rule of truth. God does not will contradictories, that something should be and not be at the same time. But contraries can be and not be at same time *in diverse ways.* Thus it would be contradictory and therefore false to say that Christ's humanity is both local and illocal. But it is true to say that Christ's humanity is local in one way and illocal in another. Human nature is local but in Christ, by reason of the person of the Son of God, it is also illocal; it shares in the illocality of God. Thus while the human properties of Christ always remain and the risen humanity of Christ is locally and circumscriptively in heaven, that same humanity is illocally on earth because it is united to the person of the Son of God. Therefore there is no *contradiction* here, but rather *contraries,* which can be said of the same thing, not simply but in different respects.[43] Andreae thereby defended the communication of properties between the natures of Christ.

In the *Acta,* Beza was allowed so few words that one must turn to his *Responsio* for a defense of the enhypostatic Christology he advocated. Beza distinguished abstract and concrete predications. Thus one could say that Christ is omnipresent, omnipotent, or even that the man Christ is omnipresent and omnipotent because such a concrete subject refers to the person. On the other hand, one may not say that the humanity is omnipresent and omnipotent because this would abolish the distinction between the human and the divine natures. So one can say that God suffers, but only *kat'allo* or according to the other nature, the passible human nature, possessed by the person, Christ. Another way of saying the same thing is to distinguish between the whole Christ and the whole of Christ, *totus Christus* and *totum Christi.*[44] In the *Acta,* Beza explained that *totus* refers to the person, *totum* to the natures. So the whole Christ is omnipotent, but not the whole of Christ.[45] Thus one can say that the whole Christ suffered, but not the whole of Christ because his divinity did not suffer. It is in this sense that Beza affirmed the presence of the whole Christ to his church while denying that the whole of Christ is so present since the body of Christ is in heaven until the Second Coming. The divinity can act, therefore, outside of, beyond, the humanity.[46] There is no need to posit the ubiquity of Christ's humanity either locally or illocally.

Andreae countered that Beza was indulging in sophistry. The two words, *totus* and *totum,* mean the same thing. If Beza insists on using the two terms differently, he can do so if he means by *totum Christi non est omnipotens* that Christ's humanity is not omnipotent *in se* or *per se* but only because of the union of the natures in Christ.[47] Beza could have picked up on this to press Andreae for agreement that it is only in the person of Christ that one can claim omnipotence for the humanity of Christ, but instead, Beza insisted that the human nature cannot be said to be omnipotent and the argument continued with no better understanding on either side.

The collocutors turned to the difference between the indwelling of the Holy Spirit in Christ and in holy persons. The discussion concerning the "fullness of the Spirit" attributed to Christ raised the problem of the capacity of the human nature of Christ to receive infinite properties. Andreae argued that this text referred to the Holy Spirit, who communicated divine attributes to the human nature of Christ. The discussion of this point began with one of Andreae's syllogisms:

> To whomever is given the Spirit without measure, to him omniscience is given.
> But the spirit is given without measure to Christ the man or according to the human nature.
> Therefore omniscience is given to him.[48]

Beza agreed that the Holy Spirit endowed Christ with every gift beyond measure, but he insisted that the gifts were created qualities, not infinite properties. (In other words, Andrea's first premise is the point of the dispute and not, therefore, a valid first principle for the argument that follows.) Beza continued, saying that although Christ now in glory knows all, during his life on earth his knowledge was limited and subject to growth. Beza again appealed to Luther's sermon. Andreae countered that Luther changed his teaching on this point and that what one should follow is Luther's Large Catechism, not an early sermon.[49]

Two interchanges lighten the reading, if not the actual colloquy, in this discussion. Andreae accused Beza of being a Turk because by denying Andreae's interpretation of the communication of properties, Beza denied the divinity of Christ. The French audience understood the accusation and began to murmur against Andreae. Andreae pressed the point, however, even quoting passages from the "Alcoran" in which Christ is considered to be a major prophet.[50] Beza not only denied such an outrageous allegation but insisted that Andreae desist from making it again. Andreae did not answer Beza's request and, indeed, repeated the charge.[51] But he went too far, and the Montbéliardais were incensed. Andreae apologized and turned the occasion into an opportunity to address the audience, even citing the Koran as evidence that its doctrine and the Nestorianism of Beza were alike in their denial of Christ's divinity.[52] After bitter exchanges, Andreae agreed not to compare Beza's doctrine to that of the Koran. Beza asked again that they abstain from bitter accusations and pursue peace.[53] In this pursuit, Beza said that he would concede all if only Andreae would admit that the *man* Christ was omnipotent and stop insisting that the *humanity* of Christ was omnipotent. Andreae refused. He reiterated that *man* is not to be taken as concrete because it represents the species and so is said abstractly.[54] Besides, arguments about what is concrete and abstract are over the heads of the audience. It would be better to stay with familiar analogies like hot iron.[55]

The second exchange involved the knowledge of Christ. Beza agreed that Christ knew what he willed to know. Andreae asked Beza whether Christ would not have wanted to know everything. Beza responded that he could not answer since he had had no opportunity to discuss the matter with Christ.[56]

Beza's *Responsio*[57]

Beza's discussion of the person of Christ addresses Andreae's arguments as they were given in the theses and marginalia, but the *Responsio* was developed as a long essay with clear themes and frequent reliance on Aristotle and Thomas Aquinas with regard to the Incarnation, the Trinity,[58] causality, psychology, and epistemology.[59] From time to time in the *Responsio,* Beza appealed for peace based on points of agreement. Andreae would have none of it. In fact, in the *Brief Recueil,* the French edition of Andreae's *Epitome,* his response to Beza's *Responsio,* Andreae argued that heretics like Beza should be prosecuted by the civil police.[60]

Beza attributed most of Andreae's errors to his inability to distinguish concrete and abstract terms and his failure to understand the nature of a property. Both errors came from not knowing basic Aristotelian epistemology, from which one learns how to distinguish a species from an individual member of the species. Beza located another of Andreae's "errors" in the Lutheran's insistence that the hypostatic union and the communication of properties are not the same but rather that the latter is a result of the former.[61] Beza taught that the two are distinct, however inseparable. The communication of properties, said Beza, is only through the person of Christ. To separate the hypostatic union and the *communicatio idiomatum* is to confuse the two natures with each other and with the person of Christ and repeats the error of Eutyches.[62] Beza accused Andreae of two conflicting errors: On the one hand, by identifying the hypostatic union and the *communicatio idiomatum,* Andreae reduced Christ to one nature and was therefore a Monophysite. On the other hand, by talking about the human nature of Christ in terms of an assumed man, Andreae made the human nature a reality separable from its existence in the hypostatic union, which leads to Nestorianism. All of these errors could be avoided, argued Beza, if Andreae would acknowledge the difference between concrete and abstract terms.[63]

It was in this context that both theologians often used the analogy of red-hot iron found in John Damascene's *On the Orthodox Faith.* When the hot iron is applied, it burns. But the fire and the iron are not the same even though their union has a common effect. Andreae argued that the nature of the iron and the nature of the fire are, in effect, communicated to one another. Beza maintained that each retains its nature; the iron burns because of the heat of the fire; the fire can be applied as a cauterizing agent because it is contained in the iron. But Beza's best argument here was that iron and fire are both created things while the two natures of Christ are incomparable because one nature is uncreated and infinite and the other is created and finite. To say that the finite can encompass the infinite is to assert a contradiction, that is to say, a lie. Contradictions, lies, are not possible to God who is Truth. Thus the argument circled over the same points, missing opportunities to find language that would have bridged their differences with regard to spiritual and illocal presence, for example.

Another of Beza's strategies in his *Responsio* was the use of Lutheran documents that contradicted Andreae's arguments. To this end, Beza cited Luther's treatise against Erasmus to support the Genevan doctrine of predestination[64] and John Brentz's *Recognitio*[65] against Andreae's Christology, especially with regard to the manner of the presence of the Holy Spirit in Christ and in Peter.[66]

Beza contested Andreae's notion that when John said that Christ received the Holy Spirit without measure, he meant that Christ's humanity received the whole Holy Spirit. No; "without measure" is not the same as "infinite," argued Beza. Christ received gifts of the Holy Spirit without measure, not the Holy Spirit as though the created humanity were capable of receiving the uncreated divinity. Beza quoted Andreae's syllogism: "Whatever is without measure is immense and infinite. But Christ as man was given the Spirit without measure. Therefore the knowledge of Christ is without measure."[67] Beza appealed to logicians to judge that verbal leap. But then Beza ironically asked to be excused for appealing to logic when Andreae did not know logic.

Beza belittled Andreae's knowledge of theology as well and explained the place of the Holy Spirit in the Trinity.[68] Although Beza did not stress the following point, I think it deserves comment here. For Beza, the *virtus,* or power, of Christ is the Holy Spirit to whom, as Second Person of the Trinity, Christ is united. It is only through the divinity of Christ, therefore, that the whole Christ possesses the Spirit. Because the Second Person of the Trinity assumes humanity, providing subsistence for the substance (body and soul) of the humanity,[69] that humanity is endowed above all others with the *gifts* of the Holy Spirit. But only the person of Christ (who assumes human nature) possesses the Holy Spirit, the Power of God and the Third Person of the Trinity.[70]

It is at this point that Beza cited the *Recognitio.* Beza then attacked the Brentian and Andrean doctrine concerning Peter and Christ. What was given Peter in measure, was given Christ unmeasured, taught the Württembergers. Beza claimed that Andreae taught that the difference between the way the divinity is united to Peter and to the man Christ assumed is seen in the fact that Christ the man resuscitated the dead and performed miracles by his own proper power (*virtus*), while Peter did these things by the power of another.[71] In other words, Andreae taught that Christ's humanity was so endowed by the Holy Spirit that it could, on its own, perform divine actions. This argument lead to an exegesis of Philippians 2:5–11. Andreae claimed that the "form of God" does not refer to divinity alone or "form of man" to humanity alone, but the divinity as united to a low condition and the humanity as adorned with an unspeakable glory, Chemnitz's "majesty."

The doctrine developed by Martin Chemnitz,[72] the *genus majestaticum,* was discussed in relation to thesis XVI. This doctrine teaches that Christ's humanity is endowed with the majesty of omnipotence, omniscience, ubiquity, and the power to vivify. Christ displayed it only "on occasion"; the rest of the time, Christ remained "in form of a servant" so he could suffer and die. Andreae's marginalia declare that the gifts poured out subjectively into Christ's flesh are not the majesty possessed as accidents in either God or man but are essential in God and poured out as personal gifts in the man the Word has taken to himself. The question Beza asks, then, is, if these gifts are neither accidents nor of the essence of the man, what are they?[73] Later, Beza referred to Andreae's thesis XXI, in which Andreae affirmed that there is no other presence of God in Christ than in other creatures. The difference is that Christ has it in plenitude.[74] The argument has therefore returned to the debate concerning the way in which Peter and Christ receive divinity.

Beza defended the exegesis that "form of God" is the equivalent of "essence of God" and "form of a servant" means the humanity of Christ. The one cannot be bestowed on the other. The argument repeats that of the *communicatio idiomatum.*[75] Beza set it in context and then went through a list of christological heresies, showing how each is refuted by Paul's passage interpreted as Beza understood it. Beza claimed that Andreae took "form" to mean the *communicatio idiomatum* and not the divinity, so that Andreae mixes concrete and abstract words.[76] Beza means by "form of God" the person of the Word. Beza quotes *De fide Orthodoxa* (bk. 1, chap. 3), in which Damascene states that a nature cannot receive into itself contrary differences such as finite and infinite.[77]

Other arguments regarding the omnipotence, omniscience, and vivifying power of Christ followed the same lines and need not be repeated.

In both the *Acta* and Beza's *Responsio,* there are long references to early christological heresies, particularly to the doctrine of Nestorius. Beza and Andreae accused each other of repeating Nestorius's error, and each interpreted the history of the Council of Chalcedon to support his own Christology. Beza claimed that Nestorius would not have made the mistake he did had he been able to discern the difference between abstract and concrete terms.

Beza summed up his doctrine in the context of the errors of Nestorius and Eutyches:

> Against Nestorius [I teach] that as there are two natures, so there are two essential properties, two wills and two operations tending to one common and final effect attributed to one single person: because Jesus Christ is but one being subsisting in two natures. He is one being gifted with all the essential properties of his two natures: one being willing through two wills, different things differently, that is to say the divine divinely, and the human humanly. He is also one being doing things not less diverse than the operations are diverse. But just as there must be no separation against Nestorius, so also there must be distinction against the error of Eutyches and the followers of Brenz, and so I draw to a single end and common effect all this diversity of the two natures whether of their essential properties or of their wills and operations, distinct whether in teaching or in working miracles, and especially in the work of our redemption are nevertheless done so that the humanity is not a mediator of our salvation without the divinity nor does the divinity redeem without the humanity.[78]

As he had done for the Lord's Supper, Beza ended the section on the person of Christ with lists of propositions on which the collocutors agreed and disagreed.[79] There are seven on which Beza considered they agreed and only three about which disagreements remained. While these points are too lengthy to reproduce here, suffice it to say that Beza was not altogether accurate, or perhaps he was being optimistic. It comes as no surprise, then, to learn that in his *Epitome,* Andreae repudiated the seven agreements, especially as interpreted by Beza in his comments.

Andreae's *Epitome*[80] sheds no further light; rather, it reduces the arguments to a virulent, one-sided polemic. In the first three lines, these words occur as descriptive of Calvinist doctrine: *horrenda, horribilior, Diabolum.* Beza and the "sacramentarian Calvinist" are accused of not wanting to honor God's word, of sophistry, and of rationalism. The Calvinists, wrote Andreae, find it absurd to say that "the man is God" and that the "bread is body." The devil is never happier than when he persuades people to credit reason over Scripture. With such an opening, it is clear that the *Epitome* did not advance the argument but further obscured it. Andreae's references are to his own *Acta.* He bypasses Beza's *Responsio* except to dismiss it.[81] The *Epitome* is purely polemical and so need not receive further comment with regard to the issues discussed at Montbéliard. In fact, Andreae claimed in his preface to the Latin edition that he had been a faithful minister for forty-two years and that during that time and to his last breath he had and would detest the errors and blasphemies of the Calvinists.

But it was Beza who had the last word. Andreae died in 1590, and in 1593, Beza published a pacific treatise, *De controversiis in Coena Domini,*[82] which he dedicated to "those who follow the Augustana."[83] In this carefully reasoned, noncondemnatory explanation of the Reformed doctrines of the Lord's Supper[84] and the two natures of Christ, Beza tried to point out in what ways the Lutherans misunderstood Reformed theology and in how many areas they agreed with one another.

It is not surprising, then, that Andreae alarmed Beza and his colleagues by demanding that the colloquy be continued to include subjects for which the Swiss were unprepared since they had not been told that they would discuss more than the Lord's Supper. Against Beza's protests, the colloquy proceeded to three more items: the destruction of churches; music, and statues in the churches; baptism; and predestination.

Notes

1. See chap. 3 for the debate over the *manducatio oralis* and the *communicatio idiomatum* in the context of the Lord's Supper.

2. See p. 122, n. 57.

3. See p. 122, n. 60.

4. See chap. 6, pp. 164–65.

5. *Triglot Concordia,* 1014–15, Thorough Declaration of the Formula of Concord [hereafter Thor. Decl.], VIII.

6. *Triglot Concordia,* 1018ff., Thor. Decl. XIIff. These passages lead into a discussion of the two natures of Christ.

7. *Triglot Concordia,* Thor. Decl. VIII, 31ff.

8. For a careful interpretation of Luther's doctrine of the *communicatio idiomatum,* see Siggins, *Martin Luther's Doctrine of Christ,* 221–40.

9. *Triglot,* 1042–45, Thor. Decl. VIII, 76ff. The interpretation given in the preface (183–84) is not upheld by the text itself. The attitude of the writer of the preface is clear when he insists that Calvin is a Zwinglian (174).

10. "Property" is used in the technical scholastic sense of an attribute that belongs uniquely to a particular nature (or, in the case of created beings, species) and that cannot be communicated to another nature. The example given by Aristotle and used by medieval theologians is that "human beings are rational animals." The property, or specific difference, separating human beings from all other creatures and indeed from God is reason. Reason is here taken to mean that process of thinking that moves from one premise through another to arrive at a conclusion. This is a process unique to embodied souls. The intellectual powers of nonbodied spiritual beings such as God and the angels operate through intuition. God knows all in a single, simple act of knowing. In medieval angelology, the ranks of angels are determined by the number of ideas required for them to know what they know. The higher angels understand more

through fewer intuitions or ideas. Animals have neither intelligence nor reason but act through instinct and so differ specifically from human beings. Divine properties are simplicity, omniscience, omnipresence, omnipotence, and other infinite attributes that cannot be shared with created beings.

11. In the *Acta,* the Responses [Resp.A] to the theses go from pp. 203 through 212. The Responses to the dogmatic statements considered contrary to Scripture run from pp. 213 through 216 and are followed by discussion that continues to p.373!

12. *Responsio,* 83–84: "Ad.6. Immò omnis & D. Andreae & ipsius sociorum inde error promanat, quòd inter Abstractas & Concretas voces non distinguant, cuiusmodi sunt in hoc argumento Deitas & Deus, Homanitas & Homo, in unico Christi supposito: & idcirco quecunque huic Homini tribuuntur, tribui etiam volunt Humanitati, Eutychiano prorsus errore, contra hypostaticae unionis definitionem. Sciendum est igitur, Abstracta Humanitatis voce naturam humanam significari, qualis est in sese, suis essentialibus proprietatibus à caeteris naturis distincta, et sibi ut subiecto insitis qualitatibus praedita." (*Response,* 122: "6. Au contraire tout l'erreur de D. André, et de ses compagnons, procede de ce qu'ils ne savent pas distinguer entre les mots emportans Abstraction, & les mots emportans Concretion, tels que sont en ce traicté les mots de Deité et de Dieu, d'Humanité, et d'Homme, en ce seul & mesme subiect Iesus Christ.")

13. Ibid., 84: "ut recte et accurate scribit Thomas" (*Response,* 123). Beza wrote this after he discussed the Trinity in relation to abstract and concrete terms. The praise of Thomas may be extended to Beza's Christology and doctrine of abstraction, however, since Beza's doctrine seems to be drawn from Thomas. Beza's insistence that properties do not leave their subject and the distinction between the grace of union and habitual grace are also Thomistic doctrines.

14. Ibid., 84–85. This argument is also drawn from Aquinas's epistemology.

15. Paul of Samosata was bishop of Antioch (260–268 c.e.). Paul was accused of using the term *homoousios* (consubstantial) in a modalist sense. He thereby denied the divinity of the Son and the Spirit and is supposed to have been one of the founders of Adoptionism. See the *New Catholic Encyclopedia* 11:26. Cf. Jaroslav Pelikan, *The Christian Tradition: A History of the Development of Doctrine,* vol. 1, *The Emergence of the Catholic Tradition (100–600)* (Chicago: University of Chicago Press, 1971), 176, 198.

16. *Responsio,* 121, where Beza gives Damascene's explanation of the incandescent sword in *De fide orthodoxa* 3:15, which supports Beza's interpretation. For Damascene's bibliography, see n. 18.

17. Ad IX in *Acta,* p. 206, but this is an error since it follows X and precedes XII.

18. *Acta,* 207; *Responsio,* 132–33 (*Response,* 175.) Cyril: Lib. de Trinit.5.; *Nyssus, contra Eunomium;* Damascene, *De Orthodoxa fide,* lib. 3, cap. 15. For Damascene, see *De Fide Orthodoxa: Versions of Burgundio and Cerbanus,* ed. Eligius M. Buytaert, OFM (St. Bonaventure, N.Y.: The Franciscan Institute, 1955), 238: "Unam autem naturalem actionem Dei et facturae nequaquam quis sapiens dabit, secundum beatum Cyrillum: 'Neque enim vivificat Lazarum humana natura, neque lacrimatur divina potestas; nam lacrima quidem humanitatis propria, vita autem enhypostatu (id est personalis) vitae.' Sed tamen communiter utrorumque alterutra propter identitatem hypostaseos. Nam unus quidem est Christus, et una eius persona vel hypostasis; sed tamen habet duas naturas, deitatis et humanitatis eius. Igitur ex deitate quidem gloria naturaliter proveniens, alterutrius communis propter hypostaseos identitatem facta est, ex carne autem humilia alterutrorum communia. Unus enim est et idem qui hoc et illud est, scilicet Deus et homo, et eiusdem et quae deitatis et quae humanitatis. Nam

divina quidem signa deitatis operabatur, sed non sine carne; humilia vero caro, sed non sine deitate. Etenim patienti carni copulata erat deitas, impassibilis permanens, et passiones perficiens salutares; et agenti Verbi deitati copulatus erat sanctus intellectus, intelligens et sciens quae perficiebantur."

19. This is one of the points where, had they wished to find common ground, Beza and Andreae might have done so. The Damascene passage is patient of both interpretations as, in fact, both interpretations may be taken as different ways of expressing the same doctrine. But Andreae and Beza came to the colloquy convinced that they would be unable to persuade one another of the truth of their own position. They were equally convinced that there could be no ambiguity in the expression of the doctrine.

20. *Acta,* 207, marginalis h): "Forma servi non est humanitas, sed sevilis conditio hominis Christi."

21. Peter Lombard, *Sententiae,* lib. I, dist. 37. Cf. discussion on early scholastics in A. M. Landgraf, *Dogmengeschichte der Früscholastik,* in 3 vols. (Regensburg: F. Pustet, 1954). Vol. 3, 41–56.

22. *Acta,* 312: "Una quidem est divinitas Spiritus sancti in homine Christo, & in aliis sanctis hominibus, qui sunt Christi membra: sed non una & eadem est eiusdem participatio seu communicatio. Nam in homine Christo omnia sunt sine mensura, hoc est, increata, immensa, & infinita: in omnibus aliis autem sanctis hominibus, Christi membris, omnia sunt creata, mensurata, finita, dona communicata."

23. Ibid., 313: "Quicunque implet omnia, ille ubique praesens est. Homo à Filio Dei in unitatem personae eius assumptus, implet omnia. Ergo homo ille assumptus ubique praesens est."

24. But see p. 122, n. 55 for Andreae's refusal to see any difference in the terms *humanity* and *man.*

25. At this point it becomes still more evident that Beza and Andreae were speaking at cross-purposes. This was the case constantly with regard to the Lord's Supper and was the point at which the Lord's Supper arguments became christological arguments. How could the body of Christ be present to believers in communion when Christ's human body was circumscribed and localized? The answer of the Württembergers was that the human nature shares in the ubiquity of God and therefore can be everywhere, especially there where Christ wills to be in the church's Supper of the Lord. This doctrine does not, the Lutherans affirmed, detract from the full humanity of Christ or from the circumscription of his human body, but is rather a supernatural mode of presence. The answer of Calvin and his followers was that the body of Christ can be shared with the faithful only through the power of the Holy Spirit uniting them with Christ in heaven, where he dwells at the right hand of the Father.

26. In technical theology, only God can be adored. The word meant to worship as divine and did not have the many lesser meanings it has since acquired.

27. *Acta,* 256–65. Behind Andreae's argument lies an interesting view of creation as "imperfect" over against the perfection of the Divinity, a Platonic notion. For Beza, following Aquinas's Aristotelian line, creation is perfect because it is as God made it and God is a perfect maker. There is therefore a finite perfection appropriate to each species, which individuals within the species approach more or less. Christ as man was and is the only perfect individual possessing a human nature whose perfection requires the retention of finite qualities.

28. They are one in the person of Christ.

29. *Acta,* 264–65: "Andreae: Supra dictum est & demonstratum, quod pluimum inter se differant unio naturarum, & proprietatum communicatio. Nam communicatio

proprietatum, est unionis naturarum quasi effectus, & consequens. Quare etsi tempore simul sunt, ratione tamen ordinis naturae habent se sicut prius & posterius.

"Quapropter sicut naturarum unio non est nuda & simplex unio, sed vera & realis communicatio, qua divina dat, & humana accipit: ita communicatio proprietatum non est talis unio, qua naturae nihil sibi invicem propriorum suorum communicent: sed etiam vera & realis communicatio, qua logo seipsum, & omnia sua assumptae naturae communicavit.

"*Beza:* Unum sunt, unio, & communicatio: & sicut divinae Naturae non communicata est passio, ut eam IN SE habeat: ita quoque humanitati in Christo omnipotentia non est communicata, ut EAM IN SE habeat. Quemadmodum igitur Deitas est crucifixa: ita humanitas est omnipotens facta. Sed illud non est; Ergo neque hoc, quod dicis, humanitatem omnipotentem factam esse.

"[p. 265] *Andreae:* Non esse unum & idem Unionem naturarum, & Communicationem idiomatum seu proprietatum, satis demonstravi. Sic quoque non esse rationem eandem harum praedicationum : Divinitas est crucifixa; & humanitas est omnipotens facta: supra dixi: idque propter naturarum diversitatem. Ideoque ostendi, longe aliter humanam naturam omnipotentem factam, quam divinitatem passam, aut crucifixam esse.

"Nam divinitas nullam, neque perfectionem, neque imperfectionem IN SE recipit, propter naturae suae immutabilitatem. Sed human natura IN SE recipere potest, & in persona filii Dei vere recepit summam Maiestatem, quae Deitatis est propria: sicut verbis S. Patrum declaravi."

30. Beza did not pick up on this argument of Andreae to point out that the human nature of Christ was and is perfect as a human nature. Therefore one would have to say that, could it communicate anything to the divine nature, the communication would be limited and finite but not "imperfect."

31. See p. 120.

32. *Acta,* 214: "Humanitas Christi aeque ac alius sanctus et naturalis homo, non semper omnia cogitavit, dixit, voluit, animadvertit, sicut quidam omnipotentem hominem, ex ipso faciunt, imprudenter confundentes duas naturas, et earum operationes."

33. *Responsio,* 7: "D. Andreae verò quinam sua dispicere, expendere, expolire, (sicut ab illo factum fuisse res ipsa evincit,) mea verò pro arbitrio mutilata, interpolata, diminuta proferre in manus hominum licuerit? Et ut licuisse demus, quorsum illa mea ne sic quidem intacta relinquere, sed observationes & refutationes adiicere fas fuit?" (*Response,* 9: "Mais qui a donné ceste auctorité au D. Iaques André, de relire, d'examiner, de polir et enrichir son dire, comme chacun voit qu'il a faict, en mutilant le mien, l'agenceant et le rongnant à sa fantasie contre tout droict equité?")

34. It is easy to make such comparisons since Andreae's speeches are printed in ordinary type and Beza's words are printed in italics.

35. *Acta,* 217: "Nam Petrus Martyr in suo Dialogo expresse scripsit: NULLA VI FIERI POSSE, ut res creata sit ubique. Et haud ita pridem Lampertus Danaeus in libello Genevae impresso scripsit: CHRISTUM ne quidem VELLE POTUISSE, ut corpus ipsius simul et semel in pluribus locis praesens sit, quia praestare non possit." In his marginal note, Andreae further identified Danaeus's work as *assertio contra D. Iacobum Andreae.* Danaeus's treatise, *Assertio . . . Contra . . . Andreae . . . scriptum de Adoratione Carnis Christi,* was published in Geneva (Eustathius Vignon) in 1585 as an answer to Andreae's tract *Refutatio blasphemae apologiae Lamberti Danaei Galli de adoratione carnis Christi* (Tübingen, 1583), which was itself an answer to Danaeus's *Apologia Seu Vera Et Orthodoxa . . . Interpretatio, De Adoratione carnis Domini* (Antwerp, Aegidius Radaeus, 1582). The citations given here are from Olivier Fatio, *Méthode et*

théologie: Lambert Daneau et les débuts de la scolastique réformée (Geneva: Librairie Droz, 1976), 65*, 60*, cf. 123*. The full title of the *Assertio* is found on p. 195*. [See p. 160 for a brief but clear explanation of Daneau's opposition to the Lutheran doctrine of the *communicatio idiomatum* and Daneau's use of Damascene.]

36. *Acta,* 217: "et in Thesibus vestris de Coena Domini, idem quoque affirmatur, de quo in praecedenti articulo etiam dictum est. Quod in Responsionibus vestris de persona Christi repetitum est, ubi contenditis, Deum propterea non negari omnipotentem, etiamsi hoc praestare non possit." Cf. Andreae, *Epitome,* (Latin) p. 24, (French) p. 58, where Andreae repeats this argument.

37. *Acta,* 216–17: "Quoniam Christus non solum sit verax, qui fallere et mentire non possit, sed etiam omnipotens, apud quem non est impossibile omne verbum, sicut Angelus Mariae loquitur. Ibi ab adversariis nostris de potentia non solum Christi hominis, sed etiam de absoluta potentia Dei disputari coeptum est."

38. For an explanation of these terms and their use, see Oberman, *Masters of the Reformation,* 96–97, together with the text given in n. 152.

39. *Acta,* 258: "Natura autem humana omnipotentiae plene capax est, sicut Oregines loquitur, ut possit etiam plenitudinem divinitatis recipere: ideo ipsa alio modo realiter omnipotens effici potest, quam divinitas passionum capax dicitur." (The margin identifies the Origen citation as Orig. *de princ. lib.4.*)

40. Oberman, *Masters of the Reformation,* 166, 169.

41. To see the relation of Beza's Christology to Calvin's and the development of Beza's Christology, see Jill Raitt, "The Person of the Mediator: Calvin's Christology and Beza's Fidelity," *Occasional Papers of the American Society for Reformation Research* 1 (December 1977): 53–80.

42. *Responsio,* 100: "Denique quum D. Andreas hac Omnipotestate potissimum ad stabiliendam illam suam Omnipraesentiam abutatur, (qua tamen posita, veritatem carnis Christi aboleri necesse est, quum corpus, ac proinde Quantum & in loco esse, & ubique simul, id est Non quantum esse, contradictoria sint, nec simul vera esse possint) perinde facit, ac si Christo diceret potestatem quoque esse concessam contradictoria volendi, id est in alterutram partem, absit verbo blasphemia, mentiendi." Ibid.: "unde recte concludunt Scholastici, fieri non posse, ut ulli creaturae communicetur: adeo quidem, ut Christus, neque corpore, neque anima potuerit, aut possit consuetum naturae ordinem immutare, nisi prout fuit Verbi Dei sibi personaliter uniti instrumentum." (*Response,* 145: "Il fait donc tout de mesme que s'il disoit, que la puissance de vouloir choses contraires a esté donnee à Christ, c'est à dire (ce qui soit dit sans blaspheme) Avoir le pouvoir de mentir [*sic*]." Ibid.: "tellement que les Scholastiques ont tresbien conclu, qu'il ne se pouvoit faire, que ceste Toutepuissance fust communiquee à aucune creature: de sorte que Christ n'a peu ni ne peut, ni en son corps, ni en son ame, changer l'ordre de nature: sinon entant qu'il a este instrument de la Parole de Dieu, à laquelle il a esté uni personnellement.")

43. *Acta,* 327.

44. *Responsio,* 108–9; see also 103, where Beza cites Damascene, *De Fide Orthodoxae,* 3, 7, on the *totus/totum*. [Cf. pp. 127–129.] Beza's doctrine is very much like that of J. Jacob Grynaeus in his 1584 debate with Andreae at Heidelberg. I must admit that I find Grynaeus's explanation clearer than Beza's. John Jacob Grynaeus. *Synopsis orationis. / quae habi / ta est in celeber / rima academia Heydel / bergensi a Iohanne Iacobo / Grynaeo, quum is, Aprilis die XV Anno Christianae / Aevae, 1584. finem imponeret Disputationibus / Teologicis, de Controversia Euchari / stica, per ociduum habitis.* Heidelberg: Typis Iacobi Mylii, 1584. P. 5. "III. Verbi gratia Enunciationem istam: Totus Christus est ubique, sed non totum Christi, exposui verbis Damasceni, . . . Totum

denotat naturam, totus autem personam. Professus sum me agnoscere, Christum qua homo est, ubique esse: sed ut beatus cyrillus ait, καθ αλλο και αλλο: quando humanitas Christi ubique est, non in se ipsa, sed in alio ut dixit Leo Romanus Episcopus. 1. Non est tropus in subiecto & praedicato huius Enunciationis: Panis est corpus Christi. Ergo nul / [p. 5v] lus inest tropus." [This is followed by a 1584 treatise of Andreae:] Jacob Andreae Admonitio / pia et necessaria, / de / synopsi ora / tionis ioannis iacobi / grynaei, professoris theo / logi Zwingliani in Academia / Basiliensi: / qua disputationi de coena / Domini, Heidelbergae Anno 1584, die 4. Aprilis / propositae, 15. eiusdem, finem / imposuit. Autore / Iacobo Andreae D. Praeposi / to Tubingensi. / Tübingen: Georg Gruppenbach, Anno 1584.]

45. *Acta,* 308: "Totum Christum, non autem totum Christi . . . omnipotentem esse dicimus.

46. *Acta,* 319. The discussion on this point continues to p. 325. Cf. *Responsio,* 118–19; *Response,* 239–40. This is the basis of the doctrine that later came to be called the *extra calvinisticum.* See Raitt, "The Person of the Mediator," 63, for Andreae's ascription of the phrase *etiam extra humanitatem* Christi to Beza. Cf. David Willis, *Calvin's Catholic Christology: The Function of the So-Called Extra Calvinisticum in Calvin's Theology* (Leiden: Brill, 1966). For Andreae's doctrine, see *Acta,* 138, 339, 350.

47. *Acta,* 309.

48. *Acta,* 301: "Cuicunque datus est spiritus sine mensura: huic omniscientia data est. Sed Christo homini seu secundum humanitatem datus est spiritus non ad mensuram. Ergo data est illi etiam omniscientia. Probatio minoris propositionis: Ioan.3. scriptum est, Quem misit Deus, verba Dei loquitur. Non enim ad mensuram dat Deus Spiritum. Pater diligit filium, & omnia dedit in manu eius." Haimo of Halberstadt uses the same passage in a way that is both like and unlike Andreae's interpretation: "Aliter enim habitat [divinitas] in singulis electorum, aliter in Christo, quia illis datur Spiritus ad mensuram, in illo autem pleniter." [Cited from Landgraf, *Dogmengeschichte der Früscholastik,* 42, n. 2.]

49. *Acta,* 302: "Lutherum ipsum doctrinam suam de persona Christi revocasse. Potissimum vero illa, quae de persona Christi in Maiori Confessione de Coena Domini."

50. Ibid., 265–66.

51. Ibid., 368: "Etenim haec res & hoc Mysterium miseros & execoecatos Iudaeos & Turcas adhuc exercet & impedit, quo minus ad cognitionem Christi pervenire possint." Ibid., 369: "Hanc doctrinam Turcicus Alcoranus summam blasphemiam, & longe horribilissimum mendacium esse affirmat."

52. Ibid., 266.

53. Ibid., 268.

54. Ibid., 272. This remark makes Andreae's peculiar doctrine of the "assumed man" [e.g., *Acta,* 267, 313] understandable in an orthodox sense, but not to distinguish the concrete from the abstract in this instance does allow for confusion.

55. Ibid., 272–74. See below for a further discussion of this analogy.

56. Ibid., Beza: "Christum secundum humanam naturam nunc scire omnia, QUAE VELIT SCIRE. Iacobus: Vult ne homo Christus omnia scire? Beza: Nescio. Non sum cum illo hac de re collocutum." [It should be noted that Beza said "nunc" and therefore means Christ in glory. Andreae referred to Christ during his earthly life.]

57. Ad acta / colloquii / Montisbelgardensis / Tubingae edita, / Theodori Bezae / Responsio. / Genevae, / Excudebat Joannes le Preux. / M.D.LXXXVII [Hereafter *Resp. pars alt.*]. A second Latin edition appeared in 1588 (the one I am using here, see

ch. 3, n. 46) and a third in 1599. A French translation was published in 1587: Response / de M. Th. de Beze / aux Actes de la conferen- / ce de Mombelliard / Imprimés à Tubingue. / A Geneve, / De l'imprimerie de Jean le Preux. / M.D.LXXXVII. In 1588, a Latin edition of the second part of the *Responsio* was published: Ad acta / Colloquii / Montisbelgardensis / Tubingae edita, / Theodori Bezae / Responsionis, Pars / Altera / Editio prima. / Excudebat Joannes le Preux. / M.D.LXXXVIII. See Gardy, *Bibliographie,* for a discussion of the editions and translations about which there is some dispute over the French translation.

58. *Responsio,* 113: "(suo id quidem modo, id est non quasi Deitas sit quiddam *noeton* in hypostasibus, sicut species in individuis creatis subsistens, quum contra singulae hypostases in tota & individua Deitate subsistant, suis relationibus, *ut vere & argute dicit Thomas,* habentibus quandam in illis suae personalitatis veluti principii, rationem)" [emphasis mine]. Cf. p. 84.

59. *Responsio,* 129–30.

60. Andreae, *Epitome.* French version: BRIEF RECUEIL / DU COL- / LOQUE DE MOM- / BELIARD TENU AU MOIS DE / Mars 1586. Entre laques Andre D. / & M. Theodore de Beze. Last page (155) says: "Pour certaines occasions on n'a peu annoter toutes les pages en cest exemplaire francois: comme elles sont fidelement & diligemmentco-teez [*sic*] en l'exemplaire Latin qui se rapporte aux actes du Colloque, & responce de M. de Beze imprimez en Latin. Ou le Lecteur pourra avoir recours." For remark about civil prosecution of heretics, see p. 155 of *Brief Recueil.*

61. *Responsio,* 159f.

62. Ibid., 159–60. Cf. *Acta,* 263, 274.

63. *Responsio,* 161–63.

64. See chap. 5, p. 154, n. 54.

65. Brenz, Recognitio / Propheticae & Aposto- / licae Doctrinae, de Vera / Maiestate Domini Nostri ie- / su Christi, ad dexteram Dei / Patris sui omnipo- / tentis. / In hoc Scripto refutatur liber Henrici Bullingeri, / cui author titulum fecit: Fundamentum fir- / mum, cui tuto fidelis quivisinnit / potest, &c. / Authore Ioanne Brentio. / Item appendix publicorum testimoniorum, quibus manifeste osten- / ditur, Cinglianos nostram, hoc est, vere piam sententiam / de coena DOMINI, mala conscientia / oppugnare. / Tubingae Apud Vi- / duam Ulrici Morhardi. / 1564.

66. *Responsio,* 18–19; 136–37.

67. Ibid., 135.

68. Ibid.

69. Ibid., 137: "Homo verò Christus, (etsi verus homo est,) non est tamen individuum humanae speciei: quia sic Christus in duas personas divideretur: sed in Filii Dei subsistentia suppositatur."

70. Ibid., 136: "Spiritum qui sit sine mensura, id est essentialem illum Deum infinitum, sed hunc sine mensura datum Spiritum, qui sit ipsi datus. Spiritus ergo qui dat, tertia est illa Trinitatis persona, . . . coëssentialis videlicet illa & énhupostasis tum Patris tum Filii virtus." And Ibid.: "quum è contrario ipse sibi Christus sua Deitate, (cuius ut & Patris virtus essentialis & énhupostatos est ipse Spiritus Sanctus) in illam assumptam humanitatem prout & quando ipsi libuit effuderit."

71. Ibid., 137.

72. Martin Chemnitz, *The Two Natures of Christ,* trans. J. A. O. Preus (St. Louis: Concordia, 1971). In this volume, first published in Latin in 1578, Chemnitz frequently cited John Damascene (over one hundred times) and many other fathers and Scholastic theologians, such as Bernard and Bonaventure (p. 82). Chemnitz claimed to be following Damascene (p. 136) when he wrote that the divine nature assumed the

human nature and thereby formed the person of Christ (pp. 68–70), a departure from the tradition that said that the Second Person of the Trinity assumed a human nature. Chemnitz wrote (p. 90) that "we have come to use as equivalents the terms essence, nature, or person (Hypostasis or hyphistamenon) with reference to the incarnation of Christ."

73. *Responsio,* 85; cf. 151–55.

74. Ibid., 163–64.

75. Ibid., 127.

76. Ibid., 139–41.

77. Ibid.

78. Ibid., 128: "Neque quum haec distinguo, propterea carnem, vel carnis actiones separo, sed suum cuique ut hypostaticae unitionis natura & definitio iubet, attribuo: tum adversum Nestorium duas, ut naturas, sic Essentiales proprietates, & voluntates & operationes, unicum denique *apotélesma,* uni & singulari personae tribuens, ut qui sit unus in duabus naturis subsistens, unus utrisque essentialibus suarum naturarum proprietatibus praeditus, unus duabus & numero & natura diversissimis, diversa diversè volens, divina videlicet divinè, humana verò humanè: Unus etiam non minùs diversis actionibus, nec minus diversa efficiens: sed ut citra separationem adversus Nestorium, sic servata semper distinctione adversus Eutychianam illam Bretianorum communicationem: ad commune *apotélesma,* tum in singularibus doctrinae & miraculorum operibus, tum in primis, in illo nostrae redemptionis opere omnem illam, tum naturarum, tum essentialium proprietatum, tum voluntatum, tum actionum diversitatem adducens, ut neque sine divinitate Humanitas, neque sive Humanitate divini- / tas, sit nostrae salutis mediatrix." Cf. *Response,* 184.

79. *Responsio,* 179, for agreements; p. 180 for the disagreements and p. 181 for Beza's commentary on these propositions.

80. Andreae, *Epitome.* French version: BRIEF RECUEIL / DU COL- / LOQUE DE MOM- / BELIARD TENU AU MOIS DE / Mars 1586. Entre Iaques Andre D. / & M. Theodore de Beze. See n. 60 in this chapter for French exerpt. In both the Latin and French versions, to the subjects actually debated, Andreae added, "On the promises of the Gospel" and "On the Merit of Christ."

81. *Epitome,* 10–12.

82. Theodore Beza, De / controversiis / in Coena / Domini, / Per nonullos nu- / per in Germania partim renovatis, partim / auctis, Christiana & Perspicua / disceptatio. / Genevae, / Apud Iohannem le Preux, / M.D.XCIII. A second edition, corrected and amplified, appeared in 1594.

83. The dedication reads: "Ista, sicut ab animo candido et pacis ecclesiarum syncere studioso profecta sunt, omnibus germaniae illustriss. Principib. caeterisq. Nobiliss. Ordinibus, magistratib. Ecclesiarum pastorib. Doctorib. Et populis augustanam confessionem profitentibus dicata sunto, sine praeiudicio, et absque animi acerbitate, legenda, expendenda, et in legitimo tandem conventu communi, libero, et legitimo, quum dederit dominus ex puro dei verbo diiudicanda."

84. For an expanded discussion of this point, see Raitt, *Eucharistic Theology of Theodore Beza,* 61–68.

5

Images, Baptism, and Predestination

Late in the morning of March 26, at the conclusion of the long discussion of the person of Christ, Andreae asked whether Beza had anything further he wished to raise on the subject before they moved on to the topic of predestination. Beza took the opportunity to repeat that he and his colleagues had no wish to extend the colloquy to subjects they had not expected to discuss and for which they were not prepared. Beza said that to begin a discussion of predestination would be to enter into a profound abyss. It was a subject, he argued, that required preparation on the part of the collocutors and the audience. Beza also urged that he and his companions be allowed to leave so they could return home in time to prepare for Easter. He was willing to explain the doctrine of predestination to Frederick in private, but he did not foresee disagreement on the subject in any case.[1] When Andreae insisted that the Württemberg theses be read aloud, Beza protested that the audience might incorrectly suppose that the Reformed theology was fairly presented by the antitheses. To forestall such an impression, Beza agreed that the Reformed team would read the Württemberg theses on predestination and respond to them.[2]

When the collocutors met that afternoon in the presence of Frederick and the persevering audience, Beza addressed them, saying that he and his colleagues wished nothing so much as a resolution of the controversies between the churches. They had tried to come to such a resolution and thereby to satisfy Frederick's "holy" request. Now the Reformed team was asked to discuss predestination, which, said Beza, was not a matter of an hour or even days or months. Beza therefore presented a written petition to Frederick asking that the colloquy conclude. The petition reminded Frederick that the Swiss theologians had been invited to discuss the Lord's Supper and the person of Christ. Furthermore, the councils of Bern and Geneva had not authorized their delegates to enter into other topics or to take the additional time necessary to discuss predestination. Besides, argued Beza, predestination should be discussed by theologians before trained students, not in the presence of those unable to grasp the arguments. If Frederick wanted a response to the Württemberg theses on predestination, Beza and his colleagues would be happy to take them home for discussion by their churches and send Frederick their opinions. Beza pleaded that, the colloquy concluded, each side replace name-calling and bitterness with mutual prayer and agreement wherever possible. The Reformed petition concluded by noting agreement on the basic doctrine of the Augsburg Confession and asked that the collocutors agree to disagree on what the unworthy receive in communion so that the French exiles could communicate in Montbéliard.[3] Since notaries had not taken official protocols, Beza also asked that the proceedings of the colloquy be handled with great care to avoid further bitterness. The petition was signed by the five Reformed theologians. In a marginal note, Andreae called their request "impudent." Frederick went off to read the petition and to confer with the Württemberg theologians, whose strategy may or may not have been revealed to him.

Divide and conquer was the strategy behind their insistence on continuing the colloquy on the topic of predestination. In fact, in 1554, Bern, to which Lausanne belonged, disagreed with Calvin's doctrine of double predestination and the Bern magistrates forbade that predestination be a subject of preaching or writing by theologians under Bern's control.[4] In 1558, Beza left Lausanne because of profound differences over church polity and the doctrine of predestination.[5] Andreae also knew that Pierre Toussain had taught single predestination and had had a falling-out with Calvin on the subject.[6] Montbéliard agreed with the Lutherans, Bern, and Basel, not the Calvinists, on predestination. Now Andreae urged Frederick to demand that the theologians from Geneva, Bern, and Lausanne debate predestination.

In response to Beza's requests, Andreae said that the reason Frederick had not mentioned the remaining disputed topics in his letter to the councils of Geneva and Bern was probably because he had not realized that there were matters other than the Lord's Supper and the person of Christ to discuss. But what good would it do, argued Andreae, if we were to agree on two points and there remained a third in dispute? Besides, the people need to understand the doctrine of predestination and they are capable of understanding it. Nothing contained in Scripture should be kept from the faithful.[7] Andreae added to predestination the discussion of baptism and of music, statues, and paintings in churches.[8]

To Beza's objection that his side had not come prepared on these subjects nor were books available to them, Andreae chided that Beza was a veteran disputant who had no need of books. Andreae also assured Beza that the Württembergers had neither consulted nor needed to consult books on the remaining topics. He then rehearsed the history of controversy on the Lord's Supper, assuring the audience that he and his colleagues wanted only peace. But they had a duty to resist false doctrine and so, in spite of their godly intentions, were dragged into controversy. Andreae had already declared that he was correct, had always taught the truth, and that Beza had only to admit his errors for there to be peace between them.[9] Andreae then turned to one of the problems lying behind the colloquy, namely the plight of the French churches. He assured his hearers that the Württemberg theologians were deeply affected with the misery of the Huguenots, prayed for them, and exhorted their churches to pray for them. The peace that the churches sought, he added, could be found only in the word of God taken in its clear and obvious sense.

Picking up on the theme of the French churches, Beza appealed to Frederick on their behalf, reminding Frederick that Duke Christoph had helped them and they had been favored by Frederick's father, Count George. Beza thanked Frederick for the help he had sent to France and hoped that nothing would prevent future assistance. Beza ended with an appeal to end the bitterness and the sharp polemical publications that had marred past relations between the Württembergers and the Swiss.

There was no further debate on the continuation of the colloquy since Andreae assured Beza that Count Frederick and the audience wanted it to continue. Andreae gave the Württemberg theses to Beza and his colleagues for study until the next day, March 27, when they would begin with the easiest subject, namely, the destruction of Catholic churches and the place of art and music in church services. They would then turn to predestination and baptism.[10]

The Destruction of Churches; Art and Music in Services[11]

Andreae's four theses defended the retention of altars, statues, and paintings, even those that had been installed by "papists," as long as they did not lead to idolatry. Music was not to be eliminated from church services. Andreae laid out the scriptural arguments to defend his theses. For example, he noted that although the Israelites were forbidden to make graven images, they nevertheless represented the cherubim on the ark of the covenant. The psalms not only tolerated but commanded the use of musical instruments. Beza agreed with the theses but modified them in the sense that while artistic representations need not be eliminated from churches, they could do more harm than good, given the tendency in human nature to fall into idolatry. In spite of his conciliatory tone and gentle representation of the Genevan preference for simplicity in church art and music, Andreae filled the margins with comments that could only be considered pugnacious. For example, when Beza deplored the destruction of churches, Andreae countered that the pulling down of churches in France and the Netherlands was not only wrong but was done in the name of bad doctrine.[12] Beza responded that churches, statues, paintings, organs, and the like had been destroyed all over Protestant Europe by angry crowds. That did not mean that those crowds acted with ecclesiastical approval and, in fact, the Genevan church deprecated such behavior. Andreae expressed relief to hear Beza say so, since he and his colleagues had supposed that the Reformed favored pulling down Catholic churches.

In earlier treatments of the Colloquy of Montbéliard, this section has been dismissed by remarking that Beza and Andreae agreed. That is too simple. They did agree that churches should not be destroyed, that altars used by "papists" could be used by Protestants, that art and music in church services were a matter of prudent judgment. But it should be pointed out that while Andreae argued for organs, polyphony, painting, and sculpture, Beza, following Calvin, preferred simple psalmody and felt that the Reformed churches were under no obligation to install organs. As for statues and paintings, Beza said that they were most useful in civil life but that the Reformed preferred not to put them in their churches. Both collocutors used Scripture to buttress their arguments. They agreed that Scripture gave no precise commands that must be obeyed on these matters since even the specific commandment against graven images was obviously interpreted to allow for statues and other representations in ancient Israel. On the other hand, while the psalms mentioned all sorts of musical instruments to praise the Lord, there was no specific command to use any particular instrument or any instruments at all. The final note sounded by both theologians was that in these matters the churches should exercise Christian liberty. At the same time, excess in either direction should be avoided so that there would be no cause for scandal.

Baptism

After expressing the pious desire that the remaining points of controversy be concluded so agreeably, Andreae introduced the Württemberg theses on baptism. The pattern was the same as previously: points considered noncontroversial, doctrines the Lutherans considered contrary to Scripture, and theses upheld by the Württemberg churches. It is intriguing to note that Andreae's marginalia became so extensive that they ran across the bottom of the pages as well as down the sides. Beza's responses appear in frames of editorial comment and contain fewer words than the marginal notes.[13] As before, Beza's remarks were much shorter than Andreae's perorations.

The noncontroversial points are simply summarized:

1. Baptism consists of water and the Word of God.
2. It replaces circumcision.[14]
3. It is to be administered to infants.
4. Baptism is not just a sign and seal but actually confers regeneration in the Holy Spirit.
5. No one who is not regenerated can enter heaven.
6. Regeneration is not earned by human works but conferred by God's mercy.
7. To be baptized is to put on Christ, to die, to be buried, and to rise with Christ to a new life.

The doctrines given as contrary to Scripture, and by implication ascribed to the Reformed, were:

1. Baptism signifies but does not necessarily effect what it signifies.
2. Baptism is thereby reduced to an unnecessary sign of membership in the external church.
3. Baptism is effective only in the elect and, even in the case of the elect, not necessarily at the time it is administered.
4. There is no need for midwives to provide emergency baptism.

Since there had been no time for Beza's team to prepare written theses at this point in the colloquy, they did so at its conclusion. Andreae explained that he set them at this point in the *Acta* so that readers would have everything set out in an orderly fashion. In his *Responsio, Second Part,* Beza did not object to this arrangement.[15]

Andreae's theses, as was the case with regard to images, presented positions that misrepresented Reformed theology. Beza's task was to set the record straight, at least for the audience at Montbéliard. He objected that thesis I did not mention that baptism represented washing in the blood of Christ figured by the water. Theses II and III, which stated that baptism replaced circumcision and should be administered to infants, were not disputed. For the rest, Beza's answers were true to Calvin's theology of baptism.[16] All that is signified by baptism, remission of sins, regeneration, and adoption by God, is offered by God through the Holy Spirit to all the baptized. But not all are able to receive what is offered since the external actions are effective only through the power of the Holy Spirit. The sacraments and their benefits are "distinct but not separate." Since the benefits of baptism are truly offered, said Beza, the signs are not "nude."[17] To thesis VI, Beza answered that his side approved all the scriptural citations dealing with the institution of baptism and its effects in those who, through their unworthiness, do not repudiate its offered benefits.

In his marginalia, Andreae remarked that the water does not signify the blood, but rather is a means through which, in the blood of Christ and the power of the Holy Spirit, the baptized are regenerated. Andreae also understood the parallel with the Lord's Supper, namely, that the benefits are offered to but not conferred on all those who are baptized. Andreae did not allow the principle of "distinct but not separate" and claimed that Beza did indeed make two baptisms, one in water, the other in the Holy Spirit. With some relish, Andreae then picked up on Beza's sixth response. He interpreted Beza to mean that only the elect receive the benefits of baptism. It is horrible to hear, said Andreae, that thousands of baptized, whether children or adults, before they have done good or ill, are not regenerated but damned in spite of the sacrament.

The discussion moved on to the eleven points that the Württemberg theologians considered contrary to Scripture. Beza said that it is idolatrous to ascribe any latent power to any water, even sacramental water. God does not transfer divine power absolutely to any created thing. Andreae responded that they were not talking about "any water" but about water made effective through the power of the Holy Spirit. If there is no latent power in the sacramental sign, is it not a "nude" sign? Once again, the argument is whether the sacramental sign is permanently affected by its cultic use or is an instrument through which God acts only during its use. In the first instance, the signs become objects of divine action; in the second instance, the signs are instruments through which divine action passes to the believer who alone is its object. Beza argued that salvation depends not on baptism but on one's faith; as for damnation, it is due to contempt for salvation and for the instruments God uses to elicit faith.

To explain the way the signs are related to the reality they signify, Beza employed metonymy, a term already familiar in explanations of the Genevan theology of the Lord's Supper.[18] Simply put, sacramental metonymy takes the sign for the effect; baptism signifies the work of the Holy Spirit, which, through the blood of Christ, cleanses interiorly. One can then say, by metonymy, that baptism is washing in Christ's blood. Andreae countered that baptism was not instituted by Christ *as a sign* of regeneration but *to confer* regeneration. It is clear from Andreae's argument that he, as well as Beza,[19] understood the sacraments of baptism and the Lord's Supper in tandem. Beza continued to insist that when children or adults are baptized, they receive the benefits of it only when the Holy Spirit gives them faith to receive those benefits. This gift, he explained, may be given at any time, the moment of baptism or at some later time. Nevertheless, infants should be baptized so that they are brought into the covenant to which they belong through their parents.

At this point, Beza made a curious concession. He said that infants also probably receive remission of original sin and the fruits of adoption as long as they do not repudiate these benefits as adults. This is a strange admission and seems to be an inconsistency in Beza's theology. If an infant receives remission of original sin and adoption, then is it not saved? And if it is saved, is it not regenerated? Surely it will not be doomed to hell if it is not guilty of original sin and is too undeveloped to be guilty of sins of its own. Was this concession made to try to win his hearers who evidently shared Andreae's horror at the thought that, in spite of their baptism, infants might be reprobates and condemned to hell? But Beza added "probably." With this word, he retained his theological consistency since he had always taught, as had Calvin, that the children of believers are *probably* elect.[20] Beza then added "as long as they do not repudiate these effects as adults." Were they to repudiate their baptism, they would evidently be reprobate from the beginning. In that case, they did not receive any benefits from baptism, something that could not be known at the time of baptism since in Reformed theology, the action of the Holy Spirit is God's secret and cannot be commanded by human actions, even sacramental actions. Beza insisted that it is absurd to say that infants are regenerated when they are baptized since their understanding is not able to receive the word of God and thereby to apprehend Christ through faith. Andreae, scandalized, said that baptism effects regeneration because God's promise is attached to it. As for children's faith, it is purer, less impeded by reason, than is the faith of adults. If these things were not true, how could baptism console? Doubt would overtake confidence in God's mercy.

Behind Beza's position lay a determination to maintain the relation of natural faculties to supernatural gifts. Faith was not something dropped into a vacuum but was given to a mind that, through grace, had understood the word of God. Before understanding developed, there was nothing to respond to grace, understand the word, or receive faith.

The last point, emergency baptism by midwives, involved two concerns: the necessity of baptism for salvation and the appropriateness of women's ministry or even laymen's ministry. Beza began by pointing out that baptism is part of the church's public ministry. It is therefore not legitimate for private persons, whether men or women, to administer it. Nor is there any need for the laws of public ministry to be broken since one can miss being baptized without being guilty of contempt for the sacrament.[21] Beza had already said that damnation resulted only from contempt for salvation and the means God instituted to offer salvation.

Andreae's marginalis to this response is well worth noting because he did not seem to understand the full import of his own argument. Andreae objected that *the Scripture did not forbid any ministry to women*[22] but only that they should not speak in church or when there are men present. But in a case of necessity, when there are no men present, women may not only baptize but teach. Andreae invoked Galatians 3: In Christ there is no longer male nor female but all are one in Christ Jesus.[23]

The example provided here of proof-texting to support a doctrinal position that also involves unexamined assumptions is a telling one. Again and again in the history of theological development, theologians fail to see the implications of their arguments. In this instance, the use of Galatians 3 ought to have been determined as describing a universal situation: Men and women are equal in Christ, hence women may be called to minister as are men. Or it may describe, as Andreae thought it did, an emergency situation, in which case the inequality of men and women for ministry should have been recognized as a matter of human, not divine, law; of polity, not nature. Calvin recognized that this was the case. Calvin did not foresee, however, that ecclesiastical custom barring women from ministry would change. In fact, Calvin found the idea that women baptize horrifying. But his theological basis was consistent in that he rejected the idea that ecclesiastical order should be broken by the ministry of laypersons, male or female. Order ("police") in the church had to be maintained. Unless the whole order were changed, there could be no changes in this or that aspect of the order.[24] Nor were there any "emergencies" that could justify such changes, since the decree of election did not depend on human activity but solely on God's good pleasure.

The next discussion revealed why Beza insisted, in reply to thesis I, that the water signified Christ's blood. Beza asked Andreae in what baptism consisted. Andreae answered that it included all those things necessary for the substance (a word Andreae used frequently in this debate) of baptism: the external elements, the word of command, and the promise of God. Beza responded that insofar as Andreae was speaking of the external baptism, yes, it did consist of the elements and word. So far they agreed. But if one speaks of the interior reason for baptism, the Reformed called Andreae's answer insufficient because baptism is not only the word and element or sign but also the signified thing, the *res significatum,* that is to say, the blood of Christ, which is the most important thing in baptism. Beza then used the Lord's Supper as an example of a sacrament that consists not only of external signs but of the interior signification of the body and blood of Christ truly offered to faith. The same is true, he said, of baptism. The blood of Christ there signified washes the baptized from all sin. Baptism also signifies, continued Beza, immersion in the death of Christ by which the old man, Adam, dies and the new man rises spiritually from sin to justice and newness of life. All of these benefits are offered in the blood of Christ through their representation in the external application of water and the word. It is not correct, therefore, to say that the sacrament of baptism consists only of water and the word, its external elements. It includes also the interior washing and rebirth effected by the blood of Christ through the power of the Holy Spirit. Beza concluded by saying that he was speaking not of a bare signification but of a representation by which, through external signs, an internal reality is offered.[25]

Andreae answered at length. He said that the Württembergers included in baptism the action of the Holy Spirit, who makes it the laver of regeneration and renovation. Baptism is not two things, one internal and the other external, argued Andreae. Rather, action and effect are so linked that they cannot be separated and always occur together. Andreae continued by denying a similarity between baptism and the Lord's Supper. He failed to recognize that he had already made such a parallel by linking the content of the sacraments to their sacramental elements and their application regardless of the faith of the recipient. As the body and blood of Christ are substantially present and given to be eaten by worthy and unworthy alike, so the power of baptism effects what it signifies in the baptized infant. (Presumably the disposition of an unwilling adult would nullify the effects of baptism and render the adult guilty of condemnation as in the case of the unworthy communicant who ate damnation.) But Andreae did not make such theological distinctions at this point; he was more concerned, it seems, to refute Beza on every point rather than to find any basis for agreement. Andreae continued that baptism and the Lord's Supper differ in many ways: the elements, the actions, the words, their final causes. In baptism, the final cause is regeneration; in the Lord's Supper, communicants are not reborn but, having been reborn by baptism, are re-made. Andreae conceded that in both sacraments, the blood of Christ is applied but for different ends. The discussion then disintegrated into long speeches by Andreae and very short lines from Beza while the two collocutors fruitlessly rehearsed the arguments already given.

The next exchange continued the comparison of baptism and the Lord's Supper. Beza emphasized that faith is necessary for the benefits of either sacrament to be received. Thus those who are baptized without appropriate interior dispositions are washed externally by the water but not internally by the blood of Christ. They are offered baptism's benefits but have no hand to grasp them, no receptivity. As he countered this argument, Andreae failed to distinguish the effectiveness of the Lord's Supper and that of baptism. Rather, he continued to insist that both sacraments not only offer but confer what they signify. In both sacraments, the word *est* means "is," not "signifies." Baptism is the laver of regeneration. The discussion here regarded infant baptism and its likeness to circumcision. Through baptism, as in circumcision, the child is made a child of God. There are no tropes in either sacrament, insisted Andreae.[26]

No, responded Beza, the water has no latent power; it is not, of itself, effective. Only the Holy Spirit can make a sinner a child of God, and the instruments the Holy Spirit uses are external signs, water and words, and internal dispositions: faith to receive the ablution of Christ's blood. Therefore the waters of baptism represent but cannot be said to be the laver of regeneration. For this reason, the effects of baptism may be activated whenever a person hears God's word and is given faith as happened before baptism in the case of the centurion Cornelius and after baptism in the case of one who lacks faith at the time and comes to it either during baptism or at some later time.

Not surprisingly, Andreae refused to allow that a sacrament is other than a "bare sign" if it is not identified with the reality it signifies. Andreae would not allow that a relation between sign and signified is sufficient. Andreae therefore objected to distance between sign and signified whether in time (baptism) or space (Lord's Supper). Andreae objected to Beza's doctrine on two more points: There is no need for the Holy Spirit to delay acting on someone who is baptized; there is no point in baptizing at all if the ritual makes no difference with regard to election and reprobation. Beza answered Andreae by repeating the Reformed defense of their sacramental doctrine, that baptism and the Lord's Supper are ordinances of Jesus Christ and as such must be obeyed. Not to obey Christ's commands would be to hold Christ in contempt, a sin meriting damnation. The sacraments are also visible words and as such are instruments of the Holy Spirit as is the preached word. When they are received with faith, they communicate Christ and all his benefits.

Beza's next question elicited Andreae's answer with regard to the difference between adult and infant baptism. Was Cornelius adopted by God prior to his actual baptism?[27] Andreae admitted that adults are capable of coming to faith through hearing, and hence justification, while infants are not. But, Andreae continued, it is an Anabaptist error to say that without a developed intellect one cannot have faith. Faith is not dependent on an active intellect; on the contrary, God can easily work faith in infants, as in John the Baptist in his mother's womb, who leapt when he heard Mary's voice. Baptism, Andreae argued, regenerates the infant in soul and body so that it is no longer a child of hell but of God.

Beza responded that the Reformed teach that while the action of the Holy Spirit may not occur until the baptized person is able to hear and to respond to the word of God, nevertheless children are to be baptized. It is done, he said, according to the formula of the covenant by which God said to Abraham and his posterity: I will be your God and the God of your seed after you. It is enough, affirmed Beza, for the parents to have faith and to apprehend this promise for their children, and therefore it is proper that the children be baptized. Furthermore, that John the Baptist leapt in his mother's womb was a singular event. Scripture nowhere promises such an extraordinary response for all infants. Beza's last point was that although all children, like all people, are invited to hear and respond to God's word, not all do or will respond in the course of their lifetime. Baptism is therefore a probable, not a certain, sign that baptized children receive the fruit of adoption. To say otherwise would be to make God's choice dependent on human actions.[28] Andreae objected that the sacraments would not be sources of comfort if they become sources of probability rather than certainty. Nor does the adoption of an infant depend on the faith of the parents but on the sacrament, just as inclusion in the covenant did not depend on the faith of the parents but on circumcision.

If faith is not given until the Holy Spirit endows an individual with faith, is this action of God equivalent to election and hence without repentance? In other words, is faith amissible? The possibility of losing faith and adoption once these had been given by God became the subject of the next portion of the colloquy. Beza asked whether Simon Magus, who had been baptized as a believer, lost his adoption into the kingdom of God by his impiety. Andreae affirmed that grace could be so lost. Beza disagreed. Simon only pretended to believe, but he did not truly believe and thus he was accursed.[29] Beza said that true faith, given by the Holy Spirit, is inamissible. Andreae therefore asked whether or not faith and the Holy Spirit remained with David during his adulterous act with Bathsheba.[30] No, answered Beza, he retained them. Andreae expressed shock. (Andreae knew how to play his audience, as his frequent turning to them and addressing them imply. According to the *Acta,* Beza never included the audience.) In spite of the buzz of disapproval, Beza insisted that even in the middle of his adultery, David retained faith and the Holy Spirit, illustrating his point by saying that a drunkard does not lose intellect and reason even though he may act contrary to both. In the same way, grace, faith, and the Holy Spirit remain in the elect who fall into sin and recall them to repentance.

Andreae protested that the faculties of intellect and reason that belong to persons because they are human beings are not the same as the divine gifts bestowed on baptized persons, so the example Beza used was inappropriate. What God has given can be lost, insisted Andreae. In fact, Scripture itself testifies to cases in which they were lost, such as the psalmist who prays, "Do not take your holy spirit from me, but give me the joy of your salvation." As the argument continued, Andreae became indignant at the impiety of Beza's assertion that in the midst of perpetrating sins against conscience, sins of impurity and adultery, the elect retain faith and the Holy Spirit. Beza challenged Andreae to show him anyone who is without sin who is at the same time a human being of flesh and blood. There is a difference, insisted Andreae, between human failings and manifest sins against God's law. The former are venial sins, that is, sins not imputed to believers and the elect and into which the just person falls seven times a day and rises up through the Holy Spirit. But the latter are, according to Paul, mortal sins that punish the flesh with eternal death.

Beza responded rather hotly that no sin is venial; all sins are mortal, that is, worthy of death. The papist distinction among sins has no place in this discussion, he said. On the contrary, returned Andreae, Paul speaks of venial sin in Romans 7 when he says that he does not do what he wishes to do and performs what he does not wish to do because the habit of sin works in him. Beza said that the Reformed are far from teaching that all sins are equal, a Stoic opinion, but that nevertheless all sins are by their nature mortal. Sin is venial in the elect except for the one sin of which John speaks that is against the Holy Spirit. In the elect, however, faith and the Holy Spirit remain like fire under banked ashes. Andreae than asked what would have happened to David had he died before he repented. For Beza such a question made no sense because David was elect; God would see to it that he repented before he died. No pun was surely intended when Andreae referred to God's gifts being without repentance. That means, said Andreae, that once baptized, even if one falls, there is no need to rebaptize. Andreae continued that although God's promise cannot fail, human beings can fail. In such an instance, God's promise remains valid and can be grasped by the newly repentant sinner. Beza protested in the same terms as before that election determines the permanence of faith and the Holy Spirit, that these may have their effect at any time in a person's life, and that baptism is of no avail to those who are reprobate.[31]

Andreae reminded Beza that they had agreed not to mix topics and that it was not the time to introduce the subject of predestination. At this point, Andreae preferred to continue the discussion of baptism and especially the problem of consolation in the face of doubt. He asked how one could be at peace if one's adoption as God's child remained uncertain. Beza answered that it is not God's fault if one baptized is not regenerated; rather, it is the fault of the impious person, to whom God owes nothing as long as that person remains impious. The consolation of adoption into God's kingdom is to be prayed for as an effect of the Holy Spirit. So, for instance, one may feel the motion of the Holy Spirit testifying that one is truly regenerated and adopted as a child of God. Andreae failed to charge Beza with avoiding the question as he had posed it. It is not a matter of placing blame but of assuring consciences. Beza's reply on that score was scarcely more helpful since it reduced assurance to subjective feeling, a veritable Pandora's box of pastoral problems.

Andreae raised the pastoral side when he asked how one who is being tempted and is unaware of any motion of the Holy Spirit, in fact one whom Satan is inspiring with contrary thoughts, can be kept from despair. One might conclude that one is not elect. How can one have the consolation of knowing one is elect if the decree is hidden in the eternal and secret decree of God? Andreae likened such a battle in conscience to David's battle with Goliath in which he had a certain hope of victory because he relied on the fact that he had been circumcised in infancy. Who, he said, is this uncircumcised Philistine? Andreae had raised the questions that were to plague Calvinists thereafter. How could one be certain of one's election; what were the signs? Calvin had said that such questions were inappropriate, since election did not depend on the believer but on the certainty of Christ's death and Resurrection. In spite of one's feelings, doubts, and temptations, if one kept one's eyes on Christ and held on to God's promise, election was certain.[32] Beza denied that the Reformed teach that there is no consolation in the sacraments but only that external baptism does not guarantee internal regeneration. Only when the elect hear the interior testimony of the Holy Spirit may they repose their confidence in the external baptism of water. Once they have been so confirmed, they should return to that experience of external and internal baptism for comfort whenever they are tempted, in doubt, or disturbed.[33]

At this point, the two theologians repeated arguments already heard. They adduced more scriptural examples, such as Saul, who was circumcised but not saved. Beza spoke of the circumcision of the flesh and the circumcision of the heart; clearly the two are not the same, he said.[34] Beza probably lost many of his hearers when he affirmed that many thousands of baptized children are never regenerated but perish eternally.[35] Andreae's marginal note says simply: *Horrenda vox.*

In his summation, Andreae rehearsed the Württemberg arguments, leaning most heavily on the lack of assurance that the Reformed doctrine of baptism imposed on parents of baptized children and on all the baptized regarding the effectiveness of their baptism. There should be no doubt that when a child is baptized, it enters into God's adoption and love, said Andreae. There should be no "probably" but rather assurance. Beza responded that no one who feels the Holy Spirit's motion should entertain any doubts about election. Beza tried to turn this disturbing doctrine into a comforting one. The history of Puritanism, especially in England, is the record of his failure. As for other people, continued Beza, no one can judge another or know for certain whether that person is reprobate or elect. Seemingly pious behavior, like that of Simon Magus, may be hypocritical. Sinners may at the last moment be regenerated or called to repentance. The hearts of all are known to God, but they are not open to anyone else. The final resting place of one's assurance is not on behavior, one's own or another's, but on God's grace, said Beza. Returning at last to Calvin's theme, Beza said that faith is directed to Christ, not to one's self. To desire heaven, to desire to hold fast to Christ is enough to assure a person that the Holy Spirit is moving in one's soul and thereby to console and strengthen the Christian in doubt and temptation. Andreae asked the pertinent question, "What if one does not feel such a desire?" Then, answered Beza, one must be as a watcher waiting for the dawn. In the middle of the night there is no sign of dawn; all is dark. But one hopes, and that hope is not deceived because the sun of justice will certainly rise. When it does, one will then feel its rays, the motion of the Holy Spirit.

Andreae remained unconvinced by this poetic peroration. Consolation is needed in the night of doubt, he said. The nature of temptation at its worst is to question one's election and whether the sun will rise before one dies. Interior movements are too insecure, and to rest assurance on such movements leads to despair and a miserable end. Andreae was right on this point. Beza's theological consistency had led him into a psychological morass. Andreae could well insist that the only basis for consolation in temptation is the reality conferred by the word and the sacraments. The consolation Beza could hold out was that no matter how bad a person seemed during a lifetime, one could hope for a deathbed repentance and the activation of a dormant baptism. The two collocutors continued to debate these points, without advancing the argument, for the rest of the day.

The next morning, Beza gave his best argument on the subject. If faith is an act of response to the word, children cannot have such faith since they are incapable of understanding preaching. But Paul says that faith comes by hearing the word of God, for actual faith presupposes knowledge of what is preached so that one can believe it. In extraordinary cases, like John the Baptist, God can bypass the normal course, but ordinarily faith comes through the external hearing of the word of God (Rom. 10). Therefore the principal efficient cause and the instrumental cause are always joined. When faith is given or poured into a person, the efficient cause is the Holy Spirit and the instrumental cause is hearing the word of God. So children do not have actual faith but the seed or root of faith. Baptism is not, on that account, useless for children, but rather baptism is rendered efficacious when the child matures, hears the word, even in memory, and believes. Further, baptism is a sign of the covenant to which the parents belong and into which they therefore baptize their children, leaning on the faith of the church. The faith of the church supplements the faith of the parents so that one can say that probably such children will be added to the number of the children of God.[36]

Andreae objected that children can have faith through the Holy Spirit. In fact, intellect is not at issue here since reason sometimes impedes faith. Scripture says that the intellect must be brought into captivity in order to believe. It should be underlined here that Beza's argument is based on the instrumental causality of the human intellect actually working, whereas Andreae's argument says that faith is a gift that does not depend on the intellect but indeed may be impeded by intellectual activity.

The action on baptism concluded with arguments about parental duties. The two collocutors agreed that to show contempt for the sacrament by not baptizing children is sinful. But the results for the children were differently presented. Andreae said that baptism is necessary and emergency baptism can be supplied by women. Beza countered that if women can administer one sacrament, they can administer the other and on Andreae's ground should be allowed to administer the Lord's Supper when no men ordained for the task were available. Andreae replied that the degree of necessity involved is quite different. In baptism, the eternal life of the infant is at stake. In the case of the Lord's Supper, a public ceremony is at issue. Beza did not pursue this last declaration of Andreae's but argued that baptism is not necessary to the extent that nonordained persons should be allowed to administer it. If a minister is not available, God's election suffices for salvation.

There were no concluding arguments or summaries of agreed-upon points or points remaining in contention. Rather, Andreae, playing well his psychological cards, appealed to the audience to judge between them.

Throughout the colloquy so far, the philosophical differences between the two theologians were consistently maintained. Beza supported the integrity of created natures and of their instrumentality whether these were sacramental elements, the humanity of Christ, or the operation of faith on the mind. For Beza, the Spirit worked through the flesh. Andreae invoked the supernatural, bypassing natural operations, so that the sacramental elements were identified with the signified reality, the human nature of Christ shared divine properties, and faith could be effective apart from human understanding. For Andreae, Spirit worked in spite of flesh.

In his *Responsio,* Beza provided his own lists of those points on which he thought he and Andreae had agreed and disagreed. They agreed, wrote Beza, on two points: Baptism is ordained by Christ as the successor to circumcision, and baptism must be conferred on Christian infants according to the institution of Christ. Beza and Andreae disagreed on four points that are in reality only one: Andreae argued that external baptism is accompanied by interior regeneration and the gift of faith. Beza said that what happens interiorly is known only to God and may not be presumed because of human actions. Effective faith is a gift bestowed without repentance by the Holy Spirit on the elect.[37]

Predestination[38]

Because the Reformed team had not come prepared to debate the three last topics, they had no theses prepared. But, wrote Andreae,[39] because Count Frederick wanted to hear the subjects debated, they proceeded by way of the public reading of the theses prepared by the Württemberg theologians between March 13 and March 21 while they awaited the arrival of the Swiss. Beza, having learned from days of experience that Andreae dominated the dialogue, asked Frederick to persuade Andreae to "study brevity and abstain from prolixity."[40]

The theses began with four points considered noncontroversial:

1. God, from all eternity, foresaw the fall of Adam and Eve and all their offspring.
2. God not only foresaw who would be saved but elected them and predestined them to eternal life.
3. Before the foundation of the world was set, their election was in Christ as the source of all salvation.
4. The number of the elect is set by God.

The controversial points were summed up in theses V through VII, posed as questions and answers.

5. Is predestination determined by a secret and absolute decree before the birth of the elect? Are the reprobate also included in a decree that cannot be affected by penance and conversion?
6. The answer to the second question in thesis V is no. It cannot be demonstrated from Scripture that there is a secret decree of God that, without any respect for unworthiness but solely by the pleasure of his will, God has destined the greater part of humankind to eternal damnation so that they are unable to do penance, be converted, and be saved. In other words, the Württembergers reject double predestination.
7. This "thesis" provides the scriptural warrants for thesis VI so that the Württemberg theologians' theses amount to an assertion of single predestination.

Eleven theses follow, which Andreae and Osiander ascribed to the Reformed and which they condemned. All of them dealt with aspects of double predestination:

1–3. Eternal reprobation is effected by God's justice and restricts God's mercy in order to glorify his wrath, power, and justice.

4. God justly ordained Adam's sin, which was nevertheless spontaneous.

5–6. God loves some and hates others; hence their election or reprobation has no cause, including their own natures, other than God's will.

7–10. Adam's fall and its mortal results have only one cause, God's prescience and foreordination, so that Adam had no alternative.

11. God did not wish to be served by those destined for reprobation so that they had to be condemned to eternal death.

Beza's brief answers to the theses elicit long marginal comments from Andreae.[41] Because of the intricacy of the arguments and the greater interest scholars have shown in the Genevan doctrine of double predestination, I shall try to do justice to arguments and counterarguments as they occur. Beza said that generally his team affirmed that God was neither ignorant nor merely lazily aware nor unwilling that Adam and Eve should fall or that anyone who was to come into the world should fall. For without God's will and knowledge, not even the smallest sparrow falls. Andreae indignantly replied that nowhere does Scripture say that God willed the sin of the first parents.

In response to thesis IV, Beza declared that since God chose the elect, he also chose not to elect the reprobate since the choice of one means the rejection of the other. There are, therefore, a certain number of elect and a specific number of reprobate known to God from eternity. Andreae answered that there is no absolute decree of God by which God refuses to save anyone. The reprobate owe their damnation to themselves alone. Beza and Andreae had a tug-of-war over theses V and VI, since these acutely pose the problem of double versus single predestination. Beza continued to assert that since nothing could happen without God's knowledge and will, there must have been a decree in which the reprobate were included since to elect some is, ipso facto, to reject others. Andreae argued that God does not will the damnation of anyone. The damned owe their state to their own will and to the devil; God's condemnation of them is therefore just. In fact, insisted Andreae, the damned perish contrary to the will of God. As for a decree, the only place in Scripture where the elect are foreseen is in Christ.

Beza had then to explain how the decree of God is the cause of election but is not the cause of damnation. He distinguished a decree of execution or "executive order" from a decree that recognizes a state of affairs. Those who are damned are so because of their corrupt natures, with which all are born and from the fruits of which God rescues some (the elect) and not others (the damned). God does not condemn the reprobate in spite of their wish to be saved made ineffective by God's decree, but rather they are condemned because they do not want to be converted, nor are they capable of wishing to be converted. Their corruption and impenitence are willed by them, and so they are justly condemned by God. Beza cited the passages "many are called but few are chosen" and "few get through the narrow gate" as scriptural justification for his argument. Andreae answered that there is no absolute decree determining who are chosen and who are not; the scriptural passages do not support such an inference. In fact, affirmed Andreae, God wants to save all; he wants no one to perish. That many are damned is because they have contempt for the grace offered in Christ and for the Word of God. The cause of damnation is within the damned; it is not in God. Andreae expressed horror at the notion that God excluded any from his love by an absolute decree of condemnation. He was equally angered by the idea that anyone wishing to be saved could be excluded from Christ.

Beza had, of course, not said that anyone could wish to be saved contrary to God's decree. He had said that because of the Fall, all were born in corruption. Some were saved from it and others left in it; in neither case was it a matter of will but of grace. That is the nub of the matter. Calvin had understood the consistency of such a position if grace were to be absolutely free and unconditioned by works of any kind. Grace had to precede human activity, including that of willing to find grace. Beza understood Calvin's position and sought to buttress it.

As he had distinguished between kinds of divine effectiveness in the decree, so Beza now distinguished what the word *all* meant when Paul wrote that God wished to save all. *All* does not mean "each." It does mean a representation of all kinds and conditions. Had God willed that each and every person be saved, argued Beza, then since it is clear that all are not saved, God's will would be rendered ineffectual by human wills. To support this thesis, Beza had to restrict the scope of Ezekiel 18 ("God says I live and do not wish the death of a sinner but that he be converted and live") to the elect, since only the elect receive the grace of effective conversion. In other words, against the scriptural passages taken by the Württembergers to express God's universal salvific will, Beza interpreted the passages to mean not *all* in a universal sense but either *all the elect* or *all kinds*. Beza qualified the absolute universality maintained by Andreae.

When Beza said that God could not wish that every single person be saved without making the divine will subject to human will, Andreae answered that God, by his absolute will, does not wish everyone to be saved; if he did so will, all would be saved since no one can resist God's will. What Paul means, continued Andreae in a marginal comment, is that God wills all who are in Christ to be saved. Andreae thus also qualified the universal salvific will of God, leaving the way clear for Beza to say that Christ is both the foundation and the first object of the decree.[42]

The extent of God's salvific will continued to occupy the discussants.[43] Beza explained Luke 24 by saying that *world* here refers to people in an unqualified way so that Christ is saying that he does not pray for everyone but only for those whom the Father had given to him and who believe in his name.

Such an interpretation pointed toward the seventeenth-century doctrine of limited atonement.[44] The same is true of Beza's next comment. John 1:2 says, "Not for us only but for the sins of the whole world he has been made a propitiation." "The whole world," explained Beza, refers to the universality of the elect gathered from all kinds of people, Jews as well as Gentiles. Christ's prayer is not indiscriminate!

In the margin, Andreae responded fulsomely. Christ is the propitiation for everyone, for the whole world, he wrote. The Johannine text is a witness against Beza because the context is not Jews and Gentiles but the whole world. Nothing is more certain, contended Andreae, than that John meant by *world* all people universally, as other places in Scripture testify and confirm.[45]

Beza continued to bolster his limited-atonement argument by saying that it is intolerable to claim that Christ died for the damned.[46] Andreae countered that it is intolerable for Beza to say that *all* means "some." Nor, charged Andreae, can Beza's doctrine avoid making God the author of sin since Beza teaches that God the Creator, by his absolute decree, created and ordained humankind to sin and to damnation so that they were unable to be converted and saved. Andreae ended his comments on a pastoral note of concern for sinners like David who would have good grounds to question their election given their response to temptation. Such persons would fall into despair. Where, then, would the comfort of the gospel be? Of what use would be the sacraments, indeed any of the church's ministry?[47]

The dogmatic discussion[48] that followed Beza's responses to the theses and Andreae's marginalia was sometimes scholastic, sometimes scriptural. Although the beginning of this debate was scholastic enough, the language became increasingly polemical and accusatory as first one and then the other expressed horror and scandal. Beza insisted on a distinction between the efficient cause and the execution of the decree. The efficient cause of the sinner's damnation is the sinner's corrupt nature. The decree then effects punishment. Beza made the bedrock of his position clear when he said that to make incredulity, faith, works, or any other human activity the cause of God's decree of either reprobation or election is Pelagian. Andreae answered that faith is the work of the Holy Spirit and so is not a human "work"; therefore, to posit faith as the basis of election is not Pelagian. Beza missed his chance here. If faith is the work of the Holy Spirit, then why does the Holy Spirit work in some and not in others? This is the problem of the relation of grace and will that has such a long, fascinating, and continuing history. Beza and the late Augustine stand on one side of the argument; Andreae and the Council of Orange (529 C.E.) stand on the other. The collocutors did not pursue this line of argument, however, or the history of the debate as they had done with regard to the Lord's Supper and the person of Christ.

Beza protested the wording of theses VI and VII, saying that Adam sinned spontaneously but nevertheless necessarily because of the decree. In his response to eight of the "unscriptural theses," Beza addressed this problem through a long-overdue analysis of the relation of causes. He said that since, in the order of causes, God knows nothing as future other than what he has already decreed concerning it, it follows that the decree precedes knowledge and that knowledge is not the proper cause of things.[49] Such an analysis put Beza in the camp of those who, in the debate concerning God's will and knowledge, gave precedence to the will of God.

Since Beza had no written response prepared on the day of the discussion, these theses and responses were signed by the Reformed team at the end of the colloquy on March 29, 1586.[50] Andreae then reduced the whole argument to whether or not God, in his eternal, hidden and secret counsel, made an eternal, absolute, immutable decree that the greater part of humankind was reprobate. Beza began his long response by warning that the subject was fraught with danger and that the Holy Spirit must guide them since there is no part of Christian doctrine by which human sense and reason are more horrified. Beza then argued that if an architect plans a house, how much more did God plan the world and that in doing so he had a certain end in mind. Ultimately the only worthy purpose is the glory of God, a glory especially known in God's mercy and justice. For that reason, God decreed that some people, the elect, would glorify God's mercy and others, the reprobate, would illustrate God's justice. Mercy, said Beza, presupposes misery. If mercy is to be manifest, there must first be misery. Again, justice presupposes fault, without which justice cannot be exercised. Beza set up a situation that required a fall and eternal damnation of some, indeed most, of the fallen.[51] The decree stood in the place of a first cause. All subsequent actions and actors were therefore second causes or instruments of the decree. Out of mercy, then, God wanted certain people to be elected in Christ, but others, according to justice, would be rejected and condemned for their faults.

The Christian doctrine of creation affirmed the basic goodness of creation, including the goodness of Adam and Eve. How, then, did they fall? Beza said that God made them not only good and holy but mutable. God is therefore the author of good; evil entered because of the first parents' mutability and their ability to sin. Eve first transgressed the law by eating the fruit of the tree of the knowledge of good and evil. This she did of her own will, coerced neither by God nor by Satan. She consented to the persuasion of the serpent and was thereby corrupted and separated from God. This did not happen, however, without God's will and decree. Adam followed her in sin, and both, of their free will, brought the human race under the justice of God. To satisfy divine justice, God decreed that the only begotten Son of God would assume human nature in the unity of the Second Person and in that human nature, by his Passion and death, pay the debt and satisfy for the sins of the elect.[52] Beza enunciated clearly the doctrine of limited atonement and in his description of the decrees, a doctrine of supralapsarian double predestination in which the Fall followed upon God's decision to be glorified through justice and mercy. Beza rehearsed Christ's incarnation, life, passion, and death. He then explained, following Augustine and Bernard, the difference between the first parents and Christ with regard to their ability to sin and die or not to sin and to die or not to sin and not to die. In each case, free will was involved. Adam and Eve could sin or not sin. Christ could not sin because his person was divine. Adam and Eve sinned and became mortal. Christ did not sin but was born into the human condition of mortality. Nevertheless, he could have chosen not to die, but he submitted to the divine decree and offered his death to satisfy divine justice and make possible divine mercy. That God exercised mercy was therefore contingent on the fall of Adam. Adam's fall was necessary so that mercy could be exercised and spontaneous because Adam fell willingly, persuaded by the serpent.

To understand this, said Beza, we have to pay attention to immediate causes whether we move from the plan of God to salvation or, even more, if we go from salvation to the plan of God. God has ordered everything by gradations so that the fault of sin lies in sinners because they are corrupt. They are cursed because they are corrupt. We must not therefore bypass second and mediating causes or we will fall into absurdities. It is no lack of respect for this mystery if we rightly consider the secondary causes that come between the secret decree of God and its last effect, namely, salvation and condemnation. We begin therefore with Adam's sin. Even at the moment of sin, God's love was active, electing some in Christ. According to the apostle, election occurred before the foundations of the world were laid. The causes of election are first God's efficacious call, which happens through the preaching of the gospel and by the interior drawing of the Holy Spirit. By this calling, the heart is softened and turned to God by grace alone, upon which faith follows, that is, trust in Christ. Christ gathers up the elect and applies his benefits to them so that their sins are remitted and they come to eternal life. The faith that is worked in the elect by the Holy Spirit and through hearing results in the imputation of Christ's justice, that is, the merits of Christ. This marks the beginning of sanctification, by which the elect are given the Holy Spirit and renewed. The Holy Spirit brings about good works through them that are pleasing and acceptable to God on account of Christ. Thus it is through secondary and mediating causes that God acts in the elect for salvation and thus also he works with the reprobate through ordained causes.

In the reprobate, the preaching of the gospel is without effect because the Holy Spirit does not work in them. The reprobate are justly hated by God because of their corruption and are justly punished. God never loved them, and even if they are called, their calling is inefficacious. Their hearts do not hear even though their ears may do so. Their hard-heartedness is both necessary and spontaneous. Besides these, there are those who hear the word and grasp it with their minds but who are not gifted with saving faith by the Holy Spirit. Others never hear the word and so have no response at all and yet are justly condemned for their corruption. God owes nothing to anyone; when the elect are called, this is pure grace and not caused by anything in themselves. On the other hand, corrupt human beings willingly embrace incredulity and reject God's call. The fault lies in them, not in God.

Salvation and reprobation are not caused in the same way if one considers them in the execution of election and of the plan of God. The cause of salvation is in God; the cause of damnation is in the damned and is from the devil, not God or God's decree.

How can one know whether one is elect or reprobate? Beza answered this most difficult pastoral question. You must, he said, believe that Christ died for you and that your predestination is secure in Christ. You must believe this against all the temptations of Satan and human conjecture. You must be as certain as though you had heard it from the mouth of God. And you can so hear it when you hear God's word preached and you are called to Christ. Consider, then, whether you are justified and sanctified in Christ. You will know this through the Spirit of Adoption crying within you, "Abba! Father!" and also because through the power of the Spirit you both feel and show it. Even though sin may still dwell in you, it will not reign in you. If you do sin, you will hate your sin and return to the merciful Father and call on him. These are the effects of faith and indicate that you are efficaciously called and drawn by God.

This is not a doctrine for children, said Beza. It is not milk but solid food. So this doctrine should not be lightly proposed. It should be used only with great prudence and only among those who are capable of understanding it and who are rightly disposed. It should be discussed only by those who have been well instructed concerning sin, the law, and justification by faith since this is the way Paul approaches it in the Epistle to the Romans.

This long speech was apparently still longer. Andreae wrote that Beza took seven hours to give it and that more than seven times Count Frederick asked Andreae to interrupt Beza's "sermon." But Andreae refused and asked Frederick to hear Beza out patiently. Frederick agreed but with considerable restlessness and said from time to time, "Dr. Beza, conclude, conclude." When Beza had finished, Andreae asked him whether he wished to add anything. Beza said that he had no more to say.[53]

Andreae accused Beza of misrepresenting the doctrine of predestination and promised his hearers that his response would be brief. Andreae said it sounded as though Beza were sitting in the council of the Holy Trinity since he knew so much about the decree, its purposes, its order, and its execution. Beza answered quite seriously that he was not God's confidant nor had he explained the doctrine according to human reason but according to the Holy Spirit in Scripture. Andreae proceeded, in a few pages, to sum up Beza's arguments quite fairly. (Andreae wanted to let Beza go on at length and was scrupulous about presenting Beza's doctrine because Andreae was confident that most of their hearers would not accept double predestination or the elaborate presentation of the decree and secondary causes.) He then said that he and the other theologians of Württemberg rejected and condemned this doctrine as false and contrary to God's word. God never thought of such a decree, insisted Andreae. Nor can the will of God be known by human reason but only from the word of God, which is not all that obscure. Scripture witnesses to God's love for all creation and for all humankind, as John 3 testifies: "God so loved the world that he gave his only begotten son." Beza's unqualified assertion that God hates the reprobate is contrary to Scripture. The word *world* does not mean the "elect," said Andreae. It means the whole human race, as all of Scripture certifies. Andreae then rolled out seven passages from the Old and New Testaments and proclaimed that Beza had no warrant for interpreting *all* as "some." Andreae then attacked Beza's doctrine that God calls many but that he intends, indeed decreed, that for many the call is inefficacious because they refuse to respond. For example, said Andreae, how foolish Count Frederick would be to call all his citizens to come to him while intending that only a few actually do so.

Andreae turned to the pastoral side of the argument and said that Beza's doctrine would make consolation impossible. Consciences and hearts would be in perpetual doubt concerning their election or reprobation. How could they know God's secret decree or the nature of the intermediate causes? Andreae was even more disturbed that Beza would teach that in order to be more certain of election one should sense in oneself the movements of the Holy Spirit. Some people might feel nothing of the kind and so fall into despair. They might hope to be regenerated at some later time, according to Beza's doctrine of baptism, but would they not be miserable until that day?

Beza returned the discussion to the word *world* and cited John 17: "I do not pray for the world," together with Augustine's interpretation of it. The word *world* refers to the reprobate, said Beza, and so commented Augustine in his letter to Simplicianus. Andreae agreed that in this case the word *world* was restricted to those who were contemptuous of Christ. The context of the passage makes it clear. But that is not the case with other passages, and Andreae repeated his earlier argument. The two continued to debate this point of exegesis without advancing their arguments. Beza then reiterated his belief that Christ died only for the elect since if he had died for the damned they would not be damned! Beza could not bear to think that Christ's blood was shed in vain for anyone, while Andreae was horrified at this doctrine of limited atonement. Turning to the audience, Andreae invited them to be horrified with him. He said that the damned are so not because of God's decree but because they refuse to apply through faith the benefits of Christ, who died for them and satisfied for their sins.

Andreae turned to Frederick and asked that the discussion be terminated since Beza was committed to a doctrine that was so absurd in the light of Christian faith and Scripture. In addition, it deprives people of consolation and reliance on the gospel and the sacraments. Baptism, said Andreae, assures the baptized of their election and salvation since in it the Trinity promises everyone baptized propitiation for their sins and the grace of Christ who died for them and for the whole world. In the eucharist, they receive the very body and blood of Christ given for their salvation.

Beza denied that the doctrine he expounded perturbed consciences or robbed people of consolation since the Holy Spirit is given to the elect and testifies to their spirits that they are indeed children of God. Indeed, claimed Beza in the first part of his *Responsio,* the Genevan doctrine was in accord with Luther's treatise against Erasmus. To prove it, Beza quoted Luther at length.[54] In fact, Beza wrote nothing more in his *Responsio* and allowed Luther to speak for him.

After further restatement of earlier arguments, Andreae began a lengthy and repetitious lecture. His summation was done in the light of baptism and the Lord's Supper and was notable for an eloquence lacking in earlier presentations. No new information was communicated, however. Beza responded that Andreae passed judgment as though he were sitting on the throne of God's tribunal and as though Andreae alone had the power to determine religious truth. Beza mounted counterarguments that also contained neither new information nor new positions regarding the sacraments and predestination. Beza then scored by pointing to the martyrs in France and the Lowlands and to the disunity of the Lutherans in spite of their Book of Concord. Beza accused Andreae of teaching eucharistic and christological doctrines different from those of Chemnitz and Heshus. He concluded by saying that he prayed that both sides would some day come to know which one was right.

Andreae appealed to Frederick and to the audience concerning his fairness to Beza. They should determine who is correctly interpreting Scripture and who is glossing it with merely human interpretations. He defended the unity of the Lutherans and then prayed not that each side should come to know the truth but that Beza's side might see the truth, admit their errors, and take the word of God in its open, simple meaning.

Beza said that his side would pray that Andreae increase in charity.

So the colloquy ended. The Württembergers asked Beza and his colleagues to give written responses to the Lutheran theses on the last three major points: the use of churches and externals, baptism, and predestination. Andreae thanked Frederick for his hospitality and his patience. Andreae was sure that Frederick now understood on which side truth resided and could make some kind of judgment. Beza thanked Frederick and promised to pray for him. Frederick responded in French so that the Frenchmen present could understand him, but Andreae reproduced it in Latin in his *Acta*. In his address, Frederick expressed his hopes that the colloquy might result in peace and concord at some time in the future. At this point, he said, there was no more to be done. Perhaps God does not will that concord be achieved, so we must be patient. Frederick thanked the collocutors, especially the Swiss, who had traveled so far.

Andreae then summarized the whole colloquy, the major issues, and the manner of proceeding. The summary was signed by the theologians and politicians from Württemberg and from the Swiss cities. Although there had been no official notaries in order to keep the discussion as uninhibited as possible, nevertheless three of the Württemberg side had taken notes. The Swiss could proceed as they wished. At this, the Swiss begged that nothing taken down so informally by the opposition be given the power and authority of a protocol. The Württembergers expressed astonishment that the Swiss should feel so strongly about this, but they agreed to the request—or said that they did. In reality, Andreae seemed to have intended to publish the results since he argued that the notes were taken in all fairness and both the audience and Count Frederick could vouch for the justness of the transcription.

It was time for farewells. Beza expressed the hope that eventually they might achieve concord, and he reiterated his prayer that God illumine minds on both sides so that wherever there were errors they might be brought to truth in the Holy Spirit. He also prayed that each side abstain from bitter writings until the Lord should, in his goodness, bestow peace. Beza, in the name of his companions, saluted the others and offered the right hand of brotherhood, that they might show that they do indeed seek concord and peace.

Andreae responded. He said that they too were sorry that they had not reached consensus on the controversial articles. At least it had become clear who explained Scripture plainly. Had the other side refrained from human glosses, said Andreae, they probably would have reached agreement. As it was, Beza's errors were a matter of public record and as long as the other side continued to hold such doctrines there could not be much hope for concord. Andreae said that he prayed that God would illumine Beza and his companions and that the Holy Spirit would illumine their minds so they would reject their terrible heresies and horrible errors. Andreae, like Luther nearly sixty years earlier, refused to extend the right hand of brotherhood. How can we do so, he asked, until they revoke their heresies? How terrible they are has been demonstrated by this colloquy, so we cannot acknowledge them as brothers. Andreae's intent was revealed when he said that his side would certainly correct any errors that might appear in print. Andreae then conceded that although he could not extend the hand of brotherhood, he could extend the hand of humanity. Beza, rightly offended by Andreae's high-handed tone, replied that if the opposite team would not shake hands in brotherhood, neither would his side accept the hand of friendship. Thus the colloquy ended. It was to have a bitter aftermath.[55]

Notes

1. *Acta,* 372.
2. Ibid., 373.
3. Ibid., 376: "Deinde & hoc petimus, ut cum in causa sacramentaria manifeste conveniamus in iis, quae vere sunt essentialia, veluti in vera rerum significatarum veri corporis & sanguinis Domini perceptione; quamvis de praesentiae Sacramentalis modo inter nos nondum conveniat, neque de impiorum manducatione, quorum causa indignum fuerit, pios inter se divelli; liceat nostrae Confessionis fratribus, suam confessionem sine ullo alterius praeiudicio, retinentibus, sacram Coenam ex aliorum manibus percipere, & ita mutuam fraternitatem colere ac testari. Andreae wrote in the margin: Non minus de dignorum, quam indignorum manducatione controvertitur. Impudens postulatum."
4. Geisendorf, *Théodore de Bèze,* 74–75.
5. Ibid., 96–103, esp. 100.
6. See p. 00.
7. There is irony in Andrea's argument. Calvin had argued that nothing in Scripture should be kept from the faithful, including predestination, difficult doctrine though it was (*Institutes* III, xx).
8. *Acta,* 378–81, for Andreae's exhortation to Frederick.

9. Ibid., 268–69.

10. Ibid., 388.

11. Ibid., 389–427. Because there was general agreement on this topic, I shall discuss only those points that have historical or theological relevance without presenting the complexities of the debate.

12. Ibid., 394.

13. It should be recalled that the marginalia were added at the time the *Acta* were edited by Andreae. His part of the discussion at the colloquy forms by far the larger part of the main text.

14. There is no discussion of the necessary restriction of circumcision to boys and the extension of baptism to girls. Calvin discusses this point briefly (*Institutes* IV, xvi, 16). Nor is there any discussion of baptism as a Christian form of passing through the Red Sea.

15. *Resp. pars alt.,* p. 41. That is to say, there was nothing at all said about it as Beza began his response.

16. Raitt, "Three Inter-related Principles," 51–61.

17. *Acta,* 432–33: "Neque nos Sacramenta docemus nuda esse signa, sed externae tamen actioni negamus tribuendum esse, quod est unius Spiritus sancti. Sicut a Ioanne, Matth.3.v.11. & a Petro, I.Epist.3.v.2. non separantur quidem, sed distinguuntur: dicente etiam Apostolo, de universo Ministerio; eum, qui plantat & rigat, nihil esse." For the importance of the principle: "not separate but distinct" in Calvin's theology, see Raitt, "Three Inter-related Principles."

18. See Raitt, *Eucharistic Theology of Theodore Beza,* 55–56.

19. Cf. *Resp. pars alt.,* 41, 61.

20. See pp. 142–43.

21. *Acta,* 435: "Baptismus pars est Ministerii publici, quod est expresse Dei verbo mulieribus, imo etiam privatis personis interdictum: neque vel Baptismum videri potest contempsisse, qui nulla sua culpa excedens ex hac vita non baptizatur: neque necessitas ulla incidere potest, publici urgentis ministerii leges transgredi."

22. Emphasis added.

23. Apparently, only in emergencies is there neither male nor female in Christ.

24. For a detailed discussion of the relation of divine, natural, and ecclesiastical order with regard to the "place" of women in Calvin's view, see Jane Dempsey Douglass, *Women, Freedom and Calvin* (Philadelphia: Westminster Press, 1985).

25. *Acta,* 437–38.

26. Now while that argument may be made for the Lord's Supper so that the unworthy receive the body and blood of Christ to their condemnation, that is, without the vivifying fruits of their communion, can the same be said for adults dragged unwillingly to be baptized or who pretend to desire baptism? Are the sins of such persons washed away in spite of their resistance or duplicity? This point was not raised by Beza or Andreae, however obvious it may seem.

27. *Acta,* 458.

28. Cf. *Resp. pars alt.,* 91–92.

29. The discussion regarding Simon Magus occurs in the *Acta,* 461–63.

30. *Acta,* 463: "Quaero igitur: num David adulterium perpetrans cum Bathseba, uxore Uriae, fidem & Spiritum sanctum amiserit?"

31. Ibid., 469–70.

32. *Institutes* III, ii, 17–25.

33. *Acta,* 472.

34. Ibid., 478.

35. Ibid., 479: "Idem in Baptismo quoque fit, quem multa millia infantum accipiunt, qui tamen nunquam regenerantur, sed in aeternum pereunt."

36. Ibid., 490–91.

37. *Resp. pars alt.,* 145–46.

38. In the *Acta* this topic extends from pp. 502 through 552. The relative brevity of this section reflects, perhaps, Beza's reluctance to address the subject as well as the need of the Reformed to return to their churches in time for Easter. On this topic cf. Gottfried Adam, *Der Streit um die Prädestination im ausgehenden 16. Jahrhundert: Eine Untersuchung zu den Entwurfen von Samuel Huber und Aegidius Hunnius* (Neukirchen: Neukirchener Verlag, 1970). Pt. 1 contains a section on the dispute on predestination at the Colloquy of Montbéliard (pp. 29–49). In his interpretation of Beza's doctrine of predestination, Adam is in the Bizer/Kickel school.

39. *Acta,* 502.

40. Ibid.: "cum D. Iacobo Andreae ageret, ut brevitati studeret, & a prolixitate sermonis abstineret."

41. These pages of the *Acta* indicate Andreae's verbosity, as Beza's responses are almost lost in the framing marginalia (pp. 507–21). The pages that record the ensuing discussion (pp. 521–52) allow Beza thirteen pages of uninterrupted discourse (the longest single segment given Beza in the *Acta*), followed by twenty-six pages of response from Andreae within which Beza's comments total roughly three pages.

42. *Resp. pars alt.,* 156–57.

43. Ibid., 192ff.

44. But see Calvin's commentary on John 3:17, which points in the same direction.

45. It is not my intention to establish the meaning of this text, which has long been disputed. Twentieth-century interpretations would not alter the course of the sixteenth-century argument or its meaning for subsequent history.

46. *Acta,* 514: "Et certe nobis intolerabilis vox vestra visa est, Christum esse mortuum pro damnatis."

47. Ibid., 516: "Ruunt interdum etiam electi filii diaboli, quemadmodum David in adulterium, homicidium, &c. Ubi ergo consolatio & certitudo electionis eorum? aut unde petenda aut sumenda erit? Quae in promissionibus Evangelii universalibus, in Baptismo, in Coena Domini, in Absolutione, secundum opinionem Bezae & sociorum eius, non est certa."

48. Ibid., 516–21.

49. Ibid., 519–20: "Cum ordine causarum nihil prius sciat Deus futurum, quam quod decrevit futurum, nisi (quod absurdissimum esset) absque Dei decreto aliquid esse vel fieri censeamus; consequitur decretum scientiae praeire, nec scientiam esse propriam rerum causam." Or, asked Beza, is it possible for something to come to pass without God's knowledge and will? The basis of the argument is the same as Calvin had laid down. Although human minds are bound to categories of time, God is not. Eternity is not sequential time. There is, therefore, no before and after in God. God's knowing and willing are likewise not bound by time, but one may speak of an order in causes that are themselves simultaneous. Thus one may say that knowledge precedes willing. But in the case of God's decree, knowing and willing, decreeing and seeing, electing and reprobating are all one.

50. Ibid., 521.

51. This initial analysis of the requirements for justice and mercy could be equally faulted by medieval and modern philosophers and theologians who understood and understand that justice is broader than punishment and that mercy can be exercised apart from an eternal destiny.

52. *Acta,* 526: "Quapropter in eodem arcano & aeterno consilio suo, sancta Trinitas decrevit, ut Filius Dei Patris unigenitus, in persona suae unitatem, naturam humanam assumeret, in qua poenas peccati secundum iustitiam Dei debitas perferret, & sua passione & morte pro peccatis electorum satisfaceret."

53. Ibid., 535–36.

54. *Responsio,* 182–96 (Response 262–82). Cf. Luther, *De servo arbitrio,* WA 18, 684–787. (For the English version, see Library of Christian Classics, vol. 17, Luther and Erasmus: Free Will and Salvation, ed. and trans. E. Gordon Rupp et al. (Philadelphia: Westminster Press, 1969). See also App. 3, pp. 207–10.

55. It is interesting to note how polemics continue for centuries. Gensichen, in *We Condemn,* wrote: "The manner in which Theodore Beza waged war on Lutheran 'cannibalism' (*sarcophagia*) seemed to warrant the conclusion that he was condemning the Lutheran doctrine of the Eucharist. The fact that at Montbeliard in 1586 Beza had refused the 'right hand of fellowship and humanity' proffered by the Lutherans in spite of the doctrinal dissent could only strengthen this impression later on" (p. 197). Since Gensichen referred to the *Acta,* one may assume he had read the text and knew that Beza had been the conciliatory collocutor and Andreae the one who refused to yield and maintained the condemnation of Calvinists.

6

Aftermath (1):
Polemics and Politics

The colloquy not only failed to unite Lutherans and Calvinists but fanned polemical flames and resulted in a bitter publishing war. In spite of Beza's plea that notaries be engaged to produce a protocol that the collocutors could sign, this was not done. Instead, Lucas Osiander and others of Andreae's party kept notes that Andreae then used to produce *Acta* of the colloquy, thereby touching off an exchange that ended only with a publication from Andreae so vitriolic that Beza chose silence.

The declared reason for publishing the *Acta* was a scurrilous pseudonymous letter that was a Calvinist response to published letters from Tübingen exulting in the Württembergers' victory, saying that Beza had been so soundly defeated that he had left the colloquy in tears.[1]

None of the postcolloquial claims were borne out by the brief, sober summary of the colloquy that was written and signed on March 29, 1586. The document briefly states the reason, conditions, and results of the colloquy, namely:

1. Count Frederick convened it at the instigation of the French exiles.
2. There was no official protocol made so that their discussions could proceed peacefully and informally.
3. The collocutors were not speaking for their churches but as individual theologians.
4. While there was agreement on the fifth article regarding images in the churches, there was so little agreement on the remaining four articles that neither side was reconciled to the other.
5. In fact, the collocutors referred to their own publications and came to no new conclusions.
6. Lastly, whatever notes had been taken were not to have the force of an authentic, authorized protocol.[2]

The summary document was signed by the members of each team.

In spite of this agreement, Andreae set about preparing for a major publication that would look like a verbatim account of the colloquy. His actions had been predicted by Ludwig Lavater in a letter to Beza dated January 19/29,

1586: "Be sure to have a notary take everything down so that you don't give occasion to Jacob to tell a false tale."[3] To justify the *Acta* and as part of its long title, Andreae affirmed that he felt constrained to publish a nonofficial but authorized version to refute widespread rumors embodied in a scurrilous letter.[4] By July 1586, Andreae had arranged for copies to be made of Osiander's notes so that he could edit them for publication.[5] In August, Lucas Osiander wrote that while it was necessary to publish a protocol of the proceedings of the colloquy in order to squelch rumors, it would not be printed in time for the fall book fair.[6] The same group of letters, all dated August 6, contains the information that Count Frederick not only wanted the protocol published but would sign it after he had studied it. To Frederick's concern was added the powerful voice of Duke Ludwig, who wrote to Andreae that he had received letters from Beza and other Calvinists who challenged reports being circulated about the colloquy. In addition: "Many well-meaning, even noble persons would like to have a certain and adequate report concerning the disputes during the colloquy at Montbéliard. Thus our gracious command is to see to it that the scribes who prepare your draft make the copies ready without further delay. And as soon as one or two copies are prepared and properly inspected, it should be sent to us immediately."[7] Duke Ludwig supported Andreae and Osiander and suspected Beza "and his ilk" of seeking not truth but their own glory (*Glimpf*).

The correspondence between Ludwig and Frederick concerning the numbers of French refugees in Montbéliard is evidence of the pressure Ludwig was putting on Frederick to take a stand regarding religion. This point should be kept in mind when assessing the conflicting reports about Frederick's behavior after the colloquy. From the preface of the *Acta,* it seemed that Frederick had been completely won over to the Lutheran theology. He declared that he was particularly annoyed by the "scurrilous letter," and the preface gives the following reasons for calling the colloquy: to establish the truth of his confession of faith and its fidelity to the Evangelical (read Lutheran) confessions recognized in the empire, and to accede to the requests of the French exiles.[8] The preface also says that anyone present was free to take notes, while Frederick himself assigned some to take notes in order to satisfy the desire of some who were absent to know what took place. In other words, the preface justifies the publication of the *Acta* by saying that Frederick had foreseen that likelihood and provided for it.[9] Frederick declared that he himself noted down what the "adverse party" said against "pious, simple and sincere doctrine" and gave those he thought most egregious.[10] The marginal comments were justified, he wrote, on the grounds of educating the Tübingen students. In spite of all these clearly Württemberg-inspired comments, Frederick claimed impartiality.

Nearly seven pages of the preface are devoted to refuting the letter ascribed to a Calvinist, and the last two pages of the appendix also refer to it.[11] In these pages, the claim in the letter that most annoyed Frederick concerned a certain Instrument of the French refugees. Frederick says that it was the "fictitious Schonberg" who first mentioned the Instrument.[12]

The Latin letter was printed and apparently distributed widely enough to cause the consternation expressed in the *Acta*. A rare copy in the Bibliothèque Nationale was published together with a French translation in 1897 by Armand Lods.[13] It is dated August 4, 1586, by the author, who signs himself Eusebius Schonberg, although this name was labeled fictitious by Frederick in his preface. Since it was published in Germany for distribution there primarily, it is interesting that the language is Latin. One might suppose that a scholar who was not familiar with German wrote it. In addition, Beza had written something similar to one of the most offensive claims in the letter[14] and so the finger was pointed not simply at a French Calvinist but at Beza himself. Hence Beza's vehement denial.[15]

"Schonberg's" letter begins by referring to the letters of a Tübingen student and of Lucas Osiander, letters that Beza would refute at length in his *Responsio*. It was these incredible claims, widely discussed in the German *gynoecea* (women's gatherings),[16] that piqued the curiosity of the writer and caused him to travel to Montbéliard to seek the truth of the matter. The letter attacks Andreae and defends Beza, asserting that Andreae could not answer Beza's arguments regarding the Lord's Supper and the person of Christ and therefore extended the colloquy to include the three last points. "Schonberg" also indicated that Andreae enjoyed the local wines and so sought to extend the discussion. The most damaging passage, however, regarded the actions of Count Frederick: "After the colloquy, the illustrious count was so good to the refugees that he allowed them what he had not allowed before, namely that they could take communion in Montbéliard after professing their loyalty to the Confession of the French churches. This fact was attested in the presence of the local notaries and pastors."[17] This is the infamous "Instrument" mentioned in the preface and the appendix.[18] The same claim was made by Beza in a letter to Lorenz Durnhoffer dated May 3/13, 1586: "The prince, however, after Andreae had left, allowed the French exiles, while testifying to their perseverance in the French Confession, to receive communion from the hands of Montbéliard pastors (which before was not granted them)."[19]

Frederick firmly denied that the French refugees were allowed anything of the kind. In fact, he had repeatedly denied their petitions for just such a privilege, and on December 22, 1586, he made his position absolutely clear to all, including his uncle, Duke Ludwig, by imposing on Montbéliard his own confession concerning the Lord's Supper.[20]

To make firm the Lutheran report concerning the colloquy and having rationalized away the signed agreement that no notes taken at the colloquy were to be given the status of a protocol or official authorization, Frederick ordered that Osiander's notes be published with Frederick's own signature and imprimatur.[21] Andreae undertook the task, which he had probably initiated in the first place by advising Duke Ludwig to write the letter quoted above.[22] By February 1587, the *Acta* was published by Georg Gruppenbach in Tübingen.

By May 1587, Gruppenbach wrote to Lucas Osiander that during the Frankfurt fair he had already sold 1,100 copies of the Latin edition of the *Acta* to book dealers from various localities. Some fifty copies were sold to dealers from Leipzig, Wittenberg, Magdeburg, and Braunschweig, but Gruppenbach had no idea how the *Acta* would sell in Saxony ("*in Sachsen nit klecken*"). He had sent over 500 copies to Leipzig dealers for the Leipzig fair, and he hoped to hear soon how they sold. Gruppenbach hoped to sell the six hundred remaining copies at the next Frankfurt fair. He noted a great demand for the German translation of the *Acta*. In fact, he already had an order for two hundred copies. Before he printed more copies, however, he needed instructions and payment.[23]

In June, Frederick asked again for copies of both German and Latin editions as soon as possible. He expressed concern for Andreae's long illness, which may have accounted for delay in readying the German editions.[24] In response, Andreae wrote on June 4, 1587, explaining that his illness caused delay but that he would hurry it along. Frederick should know, however, that the Calvinists were not like other men but were truly incarnate devils. Andreae said that he had to be sure that the German version was clear and simple and that to produce such a translation took time, but with God's grace he would have it done as soon as possible.[25] During the summer, a French translation was also undertaken by Caspar Lutz, a German pastor serving the Montbéliard church. Lutz wrote to Duke Ludwig to assure him that he was working on such a translation at the request of Ludwig's nephew, Count Frederick. Ludwig had written to Frederick to request that a French version be prepared.[26] By November, Ludwig had the French version and wrote to Lutz promising payment of twenty-five gulden for it. The French version of the *Acta*, printed by Jaques Foillet, was the first book published in Montbéliard.[27]

When the *Acta* appeared, however, Beza could not allow the ball to remain in Andreae's court. In 1587, he published his *Responsio, prima pars,* and early in 1588, his *pars altera*. In his preface, he claimed that he wrote his response against Andreae, not against Count Frederick, whose humanity and sincere desire for peace Beza said he had experienced firsthand.[28] Beza challenged both the motive and the content of the *Acta*. The author put words in his mouth, said Beza. The colloquy was called by Frederick, and Andreae ought not to diminish the honor of the count by ascribing the reason for calling the colloquy to the French refugees. Beza also suggested that the preface ascribed to Count Frederick was probably dictated by someone else.[29]

Beza then asked the prince to consider Andreae's reasons for publishing the *Acta* and Beza's counterarguments. There was no need to use the *Acta* to teach students about the points of theology since both theologians had already published widely on all the subjects of the colloquy and neither had advanced anything new. Even if there were some benefit in publishing the theses, by what right did Andreae annotate Beza's theses and arguments? Was it not rather to provoke new disputes?[30] Beza voiced his suspicion that Osiander was the scribe, together with the superintendent of Montbéliard. Andreae then corrected and polished it, enriching his own speeches while mutilating Beza's. In short, while Beza would rather not dignify the *Acta* by responding to it, he must do so lest it be thought that he approved it.[31]

With regard to the letter mentioned by Andreae in the title of the *Acta* and refuted at length in the preface attributed to Count Frederick and again in the appendix signed by Frederick, Beza said that he neither wrote nor allowed others to write anything against the count. He called on God as his witness that the letter was not written by him nor with his consent. On the contrary, Beza praised the count's hospitality and patience. In fact, Beza wrote letters to Andreae asking him to use his authority to stop his overeager partisans from writing lies. Since Andreae did not answer this request, Beza wrote to his friends refuting the lies of the Lutheran team. Beza declared himself willing to publish these letters since there is nothing in them of which he need be ashamed.[32]

Beza then reproduced a letter by a Tübingen student dated May 24, 1586. The letter says that Beza left in tears, that Andreae easily refuted Beza on predestination, that the count, who had favored Calvinism, now held it in horror, and that six French ministers rejected the opinions of Beza as unknown to them.[33] In his refutation of the letter, Beza defended his doctrine of predestination:

> What do you do with these men who neither know nor want to know about the series and connections of the opposing causes of salvation and perdition or the distinction and antecedent order among all the second causes of God's decree, and the execution of his decree? And who, with regard to the dispute over the Supper, esteem Dr. Luther as a great and irreproachable theologian, and yet do not realize that by accusing us of impiety and blasphemy with regard to the doctrine of Predestination (which is truly the foundation of the doctrine of Justification by faith; indeed of all the doctrine of Christianity) they involve Luther in the same accusation?[34]

Beza's preface continues in similar defenses, quoting in full two more letters, one from Strasbourg, dated May 13, and another from Osiander himself with no date given. These letters too were full of "the most impudent lies."[35] It is not surprising to see that both letters dwelt at length on Beza's doctrine of predestination. Osiander's letter also provided Beza with an indication of whose notes were used for the *Acta* since it reproduced parts of the letter.[36] The rest of the preface[37] is a refutation of Osiander's letter and answers the representations of Beza's doctrines on the other subjects of the colloquy.[38]

The first edition of Beza's *Responsio* appeared in French as well as in Latin and, with the exception of the preface, dealt only with the Lord's Supper and the person of Christ. A second corrected Latin edition was published in 1588, as was a German translation of part 1 and the Latin part 2 that dealt with the three remaining subjects. In 1589, third editions of both part 1 and part 2 were published and the following year, a third edition of the Latin part 1.[39]

Andreae returned the ball, and by February 1588 he had written a refutation of Beza's *Responsio*. Andreae wrote to Duke Ludwig asking permission to have it printed, and within the year Andreae's *Epitome* appeared in Latin and German. Frederick had requested a short summary in German that could be read by those who knew no Latin and who had little time for the long *Acta*.[40] Throughout the letter to Ludwig, Andreae refers to the Calvinists as "devils,"[41] as indeed he does in the *Epitome* itself. In fact the *Epitome* is so virulent that it reveals the hatred for the Calvinists that motivated Andreae to write a book the language of which is so extreme that it discredits its own arguments.[42] A few days later, Andreae asked that the German version of the *Epitome* be sent to theologians to judge since Ludwig himself was studying the Latin edition.[43] A French translation from the Latin edition appeared in 1588 without the printer's name or the place given.[44]

The interest in and ability to understand complex theological arguments was not unusual among the German Protestant princes of the latter half of the sixteenth century. They wrote theological letters to one another and even hoped to resolve theological conflicts without the "pesky theologians."[45] The theologian-translators must have set to work immediately, because a note written on February 23 said that the theologians had changed some things in the Latin work. There was need, therefore, that the Latin and the German be carefully compared in order to bring them into agreement. This was done, and another hand notes that all is correct: "*Ist alles verichtet.*"[46]

Beza ended the cycle. He would not respond to the *Epitome*. He wrote to Jacob Grynaeus on January 17/27, 1588, that he would follow Grynaeus's advice and maintain an obstinate silence with regard to that petulant work, leaving his vindication to God.[47]

By November 1589, copies of all the versions by Andreae and Beza had been published in Latin, German, and French. Andreae's French copies sold so well that within a year they were hard to find.[48] Who found these long, repetitive books so fascinating that the copies were already sold out so soon after their publication? Part of the answer lies in the continuing struggle of Reformed congregations to maintain their confessions in territories adjacent to or within the lands of Lutheran lords. Andreae referred to his *Acta* in letters and publications damning Calvinists wherever he might help Lutherans against Calvinists.[49] Another part of the answer may be found, perhaps, in the ferment over religion that kept unholy fires burning across Europe. The results of a colloquy between two recognized leaders of the two major divisions in Protestantism were as fascinating to some educated readers then as are the confrontations today over the religious aspects of abortion and euthanasia.[50]

At the end of his *Acta*, Andreae included an appendix concerning the interaction of Frederick and the French exiles after the colloquy.[51] Andreae began by referring to a "little book of supplication," which, he said, he had inserted in his *Acta*.[52] The request was that the French exiles, while retaining their own confession of faith, be allowed to receive communion from the Montbéliard ministers. Beza reported its contents more fully in his *Responsio pars altera*.[53] The supplication, which was offered to Frederick at the conclusion of the discussion of the person of Christ, repeated Beza's request that the colloquy end at that point rather than continue with three more topics. Beza asked especially that predestination not be publicly debated. He also summed up the colloquy to that point and tried to urge a degree of concord. Beza said that they had agreed on the most important matters with regard to the Lord's Supper, namely, on the signs and the signified, in opposition to the transubstantiators and to those who taught bare signs. They also agreed, wrote Beza, that Christ's body and blood were truly received through faith. It was therefore time to end bitterness, cease name-calling, and part in fraternal friendship, agreeing to disagree on what the unworthy receive.

The petition was rejected in toto. After consulting briefly with Andreae about the "little book," Frederick asked that the colloquy continue. When the colloquy concluded, since Frederick had not responded to the French refugees' request that they be admitted to sacramental communion under their own confession, Beza and his colleagues asked for an answer. Frederick sent his decree concerning the matter to the inn where Beza was staying.[54] This decree, reported Andreae, was no different from the answer given the refugees before Christmas 1585. That first decree of 1585 had been read aloud by the superintendent of Montbéliard in the great hall of the castle and then shown to the French exiles. It declared that everyone in Montbéliard had to accept the confessions already required by Frederick. If the French refugees could do so in good conscience, they were free to go to communion with the other Montbéliardais. Otherwise, they should abstain. Frederick assured them that "no one, if he has properly prepared for communion and comes forward will be excluded." The decree is dated December 17, 1585, and signed by Frederick, count of Württemberg.[55] The second decree, dated the day the colloquy ended, March 29, 1586, added that if the French exiles wished to receive communion, they would have to accept not only the confession but also the church order of Montbéliard, namely that of Württemberg.[56]

At the end of the colloquy, it seems that Frederick did not yet know about an act or instrument drawn up between Frederick's first decree (December 17, 1585) and Christmas Eve of 1585. During a meeting of the leaders of the French exiles, their ministers, and some Montbéliard citizens with the clergy of the French church in Montbéliard, Richard Dinot and Samuel Cucuel, a noble exile, Seigneur de Vesines,[57] expressed the desire of the French exiles to receive communion while professing their own French Confession.[58] A local notary, Gerard Charpiot, drew up a minute of the meeting, which contained an act or instrument enabling the French to receive communion. That instrument became the object of heated argument and extended legal action,[59] especially after it was featured in the "scurrilous letter" by the so-called Schonberg.

Before the Instrument became known to Frederick in the late summer of 1586, the French in Montbéliard and some of the citizens again took the offensive with regard to Frederick's second decree and again documented their action in a minute dated April 2, 1586, and sent to Leonard Maire, imperial notary in Montbéliard.[60] The French refugees and some of the bourgeois of Montbéliard had been offended by the minister, Samuel Cucuel. Cucuel was among the first students sent to Tübingen on the scholarship provided by Count George's will. At Tübingen, Cucuel studied under Andreae and other Württemberg theologians, by whom he was won over to ubiquitarian Lutheranism. Cucuel was in the ambiguous situation of being a Montbéliardais but a supporter of the theology he had learned at Tübingen under Andreae.[61] Cucuel's character is difficult to assess. Was he a convinced "Andreaeian"? Or was he merely an ambitious man who stood on the side of power? While Cucuel realized that he had to exercise some care in his sermons to the Montbéliard folk, nevertheless, his language about the Lord's Supper and his condemnation of other Reformed churches were more than the French refugees could bear. With their allies, the bourgeois of Montbéliard, they addressed themselves to Frederick as though the colloquy had resolved nothing and Frederick's decree did not apply to them. The argument continued through 1586 and into 1587.

During the summer of 1586, polemical literature regarding the Colloquy of Montbéliard began to circulate in the German estates. The Württembergers claimed complete victory over Beza and his colleagues. In response, a letter attacking Andreae and supporting Beza was published under the name of Eusebius Schonberg. The author declared that after the colloquy, Frederick allowed the French exiles to retain their own confession and, without subscribing to the Formula of Concord, receive communion. Frederick vehemently denied that he had given such permission. In fact, when he observed some of the French going to communion at Easter and Pentecost after the colloquy, Frederick wrote that he thought this meant they had been persuaded to embrace his confession on the Lord's Supper.[62]

On October 16, 1586, the German superintendent of the Montbéliard church, Caspar Lutz,[63] joined Samuel Cucuel, Richard Dinot, and three other ministers[64] in a complaint addressed to Frederick about the French refugees.[65] The exiles had again submitted their confession for the approval of the Montbéliard clergy so that they could receive communion. They had no desire to depart from the faith for which they had suffered exile. After the conference, the French claimed that they had obtained the desired approval.

Lutz and Cucuel denied that they had given their approval, but the situation was not that clear. The ministers' complaint insisted that no approval was given *in writing*. The reader is led to surmise that the two ministers may have given an oral approval. In their complaint, however, they charged the French refugees with ingratitude to their benevolent host, Frederick, and of creating doubt in the minds of other inhabitants by proposing a confession other than those required by Frederick, namely, the Formula of Concord, the Augsburg Confession, and the Wittenberg Concord. When the French asked to receive Christmas communion in 1586 under their own confession, the ministers contended that they had to be denied, otherwise a dangerous precedent would be set and individuals would ask to communicate under a variety of confessions. Württemberg would then become a laughingstock for other Christians. It would appear to others, wrote the ministers, that the Augsburg Confession and the Württemberg Confession were not the only true and sufficient confessions, but that other confessions, which disagreed with them, were also taken as true. That would be like combining light and darkness, Christ and Belial. The ministers turned to scriptural proofs for their doctrine. The conclusion was that only by adopting the Book of Concord, with its condemnations of Calvinist doctrines, could the French be admitted to communion in Montbéliard.

On December 13, 1586, Leonard Maire, imperial notary in Montbéliard, sent a formal supplication to Count Frederick asking clemency for Gerard Charpiot, a French notary who had fled to Montbéliard fifteen years before.[66] Charpiot had drawn up the act recording the pourparler that the French exiles and some Montbéliard citizens had had the previous December with Samuel Cucuel and Richard Dinot, both signers of the above complaint, both Tübingen Stipendiaten and then ministers of the church of Montbéliard. During that conference, the refugees claimed that the ministers gave them permission to receive communion on Christmas Eve 1585 and, in good conscience, had done so without subscribing to the Formula of Concord, which contained the obnoxious condemnations of other Reformed churches. Charpiot's *requeste* said that at the end of the conference, the Montbéliard ministers did not condemn the French churches and that the French exiles did not condemn the churches of Montbéliard. In fact, they had come to a concord between the two churches, which served as a basis for their communion in the Lord's Supper. After the meeting, Charpiot's written act or instrument[67] was given to André Floret, minister to the French exiles, who in turn was to have it signed by all who had been present, including the Montbéliard ministers.

Charpiot's supplication of December 13 was answered by Frederick on December 16. He sent it to the magistrates and asked them to consider it carefully and then to respond:

> We are forced to teach our bourgeois a lesson, since we can no longer let them go on about Communion and distribution of the Lord's Supper. We must also teach a lesson to several of the French because of their written Instrument. We are hastily sending our opinion about how we think it could be done most appropriately. And we are also sending you the Supplication of the Notary [Gerard Charpiot] who wrote this Instrument. We graciously command you to give it your immediate attention, to consider this matter as it deserves and to let us know your decision and favorable reception of it on the coming Saturday when we hope to return to you, God permitting, so that the appropriate action may be taken.[68]

Count Frederick then published on December 22 his own confession regarding the Lord's Supper. It included brief explanations of appropriate portions of the 1530 Augsburg Confession and its Apology, Duke Christoph's confession of 1552, and the Wittenberg Concord. It was, in other words, thoroughly Lutheran, although not ubiquitarian, with the only mitigating portion being Bucer's irenic and open Declaration, which allowed for a crypto-Calvinist or Melanchthonian interpretation. Frederick included it because it had been part of the agreement of 1562 and was constantly called upon by the bourgeois and the French refugees. But Frederick's interpretation and the context robbed Bucer's statement of its ambiguity. The 1586 confession supported oral manducation and the *manducatio indignorum*. In the hope of gaining the signatures of his bourgeois, Frederick added that although he rejected contrary doctrines, he did not condemn churches or persons.[69] Frederick imposed his confession on all in authority, both civic and ecclesiastical, in Montbéliard.

The Nine Bourgeois, the Eighteen, and the Notables refused to sign, risking the accusation of lèse-majesté. Instead they addressed a letter in three parts to Frederick on December 23: They asked that they be given a copy of the charges made against them, of which they declared their innocence; they asserted that the act regarding the communion of the French refugees drawn up by Bernard Maigre was passed in the presence of the Montbéliard ministers;[70] and they asked that they be given a copy of Frederick's confession and time to submit it to theologians for advice. They would then give Frederick their answer within two months.[71] Frederick was angered by this response and promised to teach his stubborn people a lesson, a promise he kept during the following spring.[72]

On Christmas Eve, nothing daunted, the French refugees petitioned Frederick.[73] The petition was signed by seven of the refugees and was their response to the written directive given them by Frederick demanding that they either sign the confession he had drawn up two days earlier or abstain from communion on Christmas. The petitioners said that they wished "to communicate in the Holy Supper of the Lord according to the confession received in the churches of France." They declared in all candor that they held the French Confession to be good and Christian and not to be condemned, nor should the confessions of the English and Swiss churches be condemned. The petition expressed the loyalty and gratitude the refugees owed to Frederick for granting them the right of habitation in Montbéliard (something for which Frederick had had to fight and eventually to suffer).[74] They reiterated their acceptance of the confessions of the Montbéliard church. At the same time, they declared their adherence to the French Confession and their desire to communicate under it as they could do in England and Switzerland. An interesting reference in the letter that cannot be pursued further here is that the now-famous pourparler occurred during a meeting called to respond to the charge of the city of Besançon that a group of refugees from Catholic Besançon joined by French refugees and some Montbéliard citizens had raided Besançon on behalf of Reformed people being prosecuted there for their religious beliefs. The raid was denied, of course. When that matter had been taken care of, the French refugee, Seigneur de Vesines, said that the refugees very much wanted to receive communion under their own confession, and so the pourparler turned to this most contentious problem.[75]

Frederick's promised rebuke[76] was delivered on December 27, 1586, in two parts, one to the bourgeois and the other to the French refugees for daring to try to circumvent his orders regarding communion. Frederick wasted no words. He told the bourgeois that they were disobedient and had arrogated to themselves an authority that they in no way enjoyed. In fact, they had usurped his authority, given him by the regulations of the empire, to determine what confession his territories should follow. "What else am I to think except that you want to elevate yourselves into the equal of an imperial city having no superior."[77] Frederick ordered the bourgeois to sign the confession he had himself composed at once without further delay or ambiguous arguments. He told them that he was considering what punishment would be just for them and for the notary (Charpiot) who wrote the Instrument for them and for themselves. In the second part, Frederick accused the French refugees of acting underhandedly. While he was away, they asked for a conference with the ministers, which was a reasonable thing to do. But after the conference was over, they summoned notaries to draw up an instrument or act that recorded what they desired and not what actually took place during the conference. The Montbéliard ministers were not consulted about the Instrument and indeed knew nothing about it. Frederick indulged in sarcasm as he told the French refugees that he assumed that they meant it as a gift to repay him for his hospitality to them. To add insult to injury, they had given scandal at the last celebration of the Lord's Supper by placing a glass on the altar to be used instead of the chalice. Frederick suggested that they seek lodging elsewhere, where they could behave as they wished. If they remained in Montbéliard, then they must either conform to the decrees of the duchy of Württemberg regarding religion and doctrine or they must abstain from communion.

On December 29, Samuel Cucuel and Anthoine Sayrran presented their side of the story to Frederick.[78] It is neatly hand printed in French, but the thought is less neat. Cucuel told the story of the conference, assured Frederick that the ministers had not allowed any protocols or acts to be drawn up, and expressed surprise at the sudden appearance of the glass on the altar. Apparently other charges had been made against Cucuel, Richard Dinot, and Anthoine Sayrran. Dinot had preached oral manducation and scandalized the bourgeois, who had never accepted the doctrine. But Cucuel assured Frederick that Dinot preached according to the confessions of Augsburg and Württemberg, the Apology, and the Wittenberg Concord, which by now had become the touchstones of orthodoxy. Cucuel's letter included an account concerning Anthoine Sayrran, another minister who served the French church in Montbéliard and who had been trained under Andreae at Tübingen.[79] Sayrran wrote his own apology on December 30 in which he told Frederick that he thought the accusations brought against him by the French and the bourgeois were part of their defense against Frederick's anger on December 16. Sayrran admitted to Frederick that he had scandalized the bourgeois and the French exiles: "It is true, as Master Samuel told me after the celebration of the Supper, that I had scandalized the French, and even some of our bourgeois because I mentioned oral manducation and the manducation of the unworthy: but since these doctrines are Christian truth, I told him that the French were unjustifiably scandalized."[80] Sayrran asked Frederick to check his story and to exonerate him from the accusations made against him by the bourgeois and the French.

Meanwhile, Frederick's council had considered the material their count had sent to them and rendered a decision on December 30, 1586.[81] The points are clear and firm: The French behaved underhandedly by meeting with the ministers when Frederick was absent and by having notaries draw up a protocol (the Instrument referred to so often) of their meeting after the ministers had withdrawn and without informing the ministers they had done so. In this protocol, they claimed that the ministers had given them permission to receive communion without signing the Formula of Concord. They had also scandalized other people at the Lord's Supper in November by putting a glass on the altar to replace the chalice.[82] As to the charge of the French refugees against the minister Anthoine Sayrran, they should know that he preached according to the Augsburg Confession and the other confessions accepted in Württemberg and by Count Frederick. Since the French refugees could not accept some points of doctrine as taught in these confessions, they would have to abstain from communion. They would solve the problem better by moving to another territory, where they could live in freedom and follow their confession. But as long as they lived in the duchy of Württemberg they must conform to the decisions concerning religion that the duke laid down and that Frederick followed. As to the bourgeois, they should be ordered not to receive in their homes any refugees who profess another confession of faith than those accepted in Montbéliard.

Meanwhile, the bourgeois of Montbéliard had deputized Leonard Maire to write on their behalf, giving their objections to signing Frederick's confession. On January 5, it was delivered to Frederick, his chancellor, councilors, and the superintendents of Montbéliard.[83] The bourgeois and the French refugees asked to be excused from signing the "new confession" (Frederick's own confession). They presented their case in a series of points that had first been suggested by Floret, a minister of the French refugees and Daniel Toussain's brother-in-law, in a letter to "the Nine Bourgeois and other citizens of Montbéliard."[84] Under the first three of five points, the petitioners said that in good conscience, they could refuse to sign; they would carefully consider it before God; and they could make up a short confession on the Lord's Supper. As the French discussed the first point, they hoped Frederick would apply the argument to himself. Should one not sign? The letter advanced five reasons:

1. Other princes had refused to impose new confessions; they named some who had not subscribed to the Formula of Concord: the king of Denmark and the princes of Anhalt, Holstein, Pomerania.
2. Besides, other Reformed communities retained their original confessions, as had Nuremberg, for example.[85]
3. The petitioners then appealed directly to Frederick's own experience and his actions on their behalf. You yourself, they told him, went to Henry III in the name of the Protestant princes, to appeal on behalf of the Huguenots. You could not have done so if you believed that the French confession was inimical to Evangelical religion.
4. The theological differences are not so great that they need comment, wrote Maire, and the bourgeois of Montbéliard would prefer not to do so after the example of Strasbourg, Colmar, and Frankfurt.
5. But, based on the premise that wherever faith and love are, there is God, their faith requires that they combat at least three Württemberg doctrines:

1. The true body of Jesus Christ is taken with the bodily mouth.
2. Who eats the bread and wine, eats and drinks the body and blood of Christ whether they believe or not.
3. Wherever in the world the divinity of Jesus Christ is, there is his humanity present through the personal union of the two natures.

It would be contrary to faith and love to sign a confession that taught these doctrines, they argued. The church of Montbéliard holds to the confession approved by Frederick's father, Count George. On the doctrine of the Lord's Supper, their confession and that of the French refugees agree. The French want to keep their French Confession, and the people of Montbéliard have no objection to their doing so since all of them believe that faith alone eats and drinks the body and blood of Jesus Christ; only believers eat and drink everlasting life. Nor can they believe that Christ's body is omnipresent.

Ten days later, from his post in Heidelberg, Daniel Toussain wrote to the Nine Bourgeois of Montbéliard, advising them not to sign Count Frederick's confession.[86] Toussain wrote that he was distressed by what he heard about his homeland. He had had many letters and he responded in sympathy. Do not give in, he wrote. You are right to hang on to our true religion. Toussain rehearsed the history of the struggle of Montbéliard with Württemberg. He pointed out that the chief doctrinal supports for the evangelical theology of Montbéliard were the *Variata* and the Wittenberg Concord with Bucer's explanation.

Andreae's Appendix contains Frederick's responses to the French petitioners. The first is dated December 17, 1585, and the second response given after the colloquy is dated March 29, 1586. The Appendix then rehearses the matter of the meeting between the Montbéliard ministers, the French ministers, and some of the French exiles. Marginalia point out Richard Dinot's "Lutheran arguments." The arguments of the French minister, Floret, are roundly rejected. Andreae wrote that he had included this account so that the truth might be known and:

> through the power of the Holy Spirit the eyes of the mind of the adversaries might be opened so that they might come to know heavenly truth and love it and embrace it, and for this His Highness ardently prays. So that this appendix might also stand by his authority, His Highness, in public testimony to the truth, subscribes to this with his own hand. Done at Montbéliard in the castle, on the 11 day of February in the year of Christ 1587.
>
> *Frederick, by the grace of God, Count of Wurttemberg and Montbéliard,* etc.[87]

In spite of Frederick's fulminations, the French were not intimidated. On March 10, 1587, they complained again about Cucuel and Sayrran. But this may have been in reaction to a legal document advising Duke Ludwig about the disobedience on the bourgeois of Montbéliard.[88] In this long Latin document the Nine Bourgeois were considered seditious because of their refusal to sign the Formula of Concord. The author, Anthoine Beuson, gave grounds for challenging the election of the Nine Bourgeois. Building on the right of the prince to determine the religion in his territory, Beuson considered the refusal of the Nine Bourgeois to accept the confessions proposed to them a political act with the most serious ramifications. They were challenging the authority and damaging the reputation of Duke Ludwig. Rather than being allowed to continue such defiance, the guilty magistrates should be punished. On the other hand, since force is inappropriate in matters of conscience, some action should be taken so that the bourgeois understand the benevolence of Duke Ludwig and either conform to the just laws of the duchy or find another territory in which to live.[89]

The problem presents an interesting case that was never quite resolved during Frederick's lifetime. Certainly this count and then duke did not succeed in employing the principle *cuius regio, eius religio* with dictatorial power before which helpless vassals simply yielded. In the repeated and protracted tug-of-war between Frederick and the people of Montbéliard, there was no cool consideration of the conflicting rights and laws involved. The bourgeois had over three hundred years of recognized franchises and customs on their side. They elected their magistrates, who were not the servants of the count but of the citizens. On the other hand, the Peace of Augsburg gave the ruler the right to establish religion. In this instance, superior strength prevailed. In the long run, the citizens of Montbéliard could not withstand the power of the duke of Württemberg.

But during the sixteenth century, the Nine Bourgeois claimed their ancient privileges, refusing to yield the sort of humble and absolute obedience that Ludwig and, in his turn, Frederick increasingly demanded. Frederick also refused to back down. On May 7, 1587, Frederick seized the town's charter and other municipal documents and incarcerated the Nine Bourgeois in his castle. He then ordered the citizens to elect a new Eighteen and the corps of Nine Bourgeois. On May 11, the new officers signed Frederick's confessions and were sworn in. Upon the signing of a treaty between Frederick and the town on May 19, the deposed magistrates were freed.[90] By May 22, the new magistracy had been wined and dined in Frederick's castle and the municipal documents had been returned to Montbéliard.[91] It would seem that peace was restored, but Frederick's housecleaning did not resolve all his problems. The bourgeois exercised another of their rights, namely, the privilege of leaving Montbéliard and returning without asking permission and without prejudice to their rights as citizens. Before the next year was out, Frederick complained of those Montbéliardais who went to Basel to receive communion rather than sign the 1530 Augsburg Confession. In 1588, Frederick interdicted such behavior, threatening fines or banishment.[92] In August 1589, those affected by the ordinance of 1588 asked that they either be allowed to receive the Lord's Supper according to their conscience or be free to receive it elsewhere. Frederick responded that if they could not accept the religion established at Montbéliard, they should move to another town.[93]

The continuing struggle between the bourgeois of Montbéliard and their suzerains provides an example of how rulers tried to implement the 1555 Peace of Augsburg. On the other hand, Montbéliard presented a unique problem to its suzerains. It was French in language and custom, so much so that a native of Montbéliard writing in the nineteenth century declared: "The county of Montbéliard has never had anything in common with Germany. The national language [German] was used only in administrative acts. German was not taught in the schools. . . . We are not surprised to read at the beginning of a statistic in German: The county of Montbéliard was nearly as foreign to the inhabitants of Württemberg as the North Pole."[94] Anthoine Beuson, writing in 1587, described Montbéliard as "surrounded by provinces and peoples recognizing different lords, professing different religions, speaking different languages, and with a diverse complexity of natures which are far from agreeing with one another."[95] For Beuson, this meant that Duke Ludwig had to take stern measures to maintain his authority. Nevertheless, the history of Montbéliard during the sixteenth century was one of negotiation with its suzerains, especially in the matter of religion. Duke Ulrich had reformed Montbéliard through Farel, a Frenchman influenced by the German Swiss Oecolampadius of Basel. Ulrich had then brought in Pierre Toussain as a French minister in the Reformed tradition who spoke the language of Montbéliard and understood its religious orientation. Count George was converted to the Reformed tradition and upheld Toussain. Duke Christoph, an ardent exponent of the unaltered Augsburg Confession, tried to impose Lutheran doctrine and, after Brenz had drawn them up in 1559, the Württemberg Confession and Church Order.[96] In spite of threats of demissions of both ministers and schoolmasters, Christopher had to recognize that the people and ministers could not be forced to adopt them. A compromise was effected that included the signing of the Wittenberg Concord of 1536.[97]

On the side of the dukes and theologians of Stuttgart, however, was the educational system. Ministers trained at Tübingen were won over to the theology of Brenz and Andreae. By 1577, Montbéliard schoolmasters were made to sign the Formula of Concord, and those who refused were fired. The matter of the sacraments was crucial. It is clear from the arguments of 1585–1587 that the doctrines of ubiquity, of oral manducation, and of the *manducatio indignorum* had not been accepted by the French-speaking congregations of Montbéliard. Their objections to Cucuel, Dinot, and Sayrran were that they preached these doctrines that they had not heard before from their ministers.

Frederick himself provides a good example of a lord unable to come to terms with the Peace of Augsburg, his own training, his people, and the pressures from other lords, including his ducal and imperial suzerains. Frederick's father, Count George, died when Frederick was an infant. Frederick was raised in Montbéliard during the years when Toussain and his ministers resisted the efforts of Christoph to impose Lutheran doctrine. He was sent to Tübingen and so was taught Andreae's theology. Frederick had probably heard the refugees from the St. Bartholomew's Day massacre recount the horrors of that day. He welcomed French refugees in 1585 and helped Henry of Navarre, through John Casimir, to raise troops by providing both funds and a place to gather the mercenaries from Switzerland and Germany. On the other hand, Frederick ordered the people of Montbéliard to sign the Formula of Concord and fired ministers and schoolmasters who refused to do so. Duke

Ludwig insisted on religious conformity, and Frederick tried to comply, but with how much heart is difficult to ascertain.

Frederick's attitude after the colloquy hardened with regard to doctrine, however, for which there are at least two reasons. First one may surmise that he, along with the Montbéliardais and against the French refugees, was shocked at the Genevan doctrine of double predestination. In fact, Frederick cited examples from Beza's arguments that particularly shocked him, such as David's retention of faith and the Holy Spirit during his adulterous act with Bathsheba and the idea that baptized children are not, ipso facto, regenerated.[98] Nevertheless, as the petition of the refugees reminded him, Frederick had gone to Paris after the colloquy to plead for the Huguenots. Frederick said he had not gone to Paris to defend their doctrine but, out of compassion for them, to try to obtain permission for them to return to their homes in France. To give alms to a needy person recognizes that person's need, not his doctrine, argued Frederick.[99] Second, on April 21, 1586, Duke Ludwig told Frederick that he was "slippery and undependable" with regard to religion,[100] and that he had better get his house in order.

Frederick remained divided, therefore, between Lutheran doctrine and French politics. He was also concerned about his own authority, and the continual resistance of the French exiles and the bourgeois of Montbéliard caused him to write them angry, threatening letters. His effectiveness, in spite of the demissions of schoolmasters and ministers, was not what he wished, as further altercations reveal.

Two more disputes will serve to illustrate the point without rehearsing the entire history. In 1594, Frederick, who had succeeded Ludwig as duke of Württemberg, had occasion to write another scolding letter to Montbéliard. Once again, the ministers and bourgeois had tried to introduce a "new confession." Frederick wrote that he would not tolerate such boldness. They must retain the confessions already established. Nor may the pastors try to hold secret meetings with the citizens, that is to say, without the knowledge of the ecclesiastical superintendent, Caspar Lutz. The situation had become so bad that Lutz, after writing whining, complaining letters, asked to resign. He was replaced by another German superintendent appointed by Frederick, John Osswaldt.[101] Duke Frederick died in 1608 and was succeeded first by Johann Frederick and in 1617, through an agreement between them, by Johann Frederick's younger brother, Ludwig Frederick. On July 6, 1613, Johann Frederick received a report from one J. Leffler, recently returned from a trip to Montbéliard. Leffler informed Johann Frederick that a number of his most noble subjects and other burghers, together with their wives and children, publicly traveled to Basel at Easter and at Pentecost to take communion in the French church. Leffler inquired of other of Johann Frederick's officers in Montbéliard whether this "dangerous practice" often occurred. He was assured that it did and that it scandalized some people in Montbéliard. Leffler warned Johann Frederick that this practice might become more dangerous and indeed grow beyond control.[102] Johann Frederick answered on July 15, 1613. He asked the members of the consistory to meet with the persons who were charged with religion in Montbéliard. When they had duly considered the problem, they must give their advice on how best to end this growing and dangerous practice.[103] The tone of Johann Frederick's response lacked the anger of his father's orders. But then, Johann Frederick had been born and raised in Stuttgart. Montbéliard was a small, almost foreign county. He need not deal directly with its problems but could leave to agents and advisers the religious nonconformity of Montbéliard.

It was only in 1634 that Montbéliard became Lutheran even though, according to P. Pfister, a native of Montbéliard studying in Geneva in 1873, the people of Montbéliard never forgot their Reformed origins and the long struggle against the efforts of their rulers to impose the *Invariata* form of the Augsburg Confession.[104]

Notes

1. See n. 12.

2. AN-K 2187: "Itaque si quae sunt ab utraque parte annotata, nolumus ea ullam vim et authenticam autoritatem protocolli habere."

3. Ludwig Lavater à Bèze, Zurich, 19/29 Janvier, 1586. I have a transcription from the Musée de la Réformation, Geneva. The original autograph is in Ms. B-Gotha (cod. chart A. 905, f. 142: "notari adhibeantur qui omnia excipiant, ne Jacobo postea tergiversandi sit locus." There is a difficulty here because the Schonberg letter did not appear until August 1586.

4. See chap. 1, n. 2: "Haec acta candide et bona fide consignata, vanissimos de hoc Colloquio sparsos rumores, imprimis vero Epistolam quandam, vanitatibus & calumijs refertam, & typis excusam abundè refutabunt."

5. HAS A63, Bü 64.

6. Ibid.

7. Ibid.: "Dieweil uns je lenger je mehr anlanget, auch allerhand Schreiben des Bezae und seines gleichen Calvinisten uns zukommen, dass sie von dem zu Mumpelgarten gehalten Colloquio ungleich und der Warheit ungemeß berichten, iren Glimpf darinnen zu suchen; und abervil guthertzige, auch fürneme Personen gern ein gewissen satten Grund hetten, was im Colloquio zu Mumpelgarten gehandelt worden, so ist unser gnediger Befehl, Ir wollet bei den Amanuensibus, welche Ewr Concept mundirn, anhalten, daß sie die Exemplaria ohne lengern Verzug fertigen. Und da ein Exemplar oder zwey aller dings, wie es sein soll, absolvirt, wöllet Ir uns selbige alsbald zukonnen lassen, und daran sein, damit die Amanuenses mit die übrigen auch nicht seumig sein. Daran beschicht unser gnedige Mainung. Und sein wir euch mit allen Gnaden wol genaigt. Datum Stutgart den 10 September Anno etc. 86.

"Friedrich. An D. Jacobum Andreae Propst und Cantzlern bei der Universitet zu Tübingen."

8. *Acta*, A2v.–A3r.

9. Ibid., A4v: "Acta illius colloquii bona fide fuisse collecta."

10. Ibid., A4v–B1r: "Neque vero nos piguit, nostra etiam manu ea annotare, quae ab adversa parte contra piam simplicem & sinceram doctrinam, in Christiana nostra Catechesi comprehensam, dicebantur, atque pertinaciter asserbantur."

11. Ibid., B3r–C2r, and pp. 574–75.

12. Ibid., 574: "Et quidem ad eusdem revelationem, occasionem praebuit vanissima sua publicata Epistola, fictitius ille Eusebius Schonbergius, qui eius Instrumenti primus mentionem fecit, idque suo indicio prodidit."

13. Lods, "Les Actes du Colloque de Montbéliard," 200–206.

14. See below.

15. See p. 164.

16. Lods, "Les Actes du Colloque de Montbéliard," 201, 206. A mark of contempt implying that serious *men* would not stoop to such gossip.

17. Ibid., 206: "Tantum obesse ut comes illustris, Gallis exulibus qui Mombelgardi erant, fuerit post colloquium iniquior, ut post colloquium illud, quod ante nonerat passus, permiserit Gallos communicare Coenae Domini, cum protestatione libera, quod a Confessione Ecclesiarum Gallicarum discedere nollent: id quod coram notoriis et pastoribus illius loci testati sunt."

18. *Acta,* Preface, B34–B4r. For the *Appendix,* see Appendix 1, pp. 000–00. For the *Instrument,* see Appendix 2, pp. 203–5.

19. From a transcription in the Musée de la Réformation, Geneva. The original came from the Bibliothèque Sainte-Genevieve, Ms. 1455, fol. 186–88, Cote: 112. "Princeps tamen ille, post Andreae discessum, Gallis exulibus concessit, ut in Confessione Gallica perseverare se testati, Coenam Domini ex pastorum Mompelgardensium manu acciperent (quod prius factum non fuerat) et ut presens semper nostrae colloquuitioni intersunt, quaedam etiam ex utrinque dictis annotans, sic etiam praesens illos ad Coenam accedentes spectavit, et gallicos quoque psalmos in coetu cecinit. Quod spem aliquam facit, fore ut bonis alioqui et pius principibus Dominus oculos aperiat. This is probably one of the letters Duke Ludwig was referring to when he ordered the preparation of the *Acta.*" See n. 6.

20. Lods, "Les Actes du Colloque de Montbéliard," 211–12 [AN-K 2177]. See pp. 168–69.

21. Ibid. But see Geisendorf, *Théodore de Bèze,* 353, which argues that relations between Frederick and Beza continued to be warm during the months following the colloquy. Through his physician, Frederick asked Beza to compose a Latin sonnet in honor of the count's vineyard: "Ces échanges épistolaires et poétiques, très en faveur au xvie s., n'auraient pu se produire entre adversaires déclarés."

22. See p. 164 with n. 7.

23. HAS A-63, Bü. 64. I owe the transcription of this manuscript to the kindness of Bodo Nischan of East Carolina University.

24. All of this correspondence is from HAS A-63, Bü 64, unless otherwise noted.

25. Ibid. D: Andreae to Frederick: "Nachdem aber die Calvinisten nicht Leutt wie andere menshen sondern recte incarnati diaboli, Leughafftige teuffel, und lesterer seyen die nichts unverkert lassen, deßwegen an der Version gar wil gelegen wie auch ein notturfft das es fur den einfaltigen teutschen Lesern verstendlich, deutlich, klar und hell verdolmetschet."

26. Ibid. Caspar Lutz (in Montbéliard) to Duke Ludwig, October 19, 1587: "Durchleuchtiger hochgeborener Fürst und Herr. E.F.G. bitt ich ganz undertheniglich, sie wollen diß mein underthenig anpringen gnedig vernemmen. Wurdeger Fürst und Herr, es haben e.f.g. vor der Zeitt, an meinen auch gnedigen Fürsten un herrn, der liebe Herrn vettern, ainschreiben, und darinnen sehr nottwendige, nutzliche, und hailsame sollicitation gelangen lassen, dazß colloquium alhie gehaltten und Latine publiciert, auch Gallice uff daß fürderlichst transferiert, und lucem ermitiert würde."

27. Les Actes / du Colloque de / Montbeliardt: / qui s'est tenu l'an de / Christ 1586. avec l'aide du Seigneur Dieu tout / puissant, y presidant le Tresillustre Prince & Sei /

gneur, Monseigneur Frideric Conte du Wirtemberg & Montbeliardt, &c. / entre tresrenommez per- / sonnages le Docteur Iaques André Preposé & Chance- / lier de l'université de Tubinge, & le Sieur Theodo- / re de Beze Professeur & Ministre / à Geneve: / Lesquels ont este nouvelle-ment publiez l'an de Christ 1587. & traduitz de Latin / en Francois par l'authorité du Prince / Frideric. . . . [mentions the "lying letter"] Imprimé a Montbeliardt / Par Iaques Foillet / Imprimeur de son Excellence. / M.D. LXXXVII. On the blank facing page, someone has written: "Ier livre imprimé à Montbéliard 1587." I owe my photocopy of this book to the kindness of the librarian of the Bibliothèque Publique of Montbéliard.

28. Ad Acta / Colloquii / Montisbelgardensis / Tubingae edita, / Theodori Bezae / Responsio / Genevae, / Excudebat Joannes le Preux. / M.D. LXXXVII, p. 3: "Cum illo [Andreae] igitur mihi negotium est, non cum Illustriss. Principe: de cuius humanitate singulari & propenso in procuranda Ecclesiarum pace studio, dubitare me ipsa experientia non finit." (Beza had said the same in the preface to his 1587 French *Response*, 3.)

29. Ibid., 5–6.

30. Ibid. 6–7.

31. Ibid., 8.

32. Ibid., 8–10.

33. Ibid., 10–11: "De secundo [Praedestinatione] Beza per sesquihoram peroravit, & sua illa placita, de consilio Dei in hominibus quibusdam vitae aeternae, absque vel fidei vel incredulitatis respectu adiudicandis, protulit. Quae patienter audita sunt: & prolixè à D. Iacobo refutata. . . . Istud addo, Bezam lachrymabundum ex colloquio discessisse. Quare hoc effectum est ut Princeps Mompelgardensis, quid ad partes Calvinianas iam inclinaverat, cognita & Audita Bezae blasphemia, illud dogma exhorrescere, & detestari atque execrari inciperet."

34. Ibid., 12–13: "Sed quid istis hominibus facias, qui neque salutis & damnationis causarum oppositarum seriem & nexum, neque distinctionem inter Dei decretum, omnes secundas causas ordine antegrediens, & eius decreti executionem, non modò non norunt, sed ne nosse quidem volunt: Qui denique in hac quidem de Coena Domini controversia Lutherum habent pro summo & irrefragabili Theologo: in doctrina verò de Praedestinatione (quae sanè est doctrinae iustificationis ex fide, atque adeò totius Christianisimi fundamentumJ) per nostrum latus, apertè, ut impium & blasphemum, à se confodi non sentiunt?"

35. Ibid., 14–18.

36. Ibid.

37. Ibid., 19–30.

38. Where appropriate, these remarks have been incorporated in the preceding chapters.

39. For a complete bibliography on these editions, see Gardy, *Bibliographie*, 197–99.

40. HAS A 63, Bü. 64. Frederick to Andreae. Unfortunately, the letter has no date. "Wir wollen euch gnedig nicht bergen, das wir bedacht, das protocollum Mompelgarischen Colloquy zu Tubingen unverzogenlich trucken zulassen, inmassen wir desshalb albereit gnedigen befehl gegeben. Doch der gestallt das es, biß auff formen gnedigen befehl ["befehl" is crossed out and "beh——d" inserted]. Innen gehalten [three words crossed out and illegible; none inserted] unvermaidenliche notturfft, das auch die jenigen so der Latinischen sprach nicht erfahren, jedoch mit grossen verlangen gern wissen möchten, wie die sachen mit bemeltem Colloquio beschaffen, durch ein kurzes teutsches scripto notturfftiger bericht beschehe." The

manuscript I have is apparently a rough draft since lines are stricken and there is neither date nor signature.

41. Ibid. Letter from Andreae to Ludwig, February 18, 1588.

42. Andreae, *Epitome*. Note the new categories: on Christ's merit and on the promises of the gospel. Neither of these categories appears as such in the volume.

43. HAS A-63, Bü. 64, February 22, 1588.

44. BRIEF RECUEIL / DU COL- / LOQUE DE MOM- / BELIARD TENU AU MOIS DE / Mars 1586. Entre Iaques Andre D. / & M. Theodore de Beze. No place of publication. Octavo. The last page (155) says: "Pour certaines occasions on n'a peu annoter toutes les pages en cest exemplaire francois: comme elles sont fidelement & diligemment co-teez [*sic*] en l'exemplaire Latin qui se rapporte aux actes du Colloque, & responce de M. de Beze imprimez en Latin. Ou le Lecteur pourra avoir recours." (I owe my photocopy of this volume to the kindness of the librarian of the Bibliothèque Publique of Montbéliard.)

45. See chap. 2, p. 53.

46 HAS A 63, Bü, 64.

47. "De Bèze à Jacob Grynaeus. Genève 17/27 Janvier 1588: De Tubingensium responso, nihil prorsus laboro et ubi alteram meae responsionis partem absolvero, certum est mihi consilium tuum sequi, et obstinato silentio maledicentiam et petulantiam istorum ulcisci, vel Deo potius reliquere vindicandam." Transcription in the Musée de la Réformation, Geneva. Original from the University Library, Basel. Kirchen Archiv CI.2.,Bd.II.

48. HAS A 63, Bü. 64: Caspar Linz to Duke Ludwig, November 10, 1589.

49. For example, see Andreae's *Christliche Trewherzige / Erinnerung verma= / nung und warning vor der zur Newen= / statt an der hart nachgetruckten ver= / falschten und mit Calvinischer Gottsla= / sterlicher Lehr beschmeiten / Bibel / D. Martin Luthers. / Gestelt / durch D. Iacobum Andreae / Probst zu Tubingen.* Tübingen: Georg Gruppenbach, 1588. The foreword is to "Friedrich IV, Pfalzgraf bey Rhein und Herzogen in Bayern." Andreae claimed that the Zwinglians had falsified Luther's Bible on "This is my body" (p. 7). The occasion was the printing in Neustadt of Luther's German Bible with summaries and concordances, etc. I would call this work feverish and overwrought. Andreae claimed that all but those who believe as he does are devils, etc. In fact, nearly every paragraph has *devil* in it. Andreae goes through all the major doctrines and makes very unpleasant reading, e.g., p. 8: "Tremellius a learned Jew, but a Jew, so how can he help even with Hebrew since he doesn't believe Jesus Christ is God's son?" And again on p. 70: "Calvinists are worse than Jesuits because Calvinists teach that Christ died only for elect."

Or, again, see Andreae's publication dedicated to the prince and council of Nurenberg: *Spiegel / der offenbaren unverschambten Cal= / vinischen Lugen wider reine Lehrer / der Augspurgischen Confession / unnd / Grewlichen erschrockenlichen Losterungen / warnung sich vor disem Geist zuhuten / Gestelt durch / Iacobum Andreae, Probst und / Cantzlern bey der Universitet / zu Tubingen.* Tubingen: Georg Gruppenbach, 1588. Foreword: The Devil has got hold of their church: "Der Teuffel hat der Kirchen zu Nurnberg hefftig zugesetzt. D. Christophorus Herdesianus ein schadlicher Calvinist gewesen." In this publication, Andreae refers to the "Mumpelgartischen Colloquio" and provides an incorrect report on the debate about the person of Christ.

50. On the Genevan printers and Beza's understanding of the power of the printed word, see Robert M. Kingdon, *Myths about the St. Bartholomew's Day Massacres, 1572–1576* (Cambridge: Harvard University Press, 1988), chap. 1, "The Role of the Printing Press."

51. See Appendix 1.

52. *Acta,* 569: "Petierant D. Beza, eiusque Collegae, in Libello supplice, (qui his actis insertus est) inter alia, hoc etiam; ut liceret suae Confessionis fratribus, suam Confessionem, sine ullo alterius praeiudicio, retinentibus, sacram Coenam ex aliorum manibus percipere, & ita mutuam fraternitatem colere ac testari." The "Libello" is reproduced in the *Acta* pp. 374–77.

53. Beza, *Responsio pars altera,* p. 4.

54. But see Beza, *Response,* Preface, 11: "le bon & humain accueil & traictement que nous avoit fait son Excellence, nous ayant fait cest honneur de nous loger mesmes en son chasteau."

55. *Acta,* 569–70: "Debere illis significari, quod illius pia et pura confessio publice plus satis prostet: sub quasi communicare velint, gratos ipsos fore: sin minus, posse ipsos abstinere, & hac ratione suae conscientiae consulere. Neminem etiam, si ad praeparatoriam concionem accessurus sit, iri exclusum."

56. Ibid., 570–71: "Ad libellum supplicem Domini Bezae & Collegarum eius, quo petunt, ut liceat suae Confessionis fratribus, suam Confessionem sine alterius praeiudicio retinentibus, sacram Coenam EX ALIORUM MANIBUS percipere: respondet Illustrissimus Princeps ac Dominus, Dominus Fridericus, Comes Wirtembergicus et Mompelgartensis, etc. extare publice suae Cels. CONFESSIONEM ET ORDINATIONEM Ecclesiasticam: SI SECUNDUM ILLAM Confessionem & ordinationem ad sacram Domini Coenam accedere velint, eaque de re sententiam suam Ministro Ecclesiae Mompelgartensis aperire voluerint, repulsam non passuros. Actum Mompelgarti, 29. Martii, Anno 86." [Capital letters are given as they appear in the *Acta.*] On the church order of Württemberg, see Brecht, *Kirchenordnung und Kirchenzucht in Württemberg,* 32–52. Regarding its imposition on the Montbéliard church, see Viénot *Histoire de la Réforme* 1:209–28.

57. De Vesines was named as one of more than a hundred exiled French nobles in Montbéliard in a letter to Henry III from de Verrière, his ambassador to Savoy: Bib. Nat., 500 Colb.' 427, fasc. 399–401 Jan. 4? 1586. Addresses "vre Maieste," fasc. 399, par. 2: "Sire, Il y a bien cen ou sixvingts maistres a Montbelliard entreaultres les Srs. de Beauvoire La Nocle, de Vezines."

58. See below, p. 168.

59. Charpiot was charged with seditious behavior and after many appeals would have been severely punished had not his death intervened. See correspondence for February 17, 24, and 25, 1587 (AN-K 2187, dr. 1).

60. AN-K 2187, dr. 1: "Minute de l'instrument receu par Mre Leonard Mayre. Touchant la faict de la cene. Le 2 d'april 1586." The manuscript is probably a draft copy since it has many lines crossed out and three fairly long marginal notes in the same hand.

61. Leube, "Die Mömpelgarder Stipendiaten im Tübinger Stift," 75. Cucuel is listed as no. 14 among the scions of Montbéliard families awarded scholarships at the University of Tübingen.

62. *Acta,* Preface, C2v.

63. Caspar Lutz was "pastor of the German church" and had been sent to Montbéliard from Stuttgart to assure fidelity to the Württemberg theology and church order. It was Lutz who would translate Andreae's *Acta* into French for the edition published in Montbéliard. See n. 92.

64. Leube, "Die Mömpelgarder Stipendiaten im Tübinger Stift," 75. Leube lists the *stipendiaten* from Montbéliard's leading families. Among them are S. Cucuel and R. Dinotz, both signatories of the ministers' complaint.

65. AN-K 2187, dr. 1: "Plainte du Surintendant et des Ministres de Montbéliard contre les françois refugies. 16 Oct. 1586."

66. AN-K 2187, dr. 1: Discussions avec plusieurs bourgeois et quelques refugies francois au sujet dela ste Cene. 1586. 1587 16 pieces [on first page of a bundle of correspondence in which this letter is no. 4]. Requeste / de mre Leonard Mayre, touchant / lacte par luy donne aux sres / francois. / 13 dec. 1586 [from last page identifying this particular letter].

67. This is the instrument about which Frederick wrote in the *Acta*'s Preface and Appendix.

68. AN-K 2787, dr. 1: "Von Gottes Gnaden Friderich Grave zu Württemberg und Mümppelgartt. Unnsern grues zuvor vester, auch Hoch- unnd wolgelertte liebe Getreuwe. Unns hatt ein sondere hohe Notturfft sein geachtet, unnsern burgern zu Mümppelgartt, (denen wir nicht lennger also zusehen khünden,) von der Communione unnd aussttheilung des Heiligen würdigen Nactmals, wie auch ettlichen Frantzosen Ires uffgerichten Instrumentz halben was fürhalltten zu lassen. Derwegen wir unnser meynung kurtz unnd in der Eil verfasst, wie wir vermeinen es am füflichsten geshrehen khönne. Unnd lassen Euch dieselbig, beneben dess Nottarÿ Supplication, so, solch Instrument uffgericht, schrifftlich zukhommen, Gnedig beuelhendt, Ir wellendt Euch samentlich also baldt darüber setzen, die sach nach Notturfft betrachten, Inn Frantzösisch transferirn lassen, Unnd uns hernach Euwers Räthlichen guetbedünckhens uff künfftigen Sambstag, da wir dan, gelieben Gott, wider anzukhommen gesinnet, widerumb verstendigen. Damit die gebür zu Itziger Gelegenheit für die handt genohmmen werden möchte. Can solches unnser endtlicher will unnd meynung, woltten wir Euch, den wir mit gnaden samentlich gewogen, zue nachrichtung nicht vorhalltten. Datum Inn Unnserer Vestung Beaumont den 16ten Decembris Anno -86- Friderich Grave zu Württemberg und Mümpelgartt."

69. This confession was published for the first time, to my knowledge, by H. Tribout de Morembert, "La Confession de foi de Montbéliard," *Revue d'Histoire Écclésiastique* 65 no. 1 (1970): 5–29. The confession is printed in its entirety on pp. 21–29. The article provides parts of the confessions from which Frederick's confession is drawn and something of its history, including several other valuable documents that my research had not uncovered, e.g., the letter of December 23 cited in n. 71. The article errs, however, when it attributes the confession to Duke Ludwig. The confession is signed Friderich, comte de Wurtenberg et Montbeliard (ibid., p. 29). Cf. Duvernoy. *Éphémérides*, 485.

70. The problem seemed then to be whether the instrument was actually drawn up in their presence and whether or not the Montbéliard ministers signed it.

71. Morembert, "La Confession de foi de Montbéliard," 17–18. The letter, from its contents, was addressed to Frederick, not Duke Ludwig. The "coup d'état" mentioned on p. 18 was Frederick's act of imprisoning the Nine Bourgeois, capturing the city charter, and holding them ransom until a new magistracy was elected and Frederick's confession duly signed.

72. The punishment was Frederick's coup d'état.

73. AN-K 2187, dr. 1. [In a file of seven letters on not signing the Formula of Concord: 1586 and after. In fact, the file is on the refusal of Nine Bourgeois and the refugees to sign Frederick's confession.] December 24, 1586: "Responce des Srs francois refugiez en ceste ville, touchant une [line through ff.: pretendue Entreprise sur la Ville Besancon par quelques francois refugies a Montbeliard,] la participation a la Ste Cene [line through ff.: Par quelques francois refugiez] [signed by seven distinct hands]

Tres illustre Prince et Seigneur Comte de Wirtemberg et Montbeliard L'escript qu'il Vous a pleu faire mettre en nos mains apres que d'iceluy lecture a este faicte et en avons requis vision et coppie pour respondre au contenu, que de restre benigne grace avey accorde.

"Disons en toutte humilite que l'assemblee faicte en vostre ville dudict Montbeliard procede originelement de la plainte de doleance faict par les Seigneurs de Bezancon ayant faict entendre a vostre Excellence par lettres expresses quil y avoit entreprise sur leurdicte ville par quelques francoys et Bezanconnois refugiez et receuz de vostre humanite en vostredicte ville et Comte, lesquelles lettres ils vous pleut delivrer a Monsr. de Vezines gentilhomme francoys affin que du faict y contenu chascun respondast en verite et saint conscience et qui fut faict et chascun se purges de ladicte accusation, declarant ny avoir panse ny faict aucune deliberation ou entreprise (chose vraye et veritable comme bien vostre Excellence la cognu). En la mesme assemblee [new page] ledict Sr de Vezines proposa a feu Messieur Richard et Samuel ministres receus en l'Eglise de Montbeliard que nous desirions grandement communiquer a la sainte cene du Seigneur selon la confession receue aux eglises de France si par eux nous y estons admis et reçeus. Lesquelz franchement et librement respondirent qu'ils tenoient ladicte confession bonne et Chrestienne et ne la condamnoient nullement ny celle des eglisses d'Angleterre et Suisse et qu'ilz estoient prestes nous recepvoir soubz ceste confession a ladicte Saincte Cene. Et orés que nous n'en eussons faict la presente instance et poursuitte, si nous nous y fussions presentes ils nous y eussient receuz.

"De ce, acte fut expedié contenant les declarations et parolles desdicts ministres, ce qui nous donna occasion de communier aultrement nous en fussions abstenez bien sachant que de nostre conscience propre nous serions jugez coulpables si contrevenions a ce que nous croyons et en la doctrine ou avons este instruictes. Et soubs la reverence et correction de vostre Excellence [new page] nous n'avons jamais panse de mesprendre ny offencer envers vous ny faire rediger par escript acte instrument ny acte contraire a verite et responces desdicts ministres, bien marries touttesfoys que ayez trouve mauvais ledict acte. En tant s'en fault que nous ayons en vouloir. Et nostre intention fust de tenir secret en la cause principale et motifes de procurer ledict acte a este pour faire apparoir aux eglises francoyses quil ny avoit aucune variation ny changement en nostre foy, creance et religion. Supplions a vostre Excellence de croire que nous vous sentons et tenons grandement obligez de la douceur, benevolance et humanite dont avez este envers nous en nous recepvant et suffrant nostre demeure et habitation en vostre ville et comte. Dequoy ne serons jamais ingrats et vous en rendrons treshumble service.

"Le second point dont vostredicte Excellence faict [new page] mention par ledict escript doibt estre prins en bonne part et sans aucun scandale que nu desdicts francoys n'a jamais entendu faire ny ne voudroit et tousiours se sont contantez de calice lors quilz ont communie accoustume estre presente a tous. Bien est vray que Messieur Samuel ministre de vostredicte ville fut consulté s'yl trouvoit bon pour obvier au peril et danger de peste et contagion qui lors regnoit en ceste ville qu'on se servist d'un verre pour quelques uns, ce que n'estant accorde ny consenti n'en ferents aultre instance ny poursuitte. Cela est plus a taxer et reprendre en la personne dudict Messieur Samuel qu'en la simplicite et imbecillite de la fille qui en demanda son advis. Prions affectueusement vostre Excellence n'estre indignee ny irritee dudict faict attendu ladicte crainte de contagion. [new page] Au surplus puyse que vostre Excellence ne trouve bon qu'on soit reçeu a la cene soubz la confession des Eglises Reformees de France ainsi seullement soubz celle forme et coustume de l'Eglise de ce lieu joinct que puys naguere en ladicte seconde cene il nous a este presche par Mesieur Anthoine Sara mesmes aultrement que lesdicts feu Messieurs Richard et Samuel n'avoient acoustume. Qui fut cause que nous nous abstinnes de ladicte cene dernierement faicte. Nous suivrons vostre vouloir pour nous abstenir d'ycelle et n'adviendra par nous aucun trouble, empeschement ny scandal que nous craignons sur touttes choses, bien sachans l'offence que ferrons envers Dieu lequel prions tres instamment [last page] asseurer et rendre certaine vostre Excellence de nos bonnes volontez accroistre et augmenter vos auctorite et grandeur en toutte sante et prosperite. [signatures]"

74. See chap. 7.

75. For letters of complaint to Frederick from Catholic cities in Alsace and Lorraine, see chap. 2, pp. 00–00.

76. AN-K 2187, dr. 1. The copy I have is evidently a draft and contains marginal notes as well as crossed-out lines. It consists of eight pages. The first part is directed to the Bourgeois. The second part is directed to the French. There is no signature, but it is evidently a draft prepared for Frederick since only the count himself could sign such a rebuke.

77. AN-K 2187, dr. 1. Minute: "Car nous ne pourrions encore [marginal insertion: et faire nostre compte] aultrement ny penser, sinon que vous vous vouleriez vouluntiers eslever et egaler a quelque Cite Imperiale, n'ayant superieur."

78. AN-K 2187, dr. 1: Avertissement de Mres. Samuel et Anthoine Saray ministres de Montbéliard. Sur les Responces des Seigneurs françois refugiez en ce lieu. 29. Decembre 1586.

79. Ibid.: A tresillustre Prince et Seigneur Monseigneur Frideric Conte de Wirttemberg et Montbéliardt. This letter is neatly printed and is signed: "De vostre Excellence le treshumble et tresobeyssant serviteur en l'eglise françoise de ce lieu, Anthoine Sayrran." It is dated December 30, 1586. Sayrran said that he had preached "selon que ie l'ay apprinse, et retenue de mes tresaymez, et honnorez precepteurs de Tubingue, lesquelz je pourrois nommer en tout honneur: item de la Confession d'Ausbourg, Wirttemberg, et du livre Chrestien de Concorde."

80. Ibid.: "Bien vray est que Maistre Samuel me dit apres la celebration de la Cene, que j'avois scandalise les françois, et mesmes quelques uns de nos bourgeois, pourtant, que j'avois faict mention de la manducation orale, et touchant la manducation des meschans: mais d'autant que c'est la verite chrestienne, je luy dis 'scandalum hoc a Gallis acceptum esse iniuste et a me non datum.' "

81. Ibid.: "Advis du Conseil donne a son Excellence touchant les Responses faictes par les Sres. françois. Du 30 de decembre 1586." This brief argument contains lengthy marginal notes that reinforce the text.

82. The French claimed that the glass was put on the altar for use in a time of great fear of the plague, then threatening the town (AN-K 2187, dr. 1).

83. AN-K 2187, dr. 1. The letter was dated January 5, 1587. I have it in both German and French.

84. Ibid., that is to say, in the same collection: "Messieurs les maistres bourgeois et aultres Citoyens de la Ville de Montbeliart." Floret's letter has no date, but the content makes clear that it was the model for the petition.

85. Nuremberg was also under pressure from Lutherans and had suffered restrictions on its clergy.

86. Although it was written by Daniel Toussain and directed to the Nine Bourgeois of Montbéliard, the French refugees apparently sent it on to Frederick in their name. The address reads: "Les françois refugiez a Montbéliard supplient treshumblement qu'il plaise a son Excellence de les dispenser de signer un certain Escrit touchant la Sainte Cene." The manuscript that follows is in German; it begins "Den Ersamen

Herren den Neunern Burgermeystern der Stadt Mumppelgart" and is dated January 15, 1587. [I think the first page has been misapplied to this document and belongs rather to the petition of the French discussed earlier.]

87. *Acta,* Appendix, 575: "per Spiritus sancti virtutem adversae parti, oculi mentis aperiantur, ut veritatem coelestem agnoscant, ament, atque amplectantur, ipsius Celsitudo ardentibus votis precatur. Et ut huic etiam Appendici sua Authoritas constaret; ipsius Celsitudo, in publicum testimonium veritatis, ei propria manu subscripsit. Actum Mompelgarti in Arce, die II. Febr. Anno Christi, 1587. Fridericus, Dei Gratia Comes Wirtembergicus & Mompelgartensis, &c."

88. AN, K 2187, dr. 1: "Difficultas haud ita pridem circa electionem novem civium Magistratus officio in Civitate Montbeligardensi." The document is signed "Anthonius Beuson. D."

89. Ibid., p. 4: "Nam sapius factos cives nullo fundamento et iure suffultos [*sic*] Religionem quam Illustriss. Dux profitetur approbare subscribendo refragari, ex subiunctis radys meridiani solis clarius apparet.

"Primum enim ut praecitatam Religionem subscribant remesse omni rationi consentaneam ipsiment ultiò confitentur, de tempore saltem quando nimirum subscriptio facienda veniat contravertentes affirmantes interum rem esse prorsus indifferentem, sive ante sive post iuramenti praestationem ad subscribendum vocentur.

"Ex quo quis adeò caecitate aut mentis inopia laborat, ut audax et temerarium civium horum facinusam non perspiciat ac palpitet. Secundo eum omni dubio careat Principem nonem cives promoderanda Rebup. [*sic*] electos, ius habere confirmandi et antequam ad confirmationem progrediatur necessarium esse, ut in qualitates personarum confirmandarum inquiratur ac investigetur, ex consequentia infallabili ditendum, Religionis subscriptionem electorum confirmatione praecedere debere, ut appareat qui et quales confirmentur, ne facta confirmatione, diversae religionis sectatorem confirmatum esse, in detrimentum Repub. haud contemnendum nimis serò deprehendatur. Tertio mentionati cives hanc suam nulla ratione tolerandam inobedientiam nullo alio pretextu aut colore palliare [p. 5] excusareque desudant, nisi quod dictam subscriptionem privilegiis suis contrariam esse praetendere non erubescant, cum tamen ex ipsorum privilegiis, ne ullo quidem verbulo hic ipsorum praetextus susteneri possit.

"Quarto ab anno 1573. ex quo hic confirmandi mos salubriter, admodum introductus est, subscriptio ut confirmationem antecederet huc usque solicité observatum esse in propatulo est, ex quo concludendum, usum huius difficultatis subministrare dilucidationem.

"Ultimo cum nemo inficias ire possit, Illustr. Ducem Würtemb. tanquam statum ac Principem Imperii subiectos suos ad illam quam ipse profitetur Religionem amplectendam non tantum adigere, verum etiam totum Religionis negotium (ubi ita commodum fore arbitrabitur.) in alium statum transmutare posse, Alt. ipsius tantum quoque potestatis tributum esse, unicuique subditorum seriò iniungere etiam, cui adhaeret Religionem ore vel scriptis declarare, nemo non videt? Unde perspicuum evadit quam ne fandé hanc Religionis subscriptionem multoties allegati cives detrectare atque subterfugere tentent, neque contradictionis suae ullus subiectorum iustam in medium afferre poterit causam, potissimum autem illi, qui ad Reipubl. gubernacula admoveri sibique iustitiae et politiae administrationem concredi affectant, cum hac ratione omnis generis corruptelae quae alias in Rempubl. irrepere possent, avertantur. Et experientia omnium rerum magistra abunde edocet, in omnibus bene ordinatis Rebus publ. laudabili receptum esse consuetudine, ut ad aliquam dignitatis vel officii publici praeeminentiam electi atque evecti, priusquam [p. 6] ad iuramentum praestandum admittantur, sinceram Religionis suae confessionem edere teneantur. Quod quid effectu aliud est quam subscriptio de qua hoc nostro casu disceptatur."

90. *Mémoires et Documents inédits, pour servir à l'histoire de la Franche-Comté,* vol. 1 [no editor] (Besançon: L. Sainte-Agathe, 1838), 452–54: "Franchises et libertés octroyées aux habitants de la ville de Montbéliard, par Renaud de Bourgogne, comte de Montbéliard, et Guillauma de Neufchatel-outre-Joux, sa femme, au mois de mai 1283." These franchises were renewed by successive counts and dukes. Of interest here are the renewals by Duke Ulrich, March 2, 1535; Count Christopher, November 27, 1550; Count George, January 1554; and Johann-Frederich, 1608. See also 453–54: Traité amiable en interpretation de ces franchises, conclu entre le comte Georges de Wurtemberg et les bourgeois de la ville de Montbéliard, le 31 mai 1557. Autre, au meme effet, entre le comte Frederic de Wurtemberg-Montbéliard et ces bourgeois, le 19 mai 1587." No new treaty was made in this regard until 1708.

91. Duvernoy, *Éphémérides,* 164, 167, 168, 171, 173, 184, 187, 188. The whole town renewed its oath of fealty to Frederick on June 28, 1587 (ibid., 241.)

92. Ibid., 435.

93. Ibid., 316.

94. M. Leube, "Die Mompelgarder Stipendiaten im Tübinger Stift," 59, citing G. Goguel: "Le comté de Montbéliard n'a jamais eu rien de commun avec l'Allemagne. La langue nationale était seule usitée dans tous les actes de l'administration. L'Allemand n'était pas enseigné dans les écoles comme le prouve l'exemple de Cuvier; était une langue barbare dont les elements lui étaient inconnus lorsqu'il arriva a Stutgart. Nous ne sommes pas étonnes qu'on lise au commencement d'une statistique en allemand: Le comté de Montbéliard était à peu pres aussi étranger aux habitants de Würtemberg que les regions polaires."

95. AN-K 2187, dr. 1. Beuson, 8–9: "Considerando enim statum comitatus Montisbelg. circumvallati Provinciis et populis diversos Dominos recognoscentibus, diversas Religiones profitentibus, diversas linguas loquentibus, ac diversa naturarum complexione quam longissime inter sese discrepantibus, in hac (9) rerum facie, vim ad sanandam plebis in obedientiam adhibere summo cum periculo iunctum esse indica quia seditio semel accensa q. scintilla impetu populari repentè agitatur ac totam urbem prius inflammare quam restingui posset: Sed si hisce seditionis Principiis obstare, proque illorum suffocatione nulli operae labori ac sumptui parcere Illustr. Dux animo constitutum habet, in id omni animi contentione desudet, et in toto negotio talem se praestet, ne Alt. ipsius autoritati quicquam detrahatur, vel subditis Maiestate sua abutendi occasio exhibeatur arripienda."

96. Viénot, *Histoire de la Réforme* 1:218–28.

97. Ibid., 227.

98. *Acta,* Preface, B1r–v.

99. Ibid., C3r–v.

100. See chap. 2, n. 19.

101. AN-K 2187, dr. 1: "Stuttgartten. unser gnediger Furst vnd Herr wegen dess Newen accords so die alhiehige franzosische Minister mit den Burgern ohne participation des Superattendenten, vil weniger der raht etc. eingangen vnd vfgericht. Stuttgart, den 2ten Maii anno 1594. Unserm Grosshoffmeister, auch Vice Cantzlern vnnd Rathen zu Mumppelgartt vnnd lieben Getrewen N N. Vnnsern grus zuuor. Liebe Getrewe, Demnack vns furkhommen, alss wan sich abermaln vnnsere Mumppelgarttische Burger vnnderstehn woltten, wider die vorige ein Newe Confession anzustellen vnnd einzufuhren, welches dan nicht zugedulden, derewegen ist vnnser Ernstlicher beuelch, lhr wellend so woll die ministros alss Burger vor Euch bescheiden vnnd sie mit Ernst

erinnern, beii der hieuor gestelten vnnd einmahl verglichnen Mumppelgarttischen Confession de Coena Domini ohngeendert zu bleiben vnnd nicht immerdar Newe Confessionnes (welche vff Sthraufen gestelt) zu machen. Sonderlich aber den Kirchendienern anzaigen, furohin ohne vorwussen vnnsers Superintendenten nichtzit mehr dergleichen mit der burgerschafft hinderruckhs zu handlen oder furzunehmen. Weil auch der jetzige Superintendent M. Caspar Lutz ab- vnnd herauss begerth, seindt wir dessen auch zufriden; wellen vnnd beuelhen desswegen, dass der jtzige diaconus M. Johan Osswaldt an sein Statt geordert werde, welcher es allein (wie vor der Zeit auch beschehen), woll verstehen khan vnnd genug qualificiert ist. Daran beschicht vnnser gnedige vnnd Ernstliche meiinung, vnd seindt Euch mit gnaden gewagen. Datum Stuttgart den 2ten Maii anno 1594. Friderich HZW [Herzog zu Württemberg]."

102. Landeskirchliches Archiv Stuttgart. Bestand 1726, 720,1e.

103. Ibid.

104. P. Pfister, *Colloque de Montbéliard (1586): Étude historique* (Geneva: Imprimerie Ramboz et Schuchardt, 1873), 81–82: "Depuis cette époque, la Confession d'Augsbourg a régné en maîtresse dans notre pays, et encore à l'heure qu'il est, elle est le symbole de l'enseignement religieux dans nos églises.

"Cela n'a empêché nos églises de conserver toujours le souvenir de leur origine. Elles se sont toujours rappelé que ce fut Farel qui, le premier, leur prêcha la Réforme et que, pendant plus d'un siècle, elles furent attachés aux doctrines de Calvin; elles n'ont jamais oublié non plus que ce fut en grande partie pour des raisons politiques que les princes, faisant violence aux consciences, ont imposé aux fidèles la Confession d'Augsbourg." Cf. Florent Mabille, *Histoire succincte de la Réforme du pays de Montbéliard,* Thèse, Bachelier en Theéologie, Genève (Geneva: Imprimerie Ramboz et Schuchardt, 1873), 78–79. It seems that the two Montbéliardais were fellow students in Geneva, both graduating in 1873.

7

Aftermath (2): The Larger Scene

At the close of the colloquy, Count Frederick seemed to have been won over to the Lutheran side and continued to refuse to allow the French refugees to receive communion without first signing a Lutheran confession. Certainly Frederick became more and more adamant about confessional unanimity in Montbéliard and expressed considerable anger at the continued request of the French refugees to follow their own confession and, when they were not allowed to do so, their migrations to Basel and elsewhere to receive the sacraments from Reformed ministers.[1] Nevertheless, what appears to have been the larger purpose of the colloquy, namely, German support of Henry of Navarre and the Huguenots, was not lost. Frederick himself became, if anything, more active on their behalf.

In April 1586, Frederick led a contingent of German princes to the court of Henry III of France to plead for the Huguenot cause. The colloquy had not deterred Frederick, but Henry III's cool, even discourteous reception, or rather lack of reception, of the German delegation was more chilling.[2] The German princes reminded Henry of the duty of a prince to keep his word, which Henry III had not done when he broke the peace with the Treaty of Nemours. They found it strange, moreover, that Henry, in his letter of October 22, 1585, blamed the Reformed for the ensuing war since it was Henry's edict of July 1585 that established the "Religion Romaine" as the only religion of France and decreed the exile of the Reformed. The German princes assured Henry that they sought only his good since the pope was clearly trying to obtain power over the Gallican church.[3] If Henry wished to reestablish peace, the Protestants would help him. Henry III replied to the ambassadors on October 11, 1586, telling them that as king he knew how to govern his people and, like other sovereigns, preferred to do so without interference.[4] The rough answer given the German ambassadors seemed to increase Frederick's zeal, however, since he found the French court was still under the powerful sway of the too-powerful Guise. More than ever, the Huguenots, as fellow Protestants, required Frederick's help.

During the months following the colloquy, Frederick continued to allow the Huguenots to use his territories as one of the staging grounds for Henry of Navarre and Casimir to gather Swiss and German mercenaries who would be sent from there into France.[5] In November 1586, Henry of Navarre commissioned the baron de Clervant and Jehan de la Fin, Sieur de Beauvoir, to raise troops and supplies in Switzerland:

> Henry, by the grace of God King of Navarre, First Prince of the blood and heir presumptive of the throne. And protector of the reformed Churches of France, to all who will see these present letters, greetings. As we, for some years have been sufficiently alarmed by the practices and secret counsels of the Pope and his adherents to extinguish, by all possible means, the light of the true religion, to exterminate Kings, Princes, lords, gentlemen and others who profess it and to leave nothing undone to accomplish their intention, especially in this kingdom. Against which we have tried to do and done what duty demanded and power allowed by all the gentlest and gracious means that we could and always with a singular patience, faithful and obedient to the edicts and will of the King. We have, nevertheless, learned that [the pope] entered into a pernicious conspiracy discovered and already broken out against the person of the King and of the Princes of his blood under the name of the Cardinal of Bourbon our uncle, but in effect by the enterprise, conduct and solicitation of the house of Guise.[6]

Henry continued to explain the ends of the Catholic League, especially its mission to promulgate and enforce the decrees of the Council of Trent and to disinherit Navarre himself. Therefore, Navarre continued, advised by his council, he took to arms and began to gather mercenaries and military supplies. He especially looked to the Swiss league of Protestant cantons. To this end, Navarre sent Clervant with full powers to negotiate and to raise the levees necessary for Navarre's army and to buy munitions, artillery, and other necessary equipment.[7] As security, Navarre promised all his possessions within and without the kingdom of Navarre and the principality of Béarn, and so on. He added the chattels of the Reformed churches of France and the property of the prince of Condé, the duke of Montmorency, the viconte de Turenne, and other nobles of the Reformed religion. Navarre gave Clervant the power to negotiate, contract, and capitulate with as much authority and validity as if Navarre himself were present.[8]

Meanwhile, the duke of Lorraine, long annoyed with Frederick's hospitality to French exiles and his support of Navarre,[9] was swift to punish Frederick and from Lorraine sent an army, under the son of Charles III of Lorraine, into Montbéliard and its dependent counties.[10] The Guisards devastated the land, pillaged, burned, raped, and reduced the area to a barren waste in January, when the people had no hope of recovering their lost supplies, replanting their destroyed crops, or even finding adequate shelter from the midwinter weather. The invaders burned sixty-three villages, drove off eight thousand head of cattle, and destroyed churches before John Casimir, at the head of Montbéliard troops, drove them out.[11] Following this outrage, both Frederick and Duke Ludwig of Württemberg appealed to Henry III and Rudolph II for reimbursement. Henry III wrote a discourteous reply, and Rudolph II set up commissions to investigate the claims, but nothing came of them.[12] Relief for the stricken county came at last from collections taken in Reformed Switzerland and other Protestant lands.

Had the German princes known it, the rough reply of Henry III was no indication of his future actions. During the critical year 1586, Henry III was anything but firm about his intentions. The Guise and their allies feared, in fact, that Henry III was too ready to make peace with the Huguenots and, what is more, that his outward friendliness toward the Guise was not genuine.[13] Pressured by the Guise to capitulate, he vacillated. But the embattled Huguenots were not privy to the mind of the king and were sure that he had given in to the Guise. In fact, they feared that he had sent an agent, La Verrière, into Germany to persuade the German Protestant princes to assist the French crown or at least not to support Navarre.[14] An anonymous warning was circulated to the German princes to put them on their guard against La Verrière:

> Warning of several French, secretly adhering to the protestant Religion concerning the mission of the ambassador La Verriere, . . . sent to the Elector of Saxony and other German Protestant princes in order to make them abandon their loyalty and good will under the cover of a peace agreement demanded by the King; to say that this mission is not to be believed as it comes at the request of the [Catholic] League.[15]

The reasons given were that Catherine had agreed to the demands of the Guise and that Henry III would join with the Guise, the pope, the emperor, the king of Spain, and others sympathetic to the League.

But in fact, the Guise terms were intolerable to Henry III. They included the enforcement of the decrees of the Council of Trent, the establishment of the Inquisition in France, and a heavy tax to support the anti-Huguenot war; further, all Huguenot property was to be sold, all Huguenot prisoners of war who refused to recant were to be put to death, and additional French towns were to be handed over and fortified by the league.[16] To agree to these conditions was to abandon the Gallicanism of the French crown and to yield control of the French Catholic church to the pope. Henry's dislike of the Guise and their control of him were becoming strong enough to stiffen his resistance to them and to the Catholic League.

While they may have misread Henry's intentions, the writers of the warning were otherwise well informed. They told the Protestant princes that Philip of Spain was financing and manipulating the League and that the duke of Savoy was part of the plot along with the Catholic cantons of Switzerland. The League was well financed and had twenty-one thousand infantry and cavalry, which included French, Swiss, and German *reiter*s. In addition, there were as many more troops and cavalry in various parts of France. As for Navarre's troops and mercenaries, the report continued, they have been neither defeated nor successful. On the contrary, they wander the countryside, pillaging in order to feed themselves since Navarre cannot pay them enough. Meanwhile, the supposed peace and the emissaries of the crown and the League go about trying to undermine the support given Navarre by the queen of England and the German Protestant princes.

The details of this warning correspond to the researches of historians. The warning, however, has the flavor of urgency and comes in the midst of un-resolved conflict. Henry's vacillations and support of both sides are difficult to interpret. The Guise reported him to be losing his reason. In the light of historians' assessments of Henry III, his actions are in character, that is to say, as inconsistent as Henry himself. Henry III, unable to be firm with the Guise, pretended to agree to their terms, but in reality he had begun to plan the desperate measures that would indeed rid him of "the king of Paris," Henry, duke of Guise, and his two powerful brothers and would lead to the assassina-tion of Henry III himself.

The War of the Three Henries (Henry III, Henry of Navarre, and Henry of Lorraine, duke of Guise) began with Navarre's victory over the royal army at Coutras, October 20, 1587. Flushed with victory, Navarre overextended his lines and trusted too far the leaders of the various components of his army.[17] The leaders had no clear plan of action, and their ill-disciplined troops suc-cumbed to disease before they met the Guisard armies. The Swiss began to desert,[18] and the Germans, defeated by the royal and Guisard armies, also came to terms with Henry III.[19] It was all over by November 24, 1587.[20]

Short of cash as always, Navarre had insufficient funds to pay the troops after his defeat in 1587. The money to continue the war was advanced instead by Ludwig of Württemberg through Clervant and Beauvoir.[21] In 1596, having succeeded his uncle Duke Ludwig, Frederick would claim that the unpaid debt was due him, as Ludwig's heir, from Henry IV of France as heir of Henry III since Ludwig, duke of Württemberg, and Henry III had arranged the payment to the German-led mercenaries.[22] To prove that Navarre had en-gaged his agent Clervant to raise troops and to pay whatever was necessary to get them, the document appended Navarre's commission to Clervant and Beauvoir as well as the notary's record of the money passed from Ludwig to Clervant and Beauvoir on July 5, 1587.

While Henry of Navarre tried to raise fresh troops and the money to pay them, Henry of Guise exploited his victory and in the spring of 1588 made known his desire to enter Paris, where the people prepared to welcome him as a hero. Emboldened, the Guises no longer hid their alliance with Philip II of Spain, who was preparing his Armada to sail against England. Henry III resented the Parisians' open preference for the duke of Guise and rightly read it as dangerous. He therefore ordered Guise to stay out of Paris, but Guise no longer felt he had to obey Henry III and in May entered Paris, where jubilant throngs received him. In the face of what was rapidly becoming open rebel-lion, Henry III left Paris. Catherine de' Medici remained and was party to the Edict of Union, the terms of which signaled the complete capitulation of Henry III to the terms demanded earlier by the League. What the writers of the warning had feared in 1586 seemed to have become a reality in 1588.

But Henry III only seemed to have capitulated. On December 23, 1588, Henry summoned the duke of Guise to his chamber, where the royal guard assassinated him. The following morning Henry III put to death Guise's brother, the cardinal of Lorraine, and others of the Guisard party.[23] But Henry III had achieved a hollow victory. Neither the people nor the government of France respected him. The Guisard League survived under the leadership of the last of the Guise brothers, the duke of Mayenne.

As 1589 began, a beleaguered Henry III turned to the Politiques and to the Huguenots. Henry of Navarre responded by publishing an appeal for peace and formed an alliance with Henry III. As the two Henrys prepared to besiege Paris, an assassin stabbed Henry III, who died the following day, after blessing Henry of Navarre and acknowledging him as the legitimate heir to the throne of France. The War of the Three Henries concluded in August 1589 when Henry of Bourbon, king of Navarre and first prince of the blood, took the title Henry IV of France.

With the death of Henry III, the Protestant princes of Germany rallied to the side of Henry of Navarre, since the lines were now more cleanly drawn between the Huguenot leader and the intransigent Catholic League. It was to the greater interest of the Protestant princes to keep France strong in its Gallican politics than to see it become part of the Roman Catholic alliance of Philip of Spain and the pope. Henry of Navarre, heir presumptive to the throne of France in spite of the pope's bull disinheriting him, therefore wrote confidently to the German princes, thanking them for their support and reminding them of their financial obligations to support Henry's armies. To Ludwig of Württemberg Henry wrote such a letter on October 20, 1591, acknowledging Ludwig's help and promising to be a good ally against their common enemies. Henry included the Guises and promised Ludwig that he would do all he could to right the wrongs that resulted from the quarrel he and the count of Montbéliard had had with the duke of Lorraine.[24]

The angry Catholics of Paris, however, could not put aside their religion in order to maintain their Gallican politics. They refused to receive a king they considered to be a heretic. They went so far as to tolerate the help of Spanish troops, who strengthened the Catholic League and prevented Henry from entering Paris. But elsewhere in France, Henry IV made it quite clear that he was the master of the field, and a defeated duke of Mayenne realized that not only was the league severely weakened, but that without the continuing presence of the Spanish in France, Henry would ultimately win. After skirmishes and further Spanish interventions, the time seemed ripe for the kind of compromises that would bring peace and a French prince to the French throne. Henry therefore abjured his Protestant faith and became a Catholic in July 1593. He was crowned in 1594 and shortly thereafter entered Paris.

Henry's conversion had alienated one of his allies, Elizabeth of England, who proclaimed herself scandalized. Relations between England and France worsened thereafter, and Elizabeth continued to press for a Protestant League until her death.

After Henry's abjuration, the French Protestants began working for a legal base in France. The new king's loyalty to the Huguenots was not entirely subverted by political compromise, and he listened to their appeals. On April 13, 1598, Henry IV signed the Edict of Nantes, which was based on previous edicts of pacification but contained many more details and fifty-six secret articles.[25] It restored to the Huguenots their properties and documents and freed those who had been imprisoned. Protestants could build churches in designated towns and, in short, exercise their rights as citizens of France. But these events, the subject of innumerable essays and books, lie outside our present inquiry.

Here I must add a grace note to draw the international aspect into relation with at least one of the collocutors at Montbéliard. Henry IV met Beza on November 25, 1600, while the king camped with his troops near Geneva.[26] Hiding his pain that Henry, on whom he had pinned so many hopes for the Protestant cause, had become a Catholic, the frail old churchman rode to the village of l'Eluiset. It had been more than thirty years since they had met. Henry embraced Beza, calling him his father and his friend. The king seated the old gentleman and remained standing himself while they talked. Beza dined with Henry and, declining a royal invitation to spend the night, returned to Geneva.[27]

Notes

1. See chap. 6, p. 173.

2. Simon Goulart, *Recueil des choses Memorables advenues en France. Le Premier / Recueil, / contenant / les choses plus me- / morables advenues / sous / la ligue, / tant en France, Angleterre, qu'autre lieux.* 1590. N.p., n.d. See Paul Chaix, Alain Dufour, and Gustave Moeckli, *Les Livres imprimés à Genève de 1550 à 1600* (Geneva: Librairie Droz, 1966), 128, which gives Heidelberg as the place and Jérôme Commelin as the printer. But see the whole entry for the opinion of E. Droz that Goulart edited only the volumes subsequent to the 1590 edition. Cf. Paul Heitz, *Genfer Buckdrucker und Verlegerzeichen im xv., xvi. und xvii. Jahrhundert* (Strasbourg: Heitz, 1908). For vols. 1 and 2, see ibid., pp. 50–51, no. 168, which gives Geneva as the place but no name for the printer. The printer's mark had moved from Lyon to Strasbourg to Geneva. For vols. 3–6, see ibid., pp. 44–45, no. 146, which gives Geneva as the place and Jacobum Stoer as the printer. The Harangue is found in vol. 1, pp. 507–16: "Harangue des Ambassadeurs des Princes Protestans d'Allemagne faicte au Roy. Sire, Les tres-puissans Electeurs Palatin, Saxon, Brandenbourg, & les autres tres-illustres Princes Joachim Frideric Marquis de Brandebourg, & Administrateur de Magdebourg, Jules de Bronsvic & Lunebourg, Guillaume, Loys, & Georges Landgraves de Hesse freres: Et Ioachim Ernest Prince de Chat, avecques les quatres villes libres imperiales & principalles de toutes les autres, Strasbourg, Ulmes, Nurnberg & Francfort, tous de la Religion reformee & estans du saincte Empire, nous ont envoyé vers vostre Majeste." Hutten and Issenbourg and others had to leave when Henry III was not there to meet them in August. The time of the meeting was October 1586.

3. Ibid., 513: The Pope "d'un costé ne chercheroit d'establir sa principaute insatiable, & par ce moyen anéantir les privileges de l'Eglise Gallicane." It should be noted that the arguments of the German princes repeated those of Queen Elizabeth in the letters addressed to these princes urging them to join her in forming a Protestant League.

4. Goulart, *Recueil* 1:3v–4r. For another contemporary account of the German embassy to Henry III, see Thou, *Histoire universelle* 9:597–98.

5. Cited in Rott, *Histoire* 275, n. 9, as " 'Fleury au roi et a Brulart. Soleure, 19

janvier 1586. Bibl. Nat. f. fr. 16 026 fo. 264.' 19 janvier, 1586. Advis du Sr. de Fleury avecq les responses du sr. devilleroy [ms. p. 264ff.]: les françoys qui sont à Montbéliard Basle, Strasbourg et Colmar. Lesquels sont en fort bon nombres et se dict quil y en a plus de huict cent à Montbéliard."

6. Hauptstaatsarchiv Stuttgart, Bestand A 266, Pergament 195: "Henry, par la grace de Dieu Roy de Navarre, Premier Prince du sang heritier presumptif de la couronne. Et protecteur des Eglises reformees de France, a tous ceux qui ces presentes lettres verront salut. Comme nous eussions depuis quelques annees enca suffisamment esprouve par les practicques menees et conseils secrets du Pape et de ses adherans que leur dessain seroit destaindre par tous moiens la lumiere de la vraye religion, exterminer tous Roys Princes seigneurs gentilzhommes et aultres qui en font profession, et ne rien laisser en ariere pour parvenir a leur intention speciallement en ce royaume. A quoy nous aurions tasche et faict tout debvoir de pourveoir par les plus doux et gratieux moyens que nous aurions peu rendant tousjours avec une singuliere patience, tresfidele et entiere obeissance aux edicts et volonte du Roy, Il seroit neantmoing advenu qu'une tres pernicieuse conspiration se seroit descouverte et esclatee en cedit royaume contre la personne dudit seigneur Roy et des Princes de son sang soubs le nom de monsieur le Cardinal de Bourbon notre oncle; mais en effect par l'entreprise conduitte et sollicitation de ceux de la maison de Guise."

7. Ibid.: "Par devant moy Macquard Müller, Notaire Jure Imperial en la ville de Basle soubsigne et en presence des tesmoings cy apres nommez, furent presens en leurs personnes nobles seigneurs Messire Claude Anthoine de Vienne, Chevallier Seigneur de Clervant Baron de Couppet, Ambassadeur pour la Majeste du Roy de Navarre, Conseillier en son conseil, surintendant de ses maison affaires et finances, au nom et comme ayant charge, pouvoir et mandement de sa Majesté. . . . Et avec luy Messire Jehan delafin Chevallier seigneur de Beauvoir en la mesme qualite de plege et caution dudict Seigneur Roy de Navarre, de leur science certaine et leur bon gre ont promis et promettent a Noble Seigneur Laurent de Vuillermin present stipullant et acceptant pour et au nom de treshault et illustre Prince Monseigneur Friderich Conte de Wirtemberg et de Montbeliard faire entrer et recevoir en l'estat et roole des deniers dehu aux Suisses par la Majeste du Roy de France la somme de cent mil escu d'or au soleil pour et au prouffit dudict Seigneur Conte de Wirtemberg et de Montbeliard. Laquelle somme il pretend estre dehue par ledit Seigneur Roy de France comme heritier et successeur a la couronne de France apres le deces du feu Roy Henry seigneur et pere dudict Roy a present regnant duquel debte ledict Seigneur Conte Friderich a faict apparoir et justifier souffisament tant par comptes arrestez que aultres documens valables. Et ladicte somme de cent mil escuz provenus de solde payee et satisfaicte aux gens de guerre Allemans conduitz et menez en France de l'authorite et commandement dudict feu Seigneur Henry Roy de France. Ladicte solde fournie par feu treshault et illustre Prince le Duc de Wirtemberg et Icelle advenue en partaige audict Seigneur Friderich Conte de Montbeliard." The document recorded is a history of nonpayment on the part of Henry of Navarre, by 1596 become Henry IV of France.

8. Ibid.: "Ledict seigneur de Clervant puisse negocier, contracter et capituler avec autant de force et validite que si nous le faisions en personne." This document was copied on parchment and duly notarized for Frederick, duke of Württemberg and count of Montbéliard, on February 27, 1596.

9. See chap. 2, p. 46, for threats from the Guise to punish Frederick for harboring French refugees, especially men who might return as part of a pro-Huguenot army.

10. René de Bouillé, *Histoire des Ducs de Guise,* vol. 3 (Paris: Imprimerie d'E. Duverger, 1850), 248: "A Porentruy et près de Bale et de Neufchâtel, "ung colonel,

quelques capitaines furent tués et plusieurs desvalisés," car Guise avait "lasché la bride aux soldats qui mirent le feu dans le dit comté de Montbelliard, bruslèrent cent ou six vingt villages," et tirèrent une aveugle vengeance des dégats commis par les Allemands, au début de la campagne, sur le territoire du duc de Lorraine." Cf. Alexandre Tuetey, *Les Allemands en France et l'invasion du comté de Montbéliard par les Lorrains, 1587–1588,* d'après des documents inédits (Paris, 1883), 199–200.

11. Tuetey, *Les Allemands en France,* 212. Cf. Simon Goulart, *Recueil* 2:412–13: "Quelques temps après ledit Jamets assiege, le Sieur de Rosne, avec les trouppes d'Italiens, Allemans, Wallons, Liégeois, Lorrains, & autres qui l'assitoient, à mettre les feuz au Comte de Montbéliard (apres la retraitte de France, de l'armee d'Allemans) en nombre de sept a huit cens chevaux, & quelques regimens de gens de pied, sont venus faire le semblables es terres de Sedan, . . . Car outre les feuz, toute sortes de paillardises, Sodomies, forees & violences se commettent envers tous sexes, / & aages [*sic*], & avec cela ne delaissent de faire payer rançon."

12. Tuetey, *Les Allemands en France,* 207, 209–11, 379–82, 385–90. See Goulart, 2:416–17; 420.

13. Ragazzoni, pp. 532–36, esp. no. 258, p. 532: "Non manca chi crede, anzi così quasi è l'opinione commune, che se bene il Re Chr.mo mostra verso esso Guisa ogni segnio di confidenza et amorevolezza, nondimeno il cuore di S. M.tà non corrispondere all'estrinseco." See also no. 259, p. 533.

14. German Protestant princes did supply mercenaries to Henry III. German mercenaries fighting for Navarre reproached their countrymen for betraying the Protestant cause and the Augsburg Confession respected by the Reformed as well as the Lutherans. M. L. Cimber and F. Danjou, *Archives curieuses de l'histoire de France depuis Louis XI jusqu'à Louis XVIII,* ser. 1, vol. 11 (Paris: Imprimerie de Bourgogne et Martinet, 1836), 106–10: "Responce faicte par les Seigneurs Allemans estans au service du roy." Besides denying that the Reformed were legitimate followers of the Augsburg Confession, the response claims that the troops were aiding a legitimate king against seditious subjects, followers of "leur faulce et abominable secte de Calvin." The *Response* indicates the kind of propaganda used to recruit the troops—fear that the ferocious Calvinists would extend their war into Germany. They express their horror at the willingness of Germans to serve Navarre. It is signed by Philibert, marquis de Bade; Jean Philippes Reingraff, Frederich Reingraff; Georges, compte de Leiningen, seigneur de Wluesterbourg et Chambourg, toujours franc; Christofle, baron de Bassompierre; seigneur de Harroue; Albert, comte de Dietz (p. 110).

15. HAS 63, Bu. 64: "Warnung wider des Königs in Franckhreich an die teutschen Chur-und Fursten verschickten Legaten, La Verriere genannt, anbeholhene Werbung etc. anno 1586. zu communicieren. Warnung etlicher heimlicher Religionsverwandten in Franckreich, belangendt des Herrn La Verriere . . . zu Franckreich an den Churfursten zu Sachsen und andere Teutsche Evangelische Fursten abgefertigten Gesandten Werbung, dardurch er dieself underm Schein eines vom Khonig begerten Fridens von ihrem gueten Willen und Zunaigung abfallig machen soll; auch da dises Abgesandten arglistigen Worten (als der uff Anhalten der Liga verschickt) aus volgenden Ursachen nicht Glauben noch Beyfall zu geben sey."

16. Jensen, *Diplomacy and Dogmatism,* 133–34; 142–45.

17. Michel de la Huguerye, *Éphéméride de l'expedition des Allemends en France* (*Août–Decembre 1587*), ed. Leonel de Laubespin and Leon Marlet (Paris: Librairie Renouard, 1892), 324, claimed that Henry of Navarre and Henry III came to an understanding. La Huguerye did not give details, but the result was that Henry of Navarre did not bring his army to meet the Swiss and German mercenaries caught

between the pincers of the army of the Guise and the royal army. La Huguerye's interest in writing his memoires and the *Éphéméride* was to exculpate himself from responsibility for the disaster of 1587. A flurry of apologies from other Huguenot officers followed and appear in the volume edited by de Laubespin and Marlet.

18. Ibid., 377–78.

19. Ibid., 435–39.

20. Jensen, *Diplomacy and Dogmatism,* 89–92.

21. Duke Ludwig may have been influenced to support Navarre because of the devastation of the territory of Montbéliard by Guisard troops in January 1587.

22. See p. 188, n. 8. This is a strange claim since it would mean that while Henry III seemed to be supporting the Guise, who had also brought in German mercenaries, Henry III was playing both sides of the game financially as well as politically. Henry's double-dealing is quite credible, however. See Jensen, *Diplomacy and Dogmatism,* 76ff. Jensen describes Henry III's preference for Navarre over the Guise in all but religion. If Navarre could be persuaded to convert, there would be no difficulty in Navarre as heir to the French throne. In fact, in 1586, "Henry [III] had given secret instruction to Biron, marshall of France and commander of the royal army, to try to make contact with Navarre and persuade him to negotiate a truce" (p. 77). Jensen credits Philip II's ambassador to Paris, Bernardino de Mendoza, with preventing an alliance between Henry III and Navarre. See pp. 89 for Navarre's use of Swiss and German mercenaries, as well as financial support from Elizabeth of England and the king of Denmark. Jensen refers to the Swiss mercenaries hired by Guise but not to the Germans hired by both Guise and by Henry III (p. 90); Jensen does not refer to Elizabeth's efforts to form a Protestant League. See n. 24 for Henry IV's acknowledgment of his debt to the duke of Württemberg.

23. E. G. Léonard, *Histoire générale du Protestantisme,* vol. 2, *L'Établissement* (Paris: Presses Universitaires de France, 1961), 138.

24. Henri IV, *Recueil des lettres missives* 3:502: A mon Cousin le Duc de Wirtemberg, Prince du Sainct Empire. Mon Cousin, Si vostre lettre, qui m'a esté rendue par mon cousin le vicomte de Turenne, est pleine d'asseurance de vostre bonne volonté envers moy, il m'en a encores, de bouche, donne plus grande confirmation, selon les bons effects que vous en avés rendus par la liberale contribution que vous avés faicte de vos moyens à l'advancement de mes affaires. . . . Et comme nous avons des ennemys communs, ainsy je desire que nous demourions joincts de bonne intellignece contre eulx; et de ma part je vous y favoriseray tousjours de ce que je pourray, mesmes aux justes querelles et inimitiez que vostre cousin le conte de Montbeliart a contre le duc de Lorraine, comme auusy je feray tout ce qui despendra de mes moyens et auctorité, pour la satisfaction et accomplissement des contractz qui ont esté passez en mon nom, avec vostre dict cousin, où je suis trés marry qu'il soit empesché."

25. Sutherland, *Huguenot Struggle,* 283–332, and Appendix 370–72.

26. Geisendorf, *Théodore de Bèze,* 410–13.

27. Ibid., 416–19.

APPENDIX 1

Appendix: In which is Taught, What was Done, Regarding the Communication and Protest of the French Exiles after the Colloquy of Montbéliard

Dr. Beza and his colleagues, in a little book of supplication, (which is inserted in these acts) petitioned, among other things, that the brethren of his confession while retaining their own confession and without any prejudice to the other [the Montbéliard Confession], they be allowed to receive Holy Communion from the hands of others [namely, Lutheran ministers] and thus cherish and testify to their mutual fraternity. But to this part of the book of supplication the Most Illustrious Prince and Lord, Lord Frederick, Count of Württemberg and Montbéliard, etc., before the Colloquy had finished answered nothing. But when the Colloquy had ended Dr. Beza and his colleagues, already preparing for their departure and dressed for the journey, again entreated that the Prince give them a response. His Highness then sent his decree about this matter to them in their inn. This decree was no different from that which just before Christmas His Highness and his counselors had given in their presence in the Great Hall. The [1585] decree was promulgated in a clear voice by the superintendent of Montbéliard. Afterward it was also exhibited in writing to them [the French exiles]. We will reiterate his opinion. The second one, which was given to Beza and his colleagues, we will append. But here is the gist of the first decree of the Most Illustrious Prince.

FIRST RESPONSE OF PRINCE FREDERICK GIVEN TO THE FRENCH
BEFORE THE COLLOQUY

After the ministers[a] of the Church of Montbéliard had submitted their petition,[b] the Illustrious Prince, their lord, the Lord Frederick, Count of Württemberg and Montbéliard, gave this response:

It ought to be signified to them that his pious and pure confession publicly

---

Acta, pp. 569–75. The translation is my own. Only the marginalia that added information to the text rather than merely summarizing it are given as lettered notes below.

offered to them stands as more than enough. If they wish to communicate under that confession, they would be most welcome, if not, then they must consult their consciences about it and they may abstain from communicating. For no one, if he has properly prepared for communion and comes forward, will be excluded. Done in the castle, 17 December 1585. Signed, Frederick, Count of Württemberg, etc.

SECOND RESPONSE OF PRINCE FREDERICK GIVEN TO THE FRENCH EXILES AFTER THE COLLOQUY

To the supplication of Reverend Beza and his colleagues, who asked that the brethren of his confession, while retaining their own confession and without prejudice to the other, be allowed to receive communion from OTHER HANDS:

The Most Illustrious Prince and Lord, the Lord Frederick, Count of Württemberg and Montbéliard, etc., responded that the confession and ecclesiastical order of His Highness had been publicly exhibited: If, according to that Confession and order, they wished to come to the Holy Supper of the Lord and if they make this intention of theirs known to the minister of the Church of Montbéliard, they would not be repulsed. Done at Montbéliard, 29 March 1586. Signed, Frederick, Duke of Württemberg, etc.ᶜ

After this decree had been promulgated on the first day of April, which was the Friday before Easter, and after the ambassadors from each side had already departed, some ministers of the French Church (who along with the French exiles had been given hospitality at Montbéliard) petitioned yet once again that this little clause be added to the decree of the Prince: "By receiving communion [in the Montbéliard church] the French did not intend, in any way to condemn their own confession." If it was not possible to obtain this concession from the Prince, namely that this short phrase be inserted into the decree, they asked that the minister of the church of Montbéliard should recite these words publicly on a platform in the presence of all the people or standing at the altar. In doing this these Gallican ministers are certainly not following Beza's counsel. Beza had previously written to the French refugees not to offend the church of Montbéliard in the least, but rather to go to communion there without too much disputation. But the petition of the French ministers was unjust. Nevertheless they continued to importune the Superintendent in the middle of the night. From him, however, they received this response: "The Illustrious Prince wishes that his dated and subscribed mandate be strictly observed and that it be changed not one iota." When they received this response one of these French ministers, on the following day, the morning of the Sabbath, with some French exiles left the city and went seeking men of their own confession elsewhere with whom they might receive communion.

But the rest of the French exiles who remained in Montbéliard called for a meeting with the French ministers of this church. At the meeting the Reverend de Vesines (who had sat at Beza's table during the Colloquy and who had listened most diligently) expressed this opinion to the French ministers of the Montbéliard church: He and his colleagues with deep emotion and desire wished to communicate as one with the Montbéliard church and to ask that they not be excluded from communion in the Holy Supper nor taken for strangers in the Church of Christ in whose name they had borne such great persecutions.[d]

To this speech Dr. Richard Dinot, minister of the French church [of Montbéliard], wished to respond (since then he has been called from this life by the Lord) but he was interrupted by some minister, a stranger and an exile, who said, "The Reverend de Vesines has not rightly or in the least declared the mind of the French clergy, for these had asked that they might be admitted to communion in the Lord's Supper UNDER THEIR OWN CONFESSION."

To this Dr. Richard Dinot responded that no one thus far had been excluded from the French church of Montbéliard whether he had come there from Geneva or elsewhere. Provided only that their sermons had first been heard and approved, they might receive communion. Why, therefore, should the French exiles be excluded now since many had already received communion with them? For he did not doubt that the French exiles had heard his own and his colleagues' sermons and had understood sufficiently the simple confession of our church which also had been thoroughly made known to them from the Augsburg Confession and its Apology and from the Württemberg Confession of Duke Christoph which was offered at the Council of Trent.[e] Or again, from the Concord of Luther and Bucer in 1536 at Wittenberg. Neither he nor his colleague could dissent from these pious confessions especially because these [confessions] were conformed to the Word of God and well founded in it. Whatever therefore had been said against these confessions were mere calumnies, lies, and manifest falsities.

To this a certain French lawyer (who often before had taken the Holy Supper in the church of Montbéliard), together with other exiles, interrupted and responded: if they disapproved of the confession and meetings of the ministers of the church of Montbéliard, they would never have petitioned that they be allowed to communicate with them. Nevertheless, at the same time they could not repudiate their French confession and condemn other churches (whether in France or elsewhere). To which Dr. Richard Dinot responded that neither he nor his colleagues wanted to condemn any churches of Christ. On the contrary, they wished them all the best. But nevertheless it is not possible to deny (if one wishes to confess the truth) that the confession of the French, especially in the 38th article, is at least ambiguous and insufficient since he could not understand who those "Sacramentarians" might be of whom the Confession makes mention.

To this Floret, a minister of the French exiles, responded that he could explain that ambiguity of the Gallican confession in this way. By "Sacramentarians" is to be understood those who reject the sign in such a way that they might say that these signs are bare. NEITHER ARE THEY CONJOINED WITH THE THINGS WHICH THEY SIGNIFY even though Jesus Christ said, "This is my body, this is my blood." Here that good man Richard Dinot in his candor (judging Floret to be a Lutheran like himself), answered: What more do we need, what remains to impede the French exiles (when they are of such an opinion), especially when they wish to come with the other faithful to the Supper of the Lord?

After that Floret asked Samuel Cucuel, Richard's colleague and a minister of the French Church of Montbéliard, whether he had anything to say that would contradict what his colleague had said. Samuel answered that he had nothing to say but rather greatly wondered what they all wished because they had so often and so many times repeated this: UNDER OUR FRENCH CONFESSION. Did they not approve of the confession of the Montbéliard church? Or, did they condemn it?

Floret, however, excused himself and his colleagues lest they seem to condemn the Montbéliard confession and repeating the thought of the lawyer (of whom we spoke above), said, we would not wish to communicate with you if we did not approve your confession. Nevertheless, (said Floret) an injury is done us if we are made to look as though we empty the sacraments. For we hold firmly that the bread and the wine are not only signs but INSTRUMENTS THROUGH WHICH THE TRUE BODY AND BLOOD OF CHRIST ARE DISTRIBUTED. But truly (said Floret) it is known that you, Samuel Cucuel, in your sermons have often rejected Transubstantiation, Consubstantiation, Ubiquity and the local extension of the body of Christ. And now, Cucuel, do you persist in this thought? To this Samuel Cucuel assented.

At length ministers questioned these two ministers [Cucuel and Dinot] of the French church of Montbéliard whether they would give communion to some of the French exiles according to their own mode and form, that is to say, give them the bread in their hand and not in their mouth? To this Samuel Cucuel answered, nothing can be gained by changing the rite of administering the Lord's Supper, for it would be too easy to offend the simple people by this change. Some French refugees pressed him further about this, but since they obtained nothing, they acquiesced and declared they thought that these ceremonies were not obstacles to their admission to the Supper of the Lord.

But when the Montbéliard ministers had already left the meeting and so were completely innocent of what was then done later by the French (this was holily affirmed by Samuel Cucuel who is still living) the French secretly, having called lawyers and some other citizens of Montbéliard, drew up a certain Instrument with such candor and faith that the Illustrious Prince and Lord, Lord Frederick, Count of Württemberg and Montbéliard, etc., would have most grave and just causes (in the preface of this work [the *Acta*]), to annul that Instrument and withdraw from it all vigor and authority. For it was drawn up not only in the absence of those whose presence, understanding and consent were required in the first place, but indeed they inserted such things of which (in the presence of the ministers of Montbéliard) either nothing had been mentioned or which had not been approved by their [the ministers'] consent. For this reason the Instrument was far from the truth of what actually happened.

But since Christ said truly there is nothing hidden which will not one day be revealed, it was not long until that Instrument, drawn up illegitimately and in detriment to the truth, came to light. The occasion of its revelation was that most vain letter published by that fictitious Eusebius Schönberg who first mentioned the Instrument, claiming he discovered it. But when that letter had been read, those who governed the Republic in the absence of Prince Frederick searched with great diligence and industry to find as many copies as they could of this secretly drawn-up instrument. But when they showed it to the Illustrious Prince on his return, His Highness was deeply disturbed by such an unjust, clandestine, bold act committed in bad faith. He took it and was deeply upset by it. Nor would the author of this instrument have gotten away with impunity, given his temerity and malice, except that death reached him before a prince and human punishment could reach him.

All of this the Most Illustrious Prince Frederick judged should be brought to light so that there would be a public testimony to the truth. And he therefore wanted the Acts of the Colloquy of Montbéliard published for posterity so that the vanity of the Schonbergian letter (in which there were as many lies as lines) might be made known to the whole world. And also so that His Highness's person might be vindicated from all false and evil suspicion of turning aside from that pious, pure and first incorrupt Augsburg Confession. And indeed His Highness had these acts published in order to promote the true and firm peace of the churches (which is founded and consists only in that very demonstration of the truth). His Excellency prays to God for this happy result and also so that the Holy Spirit might open the eyes of the mind of the adversaries that they might come to know heavenly truth and love it and embrace it, and for this His Highness, in public testimony to the truth, subscribes to this with his own hand. Done at Montbéliard in the castle, on the 11th day of February in the year of Christ 1587.

Frederick, by the grace of God, Count of Württemberg and Montbéliard, etc.

Notes

a. There are two churches, a German and a French. The primary pastor is German and at the same time also fulfills the office of superintendent.

b. That they be allowed to communicate under their own Confession.

c. [Andreae indulges in sarcasm in this marginalis and in the text itself, p. 200.] This is indeed to permit the French to do what before was not permitted. Thus the letter [Schonberg's letter] is nonsense.

d. These words, which seemed to continue the protest, were heard by the French ministers, but were neither received nor approved by them.

e. The French exiles are recalled to the Confession of the German Churches which certainly differs in many ways from the French [Confession].

APPENDIX 2

Instrument

[*—First page from a bundle of correspondence in which this letter is #4—*]
1586 \ Discussions avec plusieurs bourgeois
1587 / et quelques refugies francois au sujet de la ste. Cene. 16 pieces.
[*—From the last page identifying this particular letter—*]

Requeste
de Mre. Leonard Mayre, touchant
l'acte par luy donné aux Sres.
françois.
13 dec. 1586.

[*—Main text, page 1—*]
A tresillustre, hault et puissant
prince et seigneur Friderich,
par la grace de Dieu comte de
Wirtemberg Montbeliard.

Tresillustre Prince, Leonard Maire, votre
tres humble et tresobeissant subiect et serviteur,
notaire Imperial et procureur postulant en
ceste votre ville de montbeliard depose en
toute reverence et sincerite a votre E[xcellen]ce qu'il
y a environ trois semaines qu'il fut mande
par Messrs. de votre Conseil et interrogue
s'il n'avoit pas la minute d'ung acte donné aux
françoys qui se sont retirez par-deça soubz la
protection de votre E[xcellen]ce d'ung certain
pourparler que fut faict entre eulx et feu
Mre. Richard Dynot et Mre. Samuel Cucuel,
ministres en ceste ville, le sambedy veille
du jour de Pasques dernierement passé, a
quoy le suppliant respondit promptement qu'ouy,

I owe the corrections of my transcription and the final form of this document to Glenn Sunshine and Tom Lambert, students working under the direction of Robert M. Kingdon. Accents have been added only when necessary to distinguish two possible meanings of a word.

ne se sentant culpable de rien en sa conscience.
Et en appourta incontinent une copie a mesdits
Srs. que contenoit en substance une requeste
que faisoyt le Sr. de Vezines au nom de
tous les françoys pour estre receuz a
communicquer avec les bourgeois de ce lieu au
sainct sacrement de la cene, et la responce
faicte par lesdits ministres, selon qu'il est pre[sen]té (?)
plus au long audit acte. Et apres ledit pourparler
fini, et que lesdits Srs. ministres de ce lieu furent
retirez, ledit Sr. de Vezines s'addressa a Mre.
Girard Charpiot, notaire, et audit suppliant, et
leur demanda une acte dudit pourparler, leur
faisant entendre que moyennant ledit acte
ilz communicqueroient tous a la cene et sans
icelluy que personne d'entre eulx n'y communicquereoit
parce que lesdits ministres avoient declaré

[*—page 2—*]

quilz ne condamnoient les eglises de France et
au reciprocque lesdits françoys qu'ilz ne condamnoient
les eglises dudit Montbeliard que seroit cause
d'une concorde entre lesdits eglises, a quoy ledit
suppliant, meu d'ung zele et affection a la gloire
de Dieu pour laquelle il a quicté sa patrie et
son bien puis quinze ans encea aiant dès ledit temps
fait sa residence actuelle en ce lieu soubz votre
obeissance, accorda avec ledit Charpiot de donner
ledit acte en presence des tesmoiings qu'avoient esté
presens audit pourparler et qui sont denotez audit acte.
En quoy il n'a extimé ny peuste faire faulte,
moings offenser ou mesprendre envers votre
E[xcellen]ce, a laquelle il a tousjours desiré obeir
et y perseverer toute sa vie. Lequel acte fut
dressé, minuté, et escript par Mre. Andre Floret,
jadis ministre en cedit lieu, qui l'apporta audit
suppliant pour le signer. Mais, comme il y
avoit obmis quelques motz que le suppliant
extimoit estre de la substance dudit pourparler
quoy qu'il ne soit versé aux termes de theologie,
il les y adjousta de sa propre main en la
presence dudit Floret comme il se pourra voir
par ladite minute. Quant au reste comme il
luy sembloit que s'estoit les mesmes propos que
avoient esté leus in ladite assemblee, du moings
en substance, il le mist au net et en donna

une copie audit Floret pour la monstrer et
communicquer et la faire signer ausdits ministres
pour servir de prothocolle, ce qu'il promist faire.
Et de faict, a entendu que elle avoit este monstree
audit Mre. Richard, et que celluy declara qu'elle estoit
bien en presence d'aulcungs desdits Srs. françoys, et qu'il
n'y avoit rien treuvé a redire. Que si elle ne
fut aussi monstree audit Mre. Samuel en cela ledit
Floret auroit surprins et circonvenu ledit suppliant
qui n'en a jamais heu ny esperé aulcung proffit.

[*—Page 3—*]

Et s'il y avoit faulte, elle procederoit plus
de la simplicité et zele dudit suppliant
et par la captiosité et surprinse dudit Floret
que pour dol ou ou sinistre volunte, n'y aian
ledit suppliant studieusement ou malicieusement
aulcune chose obmis ny adjousté a la faveur
decue, que ce soit comme il le jurera
et affermera (?) en sainne conscience devant
Dieu et par-devant votre E[xcellen]ce s'il en est requis.
Et s'il plaict veoir ladite minute
escripte de la main dudit Floret, le suppliant
la rendra et delivrera a toutes les fois qu'il
plaira luy commander. Il supplie donques
bien humblement avoir bening egard a son
innocence et ne lui rien imputer dudit faict.
Et qu'il plaise a votre E[xcellen]ce lui pardonner
par sa doulceur et benignite accoustumee,
si en ce elle se retrenne aulcunement
offensee, que seroit advenu plus par mesprinse
que de propos deliberé. N'ayant ledit suppliant
chose en ce monde apres la gloire et le service
de Dieu en plus grande recommandation que
de rendre service aggreable a votre E[xcellen]ce,
en quoi il ne vouldroit espargner sa propre
vie selon que mesdits honorez Srs. de votre
Conseil, suffisans tesmoings de ses versations
et depourtemens, en pourront assurer votre
E[xcellen]ce pour laquelle il priera tousjours de
plus en plus l'eternel Dieu et souverain
createur, la vouloir maintenir et conserver
en toute prosperite et grandeur avec toute
votre genereuse maison. Actum a Montbeliard
ce 13e decembre, anno 1586.

Maire.

APPENDIX 3

Beza and Luther's *De servo arbitrio*

In Beza's 1587 *Responsio* there is no detailed response to the last three subjects of the colloquy, namely, images and music in the churches, baptism, and predestination. Rather, Beza goes from the discussion of the person of Christ directly to an *Extract from the Little Book of Dr. Luther regarding the Bondage of the Will in His Dispute with Erasmus*. He presents his excerpts rather abruptly with a simple statement that "these are the passages which I have taken from Dr. Luther's book."[1] I will indicate here what Beza included and, perhaps more importantly, what he omitted.

Beza began with that section in *The Bondage of the Will* in which Luther discusses God preached, God hidden, God's revealed will, and God's secret will. In the first passage, Beza omitted a section that dealt with Paul and Thessalonians discussing the Antichrist, and he emphasized only those parts that have to do immediately with the question of the majesty of God and his hiddenness and secretness. Beza also omitted those portions that dealt directly with arguments that were particularly Roman Catholic and directed against Erasmus's defense of the doctrine of free will. Since even Beza would not assert that the Lutherans were teaching a doctrine of free will, this is not to the point for Beza. Beza therefore skipped a considerable portion that has to do primarily with the subject of free will and moved on to the secret will of the divine majesty. His excerpts here are full and unaltered. Beza quoted Luther, arguing that "God must be left to Himself in His own majesty" and that there are matters that God "does not disclose to us in His word; He also wills many things which He does not disclose Himself as willing in His word. Thus He does not will the death of a sinner, according to His word; but He wills it according to that inscrutable will of His." All of these arguments are extremely forceful for Beza's own position.

Beza then skipped a number of lengthy paragraphs directed by Luther against specifically Roman Catholic arguments regarding free will and continued with the secret will of the divine majesty, "which," he quoted Luther, "is not a matter for debate." His quotations here leave out only small portions that he thought might be omitted without weakening his argument; neither do they undercut anything that Beza had said. He then skipped another longish portion directed against the Roman Catholic doctrine of merit and moved on through a quite long section against Erasmus.

Part of this long section (WA 700–702) is against Erasmus's use of tropes in interpreting Scripture. The reason for this is obvious, since even though Beza did not use tropes in his argument for predestination he used them as a fundamental part of his theology of the Lord's Supper. There he based his argument for his interpretation of the words of institution of the Lord's Supper on metonymy, which, of course, is itself a figure of speech or a trope. In the portion omitted by Beza, Luther is adamant against tropes. Luther says, "Look what happened to that master of tropes, Origen, in his exposition of Scriptures," and again he comments on the Arians, who, through a trope, made Christ into a merely nominal God. None of this is repeated by Beza, of course. He does pick up the end of the argument on tropes where Luther says, "For us, I say, it is not enough to say that there may be a trope here, but the question is whether there ought to be and must be a trope here. For if you do not show that a trope is of necessity involved, you have accomplished precisely nothing." This passage is then carried by Luther into the discussion of the hardening of Pharaoh's heart (WA 702–9). This section is, of course, based on Exodus 4:21ff. Throughout these passages of Luther, whenever the subject of tropes comes up together with arguments against tropes as a means of interpretation in general, Beza omitted them. But he agreed with Luther's description of Erasmus's argument as a "new and unprecedented use of grammar" so that "when God says 'I will harden Pharaoh's heart' you [Erasmus] change the person and take it to mean 'Pharaoh hardens himself through my forbearance.' " Beza allowed the discussion of tropes whenever Luther says that the trope is inappropriate in this place, as when he quoted Luther saying: "But since we are fighting with storytellers and bogeymen, let us raise a bogey ourselves and imagine (what is quite impossible) that the trope of which Diatribe dreams is really valid in this place, so that we may see how she avoids being compelled to affirm that everything happens by the will of God alone and as far as we are concerned by necessity."

Beza then returned to lengthy quotations with only short omissions throughout this long section (WA 709–14), including the passage that begins:

> [H]aving exploded the tropes and glosses of men, we can take the words of God literally, with no necessity to make excuses for God or to accuse Him of injustice. For when He says, "I will harden Pharaoh's heart," He is speaking literally, as if He said, "I will act so that Pharaoh's heart may be hardened," or "so that through my working and doing it may be hardened." How this is brought about we have heard to this effect: "Inwardly I will move his evil will by my general motion so that he may proceed according to his own bent and in his own course of willing, nor will I cease to move it nor can I do otherwise than move it; but outwardly I will confront him with the word and work with which that evil bent of his will clash, since he cannot do other than will evilly when I move him, evil as he is, by virtue of my omnipotence."

When he came to the section given in the Classics edition the title, "How God's Foreknowledge Imposes Necessity" (WA 714–20), Beza again skipped nearly all of it since it is concerned with free will. He picked up the argument where Luther says,

> Admittedly it gives the greatest possible offense to common sense or natural reason that God by His own sheer will should abandon, harden and damn men as if He enjoyed the sins and the vast, eternal torments of His wretched creatures, when He is preached as a God of such great mercy and goodness, etc. It has been regarded as unjust, as cruel, as intolerable, to entertain such an idea about God.

Here, in the middle of Luther's sentence, Beza ended this particular quotation and moved on to the section in which Luther says in effect that, even if unwillingly, all people agree that God is omnipotent in power and action or else He would be a ridiculous God.

Beza then skipped a rather long portion on the two kinds of necessity illustrated by the case of Judas (WA 720–22) and picked up the argument concerning Jacob and Esau (WA 722–27). This portion is quoted at length, although there are some sections where, for the sake of brevity, I suppose, Beza chose to include one sentence and to exclude the next. Some of the excluded passages have to do with reward. The included passages comment on the gratuity of God's love for Jacob and his hatred for Esau. The argument here includes Erasmus's refutation of the interpretation that the prophet was speaking only of temporal misfortune; Luther and Beza follow him in saying that is not the case, but rather that Paul is at least speaking about misfortune in this life and damnation in the next.

Luther's argument then deals with the potter and the clay and with the way of reason, which demands that God's justice be reconcilable to human justice, or, more succinctly, that Erasmus's way of reasoning does not let God be God (WA 703–33). This section relates to the first argument quoted by Beza from Luther, namely, that there is an explicit will of God made known through the Word and a secret will of God into which it is vain to inquire and still more vain to demand that it conform to the laws and judgment of human beings. Again, Beza omits a long portion here that deals with merit and is directed by Luther against specifically Roman Catholic doctrine (WA 731–83). This very long section again is an argument by Luther against Roman Catholic doctrines of free will and understanding of the word *flesh* in John. None of this is quoted by Beza, but instead he picks up the final section of the *Bondage of the Will* (WA 784–85), which is entitled in the Classics edition, "The Mercy and Justice of God in the Light of Nature, Grace and Glory." Beza's quotations here are integral; he omitted very little indeed and moved on to Luther's conclusion, of which he quoted the first paragraph only (WA 786), ending with "there cannot be any free choice in man or angel or any creature." This passage concludes Beza's excerpts.

Beza's use of Luther's *Bondage of the Will* should have been a master stroke. It turned against the Lutherans a fundamental work of Luther himself in which the arguments strongly underpin the very points that Andreae found so horrible, namely, that, by his secret will God could will the damnation of anyone. Beza knew that on the point of predestination, the Genevans stood almost alone. Even Zurich did not agree completely with them, and certainly Bern and others of the German Swiss cities refused to accept double predestination. Rather than carry on a fruitless argument, Beza allowed these pages to speak for his own position.

Note

1. The portion of the *Bondage of the Will* from which Beza takes his excerpts is found in WA 18, 685–786. Quotations are from the LCC edition, *Luther and Erasmus: Free Will and Salvation,* ed. E. Gordon Rupp and Philip S. Watson (Philadelphia: Westminster Press, 1959).

BIBLIOGRAPHY
OF WORKS CITED

Primary Sources

Books

Andreae, Jacob. *Acta Colloquij Mon / tis Belligartensis: / Quod habitum est, Anno Christi 1586. / Favente Deo Opt. Max. / Praeside, / Illustrissimo / Principe ac Domino, Domi- / no Friderico, comite Wirtember- / gico et Mompelgar- / tensi, &c. / inter clarissimos viros, D. Ia- / cobum Andreae, Praepositum & Can- / cellarium Aca- / demiae Tübingensis: & D. Theodorum Bezam, Pro- / fessorem & Pastorem Genevensem, / Authoritate praedicti Princi- / pis Friderici, &c. nunc Anno Chri- / sti 1587. publicata. / Haec acta candide et bona fide consi- / gnata, vanissimos de hoc Colloquio sparsos rumores, inprimis vero / Epistolam quandam, vanitatibus et calumnijs refertam, & typis ex- / cusam, abundè refutabunt. / Cum privilegio. / Tubingae, / Per Georgium Gruppenbachium, / Anno M.D. LXXXVII.*

————*Les Actes / du Colloque de / Montbeliardt: / qui s'est tenu l'an de / Christ 1586. avec l'aide du Seigneur Dieu tout / puissant, y presidant le Tresillustre Prince & Sei / gneur, Monseigneur Frideric Conte du Wirtemberg & Montbeliardt, &c. / entre tresrenommez per- / sonnages le Docteur Iaques André Preposé & Chance- / lier de l'université de Tubinge, & le Sieur Theodo- / re de Beze Professeur & Ministre / à Geneve: / Lesquels ont este nouvelle-ment publiez l'an de Christ 1587. & traduitz de Latin / en Francois par l'authorité du Prince / Frideric. . . .* [mentions the "lying letter"] *Imprimé a Montbeliardt / Par Iaques Foillet / Imprimeur de son Excellence. / M.D. LXXXVII.* On the blank facing page, someone has written: "ler livre imprimé à Montbéliard 1587." I owe my photocopy of this book to the kindness of the librarian of the Bibliothèque Publique (Montbéliard).

————. *Jacob Andreae Admonitio / pia et necessaria, / de / synopsi ora / tionis ioannis iacobi / grynaei, professoris theo / logi Zwingliani in Academia / Basiliensi: / qua disputationi de coena / Domini, Heidelbergae Anno 1584. die 4. Aprilis / proposi- tae, 15. eiusdem, finem / imposuit. Autore / Iacobo Andreae D. Praeposi / to Tubingensi.* Tübingen: Gruppenbach, Anno 1584.

————. BRIEF RECUEIL / DU COL- / LOQUE DE MOM- / BELIARD TENU AU MOIS DE / *Mars 1586. Entre Iaques Andre D. / & M. Theodore de Beze.* No place of publication. Octavo. The copy I used came from the Bibliothèque Publique (Montbéliard).

————. *Christliche Trewerzige / Erinnerung verma= / nung und warning vor der zur Newen= / statt an der hart nachgetruckten ver= / falschten und mit Calvinischer Gottsla= / sterlicher Lehr beschmei ten / Bibel / D. Martin Luthers. / Gestelt / durch D. Iacobum Andreae / Probst zu Tubingen.* Tübingen: Georg Gruppenbach, 1588.

211

————. *Epitome / Colloqquii / montisbelgartensis / inter D. Iacobum Andreae et D. / Theodorum Bezam, Anno Domini 1586. / Mense Martio celebrati. / In qua Ecclesia Christi fide- / liter monetur, ut ab horribilibus erroribus Calvinistarum / sibi caveat: quos illi de infrà scriptis articulis / fovent, atq. summo studiio propa- / gare conantur. De Coena Domini. / De Persona Christ. / De Baptismo. / De libertate Christiana, in reformatione templorum. / De praedestinatione. / De promissionibus Evangelii. / De Merito Christi. / Adiecta Refutatione solida / responsionis D. Bezae de / Actis eiusdem Colloquii. / Authore / Iacobo Andreae D. Praepo- / sito Tubigensi.* Tübingen: Georg Gruppenbach, 1588. [Text from Andover-Harvard Theological Library, t608.2 / A55.4ep / 1588.]

————. *Kurzer Begriff / des Mümpelgarti- / schen colloquii oder Gesprächs welches / zwischen D. Iacobo Andreae, unnd D, Theodoro / Beza, um Martio des 1586 Jars ist gehalten / worden. / Darinnen die Kirch Christi trewlich ver- / warnet würdt sich zuhüten vor den grewlichenn / irtthumen der Calvinisten welche sie von den nach= / volgenden Articeln haben. . . .* Gestellt / Durch Iacobum Andreae D. Probst / unnd Canzlern zu Tübingen. Tübingen bey Georg Gruppenbach. 1588.

————. *Refutatio blasphemae apologiae Lamberti Danaei Galli de adoratione carnis Christi.* Tübingen, 1583.

————. *Solida Refutatio com- / pilationis Cinglianae, / Quam Illi Con- / sensum Ortho- doxum / Sacrae Scripturae et Veteris Eccle- / siae, de controversia sacramentaria, ap- / pellarunt, in lucem ediderunt, & aliquo- / ties recoxerunt. Conscripta per Theologos Wirtembergi- / cos: in gratiam eorum, quibus gloria Christi Servato- / ris, & sua aeterna salus cor- / di est.* Tübingen: Georg Gruppenbach, 1584. In this work, Calvin is directly attacked and the Calvinists likened to Turks and followers of the "Alcoran" (p. 45).

————. *Spiegel / der offenbaren unverschambten Cal= / vinischen Lugen wider reine Lehrer / der Augspurgischen Confession / unnd / Grewlichen erschrockenlichen Losterungen / warning sich vor disem Geist zuhuten / Gestelt durch / Iacobum Andreae, Probst und / Cantzlern bey der Universitet / zu Tubingen.* Tübingen: Georg Gruppenbach, 1588.

Archives curieuses de l'histoire de France depuis Louis XI jusqu'a Louis XVIII. Edited by M. L. Cimber and F. Danjou, Series 1, vol. II. Paris: Imprimerie de Bourgogne et Martinet, 1836.

Beza, Theodore. *Ad acta / colloquii / Montisbelgardensis / Tubingae edita, / Theodori Bezae / Responsio. / Genevae, / Excudebat Joannes le Preux. / M.D.LXXXVII.* A second Latin edition appeared in 1588, and a third in 1599.

————. AD ACTA / COLLOQUII / MONTISBELGARDENSIS / TUBINGAE EDITA, / *Theodori Bezae / Responsionis, pars / prior. / Editio Secunda. Genevae, / Excudebat Joannes le Preux. / M.D. LXXXVIII.*

————. *Ad acta / Colloquii / Montisbelgardensis / Tubingae edita, / Theodori Bezae / Responsionis, Pars / Altera / Editio prima. / Excudebat Joannes le Preux. / M.D.LXXXVIII.*

————. *De / controversiis / in Coena / Domini, / per nunnulos nu- / per in Germania partim renovatis, partim / auctis, Christiana & perspicua / disceptatio. /* Theodoro Beza auctore. / Genevae: Apud Iohannem le Preux, / M.D. XCIII.

————. *Correspondance de Théodore de Bèze.* Collected by Hippolyte Aubert. Geneva: Librarie E. Droz. Vol. 2: 1556–1558, ed. F. Aubert, H. Meylan, and A. Dufour (1962), Vol. 3: 1559–1561, ed. H. Meylan and A. Dufour (1963); Vol. 5: 1564, ed. H. Meylan, A. Dufour, and A. de Heusler (1968); Vol. 7: 1566, ed. H. Meylan, A. Dufour, C. Chimelli, and M. Turchetti (1973).

————. *Response / de M. Th. de Beze / aux Actes de la conferen- / ce de Mombelliard /* Imprimés à Tubingue. / A Geneve, / De l'imprimerie de Jean le Preux. / M.D.LXXXVII.

The Book of Concord: The Confessions of the Evangelical Lutheran Church. Translated and edited by Theodore G. Tappert. Philadelphia: Muhlenberg Press, 1959.

Brenz, John. *Recognitio / Propheticae & Aposto- / licae Doctrinae, de Vera / Maiestate Domini Nostri Ie- / su Christi, ad dexteram Dei / Patris sui omnipo- / tentis. / In hoc Scripto refutatur liber Henrici Bullingeri, / cui author titulum fecit: Fundamentum fir- / mum, cui tuto fidelis quivis innit / potest, &c. / Authore Ioanne Brentio. / Item appendix publicorum testimoniorum, quibus manifeste osten- / ditur, Cinglianos nostram, hoc est, vere piam sententiam / de coena DOMINI, mala conscientia / oppugnare.* Tübingen: Ulrich Morhard, 1564.

Calendar of State Papers, Foreign Series. Vol. 20.

Calvin, John. *Calvin's New Testament Commentaries.* Vol. 4: *The Gospel according to St. John.* Edited and translated by T. H. L. Parker. Grand Rapids, Mich.: Eerdmans, 1961.

Castellion, Sébastien. *De haereticis an sint persequendi et omnino quomodeo sit cum eis agendum,* LUTERI & BRENTII, *aliorumque multorum tum veterum tum recentiorum sententiae.* Facsimile reproduction of the 1554 edition with an introduction by Sape van der Woude. Geneva: Librairie E. Droz, 1954.

Chemnitz, Martin. *The Two Natures of Christ.* Translated by J. A. O. Press. St. Louis: Concordia, 1971.

Concordia Concors. / De / Origine et Progressu For- / mulae Concordiae Ecclesiarum / Confessionis Augustanae, / Liber Unus: / In Quo Eius Or- / thodoxia, Scripturae Sacrae, Oecumenicis Symbolis, Toti Antiquitati / Puriori, et primae illi, minimeque variatae confes- / ioni Augustanae, ex asse consona: Modus item agendi, in eo conscribendo, suffragiis mu- / niendo, & tandem promulgando observatus, legitimus, & in Ecclesia Christi hactenus / usitatus fuisse, Christiano lectori evidenter & perspicue demonstratur: & Rodolphi Hospiniani Tigurini Helvetii convitia, mendacia, & ma- / nifesta crimina falsi deteguntur ac solide / refutantur. Edited by Leonhart Hutter. Wittenberg: Clement Berger, 1614.

Concordia Triglotta: The Symbolical Books of the Ev. Lutheran Church, German-Latin-English. St. Louis: Concordia, 1921.

Corpus reformatorum. Edited by C. G. Bretschneider and H. E. Binseil. Halle, 1934–1960.

Damascene, John. *De Fide Orthodoxa: Versions of Burgundio and Cerbanus.* Edited by Eligius M. Buytaert, OFM. St. Bonaventure, N.Y.: The Franciscan Institute, 1955.

Danaeus, Lambert. *Assertio contra D. Iacobum Andreae.* = *Assertio . . . Contra . . . Andreae . . . scriptum de Adoratione Carnis Christi.* Geneva: Eustathius Vignon, 1585.

————. *Apologia Seu Vera Et Orthodoxa . . . Interpretatio, De Adoratione carnis Domini.* Antwerp: Aegidius Radaeus, 1582.

Duvernoy, Charles. *Éphémérides du comté de Montbéliard. . . .* Besançon: Imprimerie de Charles Deis, 1832.

Ecclesiasticorum rituum et caeremoniarum ducatus wirtenbergensis Regula, in ursum quorundam parachorum, germanice nescientum, e germanico in latinum versa. Tübingen: Ulrich Morhardt, 1543.

Frederick the Pious. *Briefe Friedrich des Frommen, Kurfursten von der Pfalz.* Edited by August Kluckhohn. 3 vols. Braunschweig: C. A. Schwetschke und Sohn, 1868, 1870, 1872, esp. vol. 2.2.

Goulart, Simon. *Recueil des choses Memorables advenues en France. Le Premier / Recueil, / contenant / les choses plus me- / morables advenues / sous / la ligue, / tant en France, Angleterre, qu'autre lieux.* 1590. N.p., n.d. In Paul Heitz, *Genfer Buchdrucker und Verlegerzeichen im xv., xvi. und xvii. Jahrhundert.* Strassburg: Heitz, 1908.

———. Vol. 2: *Le Second / Recqueil; / Contenant / L'Histoire des Choses / plus memorables / advenues / sous / la Ligue. 1590.* In Paul Heitz, *Genfer Buchdrucker und Verlegerzeichen im xv., xvi. und xvii. Jahrhundert.* Strassburg: Heitz, 1908.

Grynaeus, John Jacob. *Synopsis orationis. / quae habi / ta est in celeber / rima academia Heydel / bergensi a Iohanne Iacobo / Grynaeo, quum is, Aprilis die XV Anno Christianae / Aevae, 1584. finem imponeret Disputationibus / Teologicis, de Controversia Euchari / stica, per ociduum habitis.* Heidelberg: Typis Iacobi Mylii, 1584.

———. *Apologia Seu Vera Et Orthodoxa . . . Interpretatio, De Adoratione carnis Domini,* Antwerp, (Aegidius Radaeus) 1582.

Henry IV. *Recueil des lettres missives de Henri IV.* Edited by M. Berger de Xivrey. Vol. 2: 1585–1589. Paris: Imprimerie Royale, 1843. Vol. 3: 1589–1593. Paris: Imprimerie Royale, 1846.

Huguerye, Michel de la. *Éphéméride de l'expedition des Allemends en France (Août–Decembre 1587).* Edited by Leonel de Laubespin and Leon Marlet. Paris: Librairie Renouard, 1892.

———. *Mémoires inédits de Michel de la Huguerye.* Vol. 3: 1587–1602. Paris: Librairie Renouard, 1880.

Johann Friedrichs V, des Mittlern, Herzogen zu Sachsen, in Gottes Wort, prophetischer und apostolisher Schriftgegrundente Confutationes, Widerlegungen und Verdammgung etlicher ein Zeit her zuvider demselzen Gotteswort und heiliger Schrift, auch der Augsburgischen Confession, Apologien und der schmalkaldischen Artikeln, aber zu Furderung und Wideranrichtung des Antichristlichen Papstthums eingeschlichenen und eingerissenen Coruptelen, Secten und Irrthumen. Jena, 1559.

Lombard, Peter. *Sententiarum libri quator.* In *PL* 192.

Lucinge, René de. *Lettres sur les débuts de la Ligue* (1585). Edited by Alain Dufour. Geneva: Librairie Droz, 1964. [Lucinge was Charles Emmanuel's ambassador to the court of France.]

Luther, Martin. *De servo arbitrio,* WA 18, 684–787. (For the English version, see Library of Christian Classics, Vol. 17: *Luther and Erasmus: Free Will and Salvation.* Translated and edited by E. Gordon Rupp and Philip S. Watson et al. Philadelphia: Westminster Press, 1969.

———. *Confession Concerning Christ's Supper. Treatise on the New Testament, AE* 36. Edited by Robert H. Fischer, Philadelphia: Muhlenberg Press, 1961. [WA 26:261–509]

Memoires et Documents inédits, pour servir à l'histoire de la Franche-Comté. Vol. 1. [No editor.] Besançon: L. Sainte-Agathe, 1838.

Pflug, Julius. *Correspondence.* Vol. 4: L'Episcopat (II) Juilet 1553–Septembre 1564. Edited by J. V. Pollet. Leiden: Brill, 1979.

Ragazzoni, Girolamo, Eveque de Bergame. *Nonce en France: Correspondence de sa Nonciature 1583–1586.* Edited by Pierre Blet, S.J. Rome: Gregorian University Press, 1962.

Registres de la Compagnie des Pasteurs de Genève. Vol. 3: 1565–1574. Edited by Olivier Fatio and Olivier Labarthe. Geneva: Librairie Droz, 1969.

Registres de la Compagnie des Pasteurs de Genève. Vol. 4: 1575–1582. Edited by Olivier Labarthe and Bernard Lescaze. Geneva: Librairie Droz, 1974.

Registres de la Compagnie des Pasteurs de Genève. Vol. 5: 1583–1588. Edited by Olivier Labarthe and Micheline Tripet. Geneva: Librairie Droz, 1976.

Salvart, Jean-François (with the help of others, including Theodore Beza). *Harmonia confessionum fidei.* . . . Geneva: Petrus Santandreas, 1581.

Scripta / Eruditorum / Aliquot virorum de / Controversia Coenae / Domini. / Anno M.D. LXI. (No editor, place, or publisher given.)

Manuscripts

Archives de Genève, Hôtel de Ville. *Registres de la Compagnie des Pasteurs de Genève,* 81, f. 47r.

Archives Nationales. Paris. Historical Section. K 2186; dr. 1, fonds Montbéliard; dr. 2; K-2187, dr. 1.

Archives Tronchin (in the Bibliothèque Publique et Universitaire de Genève). Vol. 2: Lettres Autographes de 1500 à 1600.

Bibliothèque Nationale. Paris. 500 Colb.' 427, Fas. 399–401. Letters to Henry III (January 4, 1586, and to Villeroy, Henry's secretary of state (January 6, 1586), from Fleury, Henry III's ambassador to Savoy.

Départmente de Doubs, Archives de Montbéliard, Hôtel de Ville.

Hauptstaatsarchiv Stuttgart, Bestand A 63, Bü. 54, 64, 67. Ludwig Lavater à Bèze, Zurich, 19/29 Janvier, 1586. I have a transcription from the Musée de la Réformation, Geneva. The original autograph is in Ms. B-Gotha (cod. chart A. 905, f. 142).

Landeskirchliches Archiv Stuttgart. Bestand 1726, 720,1e. Hauptstaatsarchiv Stuttgart.

Musée de la Réformation, Geneva. Transcription from an original in the Bibliothèque Sainte-Genevieve, Ms. 1455, fols. 186–88, Cote 112.

———. Transcription of an original from the University Library, Basel. Kirchen Archiv CI.2.,Bd.II.

Secondary Sources

Books

Adam, Gottfried. *Der Streit um die Prädestination im ausgehenden 16. Jahrhundert: Eine Untersuchung zu den Entwurfen von Samuel Huber und Aegidius Hunnius.* Neukirchen: Neukirchener Verlag, 1970.

Babelon, Jean-Pierre. *Henri IV.* Paris: Fayard, 1982.

Bouillé, René de. *Histoire des Ducs de Guise.* Vol. 3. Paris: Imprimerie d'E. Duverger, 1850.

Brady, Thomas A., Jr. *Turning Swiss: Cities and Empire 1450–1550.* Cambridge: Cambridge University Press, 1985.

Brecht, Martin. *Kirchenordnung und Kirchenzucht in Württemberg vom 16. bis zum 18. Jahrhundert.* Stuttgart: Calwer Verlag, 1967.

Brecht, Martin, and Hermann Ehmer. *Sudwestdeutsche Reformationsgeschichte: Zur Einfuhrung der Reformation im Herzogtum Württemberg 1534.* Stuttgart: Calwer Verlag, 1984.

Brecht, Martin, and Reinhard Schwarz, eds. *Bekenntnis und Einheit der Kirche: Studien zum Konkordienbuch.* Stuttgart: Calwer Verlag, 1980.

Broderick, J., S.J. *Saint Peter Canisius, S.J.: 1521–1597.* Baltimore: Carroll Press, 1950.

Buisseret, David. *Henri IV.* London: Allen and Unwin, 1984.

Cazaux, Yves. *Henri IV.* Vol. 1: *Ou la grande victoire.* Mayenne: Albin Michel, 1977.

Chaix, Paul, Alain Dufour, and Gustave Moeckli. *Les Livres imprimés à Genève de 1550 à 1600.* Geneva: Librairie Droz, 1966.

Cimber, M. L. and F. Danjou. *Archives curieuses de l'histoire de France depuis Louis XI jusqu'à Louis XVIII.* Series 1, volume II. Paris: Imprimerie de Bourgogue et Martinet, 1836.

Deetjen, Werner-Ulrich. *Studien zur württembergischen Kirchenordnung Herzog Ulrichs 1534–1550: Das Herzogtum Württemberg im Zeitalter Herzog Ulrichs (1498–1550), die Neuordnung des Kirchengutes und der Kloster (1534–1547).* Stuttgart: Calwer Verlag, 1981.

Dempsey Douglass, Jane. *Calvin, Women and Freedom.* Philadelphia: Westminster Press, 1985.

Ehmer, Friedrich. *Valentin Vannius und die Reformation in Württemberg.* Stuttgart: W. Kohlhammer Verlag, 1976.

Ehmer, Hermann, "Erhard Schnepf: Ein Lebensbild." Blätter für *württembergische Kirchengeschichte* 87 (1987): 72–125.

Evennett, H. Outram. *The Cardinal of Lorraine and the Council of Trent: A Study in the Counter-Reformation.* Cambridge: Cambridge University Press, 1930.

Fatio, Olivier. *Méthode et théologie: Lambert Daneau et les débuts de la scolastique réformée.* Geneva: Librairie Droz, 1976.

Gardy, Frédéric. *Bibliographie des oevres théologiques, littéraires, historiques et juridiques de Théodore de Bèze.* Geneva: Libraire Droz, 1960.

Geisendorf, Paul-F. *Théodore de Bèze.* Geneva: Alexandre Jullien, 1967.

Gensichen, Hans-Werner. *We Condemn: How Luther and 16th-Century Lutheranism Condemned False Doctrine.* Translated by Herbert J. A. Bouman. St. Louis: Concordia, 1967.

Haag, Eugène, and Émile Haag. *La France Protestante.* 10 vols. Paris, 1846–1859.

Haile, H. G. *Luther, an Experiment in Biography.* Garden City, N.Y.: Doubleday, 1980.

Heitz, Paul. *Genfer Buckdrucker-und Verlegerzeichen im xv., xvi. und xvii. Jahrhundert.* Strasbourg: Heitz, 1908.

Heppe, Heinrich. *Geschichte des deutschen Protestantismus in den Jahren 1555–1581.* 4 vols. 2d ed. Frankfurt-am-Nain: Verlag von Karl Theodor Volcker, 1865. Vol. 1: 1555–1562; Vol. 2: 1563–1574; Vol. 3: 1574–1577; Vol. 4: 1577–1581 mit fortsetzung bis zum Jahre 1583 enthaltend.

Hertel, Friedrich, ed. *In Wahrheit und Freiheit: 450 Jahre Evangelisches Stift in Tübingen.* Stuttgart: Calwer Verlag, 1986.

Hollweg, Walter. *Der Augsburger Reichstag von 1566 und seine Bedeutung für die Entstehung der Reformierten Kirche und ihres Bekenntnisses (Beiträge zur Reformationsgeschichte Bd. 8).* Neukirchen: Neukirchener Verlag, 1964.

Jensen, De Lamar. *Diplomacy and Dogmatism: Bernardo de Mendoza and the French Catholic League.* Cambridge: Harvard University Press, 1964.

Kickel, Walter. *Vernunft und Offenbarung bei Theodor Beza: Zum Problem des Verhaltnisses von Theologie, Philosophie und Staat.* Neukirchen: Neukirchener Verlag des Erziehungsvereins, 1967.

Kingdon, Robert M. *Myths about the St. Bartholomew's Day Massacres, 1572–1576.* Cambridge: Harvard University Press, 1988.

Köhler, Walther. *Zwingli und Luther: Ihr Streit uber das Abendmahl.* Leipzig: Verein für Reformationsgeschichte, 1953.

Kolb, Robert. *Andreae and the Formula of Concord: Six Sermons on the Way to Lutheran Unity.* St. Louis: Concordia, 1977.

Landgraf, A. M. *Dogmengeschichte der Früscholastik.* 3 vols. Regensburg: F. Pustet, 1954.

Léonard, E. G. *Histoire générale du Protestantisme.* Vol. 2: *L'Éstablissement.* Paris: Presses Universitaires de France, 1961.

Mabille, Florent. *Histoire succincte de la Réforme du pays de Montbéliard.* Thèse, Bachelier en Theeólogie, Genève. Geneva: Imprimerie Ramboz et Schuchardt, 1873.

Montclos, Jean de. *Lanfranc et Berenger: La controverse eucharistique du Xle siecle.* Louvain: Spicilegium Sacrum Lovaniense, 1971.

Moser, Johann Jakob. *Johann Jakob Mosers Mompelgardisches Staatsrecht.* Edited by Wolfgang Hans Stein. Translated by Georg Anders. Stuttgart: W. Kohlhammer Verlag, 1983. Veröffentlichungen der Kommission für geschichtliche Landeskunde in Baden-Württemberg. Reihe A, Quellen. 35. Band. This is a 1720 unpublished disputation, *De Comitatu Principali Montepeligardo,* plus a longer 1772 manuscript: *Einleitung in das Fürstlich Mompelgardische Staatsrecht.*

Nugent, Donald. *Ecumenism in the Age of the Reformation: The Colloquy of Poissy.* Cambridge: Harvard University Press, 1974.

Oberman, Heiko A. *Masters of the Reformation: The Emergence of a New Intellectual Climate in Europe.* Translated by Dennis Martin. Cambridge: Cambridge University Press, 1981. (Original German: *Werden und Wertung der Reformation.* Tübingen: Mohr, 1977.)

Parker, T. H. L. *John Calvin, a Biography.* Philadelphia: Westminster Press, 1975.

Pelikan, Jaroslav. *The Christian Tradition: A History of the Development of Doctrine.* Vol. 1: *The Emergence of the Catholic Tradition (100–600).* Chicago: University of Chicago Press, 1971.

Pfister, P., *Colloque de Montbéliard (1586): Étude historique.* Geneva: Imprimerie Ramboz et Schuchardt, 1873.

Press, Volker. *Calvinismus und Territorialstaat: Regierung und Zentralbehorden der Kurpfalz 1559–1619.* Stuttgart: Ernst Klett Verlag, 1970.

———. "Die württembergische Restitution von 1534—reichspolitische Voraussetzungen und Konsequenzen." *Blätter für wurttembergische Kirchengeschichte* 87 (1987): 44–71.

Raitt, Jill. *The Eucharistic Theology of Theodore Beza: Development of the Reformed Tradition.* AAR Studies in Religion, no. 4. Chambersburg, Pa.: American Academy of Religion, 1972, 1987.

Read, Conyers. *Mr. Secretary Walsingham and the Policy of Queen Elizabeth.* 3 vols. Oxford: Oxford University Press, 1925.

Rott, Edouard. *Histoire de la représentation diplomatique de la France auprès des cantons Suisses, de leurs allies et de leurs confédérés.* Vol. 2: 1559–1610. Bern: A. Benteli, 1902.

Rottstock, Felicitas. *Studien zu den Nuntiaturberichten aus dem Reich in der zweiten*

Halfte des sechzehnten Jahrhunderts: Nuntien und Legaten in ihrem Verhaltnis zu Kurie, Kaiser und Reichsfursten. Munich: Minerva Publikation, 1980.

Sattler, Christian Friderich. *Geschichte des Herzogtums Wurtenberg unter der Regierung der Graven,* III–V. Tübingen: Georg Heinrich Reiss, 1771–1772.

Siggins, Ian D. *Martin Luther's Doctrine of Christ.* New Haven: Yale University Press, 1970.

Sutcliffe, F. E. *François de La Noue, discours politiques et militaires.* Geneva: Librairie Droz, 1967.

Sutherland, N. M. *The Huguenot Struggle for Recognition.* New Haven: Yale University Press, 1980.

Thou, Jacques Auguste de. *Histoire universelle . . . depuis 1543, jusqu'en 1607.* Paris: n.p., 1734. Vol. 9, bk. 85.

Tuetey, Alexandre. *Les Allemands en France et l'invasion du comté de Montbéliard par les Lorrains, 1587–1588,* d'àpres des documents inédits. Paris, 1883.

———. *Étude sur le droit municipal au XIIIe et au XIVe siècle en Franche-Comté et en particulier à Montbéliard.* Extrait des mémoires de la Société d'Émulation de Montbéliard. Montbéliard: Henri Barbier, 1865.

Viénot, John. *Histoire de la Réforme dans le pays de Montbéliard depuis les origines jusqu'à la Mort de P. Toussain, 1524–1573.* 2 vols. [Vol. 2, *Pièces justificatives,* contains primary sources for vol. 1.] Paris: Librairie Fischbacher, 1900.

———. *Le Livre d'immatriculation au college des Montbéliards à Tubingue.* (N.p.): Imprimerie "JE SERS," 1931.

Willis, David. *Calvin's Catholic Christology: The Function of the So-Called Extra Calvinisticum in Calvin's Theology.* Leiden: Brill, 1966.

Articles

Bauer, Karl. "Die Stellung Württembergs in der Geschichte der Reformation." *Blätter für Württembergische Kirchengeschichte* 38 (1934): 3–51, and "Die Bedeutung der Württembergischen Reformation für den Gang der deutschen Reformationsgeschichte." Ibid., 267–80.

Bizer, Ernst. "Martin Butzer und der Abendmahlsstreit: Unbekannte und unveroffentlichte Aktenstucke zur Entstehungsgeschichte der wittenberger Konkordie vom 29. Mai 1536." *Archiv für Reformationsgeschichte* (1938): 203–37, (1939): 68–87.

Bornkamm, Heinrich. *Das Jahrhundert der Reformation: Gestalten und Krafte,* 262–91. Gottingen: Vandenhoeck and Ruprecht, 1966.

Brecht, Martin. "Herkunft und Ausbildung der protestantischen Geistlichen des Herzogtums Württemberg im 16. Jahrhundert." *Zeitschrift für Kirchengeschichte* 80 (1969): 163–75.

Bulletin de la Societe de l'histoire du Protestantisme français, Jan–mar 1948, "Henri de Navarre et 'Messieurs de Genève' 1570–1589." [No author given.]

Davis, Natalie Zemon. "The Rites of Violence." In *Society and Culture in Early Modern France,* 152–87. Stanford: Stanford University Press, 1975.

Ebel, Jobst. "Jacob Andreae (1528–1590) als Verfasser der Konkordienformel." *Zeitschrift fur Kirchengeschichte* 89 (1978): 78–119.

Ehmer, Hermann. "Erhard Schnepf: Ein Lebensbild." *Blätter für württembergische Kirchengeschichte* 87 (1987): 72–125.

Gerrish, B. A. "John Calvin on Luther." In *Interpreters of Luther: Essays in Honor of Wilhelm Pauck,* edited by Jaroslav Pelikan. Philadelphia: Fortress Press, 1968.

————. "The Lord's Supper in the Reformed Confessions." *Theology Today* 23 (July 1966): 224–43.

Janssen, Johann. *Geschichte des deutschen Volkes seit den Ausgang des Mittelalters.* 8 vols. Freiburg-im-Breisgau, 1878–1893. French translation: *L'Allemagne et la Réforme.* 9 vols. Paris, 1887–1914.

Kolb, D. v. "Luthertum und Calvinismus in Württemberg." *Blätter für württembergische Kirchengeschichte* 32 (1928).

Kolb, Robert. "Jacob Andreae." In *Shapers of Religious Traditions in Germany, Switzerland, and Poland, 1560–1600,* edited by Jill Raitt, 53–68. New Haven: Yale University Press, 1981.

Leube, Martin. "Die Mömpelgarder Stipendiaten im Tübinger Stift." *Blätter für württembergische Kirchengeschichte* 20 (1916): 54–73.

Lods, Armand. "Les Actes du Colloque de Montbéliard (1586): Une polemique entre Théodore de Bèze et Jacque Andreae." Mélanges de la Société de l'histoire du Protestantisme Français. *Bulletin Historique et Littéraire* 46 (1897).

Mazauric, C. "Claude-Antoine de Vienne, Sieur de Clervant (1534–1588)." *Annuaire de la Société d'histoire de la Lorraine* 67–68 (1967–1968): 83–152. This is the best available account of Clervant's life. I owe the reference to Alain Dufour, publisher, Librairie Droz S.A., Geneva.

Morembert, H. Tribout de. "La Confession de foi de Montbéliard." *Revue d'Histoire Écclésiastique* 65, no. 1 (1970): 5–29.

Müller-Streisand, Rosemarie. "Theologie und Kirchenpolitik bei Jakob Andrea bis zum Jahr 1568." *Blätter für württembergische Kirchengeschichte* 60–61 (1960–1961): 224–395.

Patterson, W. Brown. "The Anglican Reaction." In *Discord, Dialogue and Concord: Studies in the Lutheran Reformation's Formula of Concord,* edited by Lewis W. Spitz and Wenzel Lohff. Philadelphia: Fortress Press, 1977.

Petri, Hans. "Herzog Christoph von Württemberg und die Reformation in Frankreich." *Blätter für württembergische Kirchengeschichte* 55 (1955): 5–64.

Raitt, Jill. "The Elector John Casimir, Queen Elizabeth, and the Protestant League." In *Controversy and Conciliation: The Reformation and the Palatinate 1559–1583,* edited by Derk Visser. Allison Park, Pa.: Pickwick Publications, 1986.

————. "The Emperor and the Exiles: The Clash of Religion and Politics in the Sixteenth Century." *Church History* 52 (June 1983): 145–56.

————. "The Person of the Mediator: Calvin's Christology and Beza's Fidelity." *Occasional Papers of the American Society for Reformation Research* 1 (December 1977): 53–80.

————. "Three Inter-related Principles in Calvin's Unique Doctrine of Infant Baptism." *The Sixteenth Century Journal* 11, no. 1 (Spring 1980): 51–61.

Renard, Louis. "L'Ancien 'Magistrat' de Montbéliard." In *Mémoires de la Société pour l'histoire du droit et des institutions des anciens pays bourguignons, comtois et romands, (travaux) 1958–1959, fasc. 20, special no.: Le pays de Montbéliard et les régions voisines dans l'histoire et dans l'économie).* Dijon: Société pour l'histoire du droit et des institutions des anciens pays bourguignons, comtois et romands.

Schafer, Gerhard, and Martin Brecht. "Joannes Brenz 1499–1570: Beitrage zu seinem Leben und Wirken." *Blätter für württembergische Kirchengeschichte* 70 (1970).

Skarsten, Trygyve R. "The Reaction in Scandinavia." In *Discord, Dialogue, and Concord,* edited by Lewis W. Spitz and Wenzel Lohff. Philadelphia: Fortress Press, 1977.

Spitz, Lewis W. "The Formula of Concord Then and Now." In *Discord, Dialogue, and Concord,* edited by Lewis W. Spitz and Wenzel Lohff. Philadelphia: Fortress Press, 1977.

Tylenda, Joseph. "Calvin and Christ's Presence in the Supper—True or Real." *Scottish Journal of Theology* 27 (February 1974): 65–75.

Visser, Derk. "Zacharinus Ursinus and the Palatinate Reformation." In *Controversy and Conciliation: The Reformation and the Palatinate 1559–1583,* edited by Derk Visser. Allison Park, Pa.: Pickwick Publications, 1986.

INDEX

Abraham (Bible), 95

Acta (Andreae). *See throughout*

Adam and Eve (Bible), 141, 147, 148, 149, 151

Albery, Claude, 73

Anabaptists, 4, 7, 29, 52, 59, 142

Andreae, Jacob, xi, 7. *See also throughout*
- on art and music in churches, 136–37
- on baptism, 137–46
- on Calvinism, 125–26, 159
- as collocutor, 56, 58
- as conciliator, 29–30
- on consolation, 154
- on creation, 128n.27
- death of, 74
- on election, 149–50
- eucharistic theology of, 81–88
- and Formula of Concord, 31, 58
- limitations of, 103n.44
- and Montbéliard ministers, 26
- on predestination, 134–36
- and publication of *Acta,* 162–63
- and Reformed movement, 58
- refutes Beza's *Responsio,* 164–65
- rigidity of, 88
- on sin, 143–44
- and transubstantiation, 95

Antoine, King of Navarre, 7–8, 54

Anweil, Johann Wolfgang von, 73

Aquinas, Saint Thomas, 113, 122, 127n.13, 128n.27

Aristotle, 102n.25, 122–23

Art and music, in churches, 9, 135, 136–37, 610

Ascension, 22, 77, 80. *See also* Resurrection

Atonement, limited, 150, 151

Augsburg Confession, 68n.69, 167, 168, 170, 194n.14, 199
- ambiguous use of, 72
- Clervant on, 48
- Count Frederick and, 173, 201
- Daniel Toussain and, 27
- eucharistic doctrine of, 20, 26
- and French exiles, 9, 135
- German princes and, 53
- *invariata* version of, x, 20, 37n.51, 52, 54, 56, 172, 176
- and Lutheran canon, 30
- and Montbéliard church, 17
- and Peace of Augsburg, x, 4, 23, 51, 55
- Pflug and, 52–53
- presentation of, ix
- and Reformed movement, 54, 55
- as test of Protestant orthodoxy, 23, 51, 55
- *variata* version of, x, 7, 20, 29, 39n.83, 53, 56, 172

Augsburg Diet (1566), 54, 56–57, 57, 70n.92

August of Saxony, 53

Augustine of Canterbury, Saint, 57, 150, 151, 154

Baptism, 49, 70n.94, 85, 135, 137–47, 207
- Bucer on, 28
- as Christ's blood, 140
- and circumcision, 137, 138, 141, 147
- emergency, 21–22, 24, 27, 30, 137, 139–40, 146
- infant, 142, 145–46, 175
- and Lord's Supper, 138
- Lutherans on, 155
- and reprobates, 144

Belgic Confession (1561), ix

Bernard, 86, 107n.73, 151

Beuson, Anthoine, 172–73, 174, 184n.88, 185n.95

Beza, Theodore, 7, 22. *See also throughout*
- accused of heresy, 156
- advice to Montbéliard, 28–29
- agreements with Andreae, 98, 100
- and Andreae's *Epitome,* 165
- on art and music in church, 136–37, 207
- on baptism, 137–46
- and Calvin, ix, 130n.41
- on circumcision, 145
- as collocutor, 47, 48, 49–50
- on communion, 77–78
- on creation, 128n.27
- on election, 149–50
- and Henry IV, 192
- and Huguenots, 52

221

DATE DUE

DEC 26 1993			
JAN 10 2000			